The Governance of Rangelands

Rangelands are large natural landscapes that can include grasslands, shrublands, savannahs and woodlands. They are greatly influenced by, and often dependent on, the action of herbivores. In the majority of rangelands the dominant herbivores are found in domestic herds that are managed by mobile pastoralists. Most pastoralists manage their rangelands communally, benefiting from the greater flexibility and seasonal resource access that common property regimes can offer. As this book shows, this creates a major challenge for governance and institutions.

This work improves our understanding of the importance of governance, how it can be strengthened and the principles that underpin good governance, in order to prevent degradation of rangelands and ensure their sustainability. It describes the nature of governance at different levels: community governance, state governance, international governance, and the unique features of rangelands that demand collective action (issues of scale, ecological disequilibrium and seasonality).

A series of country case studies is presented, drawn from a wide spectrum of examples from Africa, the Middle East, Central Asia, Europe and North America. These provide contrasting lessons which are summarized to promote improved governance of rangelands and pastoralist livelihoods.

Pedro M. Herrera is an Environmental Consultant and President of the Entretantos Foundation, a Spanish NGO. His professional activity in Spain is shared between the Ancares Leoneses Biosphere Reserve, Gama S.L., a company he co-founded in 2000, and the University of Valladolid Institute of Urbanism.

Jonathan Davies is Director of the Global Drylands Initiative at the International Union for Conservation of Nature (IUCN), based in Nairobi, Kenya.

Pablo Manzano Baena is a Freelance Consultant and former Global Coordinator for the World Initiative for Sustainable Pastoralism (WISP), based at the IUCN office in Nairobi, Kenya.

'It is not through universities but through daily practices. It is not through few academic years of study or research but through centuries of love and interaction. It is not through greedy private ownership but through collective rights and stewardship that we, pastoralists, learned how to and did keep the rangelands for "us" and others to enjoy them, feeding our livestock, fighting diseases maintaining our souls and contributing to carbon capturing. It is time that all states and controlling parties recognize and respect pastoralists' collective land rights as a legal and legitimate way of governance so that sustainability of pastoralism is ensured, and pastoralists' contribution to food security and carbon sequestration is continued. This book is an important contribution showing many experiences of cooperation based on the traditional knowledge and the sense of ownership of the communities to rangelands. The book brings successful stories of rangeland governance where win-win situations are achieved and conflict among different communities has reduced. The variety of success stories should inspire us all to follow the proven success for a more flourishing and peaceful planet!'

Khalid Khawaldeh, Member, World Alliance of
Mobile Indigenous Peoples (WAMIP)

'A clear, empirically based, and well-argued manifesto for how to reverse decades of ill-informed policies, and instead recognise and support one of the planet's most sustainable production and land use systems – starting with the critical step of protecting the territorial rights of pastoralists'

Michael Taylor, International Land Coalition Secretariat

'It was in the early nineties and I visited Chad late in the long, dry season. In the Batha Province, north of the provincial capital Ati, I came across lush grasslands where Dorcas Gazelles abounded. There were empty villages with many granaries, all full of millet. An old man that had stayed behind told us that the herdsmen, owners of the granaries and the traditional waterholes, were still in the South, but moving northwards. They would soon be back. Granaries and grass were to feed the herdsmen, their families and livestock before the rains would arrive, new grass would grow and fields with Millet could be harvested again for the next cycle. I realized that I was witnessing some of the last vestiges of pastoral traditions in Africa. Here, traditional management of natural resources survived, respected by all stakeholders. Transhumant and nomadic pastoralists are not always popular with some governments. Their ephemeral stay in places makes them difficult to control, to tax. And yet, as the above example shows, their traditional way of life is based on sound ecological principles. There are lessons to be learned. Lessons that may need to be adapted to the requirements of modern times, but we should make sure not to lose access to this rich source of indigenous knowledge.'

Piet Wit, Chair, IUCN Commission on Ecosystem Management

The Governance of Rangelands

Collective action for sustainable pastoralism

Edited by Pedro M. Herrera, Jonathan Davies and Pablo Manzano Baena

LONDON AND NEW YORK

First published 2014
by Routledge

2 Park Square, Milton Park, Abingdon, Oxfordshire OX14 4RN
711 Third Avenue, New York, NY 10017

Routledge is an imprint of the Taylor & Francis Group, an informa business

First issued in paperback 2017

British Library Cataloguing-in-Publication Data
A catalogue record for this book is available from the British Library

Library of Congress Cataloging-in-Publication Data
The governance of rangelands : collective action for sustainable
pastoralism / edited by Pedro M. Herrera, Jonathan Mark Davies
and Pablo Manzano Baena.
     pages cm
   Includes bibliographical references and index.
   1. Range management. 2. Range policy. 3. Pastoral systems.
   I. Herrera Molina, Pedro Manuel, editor. II. Davies, Jonathan
   Mark, editor. III. Manzano Baena, Pablo, editor.
 SF85.G68 2014
 333.74 dc23   2014019066

ISBN: 978-1-138-78514-4 (hbk)
ISBN: 978-1-138-57481-6 (pbk)

Typeset in Baskerville
by HWA Text and Data Management, London

Contents

Figures

Tables

Author biographies

Mouhaman Arabi is a geographer specializing in development planning, resource management and medical geography. He first worked in environmental management and rural development projects in the Far North of Cameroon for the past 15 years. He recently joined the newly created University of Maroua where he teaches and conducts research in environmental sciences. His research focuses on the environment and natural resource management, on human and environment interaction, and on medical geography. He has been collaborating for many years now with local, national and international research institutions.

Catherine Larissa Bebisse has an MA in social sciences specializing in development and conflict resolution. She studied land use conflicts and protection of transhumance corridors in Bogo, Cameroon.

Abderrahim Boutaleb is a Moroccan national. He obtained his bachelor's degree in experimental sciences in 1979 in Oujda and continued with his graduate studies at the Agronomy and Veterinary Institute Hassan II (IAV) in Rabat (1980) and the National School of Forestry Engineering from 1981 to 1983 (ENFI) in Morocco. He worked for the Ministry of Agriculture and the Office for Water and Forest between 1983 and 2005. He also worked as a project coordinator for Med Wet Coast project with UNDP between 2005 and 2007 and for the Community SMAPIII European project between 2007 and 2009. He is currently working for the GEF-LCD UNIDO project.

Joost Brouwer is a Dutch soil scientist, (agro-) ecologist and ornithologist with 35 years of experience in Australia, Africa, Asia and Europe. Following a research and teaching career, he is now working as a consultant through his own company, Brouwer environment and agriculture. Joost lived in Niger for five years in the early 1990s, working as a principal scientist at ICRISAT Sahelian Centre. Since then he has remained involved in the agriculture, wetlands and biodiversity of the Sahel. He is the founder of the Niger Bird Data Base www.nibdab.org and can be reached via BrouwerEAC@online.nl.

Lael Buckham-Walsh holds an MSc degree in environmental science and is currently working in the Drylands Programme at IUCN. She specializes in a range of thematic areas including invasive species, landscape ecology, land rehabilitation and community engagement in the Kalahari-Namib Ecosystem. As well as being a member of IUCN's Commission on Ecosystem Management, Lael is a trained teacher and a member of the South African Council for Educators. Having lived in a number of different African countries, she has a keen awareness and understanding of environmental, social and economic issues in the region.

Jonathan Davies is an agricultural economist and an expert in sustainable dryland development and mobile pastoralism. He has worked for 20 years in Asia, Europe and Africa in the fields of development and conservation and currently heads IUCN's Global Drylands Initiative. His experiences include over 10 years living and working with pastoralist communities in eastern Africa implementing community development projects, with emphasis on governance, rights and gender equity. He is IUCN's focal point to the United Nations Convention to Combat Desertification and is actively involved in globally profiling the governance barriers to sustainable land management and demonstrating governance solutions to desertification, land degradation and drought. He holds a PhD in Agricultural Economics and Anthropology and a Master's in World Animal Production.

Pablo Domínguez is an environmental anthropologist (BSc Environmental Biology and PhD Social Anthropology). His research mainly focuses on the Mediterranean region, and especially on Berber populations of the High Atlas of Morocco and their AGDAL systems of communal natural resource management. For the last decade, he has been working on how cultural-symbolical representations and social-material uses of the environment relate to each other (www.tdx.cat/bitstream/10803/79093/1/pdg1de1.pdf), whereas his present and future research agendas focus on how to implement this knowledge, through procedures of patrimonialization within a Political Ecology framework.

Albert K. Drent has both an anthropological and ecological academic background and his research interests focus on the functioning and management of natural resources from this multi-disciplinary perspective. Since 2002 he has stayed for longer periods in the Far North Province of Cameroon. Most of this time, he has carried out research among nomadic pastoralists and surrounding sedentary groups who practise agriculture and fishing. In his research up to now, he has concentrated on 1) mobility and the relation between resource exploiters and natural resources, both from an anthropological and ecological perspective, 2) human interrelations and conflict management, related to natural resources and 3) transmission of diseases and pastoral mobility.

Ilaria Firmian has a degree in Anthropology and an MA in Cooperation and Development. She works as an Environment and Climate Knowledge Officer at the International Fund for Agricultural Development (IFAD) and is responsible for strengthening knowledge sharing and learning activities associated with IFAD-supported projects and programmes on environment and climate change (ASAP, GEF, Adaptation Fund) and for fostering partnerships with selected knowledge centres and networks on climate and environment. In IFAD, she has previously worked as a Technical Adviser on Environment and Natural Resources Management, supporting the mainstreaming of environmental and social issues at policy/programme/ project levels. This included design and implementation support missions, technical quality reviews, development of IFAD Environment and Natural Resource Management policy, and management of supplementary funds. Prior to her experience with IFAD, she has been working both on Land Tenure and Socio Economic and Gender Analysis with FAO, and as an NGO Project Coordinator for a EU-funded project focusing on indigenous peoples' livelihoods in the tropical Central African rainforests.

Fidaa F. Haddad is a development worker, with extensive experience in water management and dry land field and as a hands-on practitioner of development operation. Her main experience has been in the NGO sector and she spent the last 17 years working in international NGO interacting with the civil society sectors. Her work has included the development and the management long-range strategic plans, management, facilitation, coordination, communication. Mainly generating knowledge and awareness on gender-environment linkages necessitates both the development of targeted technical inputs and capacity building. She is also a gender specialist preparing national strategies and action plans to mainstream gender into climate change, water, and desertification for Jordan, Egypt and the League of Arab States.

Ian Hannam is Associate Professor of International Environmental Law Development and Research at the Australian Centre for Agriculture and Law, University of New England, Australia. He is Chair of the Specialist Law Group for Sustainable Use of Soil and Desertification of the IUCN World Commission on Environmental Law and has worked with many countries on environmental law reform.

Pedro M. Herrera is an environment consultant specializing in land planning and management mainly focused in rural and high nature value areas. Seduced by the participatory approach, he has oriented his work to the sustainable uses of rangeland and forests, especially those based on community management. He is President of the Entretantos Foundation, a Spanish NGO promoting citizens' participation. There, he works mainly on pastoralism advocacy and participatory tools for sustainable land use. His professional activity in Spain is shared between the Ancares Leoneses Biosphere Reserve,

Gama S.L., the small company he co-founded in 2000, and the University of Valladolid IUU (Institute of Urbanism). He is also a consultant for WISP and IUCN in pastoralism and governance, linking traditional pastoralist wisdom with adaptive ecosystem management.

Lynn Huntsinger is Professor of Rangeland Management at the University of California Berkeley. Her research focuses on the conservation and management of grasslands, particularly the interaction of social and ecological systems in working landscapes in the western United States. She has published numerous articles on topics including grazing ecology, ranching, and pastoralism in China. Her 2013 book, *Mediterranean Working Woodlands: Dehesas of Spain and Ranchlands of California*, is available through SpringerLink. Dr Huntsinger majored in Chinese History as an undergraduate and she has long-standing interest in China. She serves as Chair of the Society and Environment Division of the Department of Environmental Science, Policy, and Management.

Saïdou Kari is a Co-Director of the Centre for Support to Research and Pastoralism (CARPA) and has years of experience working in pastoral development in the Far North of Cameroon.

Luke Macaulay grew up in Temple, Texas, and graduated with a BA in Philosophy and Literature from the University of Notre Dame. He worked for the U.S. Department of Justice for several years, ultimately working as the spokesman for the U.S. Attorney's Office in San Francisco. He changed his professional direction in 2007, when he decided to pursue his passion for working in rangeland and wildlife management, earning a master's degree in range management in 2010 at University of California Berkeley. He is currently a PhD candidate at University of California Berkeley and his research focuses on the economic and conservation potential of paid hunting programmes on private lands.

Pablo Manzano Baena works with the International Union for Conservation of Nature as the Global Coordinator for the World Initiative for Sustainable Pastoralism (WISP). A Spaniard by nationality, Pablo is a rangeland ecologist who has worked with pastoralism issues during the last 10 years both in the field of scientific research and international development. His international experience includes Spain, Argentina, Germany, Bosnia and Herzegovina. In his current position based in Nairobi Kenya, he works at influencing policies from the local to global levels through mainstreaming the understanding of pastoralism with evidence-based arguments.

Mark Moritz is an Associate Professor in the Department of Anthropology at the Ohio State University. His research focuses on the transformation of African pastoral systems. He has investigated how pastoralists have adapted to changing ecological, political and institutional conditions that affect their lives and livelihoods. He has also been conducting research with pastoralists in the Far North Region of Cameroon since 1993. The long-term research has resulted in strong collaborations with local researchers, which has allowed him to develop new interdisciplinary research projects with colleagues at the Ohio State University. All his research projects examine pastoral systems within the analytical framework of coupled human and natural systems using a regional approach that situates the Far North Region within the larger Chad Basin.

Cathrine Chipo Mutambirwa is a Senior Programme Officer based in the IUCN South Africa Office managing the Drylands and Water and Wetlands Regional Portfolio of projects implemented in Southern Africa. Ms Mutambirwa has a Bachelor of Science Degree with majors on Geological and Biological Sciences and a Masters in Sustainability Sciences. Her experience is mainly in project management, natural resources management with a focus on water resources and biodiversity, state of the environment assessment and reporting, policy review and influencing processes as well stakeholder engagement and participatory planning processes.

Guyo Roba is a Senior Programme Officer with the IUCN regional drylands programme in eastern and southern Africa. He has a background in environment, energy and public policy studies and has worked on issues related to energy and natural resources management for over seven years. This includes experience in Kenya and other eastern African countries with half of his career spent in providing research based public policy advice and capacity building to the government of Kenya, local communities and to the private sector in order to contribute to the attainment of development and conservation goals. He has worked as a policy analyst in Kenya and has influenced policy and practice at different levels of infrastructure, environment and energy sectors. Accordingly, he has trained, written and published in the areas of infrastructure, resource and environmental management and public policy.

Elsa Sattout is a PhD and conservationist with over 15 years of diversified experience in spearheading research, teaching and development initiatives in the conservation and sustainable management of natural resources and biodiversity with a focus on terrestrial ecosystems and nature reserves, biodiversity assessment and monitoring, collaborative management of forest resources and environmental resources economics. She has served in national, regional and international organizations on development projects and on building up platforms and communities of practices for the implementation of the biodiversity related conventions.

Nathan F. Sayre is Associate Professor and Chair of Geography at the University of California Berkeley. His research centres on semi-arid rangelands, especially in the south western United States: how they have changed, how they have been understood and managed, and the politics and economics surrounding land use change, fire restoration, and endangered species conservation. He has written three books and dozens of articles on these topics. He is an affiliated social scientist with the USDA-Agricultural Research Service-Jornada Experimental Range in Las Cruces, New Mexico, and the Jornada Basin Long-Term Ecological Research (LTER) site funded by the National Science Foundation. He is currently writing a book on the history of range science and rangeland ecology for the University of Chicago Press.

Paul Scholte is an ecologist leading large programmmes and organizations in Conservation and NRM in a development context. He has 26 years' experience in protected-area and rangeland management, biodiversity inventories, governance, rural development, ecotourism, training and education (Wildlife colleges of Garoua (Cameroon) and KCCEM (Rwanda), Universities of Wageningen, Leiden, Yaoundé, Chad and Rwanda), and has authored some 100 publications. During his assignments Paul monitored on-the-job training of staff and supervised (postgraduate) students. His interventions, at the interface of practice, policy and science, are further based on: networking and consensus building among specialists; first-hand knowledge of international cooperation policies and financing mechanisms, andmarketing of conservation through mass media.

Introduction

To many of us, the rangelands are places of boundless inspiration and beauty. They cover a third of all the land on our planet and include savannah, prairie, steppe, pampas and mountain pastures. They appear to represent the ultimate wilderness – the last frontier – and their dramatic landscapes, powerful forces of nature, and astonishing biodiversity evoke powerful emotions. Yet the rangelands are seldom the natural wilderness that we want to believe. They have been managed over the centuries by human beings using tools such as planned herding and controlled burning, mimicking nature to carve out a thriving livelihood in these unpredictable and comparatively unproductive lands.

How do they achieve this? How do communities manage such vast areas effectively, providing not only for their own livelihoods but providing environmental services that benefit millions of others? Why does 'modernization' so often lead to the breakdown of effective management and contribute to degradation of the rangelands? How can we support pastoralists to continue their development whilst safeguarding the sustainability of what they do?

The rangelands are so vast and so unpredictable – whether it is the uncertainties of drought, flood or blizzard – that communal management has always been the key to survival. Rangeland productivity depends on certain patterns of herbivore action that demand herd mobility, and access to the most valuable resources is often seasonally limited, meaning that communal management must take place across vast areas that are often geographically distinct. Communal management may sometimes be between a relatively small community, but in some times or for some resources cooperation is needed between large numbers of people, and often between people from different ethnic groups and even from different countries. Over centuries of experience, this has given rise to elaborate customs and norms along with complex social arrangements, rules and regulations for management of many different rangeland resources, including pasture, water, trees and salt pans.

It has been reported that where livestock mobility and institutions for communal governance are found, rangeland degradation is scarce. Despite this, government policies often erode the social fabric on which governance depends, and places limits on herd mobility. This poses a number of challenges for pastoral communities. Where institutions have broken down, how can they be restored or adapted to the modern world? Where institutions remain operational, how can communities maintain or adapt them whilst embracing the many opportunities offered by development? In communities who have no tradition of communal management, can communal practices be developed from scratch?

This book provides examples that help to answer these questions. The chapters on rangeland management in Jordan and Lebanon, for example, illustrate how governance systems can be resurrected, despite having been dormant for many decades. Examples from Kenya and Morocco illustrate how persisting governance institutions can be protected and strengthened if appropriate development processes are followed. The Botswana example provides a clear illustration of the natural inclination of human beings to develop collective action on a small scale, and shows the early stages of the emergence of new governance arrangements on communal rangelands. Although strengthening community-level arrangements can be highly challenging, other chapters show that governance is more complex than relationships at local level. Effective governance needs rules and regulations not only locally but nationally, and in many cases internationally. It also requires governance systems to be aligned at these different levels without undermining the self-enforcing nature of effective local governance, and whilst maintaining a principle of subsidiarity. As the chapters in this book illustrate, this demands local solutions supported by national laws. However, what emerges is a number of common principles that can guide future work and widespread scale up of success.

The opening chapters of this book on the 'Principles of pastoralist governance and land management' introduce the mechanisms and tools used by pastoralists to manage rangelands and provide an overview of the ecological and economic basis to support them. 'Drivers of pastoralism and rangelands governance in a changing world' identifies and analyses pastoralism and rangeland management drivers, constraints, impacts and consequences in order to support the recommendation that the recovery of rangeland governance by pastoralists could indeed solve several of the diagnosed problems. The *eleven case studies* of pastoralism and governance describe different situations including the organization of land use and infrastructure by the open access nomadic pastoralism in the centre of Africa, the bylaw of traditional land management systems in Kenya, the perspectives of traditional land management systems and their upgrading to modern cooperative systems in Morocco and the adaptation of land tenure systems to extensive cattle production in Botswana. Pastoralism in the Middle East is addressed in two case studies that describe the recovery of the Hima system in Lebanon and Jordan. An Asian perspective assesses Mongolia, one of the hotspots of pastoralism, with millions of hectares dedicated to mobile pastoralism. Europe and the United States are also represented with reports addressing the effort to recover the voice and visibility of pastoralists. Finally, 'Rebuilding pastoral governance: Lessons learned and conclusions', summarizes the lessons and good practices extracted from the reports, organizing them in a common framework related to previous chapters.

Developing new models of rangeland governance

Pastoral systems, which extend all over the world, provide valuable ecosystem services in a wide range of landscapes such as maintaining high levels of biodiversity, increasing vegetation soil cover, reducing erosion, preventing wildfires, maintaining infrastructures, dispersing seeds, allocating nutrients, and defragmenting landscapes. Rangeland ecosystems are quite fragile, and as such they are threatened by degradation and global change, relying on insightful management to preserve their integrity and avoid erosion and desertification. Pastoralism also produces important commodities (including, but not limited to meat, dairy, leather and manure) often extracted in a sustainable way from unproductive ecosystems managed from prehistoric times. Moreover, pastoralism represents a cultural and intangible heritage that should be valued, understood and preserved.

The significant contributions pastoralists express, in terms of land planning and management, provide working tools and mechanisms for ecosystem management under particular conditions. The wisdom of traditional pastoralists in land governance has been refined over many generations through a cumulative body of knowledge, practice and belief. Traditional knowledge has evolved through adaptive processes and been handed down through generations by cultural transmission that maintains the relationship among people, livestock and the environment. Pastoralist management systems work under customary rules that guarantee open rights and open access to common resources. Such management frameworks must continually adapt to changing political, social and legal contexts, whilst addressing questions like participation, equity, voice, gender and transparency.

Recovering pastoralist governance depends on empowering pastoralist communities to manage their own territory: approaches that have many labels that can be broadly classified as Community Based Rangeland Resource Management. Pastoralist empowerment can be supported by grassroots pastoralist organizations defending their interests and can be promoted by initiatives such as farmers' associations. Herders would give voice to emerging organizations or platforms and play a key role in governance.

Pastoralist governance manages wide swathes of less productive lands such as rangelands, drylands and woodlands, usually public or communally owned and managed, although management rights are often nominally vested in governments. Conflicts emerge because of the prevailing tendency in most countries to allocate delimited and individual ownership rights to manage common lands in the belief that this encourages users to generate higher financial returns. This choice can lead to undesirable consequences like encroachment or abandonment, which can fuel the degradation of such lands. Private tenure can also undermine the financial returns in highly variable landscapes where flexibility and mobility are key to cope with variations in plant productivity.

Management systems based on allocating communal rights of access, decision-making and control is a viable alternative, more suitable for rangelands. However, those systems need to ensure the security of tenure and access to resources by their legitimate users, as otherwise they will not allocate efforts in long-term sustainability measures. The long-term security of land tenure and access rights constitutes a major constraint in the viability of governance systems and it could threaten the viability of promising projects. Nevertheless, the keystone for security is government commitment to supporting the empowerment of pastoralists.

Regional and local government agencies must be active agents in the participatory processes that formalize customary systems, which is key to incorporating those systems into legally supported land planning tools. Political decentralization and co-ordination among government institutions appear to be significant conditions for restoring and improving the governance of pastoralist lands.

Towards an agenda for conservation-based land tenure reform for rangelands

The reports synthesized in this work provide a plausible set of resources to improve pastoral governance. A roadmap to recover and implement prudent governance could be based on any one of the reports in the book.

The first actions to build a pastoralist governance agenda ought to include legal measures, thereby securing legitimacy. Those steps may be implemented at international, national and regional levels, *to promote an international political framework for recognizing pastoral governance*, to *develop national laws* to protect pastoralism or to *translate traditional governance systems into legally recognized and secure regulatory tools* using participatory approaches. The increased participation of pastoralists in national governance can also help *mitigate conflict in pastoralist areas* by reducing the struggle for resources and incorporating nation-wide conflict resolution as an important component of modern democracies.

The roadmap laid out in this work includes actions to implement conscientious governance models, developed *from traditional management systems, recovering and updating* them by implementing community based management, participatory tools or institutional reforms for local communities. *More equitable and participatory community management systems* are needed in conjunction with *new markets* to help pastoralist economies flourish. Diversifying production promotes multi-objective governance systems with an integral vision of land management, including *rangeland uses and services*. The promotion of pastoralist networks that *give voice and visibility to* pastoralists will confer the authority necessary for interlocution to defend their governance systems. The most expedient way to enhance the information and research needed would be by *sharing knowledge between researchers and pastoralists* and developing new research programmes based on collaboration that develops a shared wisdom about sustainable rangeland management.

There is no doubt that communal management of the rangelands is critical not only for the future of the rangelands themselves and of pastoralists, but also for the benefits that they provide to the rest of the world: benefits like climate change mitigation, biodiversity conservation and protection of watersheds as well as less tangible, though by no means less marketable, values like inspiration and culture. It is equally certain that communal governance by pastoralists is more cost effective than imposing state management and control, and the role of the state must be to enable pastoral management, as it does in many countries. Instead of prioritizing land privatization, based on the belief that we need to raise financial capital investment in order to get more financial capital back, we need to recognize that pastoralists already invest intensively using different forms of capital – human and social capital – and the investments and returns need to be measured and valued differently for the benefit of all society.

1 Principles of pastoralist governance and land management

*Pedro M. Herrera, Jonathan Davies and
Pablo Manzano Baena*

Introduction

Pastoralism, as a complex system of livestock and rangeland management, provides many examples of natural resource governance that combines people's livelihoods with nature and biodiversity conservation in extremely challenging climatic, territorial, economic and social conditions. Examples of these governance systems exist throughout the world, adapted to the great variety of circumstances and local contexts. The sustainable management of natural resources depends on the existence of regulations, compliance and enforcement of the processes by which they are governed. Failures in rangeland governance are often at the heart of biodiversity loss, breakdown in ecosystem function, land degradation and loss of resilience. Governance failures are also frequently identified as the cause of wider development challenges and vulnerability among populations that depend on such land.

There is considerable uncertainty worldwide concerning the extent of rangelands degradation, particularly in developing countries where resources are most scarce and monitoring of rangelands is typically absent. Yet the majority of countries have formulated National Action Programs to combat desertification, with major emphasis placed on rangelands. These plans generally recommend improved application of good practices to achieve sustainable land management, and minimal attention is given to the rules and regulations governing natural resource management. Many countries are unaware that their rangeland users are abandoning tried-and-tested land management practices as a result of governance failures and that this is a significant contributor to degradation.

This book provides evidence that improved governance can create a platform for sustainable development and natural resource use, and it demonstrates the sort of conditions under which governance can be made more effective. More specifically, the book will:

1 Examine the nature of governance at different levels – community, state and international.
2 Document challenges and changes to governance at different levels.
3 Present experiences and solutions to strengthening governance at different levels.

4   Show evidence of the impact of good governance on livelihoods, natural resource sustainability and biodiversity (including ecosystem function) and examine weaknesses and opportunities for improvement in documenting the evidence.

5   Present and analyse the richness and complexity of governance as a subject along with common solutions or approaches that can simplify governance in its practical application.

This study is designed to inform practitioners of successful approaches and principles, to enable advocates to make a more convincing and evidence-based case for improving governance, and to enable policymakers to identify policy gaps and bottlenecks that are undermining efforts to sustainably manage rangeland resources.

The definition and basis of governance

Governance is interpreted differently according to the needs of different institutions and individuals. Interpretations differ in terms of definition and in how good governance can be achieved. The World Bank defines governance as:

> The traditions and institutions by which authority in a country is exercised for the common good. This includes (i) the process by which those in authority are selected, monitored and replaced, (ii) the capacity of the government to effectively manage its resources and implement sound policies, and (iii) the respect of citizens and the state for the institutions that govern economic and social interactions among them.
>
> (Kaufmann *et al.*, 1999)

This definition is biased towards the role of government in governance, and this conflation of terms is widespread. The Food and Agricultural Organization defines governance as

> The way in which society is managed and how competing interests of different groups are reconciled... governance is concerned with the process by which citizens participate in decision-making, how government is accountable to its citizens and how society obliges its members to observe its rules... it is the rules, institutions, and practices that sets limits and provides incentives for individuals, organisations and firms.
>
> (FAO, 2008: 5)

IUCN's Commission on Environmental, Economic and Social Policy (CEESP) group on governance equity and rights (TGER) notes that

> For some, improving governance means curbing the power of the state, releasing a country's trade barriers and opening up as much as possible to the

influence, the values and the working style of the private sector (...) For others, it means highlighting debate, fair procedures, negotiation processes and the seeking of consensus among a plurality of actors as the best foundations for decision-making in society (deliberative processes, participatory democracy) ... For others still, 'good governance' is the meeting point of performance and equity, an evolving process through which fundamental principles and values, including environmental rights and human rights, can percolate in society.

DFID (2006) considers good governance to be 'how citizens, leaders and public institutions relate to each other in order to make change happen', and it hinges upon three factors:

- State capability: the extent to which leaders and governments are able to get things done.
- Responsiveness: whether public policies and institutions respond to the needs of citizens and uphold their rights.
- Accountability: the ability of citizens, civil society and the private sector to scrutinize public institutions and governments and hold them to account.

Governance is therefore more than government. Governance includes interactions between the state and its citizens, but it also means the interaction between citizens, even in the absence of government. There are places where government does not exist (e.g. some areas in Somalia at the time of this writing), and more commonly, particularly in pastoralist lands, there are places where state influence does not penetrate strongly. Yet in these places, people often manage to govern their natural resources effectively.

Without attempting to define natural resource governance, we use the term in this publication to refer to the rules and regulations that determine (or 'govern') natural resource use and the way those rules and regulations are developed and enforced. Governance essentially refers to the rules (laws and other norms), institutions and processes that determine interaction among citizens, between citizens and the state, and amid states. Governance is therefore a complex issue about power relationships between different actors. The World Bank simplifies governance by identifying six dimensions: i) voice and accountability, ii) political stability and absence of violence, iii) government effectiveness, iv) regulatory quality, v) rule of law and vi) control of corruption (from Kaufmann *et al.*, 1999).

Principles of pastoral governance

The following subsections examine some of these dimensions in more detail and consider other principles that may be relevant to natural resource management in drylands, such as strengthening capacity and reinforcing customary institutions.

Participation

The first principle underlying governance, and probably the most widespread, is participation, which is addressed in almost every project reviewed in this book. However, the principle is often misaddressed, starting with the concept of participation itself (Botes and Van Rensburg, 2000). It is difficult to establish a common definition of participation since it is a complex notion that has arisen from successive ideas, levels and typologies (Reed, 2008). Definitions of participation show a variety of alternatives highlighting the complexity of its nature and the enthusiasm it raises in many countries, policies and projects since historical times. However, some authors have tried to purify the concept by simplifying it, linking participation to citizen's control (Arnstein, 1969). One useful definition could be extracted from Elcom and Baines (1999), based on the semantic significance of the word as 'taking part'. So, participation means individual and group stakeholders actively identifying the issues, policies and solutions they need and taking part in the implementation of these policies and actions by contributing their ideas, labour or other resources. Be that as it may, in terms of governance (and environment), participation has always been considered as people's direct implication in decision-making affecting management and problem solving.

It is also established that participation has many different levels, from simple information to active citizen's control (Wilcox, 1994), each of them involving different degrees of involvement and commitment. Addressing different levels could be useful and legitimate for different kind of projects and purposes. Participation is used in many ways, from better diagnostics to conflict prevention, legitimacy or higher resource mobilization (Heras, 2003) but it could go further and establish truly democratic ways for managing land and resources, as intended in Community Based Management systems. Participation, however, is not always the perfect way to address everything, and some authors have pointed out that the wrong approach to participation could generate worse problems than those solved (Irvin and Stansbury, 2004) or at least delay and increase the cost of implementing solutions.

In any case, the participation level needed to improve land governance (especially in rangelands) is often related to the direct involvement of stakeholders in decision-making (Reed, 2008). This is also a key issue in pastoralists' participation. Not just because the only way to incorporate pastoralist wisdom about rangeland management is to allow them to participate directly in land use decisions but also because participation could be a necessary step to adaptive capacity, resilience and even survival of pastoralist communities (Robinson and Berkes, 2011).

Participation always depends on long, complex and expensive processes that demand trained facilitation teams and deep involvement from their promoters (in addition to participants' commitment, of course). Moreover, the more fragmented, impoverished or marginalized the target community is, the longer and more complex the process will be. It is not easy to develop good participatory processes; many fail when they cannot live up to the expectations generated, or when governments opt out of the process (Heras, 2003) or when participation is circumvented and funds are diverted to more attractive short-term projects. Thus, participation needs to be properly designed, funded, facilitated and evaluated, and it needs long-term commitment from many stakeholders.

There are several prior conditions to develop successful participatory processes, and most of them are related to other governance principles exposed in the following subsections. Participation in decision-making cannot be developed without properly addressing questions like capacity building, equity, voice, empowerment, gender or transparency. All of these issues can be approached through participatory processes applying contact, dialogue and social tools in meetings, workshops and other social activities. Participation also depends on the commitment of the agents involved, and this commitment is also something worth working on. The success of participation often relies on the establishment of social links among participants and, most important, the acceptance of a common arena and objectives that could benefit the entire community.

Voice and empowerment

Empowerment can be defined as a fundamental need to reach a certain level of human rights. It comprises economic, social and political dimensions. The term varies according to context, but here we emphasize elements of participation, voice, confidence and capacities. These elements of empowerment often emerge as an unplanned outcome of interventions and policy change. In some cases, communities have been empowered through their participation in natural resources management committees or other project activities and through support for collective action. In order to establish an equal dialogue with external interlocutors, it is very important that the community representatives either have certain degrees of technical knowledge or are supported to express them, so that they can defend the elements of their practice (Manzano Baena, 2012: 111). The acquisition of financial capital has been another source of empowerment which has enabled some communities to negotiate access to decision-making, particularly in drylands where local administrations are typically short of resources.

The establishment of representative structures and local agreements over resources can sometimes impede community empowerment. For example, a government may return decision-making powers to a lower level of government, but this can remain inaccessible to local communities. Support for community empowerment must recognize power relations among the various levels of governance and relations both within communities (e.g. between men and women) and between the community and their government. Empowerment needs to go hand in hand with building relationships among central government, local government and communities, but it also requires an inclusive approach within the community. The aim should be to strengthen accountability and enhance the capacity of local communities to take part in decision-making processes about natural resources.

Equity and gender

Good governance demands gender equity to ensure that both women and men have opportunities to exercise their rights over natural resources in order to improve their wellbeing. Tension can be created when governance is strengthened by restoring power to traditional authorities, which are not always gender sensitive. It would be inconsistent with other governance principles if power and control (e.g. rights over land), were restored to one group of users at the expense of another group.

Women and men are often responsible for the management of different resources and this should be reflected in decision-making processes. Often pastoralist women are marginalized within their societies and suffer from limited opportunities to participate in governance (FAO, 2002a). Actually, their involvement in pastoralist initiatives and fora has been lower than expected. Despite the many challenges they face, women pastoralists can be influential forces for change and they contribute with capacities, skills and visions that are vital for pastoralist development (Rota, 2010). In fact, projects with a good gender approach leading pastoralist women to deep levels of involvement and participation are achieving very interesting goals and improving environmental services delivered to the society (Köhler-Rollefson, 2012; Haddad, this volume).

Equally important is the respect for human rights and the empowerment of women. IUCN's Commission on Environmental, Economic and Social Policy (CEESP) group on governance equity and rights (TGER) regards good governance as the 'meeting point of performance and equity'.

Accountability and transparency

Accountability and transparency are important at different levels of authority to ensure good governance. At the national and local levels, accountability and control of corruption can be important to ensure that resources are used effectively, and according to priorities agreed through participatory processes. Accountability can therefore foster trust between local institutions and government authorities, strengthening partnerships for sustainable and responsive development.

At the community level, both internal and external accountability are important for effective governance. For example, customary institutions may be considered accountable within a community but may need to go to greater lengths to convince local authorities. Internal accountability can be challenging where new institutions are created, for example to handle revenues from conservation activities, and the misappropriation of funds has jeopardized efforts to strengthen community based natural resource management. Accountability may be jeopardized by internal power relations at the community level and in some cases accountability as well as representation of traditional leadership is contested; for example, when local leaders have been appointed by government or past colonial administrators rather than identified through traditional means, a 'decentralized despotism' can emerge (Mamdani, 1996).

Capacity

Secure rights under accountable and responsive authority are an important foundation for decentralized management and local level governance of resources. However these efforts are inadequate if rural communities cannot manage their natural resources due to capacity constraints, limitations of management rights or insufficient institutional support. Capacity is critical for the successful governance of resources as is the power to make decisions and the ability to claim rights accorded in policy and institutional frameworks.

Often the potential of local institutions such as village development committees, women's associations, traditional and in some cases local leadership or government structures remain untapped due to constraints to their capacity (Schuster and Steenkamp, 2007). Sometimes a lack of confidence of pastoralists in their own governance systems and the long-term practice of top-down approaches in decision-making can also undermine their capacity to participate (Sommerhalter, 2008). Weak capacity at the local government level often creates a bottleneck in implementing national decentralization policies. The key to strengthening governance is often to give people the appropriate tools, skills and framework to collaborate, which allows them to work out how to make decisions and to take ownership of the process of strengthening governance.

Rule of law and policy coherence

In the past, policies and legislative frameworks have sought to govern the use of natural resources through command and control. Recently, however, there has been a trend towards decentralizing state power and its devolving responsibilities to local bodies. Tools for decentralizing control of natural resources include national policies that facilitate community based conservation, for example through sectorial land, forestry or wildlife policies. However, specific policies on community conservation or natural resource management are rare and opportunities are usually created through a collection of sectorial legislation relating to issues such as local government, land, forests and wildlife and fisheries (Roe *et al.*, 2009). These can be very complex and may present barriers to the successful governance of natural resources at local level.

Coherence within policy and legislative frameworks is frequently lacking. Some governments have adopted the rhetoric of decentralization, devolution and local empowerment without enacting the necessary institutional reforms. In most cases the constitutional or legislative changes required to decentralize authority over resources have been truncated. Governments often mistakenly conflate policy reform with governance reform; policy statements are only one element of governance and are less important than legislative or constitutional changes (Roe *et al.*, 2009; Nelson and Agrawal, 2008; Ribot, 2004).

Other principles

The previous subsections contain a selection of principles that have emerged through this body of work as being important to improved natural resource governance in pastoral areas, but they are not treated systematically or even thoroughly. Other principles may also be significant, i.e. human rights, responsiveness, conflict prevention and management. They are all related to the principles already outlined, all of them interacting in the complex matrix of human-land-environment relationships. Even participation is explained as deeply interacting with many other principles and cannot be delinked from them. In fact, the terms are not mutually exclusive and they may describe different features of good governance, such as principles, conditions, approaches, etc.

Rangelands and pastoralists

Pastoralism has been defined as the extensive production of herbivorous livestock (Davies and Roba, 2010). In this production system, livestock and rangelands are managed dynamically to provide a stream of goods and services that are valued both locally and globally. Global dialogue on pastoralism has benefited in recent years from improved awareness of the global nature of pastoralism, and the shared challenges and concerns of pastoralists from a great diversity of regions. Nevertheless, pastoral systems are highly diverse and definitions must embrace this diversity including: systems that rely on both grazing and browsing; market-oriented as well as subsistence pastoral economies; wealthy as well as poor pastoralists; indigenous as well as non-indigenous peoples; mobile as well as sedentary peoples, etc.

Pastoral systems include semi-extensive livestock managed by settled population as well as nomadic pastoralists living and moving with their herds across huge distances. They share an adaptable regulation of grazing land that follows spatial and temporal patterns closely linked to the ecological dynamics of the rangelands. Pastoralists adjust parameters like grazing pressure, species, selection of land to be grazed or altering the grazing calendar to handle dynamic external variables in order to achieve an optimal degree of exploitation, so to preserve their own production, the richness of the pastures and the environmental services they provide. Pastoralists rely mainly on the local production of fodder and pastures and manage herders and pastures using traditional technologies that are passed on to their descendants. As such, pastoralists are heirs to a wide culture of land and livestock management that is essential for their ability to manage the environment (Montserrat, 2004). Pastoralism has proven to be highly resilient and dynamic, capable of adapting to changing climates and hazards, and embracing new opportunities offered by markets, technology and politics.

Pastoralists worldwide

Pastoralists manage their livestock over a wide range of ecosystems around the world. Estimates for the extent of extensive livestock farming ranges from 25 per

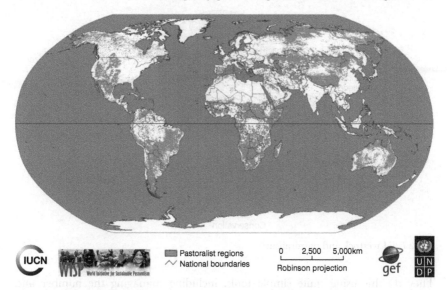

Pastoralist regions
National boundaries
0   2,500   5,000km
Robinson projection

Figure 1.1 Map of general distributions of traditional pastoralists worldwide[1]

cent (FAO, 2001) to 33 per cent (Assner *et al.*, 2004) of the world's surface, and it is estimated that provides approximately 10 per cent of the total consumption of food (FAO, 2001). Figure 1.1 shows some of the main regions of the world hosting pastoralists:

The intimate relationship between pastoralists and their rangelands is so strong that it is hard to separate the two and treat them independently. Yet despite this, the vast majority of pastoralists lack permanent rights over their land. While pastoralist development requires attention to a broad spectrum of needs – including education, health, security and markets – governance and land management must pay heed to the three main components of pastoralism: people, livestock and land, which forms the common foundation of pastoralism anywhere.

Grazed ecosystems usually occupy marginal land with low productive potential, generally grasslands but usually mixed with other vegetation communities including shrublands, open forest and crops. The relative poverty of soils and plant production potential means that pastoralism must be practised over great areas of land, which is essential to understand the environmental impact and the reality of pastoralism. While the increasing global demand for meat is driving some problems related to global change – like the loss of rain forests to create grasslands or to cultivate fodder crops – traditional pastoralist systems maintain marginal ecosystems in higher stages of maturity and biodiversity and actively promote vegetation growth, biological diversity and ecosystem function (IUCN, 2011b).

Pastoralists manage rangelands where seasonal climate extremes, aridity and drought, high climate uncertainty, rugged terrain and exposure are commonplace.

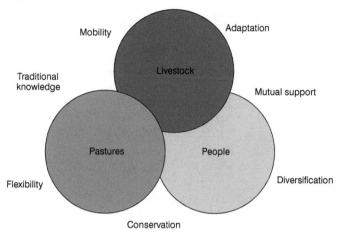

Figure 1.2 Livestock and pastoralism[2]

They do this using quite simple tools, including managing the number and composition of herds, managing herd mobility, protecting resource zones for seasonal use, resting and fallowing land, and using crop stubble. These tools are used intelligently and often employ complex rules that allow herders to manage resources over large areas.

Pastoralism is practised throughout the world and is tried and tested in a range of ecosystems and conditions. The keys to sustainable rangelands management are common throughout – from the Mediterranean to the Mongolian steppe, Australia, South and North America, the Eurasian taigas and tundras, the Sahel or East Africa – and include maintenance of high levels of biodiversity, increasing vegetation soil cover, reducing erosion, managing wildfires, maintaining natural infrastructure and dispersing seeds among other things. Importantly, pastoralism as a system can work under the harshest environments no matter what external conditions are.

Grazing regulation is the key tool in rangeland management, by adjusting factors like space, time, pressure and species. However, a sheep or a goat will not stop eating because it is not the right moment. A herder requires enough land to move herds and adjust to ecosystem constraints and – depending on fodder, climate, soil or water requirements – a lot of land may be needed to adjust grazing pressure. Additionally, vast land surfaces mean that pastoralists have to cross boundaries and borders, whether they are natural or political. This brings pastoralists periodically into contact with many other resource users and creates potential for conflict. Institutions for management of such conflicts have evolved over time but have in many cases been weakened as part of a more general weakening of governance. This is exacerbated when institutions like governments, NGOs and social services do not have the skills, tools or rules to adequately manage or support mobile people.

Ecosystem services provided by rangelands

Rangelands, like other ecosystems, are responsible for contributing to human welfare (White *et al.*, 2000). Rangeland ecosystem services are extremely valuable for people; they may even be accounted and economically expressed to show their importance (Kroeger *et al.*, 2010). Rangeland ecosystem services are perceived variously and usually people and this perception evolve following social trends. Adequate management of livestock can enhance those services and contribute to the welfare of the societies that are hosting them, but in addition, public policies should be shaped to preserve and improve such services.

Ecosystem services related to ecological processes (Maczko and Hidinger, 2008) include soil dynamics, succession, mobility, adaptation, competition, disturbance and erosion. Additionally material, water, energy and information flows are interdependent with these systems. Local populations interact with rangeland ecosystems while managing their land, which links economic, social and ecological processes through a network of relationships and exchanges. In the most advanced pastoralist communities the relationships may be considered as symbiotic, given that the ecosystem shows advanced indicators of maturity and quality and pastoralists are able to maintain their livelihood in extreme conditions.

Principal rangeland ecosystem services[3]

While pastoralism can and does maintain rangeland ecosystem services, where it is practised inappropriately it can contribute to degradation. Land degradation, in addition to being an ecological problem derived from bad management practices, is a major driver in the decline of extensive livestock. It causes a range of interconnected problems, as follows:

- Shrub encroachment that reduces biodiversity, grazing capacity/rangeland productivity, soil cover, and habitat for grassland-dependent species, and alters fire regime.
- Misuse and misunderstanding of fire as a land management tool to regenerate pastures, due to the changing major drivers acting nowadays in rangelands.
- Overdependence on climatic conditions.
- Poverty of pastoralists.
- Variability among people's perception of livestock.
- High level of interference between pastoralism land use (especially nomadic and mobile pastoralism) and intensive development and production projects.
- Bad soil tilling and protection practices leading inevitably to high soil loss.
- Affection to locally fragile biotopes, such as riverine areas, refuges for endangered species or highly specific habitats.
- Generation of social conflicts originated by degradation of production from land and common goods.

Table 1.1 Principal rangeland ecosystem services

Rangeland economic production	Rangeland environmental services	Rangeland social services
Productive soil	Soil fertility	Support for pastoral cultures
Forage for livestock	Soil stability	Pastoral way of life
Hay and stockable fodder	Edaphic processes	Pastoral societies heritage
Plants for restoration and gardening	Grass biodiversity	Mechanisms for land management
Medicinal and tea plants	Native species and relevant species populations	Hunting and fishing places
Meat production	Primary and secondary production	Social issues about fishing and hunting
Leather and other animal products	Habitats for fish and game animals	Availability of fresh water
Fish and hunting licences	Wildlife population control	Water courses for social activities
Activities related to fish and hunting, education, tourism …	Clean water	Waterscapes
Water for irrigation, bottling and economic purposes	Natural water depuration	Shadow and climate regulation
Wind energy	Ecological water dynamics (erosion, transport, sedimentation, flood…)	Woody landscapes
Wood for combustible and raw material,	Dispersal of pollutants	Tourism offer
Biofuel, charcoal and other biocombustibles	Pollination	Natural and cultural heritage
Commercial seeds for fodder and restoration	Seed dispersal	Background for educational activities
Tourism activity	Shrubs and trees diversity Spatial and landscape diversity Nutrient, litter and material recycling Carbon sequestration Limitation of carbon release in the atmosphere Genetic diversity Seed production Reduction of landscape fragmentation and maintenance of ecological connectivity	Open landscape aesthetics and scenery Scientifically significant sites Wildfire prevention Open spaces for outdoor activities Damage avoiding (floor, soil movements, Fertile soil cover and protection

Ecological basis of a managed ecosystem

Ecosystems are continuously changing, and this process is accelerated when they are disturbed and as they adapt to disruption and begin to show the evolution of some factors involved in higher thermodynamic efficiency such as growing larger (in terms of processing higher amounts of energy and materials) and increasing ecological diversity. The structure of ecosystems increases in complexity to enhance the network of relationships and the information managed as an ecosystem grows. Also the energy flows diversify and provide homeostatic and resilient mechanisms (including the rising of diversity) to stabilize and face these disturbances (Ferrer *et al.*, 2011; Ives and Carpenter, 2007). However, this evolution has a cost: primary production is increasingly invested in the development of ecosystem properties so less could be extracted from it.

The most mature ecosystems have very few possibilities for biomass extraction without disturbing this dynamic. When large amounts of biomass are extracted from an ecosystem, as in the case of meat production, the ecosystem is often simplified and driven back to an earlier stage. Sometimes, younger and simpler stages can lead to an increase in primary production, but complexity and other related properties are diminished. The ability of the ecosystem to provide high levels of biodiversity, a wide range of high quality production, better conditions of exposure, temperature and precipitation, fresh water storage, carbon retention or decontamination are compromised and the ecological properties that grant more stability, resilience and better conditions reduce their effectiveness. In naturally disturbed ecosystems, like savannahs or steppes, these conditions are generated naturally, with wild herbivores performing a similar role to that of livestock. These ecosystems can still show high levels of biodiversity and some ecosystem services, such as sequestration of carbon, could even be increased.

If the exploitation of an ecosystem is higher than its capacity to restore itself, the ecosystem continues to degrade. External intervention would be needed to avoid degradation or increase production so most agricultural or livestock systems become dependent on external inputs, usually related to fossil fuel consumption (from mechanization to fodder import), and thereby contribute to environmental impacts like climate change. There are many examples of pastoralism implementing land and ecosystem management mechanisms that have enhanced livestock production without degrading natural resources, and offering environmental services and biodiversity while maintaining acceptable conditions for up to 1,000 million people who depend more or less on livestock production.

Pastoral management of rangeland ecosystems

The ways that pastoralists manage their rangelands are closely interwoven with pastoral cultures. Pastoralist cultures enable management of land and herds following ancestral modes of organization that have prevailed over time and which are the foundation of sustainable livestock-based economies and rangeland ecosystems. Each culture has their own rules, all subtly different, yet they share a common way to profit from mature ecosystems. Pastoralists learnt a long time ago how to manage ecosystem dynamics in ways that governments and wildlife managers have not yet grasped.

Pastoral land management is not only about consumption of grasses or fodder, removing the primary production from the ecosystem. Herds decompose vegetation and distribute manure, improving fertility distribution and contributing to improvements in rangelands soils and productivity as well as soil fertility in crop farming systems they visit; for example, pastoral herds in many parts of India spend more than half the year grazing crop residues, paid by the farmers for the fertilization services they provide. The maintenance of rangeland fertility similarly relies on the behaviour of herds and the pattern of their management. Well-managed herds fertilize their way to better pastures, eat their fodder at the time of optimal production and return litter to the soil preserving the following year's fertility.

Maybe the most important technological advance from pastoralists is the way they use the information provided by the ecosystem to influence their actions. They manage complex situations by organizing the mobility and composition of their livestock following ecosystem patterns. Seasonal variations like frost, snow or drought make it impossible for pastoralists to maintain their herds within a single site, so they follow better conditions but profit along the way. This pattern of grazing is critical for effective management and mimics the bunched herding of wild herbivores, providing intensive grazing impacts for a short duration, manuring and re-seeding, before moving on, leaving the land to rest and recover from grazing, allowing grass to blossom and seed, avoiding livestock to damage crop fields, guaranteeing water and food for their animals at each time and preventing damages and health issues. Pastoralists incorporate all the information necessary for their success and express it over a complex spatial and temporal land mosaic of different uses and rules that they impose and respect with the activity of their herds. That information incorporated in the livestock activity is a key to the success of pastoral management systems and the reason why they have survived in a hostile and changing world to this day.

Pastoralists manage rangelands by deliberately protecting grazing zones and ensuring the production cycle is completed. In sedentary livestock grazing systems, where climate predictability and seasonal patterns allow continuous grazing, herders use fences or electric wires and move their livestock from paddock to paddock following a well-planned system, adjusting to production pressure. The fences act like semi-permeable membranes allowing passage when needed. Traditional pastoralists on the other hand use 'social fencing'; agreements and practices to guide grazing patterns. Pastoralists have developed complex land management systems that organize and govern land tenure, ownership and access for livestock, based on moving their animals where they need to be. Historic and current examples of these systems can be found on all continents – as illustrated in this book – and many have demonstrated that it is possible to optimize production while maintaining fertility and ecosystem services, even in the toughest conditions.

Managing the ecological effects of pastoralism

Pastoralists sustainably feed their animals, while conserving production for seasonal use, by adjusting where and when to be with their livestock. They guide their herds, sometimes helped by specialized dogs and other animals, to carefully control the time and place of grazing and passage. In this way, mature ecosystems can be maintained and enhanced, for example through distribution of seeds and redistribution of nutrients. Herds and managed ecosystems may become synchronized and establish a mutual relationship that enhances livestock production and boosts ecosystem maturity.

Pastoralists manage the land they use by effectively adjusting livestock species to suit the characteristics of rangeland grazed, and often using a diversity of species to capitalize on the diversity of rangeland products (including browse and pasture). Pastoralism makes use of several domesticated species, including but not limited to cattle, sheep, goats, horses, camels, llamas and yaks; depending on the characteristics of land, most pastoralists combine two or more species within their own system. Each species or variety shows its own preferences and adaptation to eating plants (or simply parts of the plants) and pastoralists try to match the needs of rangelands they manage to the features of the animals they own. For instance, some breeds of cattle are less selective and have a high grazing capacity while goats, equipped with narrow snouts, are able to select the edible parts from well-defended plants with thorns. As animals graze different at different heights and are selective about the pasture they eat, they can be used to manage land parcels to improve resources and to ensure their conservation. Studies have shown the suitability of local breeds for managing local rangelands in relation to pasture composition and coverage (Rook *et al.*, 2004) and there is a clear relationship between herds, herding strategies and rangeland condition that can breakdown when alternative, less adapted breeds are introduced.

Livestock grazing affects rangelands in many ways, including through the composition of plant communities and diversity (Belsky, 1992; Augustine and McNaughton, 1998), coverage or spatial heterogeneity of vegetation (Adler *et al.*, 2001), and characteristics of the soil and water. Grazing effects are influenced by many factors, including the number, species and breed of animals, quality of fodder, and resource availability (Allred, 2011). The selection of domestic species and breeds – each with a particular body size and physiology – regulates the impact of grazing over the ecosystem (Rook *et al.*, 2004). Control and scheduling of grazing patches has been shown to increase spatial heterogeneity in several pastoral environments (Pastor *et al.*, 1998), affecting plant composition, forage production, biodiversity, soil erosion, and hydrologic and carbon cycle impacts (Jackson *et al.* 2002). Grazing pressure also affects the dynamics of woody plants into rangelands preventing woody encroachment (Browning and Archer, 2011). Changes in the plant communities may influence livestock productivity (Burrows *et al.*, 1990) and long-term sustainability of livestock production. Woody encroachment must be controlled to prevent decline in rates of productivity; research shows that heavy and moderate mixed species grazing may contribute to the regulation of woody plant encroachment (Allred *et al.*, 2012).

Research clearly shows that pastoralism can, and in many cases does, maintain rangeland ecosystems as the foundation of production, contributing to biological diversity and protecting ecosystem services. This volume explores in greater depth the conditions that make such outcomes possible, and particularly the governance arrangements that underpin many of the ecological, social and economic issues that face pastoralism today. It is not enough to dispose of tools, knowledge, skills or experience to perform work; rights, safety, benefits, good conditions and opportunities are also necessary. Governance frameworks are needed that give pastoralists control of land, pastures, access rights and safety. Pastoralists can benefit greatly from interlocution with competent authorities, from conflict resolution frameworks, from facilities to set up their temporary headquarters, permission to cross borders, health services for people and animals in their home countries and many other 'enabling' factors that are considered in this book.

Traditional systems of pastoralism and rangeland management

There are many ways to describe and classify pastoralism, including species, geography, ecology and the social and economic basis of pastoralists (Blench, 2001). Focusing on land management, pastoralism can be classified into three general systems (Weber and Horst 2011): settled, nomadic and transhumant. Settled pastoralists manage their herders from a fixed location where they live throughout the year in areas where pasture is available year-round (or they can store enough hay or fodder for a short period of scarcity). Some settled pastoralists, however, move with their herds for a short period of time (e.g. up and down a mountain), driven by seasonal pastures. This system is called *transterminance* and was very common in temperate rangelands and mountain pastoralists. Nowadays, the availability of fast vehicles allows shepherds to stay at home and go visiting their herds daily, and even to milk animals *in situ* on a daily basis, which can diminish the effective consequences of the herd movement. Often settled pastoralism encourages other agricultural activities leading to agro-silvo-pastoral systems with complex management mechanisms, a situation common in the Mediterranean (like the Iberian Dehesa and Montado) and elsewhere. Ranching, considered as a modern derivation of settled pastoralism, is found in countries with low population density or strong land ownership rights; usually one sees great cattle herds on large parcels of land, typically managed with fences. This kind of land management is common in regions of the United States and in Australia. Ranching systems do not preclude managed and seasonal herd movements and there are signs of re-emergence of such management strategies in a number of ranching communities.

Transhumants have a fixed place to live during the cold or dry season that is usually close to the resources their animals need to survive the hard times.

Then they leave with their herders looking for better pastures during the growing season, travelling long distances to new domiciles where their herds graze seasonal rangelands. When the growing season is over, they head back to their homes and complete the annual cycle. Transhumance has been described in the Iberian Peninsula, Switzerland, Greece, Bosnia, North Africa, the Himalayas, Kyrgyzstan, the Andes and elsewhere. It effectively describes many of the pastoral systems in Africa where seasonal movements are made between wet season grazing zones and dry season reserves, even when those grazing zones are hundreds of kilometres apart.

Nomadic pastoralists conduct their herds through vast distances led by the feeding capacity of the rangelands their herds graze, without a fixed path or established periodic route. Most nomadic pastoralists depend exclusively on the resources provided by their livestock, so they have an extensive knowledge of the land they cross in terms of pasture availability, ecology, climate behaviour, local and regional conflicts, and market flows. Nomadic people are flexible and adaptable, relying on this flexibility for their survival. Nevertheless they know their land and can establish infrastructure to support their basic needs along the way. Nomadic communities are distributed along the toughest landscapes in the world, especially on the African and Asian continents. Most nomadic societies are ancient and have protracted histories, such as the reindeer shepherds from Siberia and Norway, Arabian Peninsula Bedouins, Mongols and Sahelian pastoralists in Africa.

Despite the great variety of pastoralist systems and cultures related to climate, ecological, political, economic, social and religious factors, the analysis of pastoralism shows a great many commonalities among them. Pastoral societies are linked by mobility, by the highly demanding care of their animals, the flexibility and knowledge of their territories and, in some cases, by historic links surviving over time. Among other things, pastoralists manage resources communally – both natural resources and livestock and their products – and these mechanisms of mutual support and social capital are critical to their management of the rangelands.

How traditional systems of pastoralist governance work

There are many traditional pastoralist management systems in the world that are based on both strengthened social relationships and a deep knowledge of local ecology, accumulated and transmitted over generations. The wisdom traditional pastoralists show in land governance is built over what Berkes (2004) has called Traditional Ecological Knowledge Systems. Such systems are cumulative bodies of knowledge, practice and belief about the relationship of living beings with one another and their environment, evolving by adaptive processes and handed down through generations by cultural transmission. Table 1.2 shows the main management practices found in traditional ecological knowledge related to pastoralist activities.

Table 1.2 Management practices based on ecological knowledge

Monitoring pasture and abundance of other resources
Surveying change in rangelands and grazed ecosystems
Protection of vulnerable life cycle stages, especially grass growing and reproduction stages
Temporal restrictions of grazing, harvesting, and other activities
Managing the production of multiple species, adapting grazing to ecosystem structure and function
Resource rotation by mobility, resting, banning and fallowing
Litter and fertility transfer
Profiting from crop residues and harvested fields
Management of successional issues
Management of landscape patchiness
Other management practices like protection of certain species, protection of specific habitats
Watershed-based management
Managing ecological processes at multiple scales
Responding to and managing pulses and surprises
Nurturing sources of ecosystem renewal

Ecological practices and mechanisms in traditional knowledge and practice[4]

The development, maintenance and governance of these systems are based on strong social and cultural relationships and institutions able to protect, enrich and transfer wisdom over time. There are social mechanisms responsible for conserving knowledge including social, cultural and religious aspects, but also a world view that provides environmental ethics and a strong ethos nurturing cultural values of respect, sharing, reciprocity and humility.

Social mechanisms involved in management practices[5]

Traditional pastoralist land management systems often show holistic alliances with the governance of great territories, considering their ecological structure and dynamics. Those territories are often classified and split in function of their habitat characteristics in functional units that constitute the basis for land regulation. Pastoralist structures are complex, ecologically oriented and locally ruled systems. These structures also share several characteristics such as regulating extended resources, including agricultural, pastoral, rangeland and forestry. They also classify land in different types and manage them implementing spatial and temporary restrictions to uses and access. Furthermore, they use mobility as a management tool and usually generate an ecological mosaic with different

Table 1.3 Social mechanisms behind management practices

Generation, accumulation, and transmission of local ecological knowledge

Reinterpreting signals for learning

Revival of local knowledge

Folklore and knowledge carriers

Integration of knowledge

Intergenerational transmission of knowledge

Geographical diffusion of knowledge

Immaterial heritage keeping

Structure and dynamics of institutions

Roles of stewards and wise people

Cross-scale institutions

Community assessments

Taboos and regulations

Social and religious sanctions

Mechanisms for cultural internalization

Rituals: ceremonies, and other traditions

Cultural frameworks for resource management

World view and cultural values

World views related to traditional pastoralism, generally imply a local conservationist and egalitarian set of principles

Cultural values of respect, sharing, reciprocity, humility and others

vegetation patches and biodiversity pools throughout the territory. Some of these systems also show a deep religious and cultural background deeply rooted in pastoralist societies that transcend the management to become part of the identity of pastoral communities.

The reports compiled in this work show several examples of functioning pastoralist systems with demonstrable benefits to local communities and ecosystems. They describe some African, American, European and Asian examples of traditional pastoralist mechanisms. Each of these case studies is unique, but all of them show wise ways of coping with extreme conditions to maintain livelihoods and land quality. The studies of these governance systems show common qualities of healthy ecosystem management, such as greater levels of production, vegetation cover and biodiversity. They generate richer, more structured, connected and heterogeneous landscapes and embody a remarkable cultural and social heritage. Moreover, these systems share their ongoing reconsideration as a genuine alternative to land degradation processes linked to changes in land use that are impoverishing people in territories and ecosystems throughout the world.

Pastoral land management systems share a set of tools that leave their footprint on territories and repeat themselves among different cultures and societies. The main features are classified into six key issues: tenure rights, mobility, timing, infrastructure, flexibility and relationships. Pastoralists from various countries and continents have developed different tools to address governance, but the following characteristics may be related to almost any successful pastoral societies. In many cases, the traditional rules are constantly evolving and these changes represent ways to improve governance and avoid constraints and difficulties.

Tenure and access rights vs. ownership

Pastoralist communities manage large areas of land, and grazing pressure must be carefully managed to avoid degradation processes. Pastoralism takes place mainly in low productive lands (drylands, marginalized territories, rangelands, steppes), which translates into large expanses of land needed. However, in most cases, high land prices discourage private land ownership, the exception being countries with specific conditions in which traditional settled livestock farmers who will own the amount of land needed to develop their activity. Territories displaying colonizer-mediated land allocation, such as North American or Australian ranches or dehesas and montados in the southwest of the Iberian Peninsula, and some very wealthy livestock owners elsewhere, provide examples of such ownership models.

The vast majority of pastoralists meet their land needs by developing land tenure rights and access rights to pastures they use. Land tenure constitutes the set of rules, institutions and policies that locally determine how land and its resources are accessed, by whom, when and under what conditions these rights to access and use may be used (Bruce *et al.*, 2010; Naughton and Day 2012). Land tenure is a common way for people to use natural resources without owning property throughout the world. Meinzen-Dick *et al.* (2005) categorizes land tenure rights in two main classes: use rights, which entitle the holder to access and use the natural resources stated, and control rights that allow the holder to manage, make decisions, transform and ban the use of the land under rights. Occasionally those rights coincide in the same territory, creating complex situations. It should be clearly stated that neither of these categories of tenure implies outright ownership or the right to sell land.

There are multiples sources of land tenure involving law, religion, tradition, self-regulation and policies (international, national and local). This creates a complex framework for governing resource exploitation. Furthermore, different resources that share the same land can have different rights, such as those for water, pasture, wood, hunting, fishing and mining. Therefore, land tenure rights over a specific patch of land can be highly complex and sometimes generate contradictions among coexisting rules and laws.

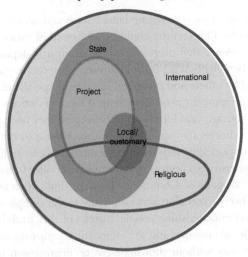

Figure 1.3 Coexisting multiple sources of property rights[6]

According to FAO (2002a), land tenure is often categorized as:

- *Private:* the assignment of rights to a private party who may be an individual, a married couple, a group of people, or a corporate body such as a commercial entity or non-profit organization.
- *Communal:* a right of commons may exist within a community where each member has a right to use the holdings of the community independently. Those lands are often ruled by locally held customary rights.
- *State:* property rights are assigned to some authority in the public sector, whether at a central or decentralized level of government.
- *Open access:* specific rights are not assigned to anyone and, unlike communal tenure, no person can be excluded. It should be noted that these categories are not mutually exclusive, so two of them could coincide (e.g. open access or communal rights within state-owned lands).

Pastoralist lands are often included in non-private land tenure systems whether communal, open access or state and rarely to private owned lands. State-owned land is usually – at least nominally – governed through specific laws, although in practice they have often become an open access system (for an example, see Chapter 3). Communal and open access systems rely on established agreements among people for effective management, and these are often unwritten. Such informal agreements can be found on any type of land and informal agreements can even be cited on privately owned rangelands. These land tenure systems, whether they come from religious, ethnic, communal or other traditions, show flexibility, complexity, adaptability, resilience and scale adjustment, which are distinctive traits of mature systems. The ability to maintain those complex systems is related to the commitment of pastoralists to good practice of access rights.

One of the main issues concerning land tenure and access is the security of rights held by people. This security could be addressed in various ways including the degree of confidence that users will not be arbitrarily deprived of the rights or the economic benefits flowing from land use, the certainty that rights to land will be recognized by others and protected in cases of specific challenges and the right to effective government protection against forced evictions (UN-HABITAT, 2008). Secured rights are vital for pastoralists because they need to be recognized throughout the territories they cross even if they belong to different regions or countries or are supported by different land tenure or access rights.

Open access systems are controversial because they offer free access to anyone. According to the 'Tragedy of Commons' (Hardin, 1968) open access to a shared resource leads to overexploitation and eventually to the complete depletion of it, degrading land and impoverishing people. Instead of this, traditional open access systems are clearly sustainable, and are supporting high exploitation rates from historic times not only without showing signs of degradation but also showing higher quality indicators than equivalent rangelands with market rights system. Researchers have shown many examples of open access successes against the tragedy of the commons (McCabe, 1990). Moreover, some studies point directly to the establishment of property rights as a cause of rangeland degradation (Blewett, 1995). Many governments, inspired by the 'Tragedy of Commons' and aware of alarming processes emerging from livestock intensification have tried to prevent land degradation by promoting ranching, fencing and property rights (Lussigi, 2008). Thus, case studies show that open access systems are being displaced by land planning projects oriented to market production in several developing countries. The result is more degradation, advancing desertification and the overall failure of rangeland management. According to this situation, land rights are being compromised, disrupting pastoral activities and pushing pastoralists into poverty and sedentarization. The former argument can be turned upside down to say that the loss of open access systems is what creates the true 'Tragedy of Commons' in terms of rangeland governance (Fernández-Giménez, 2002).

Management in movement: mobility is good for business

Pastoralist societies are often mobile: from transterminance to nomadic pastoralism, the ability to move herds and livestock from one spot to another is a key for pastoralists' business. Moving herds according to the availability of resources in rangeland systems is vastly more cost effective than moving the resources to the herds, and brings the added benefit of herds mimicking the natural ecological role of wild herbivores and thereby promoting rangeland productivity: a feature that is impossible without some form of mobility. The survival of herds and the ability to face external problems, including but not limited to drought, scarcity and violent conflicts, also relies on the ability of pastoralists to move their herds to better places. It is an adaptive strategy to profit from changing resources in an environment often affected by difficult conditions.

However, it was not until the 1980s that ecologists realized that mobile pastoralism, instead of contributing to erosion and desertification processes, was a management system, well adapted to the transitional and unstable conditions of drylands and rangelands (Adriansen, 2005). The 'mobility paradigm', proposed by Niamir-Fuller and Turner (1999) established that mobile pastoralism is a management strategy appropriate for drylands and other rangelands, with recognized benefits and improvements for some ecosystems.

Mobility can be positive and sometimes necessary for rangelands when combined with a rational management strategy. However, mobility alone is not a management system. Mobility plays an important role in the social and cultural lives of pastoralists. Identity and relationships need to be properly addressed in any future scenario for pastoralists. However, under current circumstances mobility can also pose problems for pastoralists, such as creating impediments in access to social, educational or health services during periods of displacement. Moreover, mobility can sometimes weaken the position of pastoralists in local conflicts.

Settlement, as opposed to mobility, is on the rise in many countries. Some of the factors driving this change in Africa, for example, are droughts, individualization, lack of social structure within pastoral societies, economic vulnerability of mobile herders, land-related conflicts and land grabbing (Niamir-Fuller, 2003). Government policies and agencies, specifically agricultural and environmentally related, have disrupted mobility, favouring intensive agricultural land uses or claiming great territories for protection, banning herds from traditional grazing territories, discouraging investments and otherwise constraining mobility. However, some pastoralists are also choosing to settle to improve access to services and markets. This creates a new challenge of evolving herding strategies to maintain the vital environmental services of livestock.

The way to restore balance to pastoralist mobility demands a new framework to manage common and protected lands that grant mobile pastoralists an appropriate background to develop their activity. These changes should include flexible boundaries, nested property rights, inclusive policies, participatory tools to include mobile pastoralists in decision-making, propriety for pastoralist use of land and interlocution capacity.

Scheduling land use

Pastoralism is not only land-dependent but also time-sensitive. Until now the relationship with nature has been described in terms of adaptation to singular events (some of them catastrophic like droughts, scarcity or conflicts) but most events pastoralists are adapted to show a yearly cyclic basis that is incorporated into the management system. Thus the period of non-grazing is as, or more, important as grazing time. All pastoral cultures apply intervals of no-grazing – rest, recovery and fallow – with periods of active grazing as part of their historic and traditional grazing practices (Weber and Horst, 2011). The duration of the non-grazing period may be a function of both seasonality (Voisin, 1988) and resilience or 'brittleness' of the environment (Savory, 1999).

The period of rest or recovery should constitute a positive influence on the ecosystem but has to be thoroughly applied. Bad timing could lead to local degradation if the resting time is too short or too long. Rangeland and herbivores have coevolved and need each other to develop properly. Pastoralists should measure and adjust carefully the grazing lapse to avoid overgrazing but also to prevent litter accumulation and other degradation processes (Sheppard *et al.*, 2009). Soil and plant health depends on an adequate grazing pressure to adjust ecological factors like soil organic matter (Follett, 2001) or litter to help rain-use efficiency (Weber and Gokhale, 2011).

Many traditional land management systems are based on temporary banning of grazing allowing rotation, resting and grass recovery. They also avoid grazing in the more fragile lands during the growing season to allow grass to develop fully. Overgrazing is over-cited as a major cause of land degradation but it is important to know that frequently it is the scheduling of grazing instead of the total amount of grazing pressure that is causing the problem. Adjusting the grazing load to carrying capacity involves both spatial planning and time scheduling. Moreover, managing time is an essential skill for pastoralists because they work over extremely variable conditions, and they adjust their movements and activities, which is the essence of good timing.

Most of traditional pastoralist activities are not scheduled for fixed times. Transhumants do not move at exactly the same time each year nor do they use the same tracks. Both traditional and transhumant land management systems rely on the qualified people (the herders themselves, local religious or political authorities or other leaders) to set a date for banning or for moving. The result is the maximization of both land recovery benefits obtained from regulation and also the following season's production.

Pastoralist infrastructure: the transhumant tracks

Pastoralists do not move randomly across territories. Displacing a herd is a complex task that demands a set of skills and appropriate tools. Herders also need the disposal of appropriate infrastructure to perform such movements. This infrastructure is frequently not visible but remains critical for effective pastoralism. Pastoralist infrastructure can be categorized according to the goods it provides (considering just livestock needs):

- Shelter and resting places.
- Water access and availability.
- Adequate supplies of fodder or grass to feed herds in translation.
- Tracks and appropriate ways to securely move livestock.
- Other 'on demand' services for livestock (vet services).

In addition, mobile people require infrastructure to support their travelling, including shelter, feeding, health, educational and other services.

Most traditional pastoralist territories hold a wide network of infrastructure, often maintained by the pastoralists themselves and hidden or unknown by the rest of society. This invisibility has often led to precarious situations where infrastructure is not properly addressed, maintained or protected. Infrastructure has often been destroyed due to bad practices performed by people or institutions without enough knowledge to preserve its function.

Livestock corridors and transhumant tracks are among the most important infrastructure for pastoralism. The quality and connectivity of the livestock corridor network is vital for transhumant herders not only because they use those ways to move, but also because those tracks provide enough food for herds in transition: in some cases this may be for several months of the year. Pastoralists do not repeat the same pattern of movement every year; rather, they adjust their travelling to external conditions, which means that a functional network of tracks adapted to mobility requirements is necessary.

Livestock tracks often cross populated regions, cultivated fields, roads and other intensively used areas, which brings about pressure to change their use. Their communal character means that often nobody defends those corridors. Moreover, public works like roads or power lines often are built over livestock tracks to avoid lengthy expropriation processes. The encroachment of livestock tracks means loss of connectivity and breakdown in functionality affecting not just the area encroached, but the connectivity of the network.

Delimitation and protection of transhumant corridors and infrastructures are essential for maintaining pastoralism. Pastoralist infrastructure is usually invisible and therefore difficult to map and define. Delimitation requires the participation of several agents because sometimes it is unrelated to any physical evidence or established rights. For example, a herd using post-harvest stubble as a corridor would not need a marked track, but fencing around the harvested patches would create a detour, delaying or even displacing movements. If a track is delimitated, owners could feel their property rights are affected but herders also could be affected because they should use the track but would not be able to profit from the stubble outside the tracks limits, generating a situation where everybody loses. In such cases it may be more effective to reach a no-fencing agreement between the interested parties. Delimitation is the first step; the challenge after mapping is to protect that infrastructure and its functionality. Legal protection is an expensive and complicated way to ensure real protection for pastoralist infrastructure.

Another problem is that the success of pastoralism relies on flexibility. This is also applied to mobility, meaning that pastoralists change their movements and modify their routes to adapt to external conditions. Much pastoral infrastructure consequently has fuzzy boundaries that are constantly changing. Protecting such infrastructure and its functionality also preserves flexibility, but mapping and delimitation often lead to a tidy border that boosts intensification at the track's edge, making tracks more rigid and often less functional.

Clearing cuts and other tools to get new pastures

Extensive livestock grazing is marked by change. Pastoralists tend to use the same rangelands over and over again and an adequate grazing system usually maintains rangelands in a good state of maturity and production. However, changes in the livestock load, natural events – including droughts, floods and catastrophes – wildfires, encroachment, losing grazing load, abandonment and many other factors may alter the balance between the rangeland needed and available. Pastoralists in this case need to get new pastures to feed their livestock. Shrub invasion is another problem for rangeland maintenance, especially related to places where abandonment and decrease of grazing load is a fact. The prevalence of cattle over other livestock species can trigger shrub invasion because cattle tend to be selective and abandon marginal pastures (Eldridge *et al.*, 2011). This is a particular challenge where herding practices are inadequate and cattle are allowed to be overly selective.

Pastoralists have a range of tools they use to maintain and establish rangelands, including clearing cuts, littering, and using grazing to promote palatable grasses over woody plants. Clearing cuts can be performed mechanically or be the result of using fire as a tool. There are many pastoralist cultures that have used fire as a management tool and many rangeland ecosystems are ecologically adapted to sporadic and even cyclic wildfires.

Wildfires are a major problem in some pastoral landscapes, especially in the Mediterranean, while they constitute a necessary management tool for other rangelands. Some ecosystems can generate naturally by fire and the loss of fire leads to shrub invasion and other related problems. Inappropriate use of fire for reducing shrubs is developing degradation processes including pyrophytic heathland invasion, erosion and water pollution in some places where fire was traditionally used. At the same time, banning and discouraging the use of fire in some rangeland ecosystems such as in the USA have shown similar symptoms (fertility declining, shrub invasion and quality loss). In areas with agricultural abandonment and landscape homogenization such as in southern European countries, there is a further danger of catastrophic wildfires due to the accumulation of biomass that is further exacerbated by the lack of grazing (Ruiz-Mirazo *et al.*, 2012). These situations point to a localized level of decision making where fire management needs to be addressed in particular conditions, while bearing in mind the devastating effects that uncontrolled wildfires could have.

Pastoralist relationships: agriculture, forestry and environment

Pastoralism, as an extensive activity performed over vast surfaces of land, maintains a complex relationship with other systems of land management and exploitation that could vary from strong conflict and interference to symbiosis, depending on how land uses are managed. The relationship between agricultural and pastoralist communities could be seen from the perspective of settled versus mobile interaction. Settled farmers often do not like herders moving across their lands, grazing and damaging crops, although a number of long-standing relationships have developed between pastoralists and crop farmers in which pastoralists are paid to manure crop land (e.g. India, West Africa). Mobile pastoralists do not like fences or encroachment of their infrastructure and tracks. On the other hand, livestock can benefit from some agricultural infrastructure and grazing is a much better way to treat harvested crop fields than sowing, burying or burning stubble. However, conflicts are common where pastoralists and agricultural land owners coincide and sometimes there are no adequate tools for negotiation.

Pastoralism and forestry also have a tempestuous relationship. Government agencies in charge of forestry often consider grazing to be incompatible with forestation. Forested land patches are often made inaccessible to pastoralists to avoid losing new seedlings. Recovering vegetation layers is usually the main objective for forestry agencies, so they tend to use rangelands and marginal lands as a pool for new woodlands, displacing other activities, often without enough local participation. This has been the origin of unresolved land conflicts. Moreover, extensive livestock production has been related to wildfires and other events damaging woodlands, which contributes to the mutual misunderstanding. Aggravating the situation further, pastoralists have been prohibited from traversing lands oriented to reforestation even those that have been traditional grazing lands (Rao and Geisler, 1990). Pastoralists feel banned from traditional grazing lands without advice or consideration, and react aggressively to forestation projects and forestry authorities.

Over the last two decades, some forestry managers have begun to realize that livestock grazing can be a powerful tool to manage forests (Vallentine, 2000). Livestock can be valuable in controlling under-canopy by eliminating undesired sprouts, maintaining walkability of woods, fertilizing soil, fighting shrub invasion and preventing wildfires by transferring fuel to litter – particularly when multiple species are used. Pastoralists can use more land, increase their livestock and expand seasonal grazing using forest pastures and incorporate the management of forest landscapes into the services they provide.

There are other natural resources linked to forest lands that are related to or could interfere with livestock activity such as hunting, fishing, wild plants, fruit or mushroom gathering and tourism. Despite the local conflicts those activities engender, these pursuits could be considered to be complementary activities suitable for pastoralists to subsidize their rents and provide a wider range of resources available to improve their livelihoods (Plieninger *et al.*, 2012).

Finally, pastoralists have been often seen as enemies of nature conservation and have been left out of biodiversity and wildlife policies, thus generating conflicts between government agencies in charge of nature conservation and livestock farmers. Policymakers have mistakenly considered pastoral ecosystems as potentially stable and balanced, which were destabilized by overstocking and overgrazing. They pointed to livestock overstocking as a driving force for land degradation and ecological loss. The problem and solutions were clearly addressed; there were too many cattle so it needed to be destocked. This led to the establishment of banning rules, group ranches or grazing blocks and associations which have never worked (Pimber and Pretty, 1995).

The consequence of omitting pastoralists from local conservation policies has led to unwise rangeland management in nature conservancy including policies leading to the loss of habitats of interest and biodiversity related to grassland and rangeland ecosystems. Fortunately, biodiversity policies are changing and the role of grazing and pastoralism in the maintenance, conservation and recovery of habitats of interest is clearly gaining understanding (Notenbaert *et al.*, 2012; Kerven and Behnke, 2011).

Strengthening the link between pastoralist governance and land management

Pastoralism is closely associated with the rangelands and creates identifiable pastoral landscapes. Likewise, land itself strongly influences pastoralists and their activities. The unavoidable conclusion is that pastoralists should be deeply involved in land governance. However, there are some territorial considerations that influence pastoralists' participation in land use planning and territorial policies. Some of these considerations are discussed briefly here, but the most interesting land-related questions can be found at the heart of the reports that constitute the nucleus of the book.

Shepherds without borders

Pastoralist mobility and the role of borders as they travel over wide swathes of land is the first issue related to land management. Pastoralists are influenced by borders as herders move along traditional routes year after year, often crossing regional or country borders and suffering conflicts and issues related to these borders. Furthermore, pastoralists tend to use marginal land so political borders are often drawn through their traditional territories (Nori *et al.*, 2005). Pastoral communities living in such frontier lands end up far away from decision-making centres (Galaty *et al.*, 1994).

Borders can hamper opportunities to boost trade and enhance pastoral activity, as shown in the Horn of Africa (Pavanello, 2010). Moreover, in places subject to natural disasters like droughts, boosting trans-border pastoral activities can greatly enhance pastoralist resilience and recovery ability, but this field of opportunity remains poorly examined.

Conflictual borders are clearly a major issue for pastoralists. Recurrent tensions and violence degrade the wellbeing of pastoral communities, affecting the social fabric and causing death and suffering (Pavanello, 2009). Conflicts contribute to fragility and vulnerability of pastoralist communities and hamper success, especially mobility. Border conflicts are a great obstacle to transhumance and mobility; they impoverish people and contribute to the vulnerability of herders. Moreover pastoralists' knowledge of land and their ability to move and trade (often 'under the radar') across borders are valuable skills in conflict zones that are exploited by different parties, often making them victims.

It is challenging for herders to deal with border issues to improve security, establish stable markets for their products, adapt ruling to cross border activities, promote peaceful solutions to conflicts and respect traditional rights. Regional borders, even in politically stable zones, also pose difficulties for pastoralists. Land management has been increasingly decentralized in several parts of the world, adjusting the scale of decisions to local and regional levels. Many countries have transferred environmental, land or agricultural powers to regional and local governments. This transfer of authority to regional governments, while positive in the sense of equating decision-making with citizenship, is however causing problems to pastoralists. Regionalization in some places means that mobile pastoralists are submitted to different sets of rules throughout their journeys depending on which region they are in, despite of being in the same country. Some regional governments restrict mobility due to health concerns, demanding duplicate paperwork or discouraging the use of local infrastructure for 'foreign' livestock. Pastoralists often need to fight to achieve a homogeneous ruling system over the whole territory they use; institutions and agencies are not ready to work with mobility and this rigid framework impedes pastoral activity.

Scale and land knowledge

The environment where pastoralists move is difficult to coordinate with political decisions. Too large to be local and occupying lands of various regions or countries, the scale of pastoralism is too vast to be effective for decision-makers. However, pastoralist culture has developed throughout the centuries by governing such scale and herders know how to rule these territories. They transfer matter, information and energy using that reference scale, adapted to business and ecosystem needs.

Fragmentation and other land-related issues

Land use change, an aspect of global change, has had a deep impact on rangelands, drylands and other ecosystems related to extensive livestock production throughout the world (Turner, *et al.* 2007; Foley *et al.*, 2005; Lambin and Meyfroidt, 2011). According to Lambin *et al.* (2001) agricultural intensification from the mid-twentieth century removed the nutrient connection between arable lands and livestock, separating cultivated plains from mountain and forest areas used for grazing. The conversion and fragmentation of temperate semi-natural rangelands led to a progressive loss of biodiversity, species connectivity, and means for recovery.

Landscape fragmentation is considered to be a main driver of global biodiversity loss (Primack, 2002; McGarigal and Cushman, 2002; Fahrig, 2003; Cushman, 2006). Fragmentation is a common consequence of land use change, which is more visible in developed countries. Urbanization, infrastructure location, fencing, ranching, intensive cropping and agricultural industrialization, dam building, mining and other types of land recruitment are also changing the pattern of land distribution. Reid *et al.* (2008) assert that the fragmentation of semi-arid and pastoral landscapes is a major issue that has clear consequences for people, wildlife, and grazing lands. They conclude that fragmentation and exclusivity of land use in dry grazing lands can result in declining productivity and land degradation contrary to the expected results of the application of exclusive rights.

Land, conflict, poverty and pastoralism

Pastoralists have been involved in violent conflicts throughout their history; from the Celtic tribes in the Roman Empire or the North American Far West to water and border conflicts in Africa or the Middle East (Ochieng, 2012; Omosa, 2005; Schilling *et al*, 2012). Current conflicts between farmers and pastoralists are an echo of those from Biblical times. Conflicts ranging from cattle raiding, borders (Pavanello, 2009), natural resources, and political rebellion and secessionist movements (Markakis, 2004) still go on. One example is drought, which often sparks or escalates conflict over natural resources. Pastoral groups move over larger tracts of land in search of available grazing and water sources, which can lead to fierce competition over scarce resources and in many cases it becomes a source of tension or overt conflict among both nomadic and settled communities.

While synthesizing causes and impacts of pastoralist conflicts is not the goal of this chapter, it must be brought to light that there exists a solid literature describing global incidence of conflicts in pastoralist societies (Blench, 2001; Nori *et al.*, 2005; Pavanello, 2009). Mkutu (2001) describes the main source of conflict in Africa to be government policies, socio-economic and political marginalization, inadequate land tenure policies, insecurity, livestock rustling, proliferation of small arms and light weapons, weakened traditional governance in pastoral areas, vulnerability or competition with wildlife. Clearly, there are some land rights and governance related conflicts that are necessary to address in order to understand why land rights are so important about pastoralists' security.

According to Nori *et al.* (2005), the deterioration of pastoral land tenure and management systems are boosted by encroaching interests, which range from the advancing agricultural frontier, to oil and mineral extraction, tourism-driven conservation policies and Western notions of private property and resource ownership. Changes in land tenure introduced by central governments and related uncertainties about resource access have been a major source of deprivation, vulnerability and insecurity in pastoral areas.

Land tenure issues are undoubtedly relevant for pastoralism in terms of their vulnerability. Privatization is leading to land conflicts (landlessness, insecure tenancy, eviction and violence) in several areas, particularly in Sub-Saharan Africa and Central Asia, where land privatization reforms are siphoning land rights away from pastoralist communities. This growing insecurity to resource access and to mobility options may lead to violence and conflict.

Relevant questions need to be addressed, such as why is pastoralism being displaced from territories where shepherds are the only people able to manage, improve and profit? Why are pastoralist models declining in the modern world? After all the research done and the information compiled, why is it so difficult to establish a good framework to implement pastoral models of land management allowing us to improve biodiversity and ecosystem services?

Notes

1 IUCN, UNDP-GEF and FAO, 2007.
2 Rota and Speradini, 2009
3 Kroeger *et al.*, 2010; Boyd and Banzhaf, 2007; Maczko and Hidinger, 2008.
4 Modified from Folke *et al.*, 1998.
5 Modified from Folke *et al.*, 1998.
6 Meinzen-Dick *et al.*, 2005

2 Governance of the rangelands in a changing world

Pedro M. Herrera, Jonathan Davies and Pablo Manzano Baena

Introduction: diagnosis of pastoralism and rangelands: drivers, constrains, impacts and consequences

Currently many countries around the world, including the most developed countries, consider pastoralism as a valuable economic and cultural asset (Kerven and Benke, 2011; Huntsinger *et al.*, 2012). However, literature and research from the last decade of the twentieth century show a significant increase in the vulnerability of pastoralism, which has led to its decline (Dong *et al.* 2011). The reasons for this reduction depend on local and global drivers that have affected livestock keepers in different ways. Table 2.1 shows the status and tendencies of the main global pastoralist regions and some reasons for their situation.[1]

Some of these drivers and trends may be addressed from a wider point of view, which suggests that pastoralism is evolving due to high-pressure global constraints that will continue to change pastoralism. These pressure factors are summarized in Table 2.2.[2]

Sweeping global changes, including but not limited to economics and climate, are applying great pressure on pastoralism worldwide and such impacts are likely to intensify in the future (Crane, 2010). These include changes in land use such as agricultural intensification, which displaces pastoralist activities, reduces livestock mobility or interrupts livestock tracks. Globalization implies major changes in pastoralist economies when they merge with nation-states (Galvin, 2009). There are also deep socioeconomic impacts affecting pastoralism, some of them closely related to land issues that are tearing apart the social framework of pastoralists, which often contributes to marginalization.

Despite of the global constraints addressed above, there are some common problems affecting governance and management worldwide. We try to describe the influence of common impacts over pastoralism worldwide and extract some generalizations from locally addressed factors in the case studies. Our analysis considers the different circumstances affecting pastoralists in developing versus industrialized countries. Weaknesses in governance observed in several developing countries reveals that intensification, encroachment, conflict or settlement affect territories similarly – whether caused by lack of governance or overregulation. Moreover, several social issues such as respect of traditional institutions, dealing

Table 2.1 Status and drivers of main pastoralist regions

Zone	Main species	Status
Sub-Saharan Africa	Cattle, camel, sheep, goat	Reducing due to advancing agriculture
Europe	Small ruminants	Significant decline in some countries due to enclosure and advancing agriculture, but benefits from environmental subsidies maintaining some pastoral systems
North Africa	Small ruminants	Reducing due to advancing agriculture
Near East and South-Central Asia	Small ruminants	Locally declining due to enclosure and advancing agriculture
India	Camel, cattle, buffalo, sheep, goats, ducks	Declining due to advancing agriculture but peri-urban livestock production expanding
Central Asia	Yak, camel, horse, sheep, goat	Expanding following de-collectivization
Circumpolar	Reindeer	Expanding following de-collectivization in Siberia, but under pressure in Scandinavia
North America	Sheep, cattle	Declining with increased enclosure of land and alternative economic opportunities
Central America	Sheep, cattle	Declining with increased enclosure of land and alternative economic opportunities
Andes	Llama, alpaca, sheep	Contracting llama production due to expansion of road systems and European-model livestock production but increased alpaca wool production
South American lowlands	Cattle, sheep	Expanding where forests are converted to savannah but probably otherwise static

with local authorities, social backup of pastoralist activity, and interlocution may be addressed in the same way in any region of the world.

The loss of traditional management and institutions

Traditional management systems are losing authority, management capacity, civic representation and social integration as global economies and governance shift. Tribal, traditional and common institutions, based on social ties among densely

Table 2.2 Pressure/impact table on pastoralism activity

Factor	Impact
Introduction of high-input, high-output exotic breeds	Makes pastoralists dependent on effective infrastructure where input supplies irregular, creating periodic crises
World market in livestock products	Governments import cheap meat, milk, etc., to satisfy urban demand at expense of pastoral sector
Enclosing and fencing	Collapse of traditional 'safety-nets' in terms of long-distance migration in periods of climatic extremes
Encroachment on rangeland	Rangeland is being eliminated through the use of politically attractive but often uneconomic irrigation systems
International pressure for hygiene in slaughtering and dairying	Declining market for pastoralist and handmade products
Modern veterinary medicine	Increases in productivity and greatly enlarged herds
Modern weapons	Major decline in predator threats, increasingly violent ethnic conflict and high levels of insecurity
Declining prestige of dairy products	Terms of trade running constantly against pastoral livelihoods
Ideological interference by the state	Inappropriate social and management strategies adopted and maintained by a combination of subsidized inputs and implied violence
Alternative calls on pastoral work	Pressure for children to go to school and younger people to earn cash outside the pastoral economy
Modern transportation infrastructure	Replaces systems where transport is a major element of economic production (llamas, horses)
Emergency relief, restocking and rehabilitation programs	Keeps non-viable households in pastoral areas, thereby accelerating the cycle of deficits
Conservation lobby	Pressure to turn previously pastoral land over to reserved wildlife/biodiversity regions with corresponding hard currency income from tourism
Legitimization of Indigenous and Community Conserved Areas	Growth in the number of 'Community Based Natural Resource Management' type projects with strong foundation in governance and participation and contributing to dual benefits from livestock keeping and biodiversity conservation

populated rural areas, are now weakening due to urban migration, intensification of land uses, global market influence and loss of representation. Those systems, deeply rooted in rural societies, are suffering from new constraints as a result of their incapacity to adapt to current economic, social and political pressures. The reaction of governments, which is often to dismantle such institutions and replace them with government organizations, has serious social, economic and ecological consequences.

An alternative to such government practices could be modernizing, funding, empowering, assisting and advocating traditional pastoralist institutions so established populations can retain control over rangelands. Eleanor Ostrom's pivotal work *Governing the Commons* (Ostrom, 1990) highlighted the efficiency of communal arrangements and the importance of self-regulation. Communal arrangements are more efficient than government alternatives because they do not require excessive costs for enforcement and control, relying instead on investment in social capital by the users, and the acceptance by them of certain rules and behaviours. However, these arrangements have evolved over time and it is not certain that such behaviours can be fast-tracked, although as the Botswana chapter in this book illustrates, emergence of such behaviours may be a natural tendency for some human societies.

Inappropriate government policies replacing traditional systems

Many traditional governance systems have been replaced or are on course to be replaced by government policies, which intend to be more respectful and democratic, following a western model that is based on ownership rather than on managing common rights. In many cases this substitution harms rather than helps pastoralists' ability to self-govern, which negatively impacts their herding and rangeland management strategies.

The analysis of land governance in developed countries shows a system based on hierarchical government levels (international, national, state, municipality, private owners), with specific competences implied for each rung of the governance ladder, focused and adapted to manage locally owned land. Even protected areas or state owned land are governed with the assumption of local ownership (despite the reality that owners could be public or private, local or not). Land planning tools are often static, establishing exclusive rights for exclusive uses managed by ownership. Moreover, policy makers create laws that make it difficult to manage extensive and complex areas, especially tracts of land that involve multiple regions or departments like those needed for pastoral activities.

In many developing countries rangelands have been converted to government ownership (mainly controlled by forestry and environmental agencies), without assigning financial resources or personnel to develop land policies, which leaves decision-making processes to higher levels of governance, where it is impossible to effectively manage relatively small land patches. Both processes are involved in the loss of traditional (tribal, religious, community managed and even institutional) governance systems that are currently losing their authority in political frameworks. Many drop out because of their lack of representation, insufficient funds, abandonment, or changes in political competences, all of which leaves traditional institutions out of decision-making.

There are two adaptations of traditional pastoralist systems that are missing in the systems of land governance: adjusted scale of management and land tenure rights to manage extensive areas without needing ownership. Where customary governance systems have been lost and the state has assumed ownership of rangelands, inappropriate management practices are common as pastoralists are unable to enforce rational management strategies and they are dissuaded from investing in or improving land capacities. These lands lose the application of traditional grazing methods – most notably seasonal herd movements – and thereby suffer from deterioration of rangeland productivity.

Finally, related to this flawed arrangement, there are some problems in public lands subject to fee exploitation. The establishment of fees for profiting from natural resources is not working well for rangelands because high fees are unsuitable and low fees beget poor investment in land improvements. There are very few examples of working systems of fee collection based on herd size with inducements to invest in good practices.

Privatization, claims and conflicts over ownership, rights and access

Common rights can be progressively transformed into ownership systems following recommendations of global institutions assuming that ownership will boost economic activities, investment and modernization of transformed lands. When governments take charge of communal lands they generally classify them as public property; thereafter, the legal framework proclaims such land as suitable for certain uses (e.g. for forestry, pastoralism or environmental uses). State owned lands could be leased to third parties to develop highly intensive activities – like industry, mining, wood trimming, infrastructure and urban development – even if they are governed by forestry or environmental agencies. This leads to unsustainable land exploitation that deteriorates productivity and damages pastoralist livelihoods. Often, government actions, which are intended to generate economic rights and access to natural resources like water, have the opposite effect on local communities, particularly on women who become more dependent on external institutions.

Even when livestock-breeding activity is maintained on government held lands, the absence of adequate rights management procedures results in imprudent practices that deteriorate land. Sometimes free access to public lands without traditional regulation systems effectively leads to the 'tragedy of commons', especially when livestock breeding intensifies with external inputs and is attached to demanding markets. In an open competence system, where traditional institutions are absent or overwhelmed and government is concerned only with short-term production, lack of regulation leads to deleterious practices whereby herders are unable to apply sustainable management techniques.

The lack of collective land tenure is also leading to the emergence of private ownership claims. The dominant position expressed by several governments and international institutions is to allow such claims as a way to instil a more dynamic economy, in the belief that private ownership will boost investment and production of these lands. However, private ownership of rangelands tends to give rise to overexploitation through intensive cropping, increased herds with higher rates of external inputs, which implies a loss of fertility and production capacity, and land degradation processes. Moreover, private land ownership is frequently behind some of the most common constraints upon pastoralist activity, such as grazing bans, fencing, encroachment, urbanization and closure of stock routes.

One aspect related to change in ownership rights is their relationship with poverty. Ownership in the western sense has been seen as a tool to fight poverty under the assumption that owners take care of their land more than others. Herders depend on land access rights to survive and losing those rights because of new ownership policies is driving them into poverty regardless of the intention of land ownership laws. Moreover, people living in extreme poverty are highly dependent on access to land and other natural resources for their livelihoods and when that access fails they become displaced. In general, land privatization policies by governments have helped wealthier herders and increased the vulnerability of poorer communal pastoralists.

The settlement of nomadic societies

Property claims are the first step for pastoralists to settle. Regulations and bureaucracy associated with land ownership frequently force nomadic or mobile pastoralists to abandon their activity when poverty and other difficulties arise. However, settlement of mobile pastoralists risks converting them into static livestock keepers, especially in developing countries and mostly in the same marginal territories they had previously lived. Sedenterization of herders increases pressure over neighbouring rangelands through overgrazing and intensification and misguided land management practices in fragile ecosystems. However, while herd mobility remains vital for rangeland productivity and sustainable pastoralism, settlement of the herding population does not necessarily have to be an impediment. Many pastoral societies have undergone profound change from being nomadic societies to becoming settled populations who managed mobile herds, often over large distances.

The disorientation of nature conservation policies

If contemporary societies want to preserve grassland ecosystems and biodiversity, they must apply proper grazing and livestock systems to slow down grassland degradation and maintain rangeland habitats. Research and practice indicate that preservation of other ecosystems, habitats, and landscapes also positively correlate to effective grazing management. Extensive (grazing-based) livestock production is a financially inexpensive means of conservation and is often the most effective and most profitable way to sustain valuable ecosystems like woodlands, wetlands, agro-silvo-pastoral lands, high mountain landscapes, savannah and tundra.

As a result of failure to understand the environmental benefits of pastoralism, pastoralists have been marginalized from protection policies and their activity has been frequently banned from protected areas, woodlands and fragile ecosystems, often with counterproductive results. Indeed, there are conflicts between the conservation sector and pastoralism related to two main issues: management of predators attacking herds and use of aggressive techniques in land management, like fire as a shrub control tool. Environmental conservationists and government agencies have often viewed such practices as a sign of an aggressive attitude towards nature conservation, mistakenly regarding pastoralists as their enemies.

Pastoralists have not usually been included in policies or negotiations about nature conservation, which excludes one of the most important collectives in decision-making processes concerning protected areas. As a result, those governing pastoral lands often conclude that pastoralism is a non-suitable or non-friendly activity for protected areas, discouraging herding from fragile lands, increasing bureaucracy, requiring permissions and even banning grazing in available lands.

Some opinion-forming institutions like FAO still address the environmental impact of livestock (Steinfeld, 2006) without properly disaggregating it into extensive and intensive livestock production; identifying environmental costs but ignoring environmental benefits of livestock production. Moreover, some deep impacts have been attributed to extensive livestock production without adequate characterization, assuming that extensive grazing still occupies and degrades vast areas of land and blaming livestock for impacts of global significance without distinction between the behaviour of production systems. This attitude indicates the still fragile position of pastoralism and extensive livestock and the persistent lack of public consideration for this activity.

A complex relationship with the authorities

Case studies in this work highlight difficulties in the relationships between authorities and pastoralists. These conflicts cover a variety of issues, including land tenure and property rights, disagreements with environmental agencies, lack of capacity for traditional institutions, marginalization from development and agricultural modernization policies and lack of interlocution. Moreover, mobile pastoralist and herder communities often do not fit neatly into modern political frameworks. Pastoralists often feel undefended in conflicts with settled people (who are generally closer to local authorities and more integrated within local networks) and are not able to represent their interests.

When pastoralists are hardly represented politically and badly co-ordinated, misunderstandings and strained relationships arise. Weak co-ordination between governmental agencies and local communities or municipalities results frequently in conflicting approaches to the management of land and natural resources. Herders are often damaged by these conflicts because they lack proper interlocution with local or state authorities. Authorities tend to interfere with rather than create options for low-level flexible negotiations among local user groups. When land-use zones are created by planning tools – or by state or federal laws – the possibility of negotiations between herders and other stakeholders and the ability of independent conflict resolution is remote. Despite this, at the local level in many countries traditional authorities often trump legal documents in practice when it comes to allocating land rights.

The industrialization of agricultural land use

An increasing number of people worldwide are leaving rural areas to live in urban settlements and this global urbanization, combined with global economic growth is driving up demand for meat and other livestock related products, paving the way for intensification of livestock production, especially in developing countries. This intensification has a deep environmental impact on global change (Steinfeld, 2006) and has consequences on livestock production systems, leading to a process of industrialization that is negatively affecting pastoralism and extensive production. Attempted intensification of land use is one of the major causes of reduction in pastoralism and rangelands culture. This intensification – particularly of capital inputs – varies by country and geography, but shows common patterns, particularly in developing countries. One common outcome of intensification is the concentration of production in one part of the landscape and abandonment, or major decline, of the rest. The associated losses are seldom factored into decision-making.

Intensification of agriculture and livestock production is one of the major drivers of land degradation (Benayas *et al.*, 2007). The main factors in the degradation are overexploitation of local resources, the misjudged adjustment of graze loading and dependence upon external inputs. The consequences include the loss of herd fertility, desertification and increased damage from natural disasters. Furthermore, intensification is related to the spread of poverty (Scherr, 2000) despite the fact that it is usually intended to fight against scarcity.

The growth of external inputs and market dependence

One of the most important consequences of intensification and privatization is that even when such practices boost local economies, they are also making them more fragile and overly dependent on external inputs. The intensification of agriculture and livestock production demands fuel, machinery, fertilizers, plant protection products, water and other supplies that also require financial infrastructure to establish and maintain. Dependence on these external inputs affects livestock keepers by encouraging herders to keep a large number of animals that exceed the carrying capacity of a rangeland. In an effort to boost the livestock sector, some countries have subsidized inputs, but this has similarly encouraged overpopulation and diminished the relative value of rangelands in the pastoral system, with the outcome of serious desertification. Dependence upon external inputs – sometimes subsidized to maintain competitiveness, often artificially – makes it difficult for local herders to maintain a living wage. Livestock keepers often become dependent on loans and subsidies, losing resilience and land management capacity.

The employment generated by agricultural and livestock intensification is the main goal in developing such projects, but they are not providing enough employment to compensate the population loss. There is no evidence that this form of development is adequate to fight poverty in rangelands but its application in the rangelands has been proven to be a major driver of land degradation and loss of resilience.

Vulnerability of pastoralist societies

Pastoralist societies have shown extraordinary resilience in adapting to sudden changes and natural disasters while maintaining their activity in difficult conditions in poor and marginal lands. Mobility and customary governance and social arrangements are central to enabling pastoralists to manage extreme climatic conditions that include drought and freezing depending on location. As governance systems break down, and as relationships with authorities and settled societies are affected, women and impoverished pastoralists are becoming particularly vulnerable.

Female pastoralists are key to the survival of pastoralism; according to recent studies, women are the most valuable assets for the maintenance of pastoralism (Kristjansonn *et al.*, 2010; Joyce, 2007). Women act as guardians of locally adapted livestock breeds as the sector experiences high-input and large-scale production intensification. Women's responsibilities in the reproductive economy are deeply ingrained in gender roles that restrict their range of activities. They tend to favour risk-avoiding livelihood strategies and while intensification is more often related to men's activity women tend to adhere to locally adapted systems. Women are often marginalized in land rights in traditional societies but they are increasingly heading households in a context where men are forced to migrate to urban areas in search of employment (FAO, 2012; Kleinbooi, 2013).

The legal and cultural acknowledgement of women's roles and responsibilities in pastoralist societies could lead to better frameworks and conditions for the survival of endangered pastoralist societies. On the other hand, in countries where land rights have been equal for women, there has been a process of rural masculinization where women have migrated to urban places, escaping the constraints and the conservatism of rural societies. The gender equilibrium in some developed countries has shown an increasing abandonment and fragility of rural communities.

Rangelands and global change

The decline of rangelands and pastoralism is also related to global change. Imprudent management practices and subsequent intensification of land uses contributes to global change (Society for Range Management, 2003) and climatic change. It is expected that these changes will increase the risk of land degradation and biodiversity loss. Climate change will modify the length of growing seasons, crop and livestock yields, and increase the likelihood of food shortages, insecurity, and pest and disease incidence, all of which place populations at greater health and livelihood risks (Neely *et al.*, 2009).

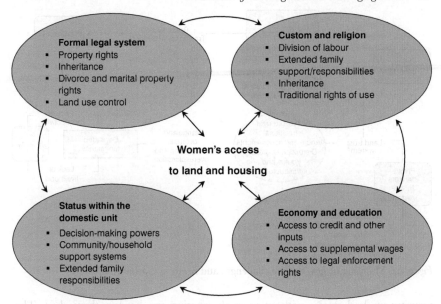

Figure 2.1 Factors in pastoral women's rights[3]

Grasslands, by their extensive nature, hold enormous potential to serve as one of the greatest terrestrial sinks for carbon. Furthermore, livestock play an important role in carbon sequestration through improved pasture and rangeland management (Steinfeld, 2006; Tennigkeit and Wilkes, 2008). Rangelands also play a significant role in conserving biodiversity, and especially in providing livelihood benefits to local herders. Healthy grasslands, livestock and associated livelihoods constitute a valuable option for addressing climate change in fragile dryland areas where pastoralism remains the most rational strategy for maintaining the wellbeing of communities (Neely,*et al.* 2009).

Complex problems demand complex solutions

We have so far described some of the key factors in the weakening of pastoralist governance in very different countries and backgrounds. However, it is also necessary to understand the way these factors interact with people and communities to create complex challenges that are particularly challenging to address. Complex systems are characterized by the constant adjustment of components in the system to changes in other components as well as to outside influences. When elements of the system are isolated and changed in order to make the system more efficient, the usual outcome is the opposite: a loss in efficiency of the system overall.

Shanahan (2012) explained the image problem pastoralism faces, making reference to the situation in Kenya. Mass media ignore pastoralists' knowledge and skills, which have led them to become a cornerstone of rangelands and drylands economy and highlight, quite improperly, the conflicts related to pastoral activity,

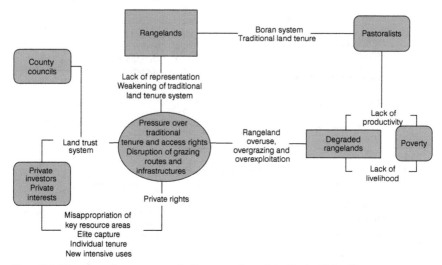

Figure 2.2 Mapping of governance challenges and needs in Garba Tula, Kenya

focusing on bad stories without properly quoting the herders themselves. The authors played a game with Kenyan journalists, asking them for five words related to pastoralism. The results are mapped out below showing vividly how pastoralism is perceived by and portrayed in the media, and demonstrating the overwhelming absence of any reference to nature conservation, land management or any other positive role. Though this refers only to the situation in Kenya, the situation is not very different in the majority of countries.

In order to respond more effectively to the complex needs and contexts of pastoralism, we need an understanding of how the different factors involved interact. To address this, we have reviewed several of the case studies, identifying the principal drivers affecting the current scenario in order to map out the relationship between them. The aim is to show the emerging picture driven by several factors acting simultaneously and put them in a contextualized map of the situation. This mapping needs to be adjusted to each particular reality, addressing local drivers. The first example corresponds to the Garba Tula case study from Kenya. This is the simplest case study to analyse this way and provides a template for two more examples below.

The schema shows how private rights and intensification weaken pastoral governance and increase rangeland degradation, leading to a lack of productivity and increasing vulnerability of pastoralists whose livelihoods are affected.

The Jordan case map shows the same main drivers analysed in Kenya, but incorporating new drivers and actors that promote degradation by overriding traditional management systems. Intensification is shown as a main factor in rangeland degradation with strong consequences for the social fabric and land rights. The chart also shows the increasing private ownership claims and how rangeland degradation is related to poverty and settlement creating a negative feedback loop that ends in rangeland degradation. The role of government and private investors are also relevant for the loss of traditional land access rights.

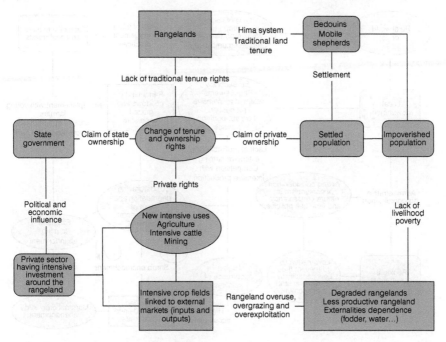

Figure 2.3 Mapping of governance challenges and needs in Jordan

On the other hand, the situation in a European country like Spain shows a close relationship between degradation and abandonment of extensive uses. Inland northern Spain, with a valuable heritage of common lands, is currently in the throes of a deep crisis affecting rural areas that is leading to depopulation and to polarization of intensive agriculture in the central region while mountains and rangelands are abandoned.

Some of the drivers behave in the same way in all cases. The lack of resources for nature conservation and land management, the failure of environmental and forestry authorities over rangeland management (represented by regional and national governments boxes), the rise of intensive agriculture as the exclusive production system are global trends, as are the loss of social fabric, interlocution and visibility of pastoralists and extensive farmers.

Facing rangeland degradation by restoring pastoral governance

Major changes like land use change, climate change, economic globalization, and urbanization, are seriously affecting rangeland and other grass-based ecosystems throughout the world. By degrading and destroying ecosystem services, these changes undermine the livelihoods of millions of poor people. One of the main drivers in rangeland degradation is the loss of traditional governance systems in

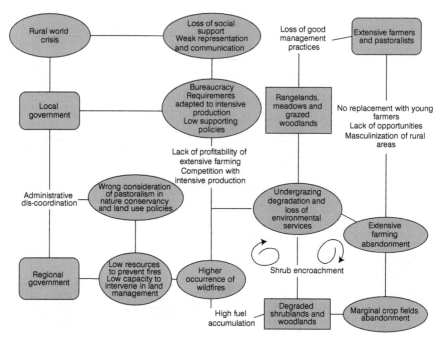

Figure 2.4 Mapping of governance challenges and needs in Spain

parallel with the abandonment of pastoral activities and the lack of involvement of pastoralists in land management.

For many people, rangelands are places of inspiration, yet their capacity to inspire is weakened when pastoralists are unable to be effective stewards. This book is intended to provide solid evidence that governance is the foundation of sustainable management, that pastoralists have the knowledge and institutions to manage rangelands effectively, and that when sustainably managed by pastoralists rangelands contribute greatly to conserving global biodiversity, mitigating climate change and providing high value livestock products.

The following cases studies give practical examples of how this can be achieved, through heavily process-oriented work with pastoral communities, strengthening their rights and their voice and enabling systems of natural resource governance to evolve within new social and legal frameworks. It is hoped that more actors will see the importance of further strengthening pastoral governance and re-enabling pastoralists to be the custodians of this hugely important part of our global heritage.

Notes

1   Adapted from Blench, 2001.
2   Drawing on Blench, 2001.
3   Extracted from FAO, 2002a.

3 Rangeland resource governance – Jordan

Fidaa F. Haddad

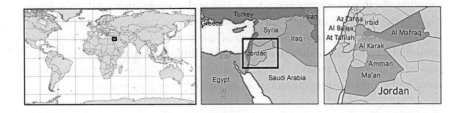

Overview

Planning is a key element of sustainable land-use management particularly in areas that are experiencing high-levels of competition for limited natural resources such as water. Integrated Natural Resource Management brings coordination and collaboration among the individual sectors, plus encouraging stakeholder participation, transparency and cost-effective local management. The Hima approach to strengthening integrated Natural Resource Management is a powerful tool for both conservation and for sustainable development. The Hima system implies a sense of accountability for the actions undertaken for resource management with emphasis on accountability and ownership by local people for sustainable land use and management, to benefit themselves and their community.

Keywords: governance, rangelands, land management, pastoralism, Hima system, accountability, ownership

Introduction

For a long period, Jordan's grazing lands, were characterized by effective traditional land tenure systems and grazing rights associated with Bedouin tribal institutions expressed by the term '*Dirah*', the area throughout which a group migrated that included pasture and some cultivated zones. They used a grazing system known as '*Hima*'[1], in which valued forage within a tribe's territories was sought out while heavily grazed land was allowed to lie fallow to recover. Within the Dirah, certain good grazing areas, such as wadis and marabs (wadi fluvial outwash zones that are typically well vegetated), are traditionally considered to 'belong to' individual families and clans whose property rights are recognized and respected by others.

This practice protected the resources in these lands and organized their use in a way that supported their conservation and sustained productivity under the prevailing harsh environmental and social conditions.

With the elimination of these systems and rights and the declaration of grazing lands as State-owned lands, open to everybody, new land uses encroached on the rangelands. Many of these areas have become overused without consideration to their resource requirements or productivity. This change in land tenure also led to a lack of incentives that would encourage Bedouin pastoralists to maintain and conserve their resources and lands and control their grazing.

Reviving the Hima system showcases how the ability to strengthen local community capacities (both women and men) to protect and manage their land resources in proper communal efforts will reflect positively on their natural resources as well as social-economic growth. Ownership of natural resources implies a sense of accountability for the actions undertaken in Hima management. The case will present analytical methods to assess the extent to which the Hima system takes social and economic integration into account for better governance.

The Jordanian context

Jordan is located about 80 kilometers east of the Mediterranean Sea between 29° 11' to 33° 22' north, and 34° 19' to 39° 18' east. The area of land mass is approximately 88,778 km^2 (DOS, 2012[2]) while the area of water bodies is approximately 482km² including the Dead Sea and the Gulf of Aqaba. Altitude ranges from less than -400m (below mean sea level) at the surface of the Dead Sea up to the 1,750m peak of Jebel Rum. The climate varies from dry sub-humid Mediterranean in the northwest of the country with rainfall of about 630mm to desert conditions with less than 50mm within a distance of only 100km.

The country has three distinct ecological zones: the Jordan Valley, which forms a narrow strip, located below the mean sea level, and has warm winters and hot summers with irrigation being mainly practised in this area; the western highlands where rainfall is relatively high, and climate is typical of Mediterranean areas; and the arid and semi-arid inland to the east, known as the 'Badia', where the annual rainfall is below 200mm. Badia is a standard Arabic word describing the arid, semi-arid and desertified lands which include the open rangeland where Bedouins (nomads) live and practise seasonal livestock grazing.

The Jordanian National Rangeland Strategy (MoA, 2001) indicates that Jordan is a country dominated by an arid climate and fragile ecological systems. The country suffered drastically from sudden increases in population due to political conditions that prevailed during the second half of the twentieth century. With a population of 6.4 million, Jordan struggles with limited natural resources and serious environmental challenges. Desertification and declining standards of living have forced locals to abandon pastoralism and migrate to urban centres. Desertification and over grazing have allowed for inevitable outcomes: poverty and unemployment (Ministry of Planning, 2009). Due to various factors, most of the country is subject to one form or another of desertification.

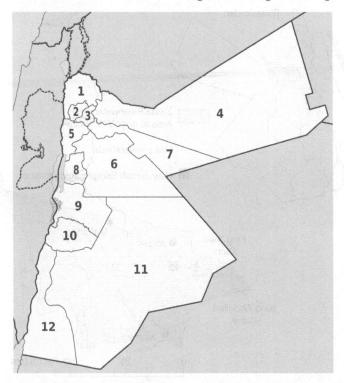

Figure 3.1 Map of Jordan with its 12 governorates. Source: Wikimedia Commons, under the Creative Commons Attribution-Share Alike 3.0 Unported license

Published 11 August 2012 | Author: TUBS | Map of administrative divisions of Jordan http://en.wikipedia.org/wiki/File:Jordan,_administrative_divisions_-_Nmbrs_-_monochrome.svg

1. Irbid, 2. Ajlun, 3. Jarash, 4. Al Mafraq, 5. Al Balqa', 6. 'Amman, 7. Az Zarqa, 8. Madaba, 9. Al Karak, 10. At Tafilah, 11. Ma'an, 12. Al 'Aqabah

Site setting

The Zarqa River Basin is one of the most significant basins in Jordan with respect to its economic, social and agricultural importance. It is located in the central northern part of Jordan and covers an area of 3,567km² from the upper northeastern point to its outlet near King Talal Dam in the west and is part of five governorates: Amman, Balqa, Jerash, Mafraq and Zarqa. Most of the land in the Zarqa River Basin is considered arid or semi-arid.

Land degradation is extensive in the basin and is largely the outcome of human mismanagement and development that has not been well informed of environmental risks. This degradation has compromised human well-being and social and economic development. Biodiversity is decreasing, and improper land use and heavy ground water extraction represent significant causes of degradation of land and vegetation. Specific factors in degradation include population increase; land tenure and ownership conflicts; lack of environmentally friendly

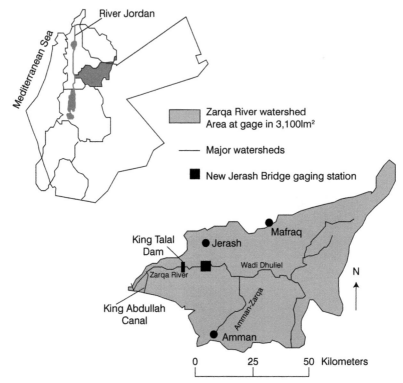

Figure 3.2 The Zarqa River Basin

national land-use management plans and policy; weak enforcement of agricultural legislation and guidelines for best practices; and other barriers that include limited knowledge, communication, and institutional coordination (MoJordan, 2007).

In both the western and eastern parts of the Zarqa River Basin, considerations of economic viability and long-term sustainability have been absent in land management decisions. Depletion of natural resources is to a large extent caused by short-term financial interests in use of land and water by affluent individuals, often having the right connections in the capital.[3] This has been furthered by external economic developments and the weaknesses or near absence of both environmentally sustainable policies and their enforcement. As a result, rural livelihood strategies are shifting from livestock production/range management and rain-fed cereals to highly intensified agriculture such as poultry, cattle production and irrigated vegetables and orchards, partly linked to export markets. Inevitably, this production takes place in a small proportion of the land but uses the majority of available water resources. The promise of short-term financial gains, even in the more remote and eastern/southern regions of the country, has also led to a trend among Bedouin tribal families, whose livelihoods previously depended on range management, to increasingly make fixed ownership claims on either tribal land or government lands (IUCN, Securing Rights Baseline study 2011d).

History of livestock management and land degradation

For many years, Jordan's rangelands were characterized by effective land tenure systems and grazing rights associated with tribal institutions. Land and water were controlled by the Ashira (clan) represented by the Sheikh (tribal leader) and were linked to the notion of Dirah. The term Dirah refers to the tribal territory, together with a system of exchange organized around the Khuwa (the forced payment to clans in return for their protection) (adapted from Bocco, 1987). This arrangement protected the resources within those lands and provided for their use in ways that helped rangeland conservation and continued productivity under the prevailing environmental and social conditions. Upon elimination of these systems and rights and the declaration of rangelands as State-owned areas that are open for everybody to use, new unsustainable land uses encroached upon the rangelands. Many of these areas were overused without consideration of the resource sustainability requirements or their long-term productivity. The elimination of tribal ownership also led to a lack of incentives to encourage Bedouins and other pastoralists to maintain and conserve resources and rangelands under their control and use (Ministry of Agriculture, 2001).

The pastoral communities continue informally to claim common tribal rights and enjoy free access and use of natural resources in their rangelands. However, these community claims are only recognized in settled areas. In all the unsettled areas, the State asserts ownership regardless of customary tribal claims. State claims over grazing lands changed the traditional welfare system, caused the breakdown of resource allocation mechanisms, and transformed secured-access rights into secured-tenure rights. Consequently, customary management rules are often no longer being enforced. State appropriation did not deny local communities access to their traditional pasture but favoured a situation of open-access to grazing and expansion of barley cultivation. In addition, water is bought and sold in pastoral areas, especially during droughts, which makes it increasingly difficult for poorer and less powerful groups in society to access water. This includes women, who then become more dependent on their husbands to provide money and access.

In the project sites in western Zarqa, very little grazing land is left (less than 3km² in each village), and range management for grazing purposes has become a marginal activity both in terms of land use and livelihoods. However, sites have been identified where it is possible to demonstrate how, under rapidly changing demographics and industrialization conditions, alternative models for an extensive range management can be established.

In short, the roots of the problem lie in the country's rapid population increase, land and water mismanagement, and lifestyle change. The roots of these problems include:[4]

* Land tenure: abolishing collective tribal land tenures led to the emergence of private ownership that exploits lands unsustainably and at the expense of traditional pastoralists in the area.

- Poor marketing of livestock and agricultural products.
- Weak coordination between relevant governmental agencies and local communities resulting in conflicting approaches to the management of land and natural resources.
- Scarcity of drinking water and lack of sanitation.
- Bedouin settlements allowing livestock to overgraze in specific areas.
- Subsidizing (barley) during the dry seasons has encouraged livestock herders to keep large numbers of animals that exceed the carrying capacity of the rangeland.

All these factors contribute to desertification and land degradation in the Zarqa River Basin. Its plant cover has fallen victim to growing water demand, leading to large-scale groundwater extraction that further depletes its aquifers. Indigenous plant biodiversity has decreased drastically, shifting productive land to arid and industrialized zones and limiting its production for fodder. This has occurred in addition to a decline in the number of livestock producers while the numbers of livestock have increased slightly over the years. This indicates an increase in large-scale commercial operations and movement of thousands of small herders out of their traditional livelihood occupation (DOS, 2011).[5] Over the last four decades, especially in the western Zarqa River Basin, the local community's response has been to purchase fodder and use arid land for livestock grazing, as well as shift from animal husbandry and rangeland management to permanent agriculture to improve their living standards (OPTIMA, 2006[6]).

Rangeland policy setting

Environmental planning and policy formulation in Jordan prior to the 1990s was based on a sector-specific approach with little consideration of environmental concerns.[7] Environmental planning and policy formulation came of age in 1991, when the Ministry of Municipal and Rural Affairs and the Environment, with technical assistance from the International Union for Conservation of Nature (IUCN) and financial assistance from USAID, led a national consultation process and formulated the National Environmental Strategy (NES).

According to the Agriculture Law (20) of 1973, the rangelands are a strong element in Jordanian culture, historical discourse, social imagery, and social history and have significant cultural and heritage value. The law defined the rangelands as 'all lands[8] registered as such and any other State-owned lands where annual rainfall is below 200mm and that do not have sustainable irrigation, or the lands confined for public use'. Thus, this law took only the average annual rainfall into consideration, and disregarded other factors which play vital roles in defining the rangelands, such as, the land topography, fertility, and physical and morphological characteristics, which have a close relationship with rangelands' utilization and sound management (MoA, 2001).

As for the Jordanian National Rangeland Strategy (MoA, 2001), this indicates 'directive top-down' policies, laws and regulations and prescriptive extension have not worked well, while much can be learnt 'from successful project and program experience with participatory approaches involving all stakeholders in rangeland management decision-making, planning and implementation.' It concludes by recommending 'an overall rangeland strategy with a complementary set of policies, regulations, and support services, to ensure that user groups and communities have the security of tenure and incentives to use the rangelands in a sustainable manner while optimizing production and their income' (Hadadin and Tarawneh, 2007).

An in-depth policy analysis illustrated that after ten years, not much progress has been made to develop such a strategy through specific policies and legislation to strengthen action on the ground. Many of the difficulties facing environmental management in Jordan, such as a lack of institutional and human capacity, as well as legislative, institutional, technical, management and implementation problems, are relevant to the management of the rangelands.

The gaps between intentions and practice in rangeland governance

In Jordan, natural ranges are defined as

the wide-open, non-fenced lands where fodder grow naturally that are not suitable for traditional farming due to lack of rain, low fertility, rough terrain and high rockiness or because of a combination of these factors, which makes the land optimum use restricted to production of fodder for animals'.

(Abu-Zanat *et al.*, 1993; Sankari, 1977)

In 1971, when Jordan introduced the Rangeland Land Law, the government declared that all uncultivated land belonged to the State and that all land receiving less than 200mm of precipitation per year, unless privately owned, was for communal pastoral use.

The 2002 provisional agricultural law addressed many articles related to rangeland and its management and Article 36 defined rangeland as lands registered in the name of the Kingdom's treasury or any other State lands in which the annual rainfall is less than 200mm, except for:

a   Lands permanently irrigated and agricultural projects and housing lands established before the coming into force of this law.
b   Lands exploited for public benefit purposes or allocated to serve the State and its institutions' interests prior to the coming into force of this law, or the lands that the Council of Ministers decided to allocate for this purpose after the implementation of this law's provisions.

Over the last 60 years, there has been a decline in the overall contribution of natural rangelands to animal feeding in Jordan, from 85 per cent in the 1950s to 30 per cent without complementary feeding in 1993 (Juneidi and

Abu-Zanat *et al.*,1993) and to less than 10 per cent in 2011 (Sidahamed *et al.*, 2011). Rangeland vegetation now provides between 90 days and zero days of supplemental grazing each year to Badia livestock depending on the location and the rainfall and when grazing is performed twice, in the spring and in the autumn (Sidahamed *et al.*, 2011). Furthermore, the government policy of subsidizing prices of imported inputs, especially during the dry season, has also encouraged livestock herders to keep a large number of animals that exceed the carrying capacity of the rangeland.

Given the extremely low rainfall, this area is not usually regarded as suitable for agriculture. Despite this, cropping is common all along the western edge of the rangelands. The most common pattern is rain-fed winter barley, and the ploughing of undisturbed rangeland is usually associated with this crop. Yields are so poor that it is difficult to demonstrate that such production is economically viable, and its function may be as much to bolster land claims as to provide cereals, which clearly replaced the communal livelihood practices such as traditional grazing (MoA, 2013).

Furthermore, a study conducted by the National Compensation Fund shows that mining and continuous land harvesting worked against natural ecological processes where significant areas have been degraded.

Our initial review of the extent to which Jordanian rangelands have an effective governance framework was based on the definition from IUCN Social Policy Program: 'The norms, institutions and processes that determine how power and responsibilities are exercised, how decisions are taken, and how citizens participate in the management of natural resources.' We can clearly conclude that the rangeland governance system is weak due to weak property rights which were associated with tribal institutions. In these conditions, it is not surprising that communities no longer feel accountable for the protection and management of land resources. Without this accountability, any intervention will fail to succeed in the rangeland governance system. However, retaining systems such as Hima has undoubtedly found support among rangeland communities and managers who recognize that past management practices and some current ones have proven the need to encourage the participation of beneficiaries in range development and management activities, especially given their traditional knowledge.

To improve the rangeland system within the Jordan's rangeland laws and the country's priorities means looking beyond the State sites, as governance may rest with the public sector, private owners or the community. Improved participatory sustainable land management 'SLM', which operates through two related and overlapping processes called *The Planning Cycle Framework* and *The Stakeholder Dialogue for Concerted Action,* is a key approach used for combining human ownership and accountability over land resources with rangeland ecosystem protection that is well known in Jordanian Islamic culture as the Hima system.[9]

Strategic planning cycle for sustainable land management (SLM)

The planning cycle framework

This first step provides a methodology that ensures the development of holistic planning where the needs of end-users are brought together with intermediate-level land managers from the local governorate and natural resources-related ministries. Taking into consideration gender and different wealth and power groups in the planning stage ensures that the poorest and most vulnerable have their equitable share and access and can exercise control and ownership over land resources. The planning process identifies and develops location-specific long-term visions and strategies for land resource management for combating desertification. These are based on a careful reflection of environmental-related problems and the development needs of the community. The process is supported by several participatory tools for collecting and analysing relevant information such as stakeholders' analysis and PRA (Participatory Rural Appraisal). Visioning exercises consist of mapping natural resources in their current state, including areas of degradation, followed by mapping of desired future states. Locals then agree on a plan of action for getting from the current state to the envisioned state, with a strong emphasis on defining the roles and responsibilities of the local community.

The process attempts to incorporate the uncertainty of the future by considering a series of different scenarios. The logic of the decisions is tested through a process of discussion and reflection. Pilot projects further check the potential of the stakeholders (who have not previously worked in this way) to develop further trust and coordination. Thus, the participating stakeholders at local and intermediate levels are able to make the technical and political decisions to begin the process of effective development and management of their land resources. Through this process of holding stakeholder discussions, the ultimate aim of building the capacity of the participants to continue this work in the future is gradually achieved.

Stakeholder dialogue and concerted action

The planning cycle process described above feeds into this second process that brings national and local level decision-makers together to further debate what is critical rangeland of national concern. Using a facilitated approach; a range of influential actors around rangeland management are challenged to come to a strategic consensus on how to work together to tackle local specific issues of shared concern. Output from local community exercises is used in meetings, to highlight the need for innovation and policy revision. Different opinions, perceptions, preoccupations, assumptions, and prejudices among the participants are made explicit, and discussion between them is always encouraged. The process is intended to open the debate regarding the urgency of the situation and the need to remove barriers for innovation, to explicitly, consider the poorest end-users, and to better understand the whole fabric of land tenure and rangeland policy.

The participation of the parliamentary representative in conducting training workshops on management and development and different tribal meetings had a big influence on the participants (local committees of the four Hima sites) and increased their sense of the importance of the subject and the seriousness of the governmental parties in working with them.

Evidence for improved local governance and benefit sharing

The Hima initiative has improved the exchange of information, social organization, and decision-making process between stakeholders and has raised awareness with respect to constraints and opportunities that affect the performance of actors as innovators. It has brought end-users, policy makers and members of parliament together to recognize that their current rangeland degradation problems and future solutions are interlinked.

To achieve this impact, the mentality that rules land management has had to be challenged. Every member of the land management structure has to attain a degree of mutual understanding and a clear, unified vision of how his or her roles and responsibilities contribute to the inalienable human rights to land resources and improved living standards. Key to this goal is the development of the different actors' capacity to participate in the management structure and fulfil people's rights and obligations. The Hima system represents a simple, practical, and resourceful

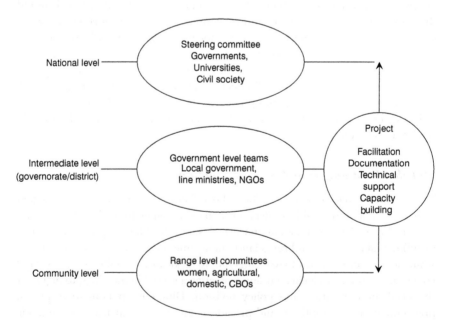

Figure 3.3 The stakeholder dialogue and concerted Action process function at three levels within society with the project team acting largely as facilitator

approach to reach this consensus, activate the power of change at the local level, and empower people to make local initiatives that can help themselves and the government to raise their living standards and take control of their land resources.

In Jordan, the Hima initiatives promote better management practices to strengthen natural resource governance. Various local Hima sites around the Zarqa River Basin established through negotiations between various branches of government and communities aim to identify land that the community could manage and restore for their own use. The four local Hima initiatives are as follows.

Hashmyia: A community standing together

The deterioration of pastures has substantial implications on the Hashmyia community. While livestock owners suffer from land degradation, pollution, and high cost of production inputs like fodder, heads of households complain about the declining ability of households to maintain food self-sufficiency. Additionally, several earlier projects had a negative impression on the community by blocking them out of any decision-making processes.

To address these challenges, a local committee was formed representing all Hashmyia community segments and different stakeholders. This committee acts as a networking hub, to spread knowledge to the rest of the community. After work began, the community requested that the government adopt an improved participatory approach to conferring management rights to the community. The government finally accepted the terms and has given the community access to 50 hectares as a trial to demonstrate that they have the capacity to restrict access and manage and restore the rangeland, on the condition that if they are not capable the land will return to government care.

Halabat: combined efforts

The community of Halabat has faced particular hardship since abandoning their former mobile lifestyle and settling. Increased unemployment and decreased income have resulted from the deterioration of pastures, which present the main source of income, with no present alternatives available. These challenges have led to decreased vegetative cover and the loss of valuable grazing plants in Halabat.

The community sought to create a Hima in their area to demonstrate sustainable management of rangeland and livestock production. However, the local community was reluctant to allocate an area from their tribal lands for that cause, pushing for an agreement with the Antiquities Department to establish a Hima on 250 dunums (*25 Ha*) of public lands and reviving sustainable traditional grazing and cultivation practices.

Duliel: adapting to change

Duliel's long history of dense tree cover and abundant water has been replaced in the past few decades by rapid desertification due to the expansion of factories and industrial waste. Another key challenge to pastoral livelihoods stems from land tenure as most of the land is either governmental (miri) or designated for military exercises. Moreover, the area lacks rainwater-harvesting techniques that can provide for pastoral agriculture in light of the poor rainfall and effects of climate change.

Working with the locals in the area, an awareness campaign targeting 200 women and other community members has used a participatory video approach to identify their problems and document their suggestions. These approaches have allowed the community to develop a vision for restoring rangeland plants by 20–30 per cent, which will later reflect on the economic and social situation of livestock owners in their areas.

A Hima was established with proper rangeland management, to aid in the revival of indigenous plants necessary for sustainable pastoralism. Livestock will be allowed to graze in the Hima when it has begun to recover, but cultivation has been excluded from the area. The aim is for managed grazing to no longer be a desertification factor, but rather to contribute to spreading desirable seeds to wider rangeland areas. The outcomes shall encourage the adoption of this method in other areas of Duliel while the resultant benefits to the community, especially women, will alleviate poverty and improve living standards.

Bani-Hashem: political support does count

Bani-Hashem consists of four communities located 21km north of Zarqa City and has a total population of 15,000, mostly of Bedouin origin. The area was originally characterized by rich plant cover and abundant water resources, which encouraged Bedouin tribes to settle there as early as the 1850s. Despite the above-mentioned factors, livestock remained a core socio-economic element for Bani-Hashem's communities, meeting some of their basic nutritional needs and providing an additional source of income. The current population of livestock in the area is around 5,000 heads (sheep and goats) whose owners have several complaints including a lack of sufficient pastures, high costs of forage, difficulties in marketing livestock products, water scarcity and the spread of livestock diseases.

To address these problems, a Hima was established with a vision of achieving ecologically sustainable rangeland management, supporting social, ecologically and economic activities. The Hima land is being rehabilitated through natural regeneration, and indigenous plants are being restored to contribute to improving living standards in Bani-Hashem. Through the Ministry of Agriculture's support, the local community obtained the Prime Minister's approval to allocate 100Ha of rangelands for use and management by the community.

To ensure sustainability, a tribal charter was drafted and signed by community members pledging protection from violations. The charter acquired an official status by involving law enforcement authorities in its application while a local committee was formed through the local cooperative society 'Community Based Organization' (CBO) to coordinate the management of the Hima following tribal traditions.

The local initiative of the Bani-Hashem Hima embraces the belief that women are important actors of change and holders of significant knowledge and skills related to mitigation, adaptation, and reduction of risks relevant to land degradation. This makes them crucial agents in this area through information and knowledge sharing, which are necessary to improve community livelihoods. Therefore, women were included in the CBO's management bodies as founding members and on the administrative board.

Protecting the pilot area allowed shrubs and grasses to regenerate, restoring the land's vegetation. Even some indigenous species, such as Artemisia herba-alba, reappeared in the Hima site. A total of 36 native plant species was recorded in the site, mainly on the north-western slope which receives the highest amounts of rainfall. After one year of activities and protecting their Hima area from herders (without using fencing), biodiversity benefits can already be observed through the increase of biomass and restoration of indigenous floral species.

Reasons for success

Capacity building: The Hima initiative set out an effective framework for capacity building at various levels to improve sustainable rangeland management. Sustainability is a central premise if capacity building is understood as being more than simply training, but rather a process of allowing people to have influence over decisions and resources that affect their livelihoods in the long term (Enabling poor rural people to overcome poverty, IFAD, 2009) This process involved collaboration between wide ranges of stakeholders, capacity building to strengthen interaction between local and national-level governance bodies and to define the existing and future decision-making of roles and responsibilities.

The key factors of the initiative's capacity building are that:

- It is problem and vision focused. That is, it addresses clearly identified problems, within the context of achieving a clearly articulated long-term vision.
- It sees the creation of a commonly owned and accepted body of key information, qualitative and quantitative, as essential to the development of effective community planning.
- It acknowledges that there will always be multiple paths to resolving problems and achieving ideals and that deciding between them is a political issue.
- It recognizes that different levels of risk are associated with different courses and that effective planning seeks to minimize immediate and long-term risks.
- It brings to the foreground the voice of local communities and end-users and tries to advocate for the rights of the underprivileged among them.

Empowerment for building local ownership: at the local level, the initiative focused on building the capacity of the involved stakeholders, mainly the civil society groups, through a non-conventional capacity building and planning approach to reach a level of competence within the civil society groups that will allow them to respond better to the actual needs of the community. Capacity building of those groups provides them with the knowledge and skills that will enable them to play a major role in the reform process and hence contribute to the welfare of the community. The SLM approach explores the substantial skills that communities already have and the ability to innovate through various tools, including PRA and stakeholder analysis.

Community empowerment will be unsustainable if it is not embedded in institutional structures. It is crucial to have linkages between the community and other stakeholders, and community empowerment needs to be accompanied by local government empowerment. The Hima approach strengthens supportive governance arrangements for sustainably managed rangelands, conserving biodiversity and supporting resilient livelihoods through local knowledge and traditional resource tenure.

The key factors in empowerment are:

- Organizing and improving community participation.
- Creating sustainable networks and communication mechanisms with various stakeholders, especially local government.
- Finding shared strategies for the development of local land resources.
- Financing pilot projects to create tangible evidence of the importance of strategic planning.
- Promoting a gender-sensitive approach to enhance the voices of women and the poor for participation in public dialogue, inclusion in the community and development affairs, and demand for greater and better service within their own communities and from local governments and institutions.

Mechanism to motivate decisions: planning and management require effort, cost money, and use up other resources. Investing in these resources only makes sense when the effort involved is outweighed by the benefits gained or the problems avoided. The achievement of real and lasting benefits is not something that can be easily achieved by one agency operating alone. It requires the building of new and innovative partnerships, which include governmental, civil society, private sector, and donor agencies. Strong partnerships bring institutional capabilities and human resources together in the form of skills, experiences, and ideas to tackle common problems that are often beyond the capacity of a single organization or community group. The participatory approach cannot be achieved unless suitable skills are acquired. These include facilitation, negotiation, appreciation of information, the art of dialogue and the acceptance of others. These skills can be acquired through the process but require a lot of patience and understanding of the local customs and power dynamics, as well as a good level of trust and respect within the working team (Laban, 2008, Rewarding Ecosystems Rewarding

People, http://cmsdata.iucn.org/downloads/rewarding_ecosystems_rewarding_people__reward_sharm_al_shaikh_report__final.pdf)

This partnership between the Ministry of Agriculture (which acknowledged the local customary law of land resource management (Hima) and encouraged the updating of the national rangeland strategy), local Hima committees (with government, community based organizations, and various other community groups including women, the landless, youth, etc.) and members of parliament discussed the problems surrounding rangeland degradation caused by human activities and agreed on the implementation of joint activities to address the problem and improve the land resources.

Partnering with government, can also help CBOs promote external linkages, and enhance the effectiveness, and reduce costs while local governments can benefit through expanding service delivery and deepening the participation of citizens in local activities. However, effective partnering requires addressing structural and legal flaws in local government design that limit local government accountability or capacity and requires ensuring an enabling environment within which community cooperatives and civil society can operate. It is important to ensure adequate political, administrative, and fiscal decentralization. Local governments need to have both the authority and resources to plan and coordinate local-level strategic plans and provide local frontline services *(A Handbook for Trainers on Participatory Local development,* 2007).

Engaging underprivileged groups in different meetings: the management of natural resources is a long-term, complex, multi-stakeholder process in which many players at different levels have to assume responsibilities and accountabilities to others (Röling and Engel, 1991). The sustainability of specific NRM measures is at risk when those directly concerned in the local communities are not involved and feel no ownership over the resource and for the way it is used and managed.

In-depth social analysis was conducted to assess community structuring with respect to gender, and different wealth and power groups to ensure that the poorest and most vulnerable have an equitable share in land resources and can exercise control and ownership over it. This process defines the conditions leading to the empowerment of women regarding the access and control of resources and the equitable distribution of benefits from reviving Hima such as the creation of income-generating alternatives for women.

What is still needed for effectiveness of Hima governance system?

The Hima model, is reviving rapidly, and there is a growing support for this method which is characterized by greater social sensitivity and broad flexibility in its approach. The issues brought to light by this Hima initiative are more encouraging at the outset for the effectiveness of the rangeland governance system.

Despite the progress mentioned above, there is clearly more work to be done to have effective governance of the rangelands. This includes ensuring that a comprehensive approach is reflected in national legislation with clear consideration of the implication of land ownership fragmentation and property rights. This process must create an enabling policy environment to institutionalize the cooperation between government and local communities. This will maintain the sustainable use of natural ecosystems to meet community needs while ensuring long-term protection and conservation of biodiversity.

Although the updated Jordanian Rangeland Strategy 2013 clearly recognizes the importance of Hima systems for reversing land degradation and reflects the desire to upscale this initiative to different sites in Jordan, our analysis suggests that the understanding of the relationship between Hima and land use[10] in Jordan remains insufficient, especially in relation to property rights.

A need exists to review the land-use policies, laws, regulations, and bylaws for effective management of resources that are managed communally. These must consider incentives for farmers and herders to improve land-use practices (sustainability, reduced land fragmentation). Also, there is a need for programs supporting breed improvement, flock management, and range management and combating the expansion of crop cultivation (usually low-yield field crops) at the expense of the fragile rangeland ecosystem. Furthermore, it is necessary to assess the threats caused by urbanization and the encroachment of human settlements in arable areas and the poor support of green belts around cities.

The effectiveness of rangeland governance is at risk when those directly concerned with local communities are not involved and feel no ownership over their natural land resource. This can be addressed when they recognize the land benefits they are sharing, have access and control over resources, have the knowledge and capacity to manage their resources, and have functional community institutional structure. All of these are critical to determining to what extent the basic rights of local people to use a resource are or can be fulfilled and will ensure the sustainability of land restoration.

After three years, Hima systems have started to improve environmental as well as social conditions in the site area. Tribal conflicts over natural resources have reduced, grazing seasons are now better managed, and the indigenous biodiversity is revived. Solving overgrazing will no longer mean keeping livestock from grazing in a protected area, but lead to better managed grazing periods. These solutions have paved a way forward that builds on the capacities of the local community and increase the involvement of different groups, mainly women. These played a major role in improving their livelihoods through securing their access and management rights and building relationships with government institutions.

Notes

1 Hima – Arabic for 'conserved area'; an ancient land use zoning concept. Its practice dates back to the pre-Islamic era (over 1,447 years ago) in the Arabian Peninsula, and was further shaped by Islamic principles for social development (WANA Forum 2012).
2 http://www.dos.gov.jo/dos_home_a/jorfig/2012/2.pdf.
3 IUCN Securing Rights and Restoring Land Project Baseline study (Zarqa River Basin) 2011 (IUCN, 2011d).

4　IUCN Reviving Hima Case study 2012 (IUCN, 2012a).
5　For example, the number of sheep and goat keepers declined from 29,650 families in 2010 to 25,469 in 2011 because of the vulnerability of the smallholders to market and environmental shocks (MOA, 2011).
6　Optimization for Sustainable Water Resources Management Project, a Zarqa River Case Study http://www.ess.co.at/OPTIMA/.
7　National Capacity Self-Assessment for Global Environmental Management (MoEnv Jordan 2007).
8　The area of these lands is about 80 million dunums (8 million hectares) or 90 per cent of the kingdom's total area of 89.3 million dunums (MoA, 2001).
9　See Note 1.
10　Land ownership in Jordan can be categorized as the following (Al-Oun, 2008):
 • Land that is privately owned and called (Miri and Mulk), which is owned by individuals that is registered and documented.
 • Tribal land (Wajehat El-Ashayeria), which is claimed by the tribe and historically distributed by the sheikhs.
 • Public land with free access to all resources (Al mawat), which is the land owned by the state and but at the same time claimed by tribes, although it is not divided among the tribe members.

4 Ranchers, land tenure, and grassroots governance

Maintaining pastoralist use of rangelands in the United States in three different settings

Lynn Huntsinger, Nathan F. Sayre and Luke Macaulay

Overview

The forms of grassroots governance that have emerged in three different land tenure settings, Arizona, California, and Texas are examined in terms of how they help ranchers maintain access to rangeland resources within each setting. Ranchers and pastoralists need a web of social and political relations to secure their ability to benefit from rangelands, regardless of whether they own, rent, or are permitted to use the land by a government agency. In the Malpai Borderlands, where much of the rangeland is leased from a few public agencies, the need to use prescribed burning, maintain access to public lands, and stave off land fragmentation and development has led to the emergence of a grassroots rancher organization with a system of conservation easements whose permanence is linked to stability of public leases, and a burn and land conservation plan that benefits both ranchers and fire agencies. In California, where a significant proportion of rangeland is private but diverse types of public and reserved land are important, the California Rangeland Conservation Coalition communicates the benefits of grazing to agency managers, and has produced a strategic plan for maintaining rangelands and ranching, in an effort to help keep the growing proportion of public and reserved rangeland available for grazing. In Texas, where the vast majority of rangeland is privately owned, wildlife management associations help ranchers to manage and market game species for hunting in an increasingly fragmented landscape. These wildlife associations help increase benefits to ranchers from game species, a common pool resource, while maintaining habitat on a landscape scale. All of these groups rely on creating connections among ranchers and regulatory or management agencies, and on sharing knowledge, labor, and resources. Each supports research and policy that benefits pastoralism in ways that an individual rancher cannot. All of them are involved in transboundary management, whether it is fire, wildlife, or maintaining a grazing calendar of several different ownerships. Finally, each group maintains that they are benefiting rangelands, including supporting biodiversity.

Keywords: governance, rangelands, land management, ranching, access

Introduction

Ranchers in the United States maintain production amidst differing configurations of rangeland control and ownership (Starrs 1998; Fairfax *et al.* 2005). As is common in grazing economies, they rely on access to large areas of land, often with tenuous property rights through leases and permits (Huntsinger *et al.* 2010). Here we examine forms of grassroots governance that have emerged in three different land tenure settings, Texas, Arizona, and California, and how they help ranchers maintain access to rangeland resources within each setting. Using the analytic framework of Ribot and Peluso (2003), we show that ranchers and pastoralists need a web of social and political relations to secure their ability to benefit from rangelands, regardless of whether they own, rent, or are permitted to use the land by a government agency (Li and Huntsinger 2011).

This approach is useful in understanding the role of these grassroots governance structures across vastly different institutional arrangements for landowners and land use in the United States. Even when rangelands are private property held individually, and the right to benefit seems most straightforward, the emphasis for a pastoralist must be on maintaining the ability to benefit despite regulatory, market, environmental, social and political relations that might seek to constrain such ability. Where land tenure is complex, with diverse owners and ownership types, the right to benefit comes through leases and permits with diverse objectives and constraints. Acquiring and maintaining the ability to benefit involves coping with multiple social and political relationships, institutional contexts, and competitors for access to the same land. When rangeland is largely owned by the government, finding points of leverage and strategies for negotiation become critical for maintaining a right to benefit, as well as ability to benefit, that in many places is growing increasingly tenuous due to larger-scale social, political, and economic changes. When land is owned by the rancher, income sufficient to support the property is critical to maintain access to the resource and to reduce rangeland conversion to other uses. In turn, government agencies with environmental goals sometimes want to influence management on private land in the context of the considerable autonomy landowners have in the United States. In each of our three case studies, grassroots governance structures act to help pastoralists navigate the contextual factors that shape their access to the rangeland resources they need.

Ribot and Peluso's work (2003) on rights and access provides an analytic frame for comparing how land tenure and regulatory arrangements influence the ability of ranchers to benefit from rangelands, and result in the emergence of different grassroots governance forms. For ranchers using extensive rangelands, the ability to benefit from the resources is as important, or more important, than the right to benefit in the form of landownership or a grazing permit. A right of use allocation like a grazing permit can grant someone the right to benefit from a piece of land, but if the rights holder does not have the ability to use the resources profitably, he or she will not be able to benefit from the land to maintain his or her enterprise. For example, if a permit or lease is granted, but the conditions that must be met in order to be allowed to graze are costly, the grazier will be unable to use the land in a way that allows an income to be returned. Of course, right and ability are often interlinked, but a right is only one aspect of safeguarding the ability to benefit, while ability is embedded in a web of mechanisms, or means, processes, and relations, and is subject to the impacts and outcomes of social relations, including forms of governance (Ribot and Peluso 2003).

The web of social relations that shapes pastoralist ability to benefit from rangelands depends, in the first instance, on the tenure arrangements for that rangeland. Fee-simple ownership implies that the owner has the right to benefit from the land as the owner sees fit, as well as the right to sell or develop the land, but these rights are usually constrained by regulations and land use designations, which may be created and enforced at local to national levels of governance and shape the ability to benefit. Being "over-regulated" was a common reason ranchers surveyed in California gave for "quitting ranching" (Liffmann *et al.* 2000). Environmental regulations can influence pastoralist ability to benefit from their own rangelands. For example, the Endangered Species Act, a federal regulation, requires landowners to protect animal species designated as endangered by the federal government. Similar requirements may be present at the state level. Water quality protections also operate at multiple levels of governance and may preclude certain land uses. Therefore although the pastoralist may have a right to use the land, it can only be exercised within the constraints of regulatory and land use planning institutional arrangements at local to federal scales. This is part of the "web of social relations" that shapes pastoralist ability to benefit from rangelands. The matrix of land uses and ownerships within which a ranch is situated can also affect ability to benefit, as when domestic dogs harass livestock, or neighbors complain about agricultural activities.

Pastoralists may lease rangelands from private and governmental entities. The terms of a lease are a contract with the landowner and vary from property to property, but usually are for specific numbers of animals for specific periods of time. Private leases spell out the obligations of lessor and lessee and may include contributions in kind from the lessee, including fixing or developing infrastructure. They are often given out on a competitive basis, or as the result of a friendship or long-term relationship. Often they grant the lessee exclusive use of the property. Government permits may include in-kind contributions as well, but they usually do not grant the lessee exclusive use of the property, reserving public access for recreation and hunting, private access for timber harvest, or government access for military operations and so on. Depending on the scope of these other uses and their requirements, this will influence the pastoralist's ability to benefit. Protection of wildlife habitat and other resource values, in addition to whatever environmental regulations may be pertinent, also influence how the land may be used and the ability to benefit.

On some government lands, where the public also holds rights to benefit based on the governance institutions for these "public lands," the amount and nature of the resources allocated to each type of use and user is a subject of contention, and sometimes costly litigation. Different constituencies seek to invoke their rights of access in order to advance their ability to benefit from public lands. For example, the Multiple Use Sustained Yield Act of 1960 and the Forest and Land Management Planning Act of 1972, hold that the Forest Service and the Bureau of Land Management, respectively, must manage public lands for multiple uses, but the statutes do not provide guidance on priorities or methods of allocation among those uses. Pastoralist ability to benefit, then, can be heavily influenced by political and managerial decisions about the rights to benefit from diverse user groups, and by changes in or interpretations of environmental regulations pertinent to livestock grazing. As a Forest Service natural resource manager commented at a 2013 symposium, "for the rancher using the national forest the [environmental] bar keeps getting higher every year." In California, Arizona, and Texas, ranchers have established grassroots local governance organizations that help them maintain the ability to benefit from rangelands in ways that fit to local tenure and institutional arrangements, and to build resilience to shifts in policy and markets that might have an impact on their ability to maintain access to and benefit from rangeland resources.

Evolution of ranching land tenure in the Western United States: a general overview

A general history of livestock grazing in the western United States begins with the implantation of livestock in the Southwest. In 1598, Spanish settlers brought cattle, sheep and goats into what is now New Mexico. For about 200 years, Spanish and Mexican land grants, thousands of hectares in size, were given to individuals and communities for farming, grazing, and woodcutting. Local tribes, such as the Navajo, adopted livestock grazing very early on (Bailey 1980). In California, a short-lived Spanish colonization began in 1769, and as in the Southwest was then superseded by Mexican control in 1822, and finally by the United States in 1848. In the Spanish and Mexican periods of California large land grants were given out to individuals for ranching, leaving a legacy of some extensive private rangeland ownerships.

In the mid-nineteenth century, settlers from eastern regions moved rapidly into the arid western territories, drawn by the Gold Rush and other mining strikes, and by abundant open land for settlement. This land was known as the "public domain" as it belonged to the federal government and it was originally designated for privatization and development through sales and grants. American land allocation policies were eventually implemented that, beginning with the 1862 Homestead Act, limited settler land claims to a few hundred acres. These claims were made in the rare areas with decent soils and water for irrigation, leaving arid and mountainous land in the public domain. In the Southwest and California, under American governance, the majority of community and individual grants given out by the Spanish and Mexican governments were abrogated by the courts, ceded to clever entrepreneurs and lawyers, or returned to the federal or state governments for back taxes, and only rarely remained in the hands of some of the grantees (de Buys 1985).

Ranchers throughout the West grazed the public domain and created patterns of livestock mobility that suited local geographies, moving stock from arid lowlands in the winter to montane meadows in the summer in mountainous regions. In regions where water and soils supported cultivation, large areas were plowed and converted to farmland. Various land allocation policies supported acquisition of farmlands. In exchange for development of irrigation or drainage infrastructure, land allocations from the public domain for farming could be quite large. At times, it was convenient to leave rangelands in government ownership to avoid the costs of owning land given the low returns per hectare from livestock grazing in arid regions. Extensive areas of government-owned arid rangelands are today embedded with small, scattered plots of claimed private lands that center on the rare water sources. The state of Nevada is the most extreme case, with more than 90 percent of the land in government ownership of one sort or another, and private lands located along rivers, creeks, and springs. Compounding this fractured tenure was the federal government's habit of ceding "sections" (640 acres or one square mile) of cadastral "townships" (6-mile by 6-mile squares) to states or to the railroads. The states were to use the lands to fund education, while the railroads were to use their alternating sections to pay for the expansion of the rails. In the latter case, the legacy is a checkerboard of private and public lands along the rail corridors in many areas, as the government lands were retained rather than sold or granted.

A strategy of "control of the range by control of the water" emerged in much of the West in the nineteenth century. Settlers, limited to small claims by land allocation policies like the 1862 Homestead Act, acquired lowland areas with arable lands and water, and grazed the surrounding public domain open range. In ranching communities, informal rules and practices evolved that helped control grazing, including legal fencing of home properties, illegal fencing of public domain range, grazing agreements among community members, and extra-legal threats and pressures to fend off outside intruders (Nelson 1995). An informal nineteenth-century rule in Arizona held that the owner of a water source had the rights to graze the public domain halfway to the next water source (Sayre 2002). Common gathers where livestock were sorted, with reciprocal labor and herding, and brands to monitor cattle ownership, reflected a nascent pastoral culture as well as Hispano influence (Farquhar 1930).

The latter half of the nineteenth century saw an influx of speculative money, funded by industrial wealth and family fortune, often from overseas, that drove the rapid development of a commercial livestock industry based on access to low-cost, uncontrolled land, with few ties to local communities. The invention of barbed wire in 1867, and its proliferation in the 1870s changed the face of open range grazing across much of the West. Barbed wire dramatically reduced the cost of enclosing cattle on vast areas of range, and of keeping livestock out of crops. Conflicts erupted between sedentary farmers and ranchers, and grazers with free-range herds who came across newly constructed barbed wire and cut fences, culminating in a "fence cutters war" that resulted in the designation of cutting fences as a felony in Texas in 1884. Many other states followed suit. Profiteering from running cattle crashed toward the end of the century with overstocked ranges, inadequate and badly placed fences, and a few brutal winters. In 1885, Congress forbade stretching barbed wire across the public domain. Enforcement of the open access character of government rangelands fostered continued tensions over pasture use between settled communities and "outsiders" such as widely roaming shepherds and speculative cattle enterprises (Nelson 1995).

The government asserted control over this range in the early twentieth century, committing to government control as a means of governing open rangelands to prevent their degradation (Ostrom 1990). Most montane range was reserved out of the public domain to create national forests, and now is under the jurisdiction of the United States Forest Service (USFS). The motive was to protect forest resources and watersheds from rapacious exploitation by loggers and graziers. Most lowland arid ranges eventually came under the jurisdiction of the United States Bureau of Land Management (BLM), with the dual objective of utilizing and conserving timber, forage, and mineral resources. Sedentary ranchers and sheep producers were given precedence in the allocation of "allotments" on these lands – areas for which the federal government gave grazing permits. Forest Service and BLM lands are known as public lands today, as they are managed in the public interest, including for recreation and wildlife habitat. Meanwhile, well-watered lands were claimed for private ownership.

Ranches today are of course a function of the culture of the settlers and the details of the local environment, as well as the way that land allocation played out (Starrs 1998). A typical western cattle ranch evolved to have a ranch house and private 'deeded acres' located on water or a water development, and a larger extent of land that belongs to the government and requires a permit for grazing. However, each of the case studies diverges from this narrative in important ways.

Case studies

With the exception of Texas, western states agreed to federal government retention of public lands as a condition of gaining statehood. However, they were granted some blocks of this land based on the cadastral survey system to support the development of education systems. When Arizona and New Mexico became states in 1912, for example, they were granted four sections per township and the right to make "in lieu" selections from the public domain to make up for sections that had already been reserved by the federal government for national forests, parks, and Indian reservations. Arizona selected prime rangelands because they were the most valuable remaining parcels available. The United States Forest Service administers most of the upland forest. The Bureau of Land Management, the largest federal land management agency, manages much of the desert. In this arid country, supporting livestock requires large amounts of land. Overall, the state is approximately 42 percent in federal ownership with 28 percent in Indian reservations under federal jurisdiction (Gorte *et al.* 2012). There is 13 percent in state ownership (National Agricultural Statistics 2007).

In California, the history of Spanish and Mexican land grants and land settlement policies for irrigation development resulted in extensive private rangelands. In addition, water resources are more plentiful, and rangelands are more productive, than in much of the arid West, making relatively small parcels viable for grazing operations. Upland forests and desert areas remained in federal ownership. The most productive rangelands in the state, oak woodland and annual grassland, are more than 80 percent in private ownership (CDF-FRAP 2010). The high value of these lands and the growing population has resulted in many types of land set aside, from local and regional parks, to land trusts and large state parks. Rangelands are owned by numerous different private and public owners. Overall, the state is about 48 percent in federal and 6 percent in state ownership, while the remaining public ownerships are uncensored.

Texas was annexed by the United States in 1845 in the midst of border disputes with neighboring states and Mexico. Texas gave up most of the disputed territories to the federal government in exchange for the U.S. assuming its 10 million dollar debt, and the disputed lands eventually became part of other states. As part of the negotiation process for annexation, Texas was not required to surrender the public domain within its borders to the federal government, unlike Arizona and California. Much of these state lands were gradually sold or traded off to fund projects ranging from the Texas public education system to construction of a state capitol building in red granite. As a result, Texas is less than 2 percent federal (Gorte *et al.* 2012) and approximately 8 percent state land (Texas General Land Office 2013).

Methods

In all three case studies, the benefits of collaboration to ranchers and agencies are summarized in a table, drawing on the framework of Taylor (2005), based on archival and primary interview data. To understand the role of conservation easements in the grassroots Malpai Borderlands Group of Arizona and New Mexico, 25 interviews were conducted in 2009. Eleven interviewees were ranchers whose lands were encumbered by easements; 14 interviewees were public agency personnel who worked with the Group (Rissman and Sayre 2012).

California interviews come from five different interview series in different parts of California. In 2000–2001 ranchers in the central Sierra Nevada foothills were interviewed about their use of public and private lands in the region (Sulak and

Huntsinger 2002a; Sulak and Huntsinger 2007; Huntsinger *et al.* 2010). A second study with the same objectives was conducted in 2005 in the San Francisco Bay area (Sulak and Huntsinger 2007). Twenty-nine interviews were conducted. In 2011, 15 interviews were conducted in the San Francisco Bay area with ranchers leasing land from public agencies, and in 2012, 25 interviews were carried out with ranchers in the northern Sierra foothills with the objective of understanding their ideas about land management and wildlife. Interviewees were selected from lists of lessors in each place, except in the 2011 and 2012 studies, where interviews were based on referrals from the California Rangeland Conservation Coalition, County Extension, and snowball sampling. Some of the founders of the Coalition were interviewed specifically for this chapter in 2013.

The Texas case study has been informed by the ongoing dissertation research of Luke Macaulay that includes four ranch visits with private landowners offering hunting on their properties, a visit to a biannual spring meeting of the Simms Creek Wildlife Management Area, and interviews with eight private landowners in Central Texas. After a literature review and archival research, semi-structured phone interviews were conducted with eight additional individuals with a particular focus on Wildlife Management Areas in 2013: three current or former biologists with the Texas Parks and Wildlife Department, one cooperative extension county agent, and four private landowners who are officers in various Wildlife Management Associations in Texas.

The Malpai Borderlands Group: "implementing ecosystem management"

Headquartered on the Malpai Ranch outside of Douglas, Arizona, the Malpai Borderlands Group (MBG) is a grassroots, landowner-driven nonprofit organization that has a goal of implementing ecosystem management on 800,000 acres of unfragmented rangelands in southeastern Arizona and southwestern New Mexico (http://www.malpaiborderlandsgroup.org/). With one important exception – the huge Gray Ranch (also known as the Diamond A) – ranches in this area comprise a mixture of private and public lands, depending for a significant portion of their forage on leases to graze on state and federal lands. Land ownership in the area is 59 percent private, 11 percent national forest, 23 percent state land (Arizona and New Mexico), and 7 percent BLM.

The rangelands around Douglas are semi-arid, with an average precipitation of 360 mm (NOAA 2000). The desert grasslands are subject to invasion by mesquite (*Prosopis velutina*) and other shrubs, which reduce grazing capacity, soil cover, and habitat for grassland-dependent species. In 1991, several of the area ranchers met at the Malpai Ranch in the San Bernardino Valley to discuss what they saw as a deteriorating situation. The ranchers were concerned about the future of the rangelands they depended on for their livelihoods. The grasslands with some shrubs were moving inexorably to shrublands with some grass. The group believed that using fire to burn the grasslands was part of the solution. As Bill McDonald, one of the founders and leaders of the group said:

> Despite widespread acceptance of the need to reintroduce fire into the natural ecosystems of the Southwest, the maze of conflicting and overlapping regulations seemed even to the agencies to be a gridlock too tough to overcome.
>
> (http://www.malpaiborderlandsgroup.org/fire.asp)

The ranchers also believed that ranching itself was under attack by environmental groups and misunderstood by the public. They were concerned about the growing demand for residential real estate parcels that was driving the fragmentation of private rangelands throughout the region. The group decided that rather than retrenching, they should reach out to critics and find common ground.

For two years, a small group of ranchers and environmentalists, together with scientist Ray Turner, met to discuss their mutual concerns about the health and integrity of the land. Calling themselves the Malpai Group, after two years they crafted a mission statement and agenda addressing the threat of fragmentation and the declining productivity and loss of biological diversity accompanying the encroachment of woody species on grasslands. The consensus of the group was that more government regulation was not going to help, but would just replace one set of problems with another. The inevitable result would probably be fragmentation into low density residential development. They decided that their solutions should involve good science, a strong conservation ethic, be economically feasible and be initiated and led by the private sector with the agencies coming in as partners, rather than with ranchers as clients.

In 1994, the Malpai Borderlands Group incorporated as a nonprofit organization, capable of accepting tax-deductible contributions and of holding conservation easements. A conservation easement is a legal document by which a landowner conveys certain specific rights, usually associated with the development of land, to another qualified entity for safekeeping. The Board of Directors includes local ranchers, and scientists and other stakeholders. The mission statement of the Group reads as follows:

> Our goal is to restore and maintain the natural processes that create and protect a healthy, unfragmented landscape to support a diverse, flourishing community of human, plant and animal life in our borderlands region. Together, we will accomplish this by working to encourage profitable ranching and other traditional livelihoods which will sustain the open space nature of our land for generations to come.

Fire plan

Fire suppression was believed to be a major factor in the accelerated encroachment of brush in the twentieth century and many ranchers, as well as others, felt it was time for fire to regain its evolutionary role in the ecosystem. The Malpai Group invited the land management agencies to work with them to coordinate fire management throughout the area. The response from the agencies was favorable. The Forest Service, the Bureau of Land Management, the State Land Departments of New Mexico and Arizona, and the Natural Resource Conservation Service agreed to cooperate with the group in identifying where fires would be suppressed and where they would be allowed to burn. Over the longer term – it took more than a decade – a Comprehensive Fire Plan was developed to facilitate prescribed fires as well. These efforts not only helped increase the amount of rangeland burned, but also helped improved inter-agency and agency-rancher coordination more generally. As one state lands manager remarked:

> Having a coordinated group helped us work together, because everything was laid out beforehand. The fire management plan designated areas such that if a fire started we would let it burn in that area, and ranchers knew that, and we would let go or suppress a fire based on the plan. Everybody knows what is going on and is on the same page.

Grassbanking

The Group also invented the concept of "Grassbanking," by which neighboring ranchers could rest their ranches from grazing by moving their herds to the Gray Ranch to enable conservation practices such as prescribed fires, reduce the impacts of drought, or in exchange for conservation easements on their private lands (Gripne 2005; White and Conley 2007). Although novel for the US West, Grassbanking is reminiscent of what has been termed "reserves" for traditional pastoralists (Fernández-Giménez and Le Febre 2006).

Land conservation

The Nature Conservancy began to work with the group on land conservation issues shortly after it purchased the 235,000-acre Gray Ranch in 1990. The Conservancy was looking to sell the ranch, and the community feared that the buyer might be the federal government. Instead, a local rancher offered to create the private Animas Foundation to purchase the Gray Ranch with conservation easements that forbid development and protect the ranch's native biodiversity (Sayre 2005).

Since that time, the Malpai Borderlands Group has acquired conservation easements on 85,252 acres of private land on 13 ranches. Nine of the easements were purchased outright for cash, with the purchase price determined by appraisals that compared the market value of the particular ranch with and without the easement restrictions. The other four easements were obtained in exchange for access to the Grassbank: the value of the easement – measured as just described – determined the amount of forage provided on the Gray Ranch, measured in market prices for private rangeland leases.

The easements apply only to the ranches' private (or deeded) acres. But they also all contain a clause which provides for extinguishment of the easement, by mutual agreement of the MBG and the landowner, in the event that the ranches' access to public lands for grazing is lost through no fault of the parties to the easement. The ranchers were not willing to encumber their private lands without such a clause, because their viability as livestock operations depends on their access to state and federal lands. Interestingly, interviews revealed that even with the clause, Malpai's easements have strengthened relations between ranchers and agencies, because the agencies recognize the benefit of preventing development of private lands to the conservation of adjacent public lands. In effect, the clause holds *both* the ranchers and the agencies to a higher standard of cooperation and effective management, as the former seek to maintain their leases and the latter seek to prevent the clause from being exercised (Rissman and Sayre 2012). As one agency employee put it:

> If grazing was abusive and not living up to the ideals of the group in the first place, we would work with the group to try to change the practices before we stopped the grazing; we would work with the group to put pressure on the rancher.

Mutual benefits

Agency personnel interviewed stated unanimously that the Malpai Borderlands Group's work benefited them in multiple ways. Urban encroachment and fragmentation of ranch lands would increase fire suppression needs and costs, make management with prescribed burning more difficult, and create conflicts between the management practices and land uses of adjacent private and public lands. Large undeveloped ranches create a buffer around public lands. Agency personnel felt that they already had a connection, a shared commitment to conservation, when they worked with Group members. As one interviewee commented:

> conservation easement [ranchers] have more of a land ethic... They manage more holistically, more for the long term ... if it [the ranch] has an easement, you know things are going to stay around. You walk into a ranch that has an easement, even the crustiest guys have long term plans and objectives. They make infrastructure investments, graze lighter, manage more effectively.

The Group also carries out a wide range of conservation programs and activities, including land restoration, endangered species habitat protection, cost-sharing for range and ranch improvements, and erosion control projects. They hold an annual science symposium attended by ranchers and agency personnel and have a science advisory panel that meets with the Board of Directors. As Executive Director Bill McDonald has explained:

> We have proved to the toughest critics that private sector leadership works by completing the first approved fire prescription ever for the Borderlands region, ending over 80 years of fire suppression. It involved two states, four private landowners, two BLM districts, two state land departments, the Forest Service, the Game and Fish departments in two states, the U.S. Fish and Wildlife Service, a proposed Wilderness Study Area, the Endangered Species Act, and the Antiquities Laws, and coordination with Mexico.

Endangered species

Efforts by ranchers to protect wildlife have also been promoted by the group (Allen 2006). When a drought in 1994 threatened to dry up the water source for two populations of endangered Chiricahua Leopard Frogs, the Magoffin Family began to haul water to a pond. They furnished about 1,000 gallons a week all summer, and the frogs were able to survive. The Malpai Group reimbursed the Magoffins for a portion of their expenses. This "frog project" has now grown into a major effort involving Arizona Game and Fish, US Fish and Wildlife Service, the University of Arizona, and biology classes in the public schools in Douglas, Arizona. Several agency- and Malpai Borderlands Group-supported projects enabled the Magoffins to drill wells and to provide pipelines and ponds to keep the frogs prospering, while providing much-needed cattle water (Allen 2006). In 2008, the MBG and the US Fish and Wildlife Service signed a Habitat Conservation Plan covering 19 rare species of fish, wildlife, and plants. The HCP ensures ESA compliance for ranching and conservation activities in the area, reducing uncertainty and legal exposure and facilitating inter-agency coordination for activities such as prescribed burning.

In March 1996, rancher and guide Warner Glenn encountered a very rare Mexican Jaguar while hunting mountain lions along the New Mexico–Arizona state line. Warner's photos of the cats were published in the book *Eyes of Fire*. A portion of the proceeds from that book is placed in a fund to compensate ranchers who can document losses of livestock to jaguars and to fund jaguar research in Arizona, New Mexico, and the nearby Sierra Madre of Mexico. Efforts of the Malpai Group to encourage research and management of this animal have resulted in an active Jaguar Management team in the Borderlands region, under the leadership of the Arizona Game and Fish Department (Allen 2006).

California Rangeland Conservation Coalition: "Working to keep ranchers ranching"

California ranchers not only work with a large number of agencies and conservation groups, but they engage in very diverse forms of production. Cattle are the predominant livestock, but there are also sheep producers and a few goat operations. Meat and dairy animals graze on rangelands, and grass fed, natural, and conventional products are produced. Proximity to large urban markets means that niche marketing opportunities influence range decisions. Ranch lands are under pressure from social demand for recreation areas, preserves, and "open space" (undeveloped land). In addition, California Mediterranean rangelands are highly desirable for suburban and ranchette development, and ranch lands are usually worth magnitudes more for development than for production. This "development pressure" has a major effect on the ranching community and is the scourge of conservationists. Although about half the state is in federal ownership and protected, this land is largely forest and desert, while the rangelands of the coast and Sierran foothills are the richest wildlife habitat in the state and are in the majority privately owned.

Table 4.1 Ways the Malpai Borderlands Group, a grassroots governance group, helps to maintain rancher ability to benefit from public and private rangelands

Obstacles to ability to benefit for ranchers using state and federal lands	Individual capacity to respond	Collaborative capacity to respond	Benefit to agency from collaborative group
Agencies: agency personnel uninformed about grazing, concerned about impacts, restrict grazing, disagreements with agency managers	Make one-on-one connections, graze only private land, hire consultants, legal actions	Work with leadership of diverse agencies; put on symposia, meetings, and events to increase communication, support research; ability to lobby agencies, political clout; network of experts	Work with and negotiate with group representatives instead of many individuals; develop networks and information; mediation of conflict; working with members is easier.
Development: urban sprawl breaks up community, restricts management options, creates neighbor conflicts	Work with planning departments, vote, put easement on own land, work with neighbors	Create community commitment to ranching landscape, healthy rangelands; coordinate and encourage conservation easements, strengthen community	Lower costs of management, buffers of private land around public lands
Resources: Lack of information and assistance about impacts of grazing, management, monitoring, available grants and programs	Advisory agencies, cooperative extension	Support for ecological and social research, university positions, extension and advisory services; network of expertise, symposia, meetings, and events for knowledge-sharing	More informed lessees, mediation, monitoring. Better management of associated private lands
Regulations: restrictions on burning, liability	Try to get attention of agency to burn or get equipment and resources to do own burning.	Fund research on benefits of fire; create cross boundary burn plan	Improved ability to conduct prescribed burns and/or use "let burn"' policy; less liability for fires crossing property lines if neighbors are in the burn plan
Context: unpredictable drought, loss of forage to fire or restoration projects	Purchase hay, sell animals, lease forage	Grassbank provides reserve forage, leased forage from Gray Ranch	Easier to carry out restoration project, restrict grazing when needed
Other users: Integration with other uses of public lands, environmentalist hostility to ranching	Rely on "multiple use" doctrine for public lands	Creates lobbying group for maintaining rancher "right to benefit" from state and federal lands; publicize stewardship of ranchers	Helps agency work with multiple constituencies

After a decade or two of combative relations, the California Rangeland Conservation Coalition was born out of a recognition that this habitat would largely be lost if the ranching and environmental communities did not work together. A ranch in the San Francisco Bay Area was the backdrop for a meeting between environmentalists, ranchers, and resource professionals from federal and state agencies in the summer of 2005. Out of this meeting of former foes came a resolution documenting common ground for the conservation of the rangeland encircling the Central Valley, including the Sierra Foothills and Interior Coast Ranges. Together these signatories form the California Rangeland Conservation Coalition. The signatories have pledged to work together to preserve and enhance California's rangeland for species of special concern, while supporting the long-term viability of the ranching industry. Signatories either conceptually support the work of the Coalition or are actively engaged in working with other partners to fulfill the underlying principles of the Coalition stated in the resolution and outlined in more detail within a strategic plan (http://www.carangeland.org/).

Unlike the Malpai Borderlands Group, the Rangeland Coalition includes a large portion of the state with both rural and heavily populated areas, and from the outset included agencies and environmental groups as well as ranchers. As urban development, conversion to more intensive forms of agriculture, and land acquisition for preserves or recreation continue to shrink the private rangelands available for grazing, California ranchers typically obtain a quarter to half of their forage from government-owned rangelands. The types of government ownership are quite variable. Some BLM and USFS land is grazed, the US Fish and Wildlife Service, regional and local parks, and utility districts lease significant amounts of lands for grazing, as do state agencies like the Department of Fish and Wildlife. Numerous private conservation reserves, large and small, lease land for grazing, including those managed by groups like the Audubon Society, the Nature Conservancy, land trusts, and a host of others. Interviews with ranchers around the state have revealed that many manage a complex portfolio of owned and leased lands, leasing from government agencies, but also from private landowners who have retired from ranching, own land for investment, or own land for non-ranching purposes. A rancher in the Sierran foothills told interviewers that he used 14 different leases (Sulak and Huntsinger 2007), while another claimed in a 2012 study to have 33 small leases scattered throughout his local area, some grazed by only small groups of cattle. Competition for leases is fierce, and it is not uncommon for ranchers to submit bids for leases that require substantial commitment to stewarding and improving the range.

The Coalition has for the past seven years held an annual Summit. The Summit is an opportunity to hear from researchers about the ecological benefits of grazing and more. Scientists, environmentalists, and ranchers present on rangeland restoration and improvement projects. The 2013 Summit was attended by more than 400 people from across the state (carangeland.org/calendarevents/2013summit.html). An important goal for the Coalition is to inform the public and agencies that ranching is not only a preferred land use compared to development, but also is an essential resource management tool and can be used to benefit wildlife.

California Rangeland Resolution

The California Rangeland Resolution states that the diversity of the species rangelands support is largely due to the grazing and other land stewardship practices of the ranchers that own and manage them. The resolution was signed by over 100 agricultural organizations, environmental interest groups, as well as by state and federal agencies. New signatories continue to sign on to the resolution on a regular basis. Developing the wording for the resolution was a challenge, because the right balance had to be found so that ranchers and environmental organizations would all feel comfortable signing on. Karen Sweet, a prominent rancher and one of the Resolution's authors, recalls:

> We needed to create a statement about what we all cared about, what we had in common. A committee of 6 was charged with authoring it including ranchers, and representatives of agencies and conservation organizations. We all cared so much about these rangelands, and we learned a lot over the course of putting the language together. Someone would suggest a word, and others would ask what it meant. We had to keep the right tone, and make it layman friendly. It was hard work, but we evolved a common language.

A critical part of obtaining so many signatories was a growing body of research, as well as a number of spectacular conservation failures, that indicated grazing is beneficial and sometimes necessary for maintaining viable wildlife habitat for a number of species of animals and plants. These include species on the endangered list, as well as wildflowers enjoyed by the public. Tim Koopmann, a member of the Coalition in the San Francisco Bay Area, has described his experience with the endangered callippe silverspot butterfly (*Speyeria callippe callippe*). The larvae eat one species of plant only, the yellow pansy, or "Johnny jump-up" (*Viola pedunculata*). On his ranch there are an abundance of Johnny jump ups, so he sold a "mitigation easement" to provide habitat for the butterfly on his ranch when a golf course was developed nearby. On adjacent land protected by the city, cattle were excluded, and the butterfly nearly disappeared. He now has an agreement with the city to graze the city's land to enhance habitat for the butterfly. As in so many cases, the flora the butterfly needed was dependent on grazing to reduce the stature of the invasive exotic annual grasses that now dominate the California grassland. As Tim Koopmann said himself:

> The biodiversity developed over 1000s of years with grazing of some kind. Previously, it was wildlife. Today, grazing can be a tool that is effective in maintaining that biodiversity.
>
> (The Independent, Livermore, 2009)

A similar case was documented for the endangered bay checkerspot butterfly (*Euphydryas editha bayensis*), south of San Francisco, and further linked to nitrogen deposition that increased grass growth (Weiss 1999). These and other similar cases have lent considerable support to the Coalition's efforts to promote rancher stewardship of wildlife and land. In Coalition publications ranching is linked to conservation and production of pollinators, birds, salamanders, game, native grasses, wildflowers, heritage values, fire resistance, and natural beauty, among other things (http://carangeland.org/stories.html).

In addition to numerous accounts by experts, landowners, and managers, the scientific literature includes findings that support the benefits of grazing for wildlife and plants. Those shown to benefit from grazing include burrowing owls (*Athene cunicularia*) (Nuzum 2005), insects (Dennis *et al.* 1997), kit fox (*Vulpes macrotis mutica*) (USDA-FWS 2010), kangaroo rats (*Dipodomys stephensi*) (USDA-FWS 1997, Kelt *et al.* 2005, Germano *et al.* 2012), wildflowers (Barry 2011), and a host of rare flora and fauna associated with vernal pools (Marty 2005, Pyke and Marty 2005). There are numerous additional anecdotal accounts. In the case of the tiger salamander, continued research has demonstrated the preference of the species for grazed, muddy ponds. Another endangered species, the red-legged frog, also seems to flourish in grazed ponds. This has come as a surprise to the ranchers themselves. As Darrel Sweet, a leader in the Coalition and member of the Board of Directors of the Rangeland Trust, described it in 2013:

> About 15 years ago I was asked to go on a tour of a local Wilderness area with members of their board of directors and senior staff… So we loaded up at the park headquarters and proceeded to climb up a rather steep road. When we stopped at a flat spot the first thing we saw was a stock pond. Obviously it was heavily used by the cattle which, as the only rancher on the bus, was why I thought this was not going to be a fun trip. After we stopped their staff biologist asked if anyone on board had ever seen a red-legged frog, which few had. So he grabbed his net and we unloaded the bus. Most walked carefully to the edge of the pond and watched as the biologist netted a large red-legged frog. He went on to explain why the park removed the fencing they had originally installed to exclude the cattle from many of their ponds as a frog protection effort. This pond had never been fenced and had one of the highest numbers of frogs of any of their 80 or so ponds surveyed/studied.

Sharing the benefits of grazing for wildlife is one way the Coalition gains support and represents its membership. Promoting a positive role for ranching not only encourages the conservation community to support efforts to maintain it, but helps ranchers gain access to public lands and NGO preserves. As rangelands are in short supply and competition for leases is high (Sulak and Huntsinger 2007), this is key to supporting the ranching community's "ability to benefit" from California rangelands.

Land conservation

Most ranchers prefer to stay in ranching and to see the landscape remain a ranching landscape. They depend on a "critical mass" of ranchers to maintain ranching infrastructure such as veterinary services and feed suppliers in an area (Liffmann *et al.*, 2000). Yet they also insist that they should retain the right to do as they like with their land, including selling it to development if needed. The Coalition works to maintain the existence of rangelands and ranching through voluntary, private sector land conservation, largely in the form of conservation easements. Because the conservation community also recognizes the value of unfragmented habitat, and the role of ranching in maintaining large areas of habitat, this is another area of focus for the Coalition.

One of the first things accomplished by the Coalition was to create a map of high priority areas for wildlife and plant conservation in the state, defining rangeland areas that should be protected from development (http://www.carangeland.org/images/Rangeland_Coalition_Map.pdf). Coastal prairies were left out of the prioritized lands because according to Karen Sweet:

> The environmental community was not sure that grazing could provide positive benefits on this type of grassland. We had to make places where there was consensus about the benefits of ranching our priority.

Like the Malpai Borderlands Group, the Coalition is committed to private sector initiatives. Conservation easements appeal to rancher members as a tool because the rancher remains in control of the land and makes the management decisions. According to Karen Sweet, a key concern of the ranching community is that "someone might take away their land or tell them how to manage it." Some ranchers do not believe that the Coalition's environmental signatories really care about the economic viability of ranching. In general the ranching community already feels "over-regulated" (Liffmann *et al.* 2000), and it is important that easements remain voluntary and that easement requirements are clear and minimize interference in ranch management. The California Rangeland Conservation Coalition also has a land trust to which they are closely allied: the California Rangeland Trust. The trust emphasizes that it was founded by ranchers and knows how to work with ranchers (http://www.rangelandtrust.org/). As stated on the website:

> We are ... proud of the trust we have established within the landowner community. From its inception, the Rangeland Trust has demonstrated that we share the same values important to ranching families. Additionally, we bring the ranching and environmental communities together to cultivate shared efforts to protect open space and the western lifestyle.

Key benefits of easements for the conservation community are that obtaining easements is less expensive than acquiring land, so more land can be conserved; and the land is managed by the rancher. Costs of management are proving difficult for public entities to sustain, as exemplified by the closure of some of the California State Parks because of a shortage of funds for management. Public agencies and NGOs alike recognize the importance of unfragmented landscapes and buffer areas to long-term conservation.

Involvement in land use planning is more fraught with difficulty. Some in the ranching community view planning as "regulatory" and fear that it sets limits on their ability to use their property without government consent or compensation. In other words, to tell a rancher that they cannot sell or develop their land is unfairly asking them to bear the conservation burden. On the other hand, the Coalition is interested in Habitat Conservation Planning (HCP), where habitat may be set aside through purchase or easement. The Coalition favors the easement approach, where the ranching enterprise remains as part of the community that supports ranching infrastructure and community. Often they find that ranch land is not recognized as agricultural land and HCP projects inadequately consider the need to maintain grazing and ranching in the area. Once again, clarifying the importance of grazing to species that are often central to HCPs can help to gain the attention of the planners.

As the subject of land conservation is a complex one for the ranchers, there have been controversies when an agency has proposed an easement project for example. The Coalition can provide advice and a network for outreach to ranchers. Hearing about one easement program proposal that engendered considerable controversy among local ranchers, Darrel Sweet commented that:

> Why didn't they have a rancher explain it to the ranchers? That's all they needed to do.

Ranchers, as with most cultural groups, prefer to learn from their peers and Coalition representatives can help with communication and outreach to ranchers on projects they support. Coalition members can also help a rancher communicate with an agency lessor, for example, when disputes arise, and vice versa.

Strategic plan

The Coalition has developed a strategic plan that lays the foundation for signatories to work together to acquire additional federal funding for conservation programs, coordinate permitting processes, garner support for cooperative conservation projects, fill research gaps, conduct outreach on the positive role of managed grazing and provide incentives for ecosystem services. In some cases, research on the benefits of grazing has led public agencies to develop complex grazing plans that ranchers, concerned about marketing their livestock, find difficult to accommodate (Germano *et al.* 2012). As one lessee remarked in the 2011 interviews:

> Regulations and standards vary between agencies, making it challenging to do business … [On some lands] public lands management has set a standard that's virtually impossible for a private landowner to follow and stay in business.

Table 4.2 Ways the California Rangeland Conservation Coalition helps ranchers maintain the ability to benefit from private and public rangelands in California

Obstacle to ability to benefit for ranchers using diverse public lands via lease and permit	Individual capacity to respond	Collaborative capacity to respond	Benefit to agency from collaborative group
Agencies: agency and NGO personnel uninformed about grazing, restricting or eliminating it on public lands whenever possible	Work with knowledgeable individuals and agency reps, graze only private land	Work with leadership of diverse agencies; put on symposia; support conservation easements and conservation grazing; Rangeland Resolution	Improved land management, better communication among rangeland managers via external and internal networks and access to research. Easier to work with leaders than many individuals
Resources: lack of information and assistance about impacts of grazing, management, monitoring	Private consultants	Support for ecological and social research, university positions, extension and advisory services	Advisory services help create a more informed lease process, mediation, monitoring. Better management of associated private lands – able to influence management
Development: Urban sprawl and loss of ranching infrastructure, rural environment; neighbors that do not understand ranching	Sell ranch and buy a ranch away from developed areas	Promote conservation easements, California Rangeland Trust	Reduce costs and habitat losses associated with sprawl; provide buffer areas
Regulations: complex and sometimes conflicting regulations, complex permitting processes for improvements, cost-sharing projects	Try to understand, hire private consultants, try to get assistance	Lobby to streamline and coordinate regulations; bring agency representatives and managers together at events and meetings; strategic plan	Lower costs of enforcement and monitoring; enhanced habitat diversity

Regulations: disagreement with landlord, private or public	Get help from private consultant, cooperative extension	Network of experts to draw on, sometimes presentations to boards, interest groups	Informal mediation of conflict
Regulations: shortage of available leases; increasingly complex lease requirements	Compete: hire private consultants	Learn how to write appealing conservation grazing bids; symposia educate lessors about needs of ranchers	More knowledgeable lessees; more successful leases that achieve conservation goals
Context: drought, variable income from livestock production	Diversify	Support incentives, payments for ecosystem services, cost-sharing programs	Positive way to work with landowners
Other users: integration with other uses of public and private land	Be friendly and compliant	Demonstrate benefits of grazing to plant diversity, weed control, wildlife, fire hazard reduction; and research showing grazing harms can be mitigated	Improved habitat, reduced fire hazard

On the other hand, agency interviewees often lamented that finding employees or ranch hands who can herd cattle, work with agency employees, and attend to the ecosystem as requested by agencies is a challenge. "Good employees who can manage cattle and rangelands at the same time are hard to find" was a common statement.

The Coalition works to inform agency managers of the economic constraints of livestock producers and to help managers learn about ranching, and at the same time helps ranchers learn about the requirements the agencies must meet.

While cost-sharing programs and other incentives programs are offered to ranchers by federal and state governments, in too many cases the oversight requirements and paperwork are quite onerous. A rancher related the paperwork and bureaucracy associated with obtaining cost share funding for fixing a pond that was home to the endangered tiger salamander. Not only was the paperwork complex, particularly because more than one agency was involved, it was very difficult to get the agencies to respond in a timely way and to come out as required to observe the work. As one Coalition member put it:

> We had to plan the repairs to avoid affecting the breeding of the salamanders, but the agency was so slow that we couldn't even do it that year, after we had gone through all the other processes to get the permit and had the equipment ready.

The Coalition tries to work with agencies to help streamline such processes, and to facilitate communication and land use decisions. One problem pointed out by Karen Sweet is that it is difficult to reach the consultants who advise the regulators and owner-decision makers. Because of this, some regulatory efforts do not fit the conditions in California, calling for fencing cattle out where they are needed to manage the habitat and so forth. The Coalition sponsors ranch tours and workshops, bringing together experts, ranchers, and regulators in an effort to get the word out about maintaining grazing and ranching.

While the Coalition's original focus was on private land conservation, emphasis has grown to include the need for grazing as a tool for public lands management as well. Among its many activities the group gives its opinions on legislation, lobbies in the state and Washington D.C., produces publications, gives presentations, and writes letters of support for research funding that they believe will build bridges among signatories, inform grazing management, and find ways to support the viability of ranching.

Texas Wildlife Associations: "enhancing land and wildlife stewardship"

In many parts of Texas, hunting of game species has been an integral part of livestock ranching, with the commercialized value of hunting increasing rapidly since the 1970s. One way to diversify, and increase total income or benefits from the land, is to manage for commercial hunting as well as livestock production.

In the United States, most wildlife is under state trusteeship. The ability to use private lands for hunting is constrained by state wildlife regulations, the wildlife resource itself, and the rancher's own management capacity. Game animals, unless they are confined domestics or exotics, cross property lines, making effective management more dependent on coordination among landowners, especially in areas with smaller land holdings. Ranchers wishing to sell hunting opportunities must comply with state hunting regulations and regulatory agencies, but are also affected by the management practices of their neighbors. Wildlife Management Associations (WMAs) help ranchers by improving coordination with neighbors and regulators, understanding of game regulations, and integration of hunting with livestock production (Lyons and Wright 2003). The first known WMA in Texas was established in 1955 and operated in the three corners region of Bee, Goliad and Karnes counties. The first modern day WMA in Texas, the Peach Creek Wildlife Management Co-op, was organized in 1973 with the help of Texas Parks and Wildlife Department (TPWD) wildlife biologists (Texas Parks and Wildlife 2004).

As the population continues to grow in the Texas, and lands are divided (often through inheritance), the overall ownership sizes of rural land tracts are shrinking (Wilkens *et al.* 2009). In addition, while livestock production produces low and variable income on a per hectare basis, the recreational value of rural land is increasing. Hunting, fishing, and recreation in scenic areas are major interests of city dwellers seeking an escape to the countryside. Newer landowners are increasingly interested in wildlife and habitat management, but highly fragmented ownership patterns make management of wildlife habitat difficult (Wagner *et al.* 2007b). Fragmentation is also affecting water and brush management, and wildlife management associations build relationships that can help with collaborative management for other resources. While primarily oriented to improving habitat for game species, wildlife management associations have helped landowners garner additional income from hunting fees, and the social organization of these associations has fostered increased communication and cooperation among landowners. This in turn has led to improvements in knowledge-sharing about livestock practices through participation in educational events and improved range conditions for both livestock and wildlife. Managing for wildlife not only augments rancher income, but incentivizes managing for native species.

In 2007, more than 85 million ha of private lands in Texas were managed for hunting enterprises, charging fees commonly ranging from $15 to $25 per ha, or more. In prime habitat hunting revenues may be greater than those from ranching or crop production (Wagner *et al.* 2007b). As a rancher in San Saba County, Texas, commented in 2013:

> Main thing is, if we do protect our wildlife, then our ranchers stand a chance of being more productive as far as the bottom line for the ranching operation. It helps the bottom line, it really does.

Mike Krueger, a retired TPWD Technical Guidance Biologist, added in a 2013 interview that:

> Running livestock is a kind of break-even proposition, some years you make money and some years not, there are a lot of input costs, but when it comes to leasing wildlife, a lot of that is pure net, not a lot of landowner input is needed to maintain a commercial hunting operation, or to maintain your habitat. If hunters want to build a cabin, they pay for it, the net profit from hunting has always been a lot greater than from the livestock operation.

The Texas Organization of Wildlife Management Associations (TOWMA) (www.towma.org) is a nonprofit NGO founded in 1996 to coordinate a large number of Wildlife Management Associations in Texas. TOWMA promotes coordination between wildlife associations by providing a forum for the exchange of ideas and information. This forum helps maintain interest among existing WMAs and supports the establishment of new associations. TOWMA currently represents over 60 WMAs in 33 counties of Texas and these WMA member landowners total more than 3,000 and control in excess of 1.5 million acres of Texas wildlife habitat. As a collaboration of collaborative programs, TOWMA argues that:

> We exist for several reasons, including the fact that there is strength in numbers. While individual wildlife associations or burn associations may consist of dozens or hundreds of landowners, TOWMA, by bringing them all together, represents thousands. Consequently, TOWMA is more likely to be listened to when addressing issues at the state and national level that affect landowners, land owner's rights, and wildlife in Texas.
>
> (www.towma.org)

Managing a transboundary resource

White-tailed deer, quail, turkeys, doves, and waterfowl are common pool resources that are typically managed for hunting in Texas. Some landowners have also begun managing for birds of interest to recreational birdwatchers. Because game animals often cross property boundaries, their management may depend on the decision-making of the many different landowners owning properties within an animal's range. Managing for quality deer hunting requires adherence to harvest criteria for males and females over a large area. Maintaining sex ratios that result in adequate mature males for harvest depends on cooperation among neighboring landowners to establish rules for hunting and make sure they are followed.

Wildlife management associations (WMAs) have become a popular mechanism for coordinating wildlife management decisions in Texas, and applying game management programs supported by the state (Wagner *et al.* 2007b). Collective decision-making can be fostered through group interaction that builds social capital, including shared norms and goals. As TOWMA puts it:

quality deer management is not a realistic goal for individual properties under 5,000 acres because mature bucks may range 6 miles or more during the rut. Even after being informed of this complication, most landowners still want to produce trophy bucks in the hope that they will occasionally see one. These small landowners must be prepared to share the fruits of their labor with their neighbors and/or their neighbor's hunters ... The concept behind wildlife management associations is founded in that simple truth. Since we are forced to share the fruits of our labor, why not share the labor as well? If we have similar goals, and can increase the likelihood of attaining those goals by working together, why not do it?

(www.towma.org/the_wma_solution.html)

Research has demonstrated that Wildlife Management Associations in Texas contribute to building social capital among landowners, especially when meetings are frequent, and landowners are resident and have owned the property for a long time. The state benefits from these associations by being able to promulgate policies for game management across large areas. Creating a setting that fosters cooperation may also help Texas landowners manage brush with fire, protect watersheds, and maintain scenery (Wagner *et al.* 2007b). In a study of wildlife management associations in the Post Oak Savannah region, Wagner *et al.* (2007b) found that association goals included making habitat improvements, increasing deer numbers through importation of deer, and balancing deer sex ratios to produce more high quality hunting animals.

Wildlife agency personnel value the ecological outcomes of cooperation among landowners, but they also recognize the social values. Quoted in a state guide for wildlife management associations, Mike Kreuger stated:

It is always gratifying to me to see a group of neighbors (who may have thought that they had nothing in common) realize that they share a common interest in wildlife ... It is amazing how getting together, whether it be for a WMA meeting or riding together in the back of a pickup truck for a deer census, can break down barriers and dispel rumors. I personally feel that the social benefits of a WMA are just as important as the biological benefits.

(TPWD 2004: 5)

A Coryell County rancher commented in 2013 that:

Our association is not all that active. The best result we get from it, it helps neighbors know one another, neighbors get to talk about an issue, a pretty large percent of landowners aren't residents, maybe 50–60%. We don't help out on livestock, but if cattle get out, get through the fence, you can call your neighbor ... That's one of the advantages.

In Texas, hunting is regulated by a central authority, the Texas Parks and Wildlife Department. It is to the benefit of ranchers to work closely with the

Texas Parks and Wildlife Department to support development of management plans that improve hunting values. For deer hunting, limits are placed on the number of deer a single hunter may harvest annually, but the number of hunters on a given tract of land is not regulated. Thus, in areas with small ownerships, overharvest of deer can be a problem (Wagner *et al.* 2007a). Wildlife Management Associations most often operate under a written wildlife management plan prepared by a TPWD wildlife biologist (Wagner *et al.* 2007b), carrying the approval of the regulatory agency. Landowners usually also agree to put forth a good-faith effort to get their hunters to comply with plan recommendations (TPWD 2004), and to collect standardized data and observations for monitoring game populations. A San Saba County rancher explained in a 2013 interview:

> We have 2 meetings each year ... one in the spring when we go through and look at all deer harvested in past year, record and age them, to see if we're taking the right deer or not. Then in the fall we tally up the results of our spotlight surveys of the summer and plan a selective harvest of deer based on age and quality.

Texas Department of Parks and Wildlife

Being a state dominated by private land, in order to influence land and habitat management, Texas has fostered a collaborative relationship with landowners through wildlife management associations. The state provides a significant reduction in hunting lease license fees for landowners who participate in an association. By participating in many of the practices of the WMAs, landowners are often able to enter into the Managed Lands Deer Program which allows for more flexibility in harvest for hunters through targeted harvest strategies for individual properties.

To encourage landowner participation in programs that include technical guidance by state biologists, Texas has passed a law prohibiting the disclosure of information about a private property when technical guidance is being provided. This law helps encourage landowners to accept technical guidance when they may have endangered species on their properties, as otherwise disclosure of the presence of an endangered species on a private property might result in additional regulatory oversight for that landowner. As a result, landowners are more trusting and open to allowing state employees onto their property to receive technical guidance. Interviewees noticed varying opinions from landowners toward endangered species, with a tendency of more traditional landowners preferring not to know about the endangered species, but a different attitude emerging from newer landowners who were often excited about having these species on their properties (Homerstad interview 2013 and Krueger interview 2013). Interestingly, sometimes landowners who are loath to admit endangered species are on their property are eager to find them if a development project is underway as a way to block a project that would negatively affect their property.

Ranchers obtain substantial benefits through the associations, and may initiate an association in their area in order to improve the number and quality of game species available for their hunting enterprises. In the early development of the first WMAs in the state, Texas Parks and Wildlife biologist Dennis Brown told an interested landowner:

> One of you has to organize it, get it rolling and stay on top of it. Otherwise it just looks like the government is interfering in private business. We'll put on a program and help set up a wildlife management plan, but the establishment of the goals and commitment has to come from the landowners.
>
> (TPWD 2004)

In the state guidelines for wildlife management associations, the point is made that as wildlife plans succeed in producing more wildlife, WMA members and their families "often turn into wildlife activists – pursuing, watching and appreciating the animals they are aiding. Landowners earnestly begin to address habitat, managing and enhancing the vegetation and supporting conditions that are essential to all forms of wildlife" (TPWD 2004: 7). This is important from a conservation perspective because Texas has a high number of rare and endangered species. Gary Homerstad, President of TOWMA, pointed out in a 2013 interview that:

> One good thing is that with landowners cooperating, knowing each other, trusting each other, there is not as great a tendency to high fence their property.

Land fragmentation

Biologists working for the Texas Parks and Wildlife Department describe two types of landowners, the "new" landowner, who is often an urban resident and has little experience in owning rangelands, and "traditional" landowners who have more experience, sometimes multiple generations, in running livestock and harvesting game on their properties. They described the benefits of WMAs in educating new landowners about the use of fire on their properties as well as the benefits of targeted grazing. As Gary Homerstad observed in 2013:

> One survey found that in Washington County, 56% of people who own property don't live in that county, but lived in nearby cities like Houston or Austin. These landowners don't have relatives with ranching background, but the coops have helped even those people realize that they need to graze, they see what happens when they don't. Mowing isn't a viable management tool compared to grazing.

The TOWMA website talks about the problems of coping with land fragmentation, stating:

Fragmentation usually ... means more access roads, land clearing for home sites, out buildings, pens, fences, utility right of ways, and landscaping, all of which reduce the amount of habitat available to wildlife. This is usually compounded by more frequent use of the land by people, motor vehicles and domestic animals. Hunting pressure generally increases because family members and friends suddenly have access to the property. Herbicide, pesticide and other chemical uses increase. Habitat quantity is reduced, its quality declines, and wildlife is forced out or suffers from increased pressure. The only workable solution for small landowners in their quest for better deer, and quality wildlife of all types, is to work together with their neighbors and jointly manage enough habitat to support quality wildlife.

(www.towma.org)

Mike Kreuger relates one case where WMA connections, or social capital, was instrumental in building support for efforts to stop an electricity transmission line from crossing ranch properties and impacting a river watershed.

Influencing policy

At the statewide scale, TOWMA believes that urban voters will ultimately control what happens on ranch lands. Like ranchers in Malpai and California, they are concerned with being "outnumbered" by a growing, non-agricultural population. However, by banding together, landowners believe that they can have more of an influence on state politics and the policies that influence them. The TOWMA website mentions the 1996 proposition allowing land shifted to wildlife management to qualify for agriculture tax appraisals, and regulations affecting which animals can be harvested, as examples of where working with legislators as a group helped to create and support policies that help ranchers maintain their ability to benefit from their lands (www.towma.org). Wildlife Management Associations actively supported the legislation. It provides significant tax savings over residential or unmanaged lands. The landowner needs to demonstrate management to propagate a sustaining breeding, migrating, or wintering population of indigenous wild animals for human use, including food, medicine, or recreation. Joining or creating a Wildlife Management Association that establishes practices that meet this requirement is one way to qualify, and is another way to share the labor required to meet requirements, conduct monitoring, and produce documentation.

Integration with grazing and vegetation management

Wildlife Management Associations can facilitate the development of other grassroots groups that help ranchers to benefit from their lands. TOWMA is seeking additional sources of funding to add full time staff in order to provide more services including support for Prescribed Burn Associations. Organizations whose functions complement TOWMA are considered for membership, including Prescribed Burn Associations, which provide fire training and promote prescribed fire in their regions. TOWMA believes that memberships of this type are beneficial to both organizations since they expand membership, share resources and act as partners in enhancing habitat and wildlife in Texas.

A San Saba County Rancher, talking about his local WMA in 2013, responded to a question about prescribed burning with the following:

> It's something we're looking into more and more as a management tool, we don't have a burning association but have been talking about getting one started, to try to do some prescribed burning. There are so many liabilities, if fire gets out, then you're facing lawsuits and things like that, but it's something we've got to develop so that we can adequately manage fire. A burn would be beneficial to both livestock and wildlife, cut back on the less desirable species like mesquite and cedar, and keep the undergrowth under control.

Sharing liability costs, training, and equipment is one benefit that has been documented for Prescribed Burning Associations in Texas (Taylor 2005). Mike Krueger mentioned that some members of WMAs have talked about forming grazing associations so that they can move cattle herds from one ranch to another in a large-scale rotation, or at least to share rangelands (interview, 2013).

TOWMA works to continue and even increase the momentum of member organizations by conducting regular meetings and sharing information about successes in wildlife management and operations. Workshops on using burning and grazing may be advertised to members though a WMA. The President of TOWMA in an interview stated that one method for educating "new" landowners about grazing was to invite Cooperative Extension Specialists to speak at WMA meetings:

> At the meetings, they would almost always discuss types of grazing, stocking rates, timing and intensity of grazing. Grazing is so critical. We don't want to see someone hammering a place to death and overgrazing, but we don't want to see a place without any grazing either.

Mike Krueger mentioned in a 2013 interview that cattle grazing and deer management are very compatible. Gary Homerstad described the benefits of grazing, as well as fire, in 2013:

> [without grazing or fire] the grass becomes very thick and dominant, less forbs, which are more important to deer, quail, and turkeys. The forage value of a weed [broad-leaved plant] compared to grass is much better for deer. Deer can't digest grass compared to a weed.

TOWMA has a goal of sharing information and re-usable templates to help organizations avoid "re-inventing the wheel." Every other year a two-day Symposium is held that brings together some of the best wildlife professionals in the United States. Additional learning resources are provided in member

Table 4.3 Ways that Wildlife Management Associations help ranchers to maintain the ability to benefit from private rangelands using fire as a management tool

Obstacle to ability to benefit from private lands	Individual capacity to respond	Collaborative capacity to respond	Benefit to agency from collaborative group
Development: Properties too small to economically benefit from wildlife resource; land fragmentation; game have larger ranges than single property size	Limited because game cross boundaries	Community-level harvest recommendations and habitat management; improved quality of wildlife and resulting income through hunting leases; meetings and events to encourage communication, build relationships, develop plan with wildlife agency, encourage hunter compliance, coordinate with neighbors; support and clout for anti-development initiatives; tax relief and other benefits for wildlife management	Outlet for information about local game conditions; compliance with game plan; peer monitoring; improved herd management, influence on private lands; better habitat
Agencies: Standard wildlife and hunting regulations and fees, low ranching income	Comply with regional regulations	Enhance habitat collaboratively in exchange for increased hunting and harvest flexibility; encourage agency willingness to work with ranchers; work with legislature; training and safety programs; more political clout; reduced license fees for commercial hunting leases	Greater cooperation, safety, peer monitoring; work with leadership rather than many individuals
Resources: not knowing absentee neighbors and who to contact with problems like livestock escape	Make individual outreach effort	Meet neighbors and landowners across the area at biennial meetings; know who to call	Landowners contact each other directly instead of reporting to county agencies

Resources: lack of knowledge about game and habitat management	Engage with state or federal employees for technical guidance; hire private consultants	Biannual meetings and symposia with education and training; network of experts, positions, university research, positions, extension and advisory services; source for credible information; support for other groups like prescribed burning associations; awards for stewardship and sharing of best practices.	Improved management, less conflict, influence on private lands
Context: brush encroachment reducing forage productivity	Clear brush or conduct prescribed burns	Learn best practices for brush control; share equipment; reduce risk and spread liability insurance cost	Improved range productivity and native species habitat
Other users: poaching and trespass	Watch own property	Neighbors watch out for neighbors	Reduced poaching
Other users: overhunting by neighbors so less game	Try to harvest it first or try to reason with neighbor	Peer pressure encourages landowners to act responsibly and to not overharvest the wildlife resource	Less over-hunting, higher quality and quantity of game species

newsletters and a website. TOWMA maintains a speaker roster for associations seeking expert speakers on a variety of subjects.

To sum up, wildlife management associations, often called "coops" in Texas, are primarily oriented to improving habitat for game species, but they have helped landowners running livestock garner additional income from hunting fees, and the social organization of these associations has led to the benefits of increased communication and cooperation among landowners. Those who have worked extensively with these associations believe that this has led to improved ability to run livestock successfully, and improved range conditions for both livestock and wildlife. WMAs work to dispel the notion that livestock are in direct competition with wildlife, and have informed landowners oriented toward hunting game animals that livestock are an important tool in habitat management for wildlife. WMAs have helped to encourage burning and have been the nucleus for development of prescribed burning associations and organizations to limit development. In some limited cases, they may even foster cooperation and sharing of grazing resources, although possibly due to the cost of transporting cattle to various small properties, this has yet to be adopted as a widespread practice.

Conclusions

In our three case studies, grassroots organization has helped maintain and increase rancher ability to benefit from rangelands. The need for a collaborative effort seems more obvious when grazing must depend on large amounts of land that are not owned by the rancher, yet even in Texas, where most grazed land is the rancher's, grassroots organizations develop to foster the web of social and institutional relationships that keep ranchers in place and help them benefit from their rangelands. All of these groups rely on creating connections among ranchers, and among ranchers and regulatory or management agencies, and sharing knowledge, labor, and resources. Each supports research and policy that benefits pastoralism in ways that an individual rancher cannot. All of them are involved in transboundary management, whether it is fire, wildlife, or maintaining a grazing calendar of several different ownerships. Finally, all of them argue that they are benefiting rangelands, including supporting biodiversity.

In the Malpai Borderlands, the need to use prescribed burning, maintain access to public lands, and stave off land fragmentation and development has led to the development of a grassroots rancher organization with a system of conservation easements whose permanence is linked to good treatment by public lessors, and a burn and land conservation plan that benefits both ranchers and fire agencies. When rangeland is largely owned by the government, finding points of leverage and strategies for negotiation become critical for maintaining a right to benefit, as well as ability to benefit, that in many places is growing increasingly tenuous due to larger-scale social, political, and economic changes. In California, the California Rangeland Conservation Coalition communicates the benefits of grazing to agency managers, and has produced a strategic plan for maintaining rangelands and ranching, in an effort to help keep the growing proportion of public and reserved rangeland available for grazing. As private land is developed, lands set aside for mitigation or recreation are becoming a greater part of the rangeland portfolio for California ranchers. The Coalition also helps ranchers and agencies establish conservation easements and collaborative management programs, and learn about recent research results about grazing and the environment.

Finally, in Texas, wildlife management associations help ranchers marketing hunting opportunities to manage game in an increasingly fragmented landscape. By unifying the associations under a statewide network TOWMA has provided increased political influence for landowners. Wildlife Management Associations meet regularly, sharing best practices, supporting research, and helping ranchers work together to manage game and qualify for tax relief. In all three cases, public agencies are participants in the associations, but in Texas, one particular agency, the Texas Parks and Wildlife Department, is a critical facilitator, and benefits from the ability to influence management on private lands through wildlife management plans.

Pastoralists need lots of rangeland, because the production per hectare is low, and because forms of mobility are a common part of the annual calendar. Creating social connections, as illustrated by these case studies, is one way to maintain access to, and the ability to benefit from, rangelands in a changing ecological, economic, and social environment. These connections are important regardless of landownership.

5 Community governance of natural resources and rangelands

The case of the Eastern Highlands of Morocco

Abderrahim Boutaleb and Ilaria Firmian

Briefing

Human activity, specifically overgrazing and cropping, and climate change are driving Moroccan rangelands in the Eastern Highlands to degradation and inability to maintain livestock anymore. This dreadful condition is becoming permanent and irreversible. To face this situation the Government of Morocco in collaboration with IFAD is running the PDPEO (Livestock and Pastoral Development Project in the Eastern region), now in its second phase, to improve rangeland management through temporary protection, plantation of fodder shrubs, reseeding, scarification, improvement of health services or fattening.

This chapter shows how the success of this project lies in the recognition of the collective rights of local tribes and the organization of herders into ethno-lineage cooperatives. The assessment of this initiative shows how common management and restoration of traditional social systems may be a successful path to enhance governance and sustainable management of natural resources.

Keywords: governance, rangelands, land management, pastoralism, community governance, pastoral cooperatives, participatory approach

Environmental profile of the zone

The zone concerned by this case study stretches across Morocco's Eastern Region from the provinces of Jerada in the north and Taourirt in the west to the province of

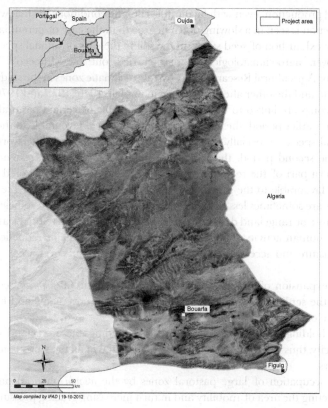

Figure 5.1 Project area

Figuig in the south. It covers more than 3.5 million hectares, most of it highlands. This vast area is a major pastoral region, carrying some 2 million head of small ruminant animals. The climate is mainly arid to desert in type, so that the area has a well-adapted steppe-type vegetation. This vegetation supports the generations-old activity of livestock production, which represents the backbone of the economy for the whole zone. It is still for the most part carried out extensively to enable the livestock to obtain most of their sustenance from the pastures.

The rangelands are no longer in a good enough condition to meet the food requirements of the livestock. Even worse, in most cases the degradation of these rangelands has become an irreversible process, leaving desert landscapes. The region experienced a climate change in the 1970s, leading to a reduction in annual rainfall. The decline in rainfall caused by climate changes affected specifically and severely the spring season in Ain Beni Mathar and Tendrara, while it affected all the seasons in Figuig. These changes in the distribution of rainfall probably accelerated the degradation of rangelands that was observed in the zone. One of the main consequences of the reduction in springtime rainfall is a decrease in rangeland productivity, inasmuch as spring is a period of active growth for most plants and any water deficit in this period will have a negative effect on rangeland production, even with favourable climatic conditions the following year. The reduction is seen in a slowing down in growth in the case of perennial species and in the exhaustion of seed stocks in the soil in the case of annual species.

Moreover, agro-climatological studies carried out by Morocco's National Institute for Agricultural Research show two agro-climatic zones in the study region: one prior to and the other after the change in rainfall (1946–1975 and 1976–2002). The two zones are linked to the climatic requirements of certain pastoral species. During the earlier period, the climatic conditions seemed favourable to the growth of pastoral species, especially *esparto* (alfa grass) and *artemisia* (white wormwood). During the second period, the zones favourable to these species extended over the northern part of the region, and the central and northern part of the region remained favourable to the growth of pastoral species. Thus, even if the climatic conditions are sometimes less than optimal for growth, they remain sufficient.

The cause of rangeland degradation in these zones must therefore be attributed mainly to human activity. The factors that have led to a major reduction in the area of pasture and acceleration in the reduction in ground cover are:

- The expansion of rangeland clearing beyond the usual *mhareth*,[1] combined with the settling of families, which curtails flock movements and limits the choice of camp sites.
- The holding of numbers of livestock exceeding the rangeland carrying capacity, thus reducing the regeneration potential in all the various ecological sectors.
- The occupation of large pastoral zones by the *attarda* phenomenon,[2] thus restricting the area of mobility and in turn increasing grazing pressure on the rangelands available for all users.
- The reduction – or even disappearance – of shrub and dwarf shrub plant species, which give way to herbaceous species, thus reducing the times spent in transhumance sites, which in turn jeopardizes the viability of the whole operation.
- Transport difficulties, particularly the loading and unloading of livestock and equipment.
- The creation of certain rested range areas or grazing bans, which some herders have reported as hampering movement.
- The replacement of transhumance by feed intensification in periods of drought or pre-drought.

This state of degradation meant that studies and surveys carried out on the ground observed the following facts between 1975 and 2001:

- Major expansion of degraded *artemisia* and *esparto* grasslands, with the area of these lands increasing from 638,700 to 890,068 hectares (an increase of about 40 per cent).
- A considerable reduction in areas of *artemisia*, which shrank from 394,770 to 35,482 hectares between 1975/76 and 2000/01.

- A similarly large reduction in areas of really vigorous *esparto*, which dwindled from 1,326,918 to a mere 353,255 hectares.

In the south (Bouarfa, Abbou Lakhal), where climatic conditions are no longer sufficient for the optimal growth of these species, any adverse action, especially overgrazing, can bring about irreversible degradation. Very severely degraded rangelands account for more than 650,000 hectares in the study area, presenting the most advanced forms of degradation. They comprise mainly areas of sand encroachment and bare ground. The intensified degradation of these steppes results in a major reduction in biological productivity. Sand encroachment, one of the most typical forms of rangeland degradation, is found mainly in the southeast of the zone.

Bare ground is another component of the very severe type of degradation. It is a result of the total disappearance of vegetation due to overgrazing and the abandonment of cultivated rangeland. Such areas are slopes that are particularly vulnerable to erosion. Bare ground composed of rocky desert is found in the mountainous zones of the south.

Socio-economic profile of the zone

The population of the zone (including the Tendrara, Bouarfa and Ain Beni Mathar urban centres) is estimated at roughly 100,000, with an average of seven people per household. The growth rate in the project zone is higher than in the Eastern Region as a whole (0.2 as against −0.8 per cent), although it is considerably lower than the national figure (0.6 per cent). More than half the inhabitants are under 24 years of age – 44.4 per cent in Figuig province, 54 per cent in Jerada and 53.9 per cent in Taourirt – while the national figure for this age group is 47.8 per cent. The predominant type of housing in the region is rural (65 per cent). The Eastern Region is fifth in terms of its poverty rate. According to the 2004 census, the poverty rate in the region is roughly 17.9 per cent, although it is higher than this regional average in rural areas, reaching about 25 per cent.

In terms of socio-economic activities, the vast majority of the region's population obtains almost all its income directly or indirectly from livestock production, mainly sheep. Thus, 67 per cent of the population practise livestock rearing, while 28 per cent practise it as a sideline with agriculture. The remaining 5 per cent are engaged in trading activities in the urban centres of Tendrara, Bouarfa and Ain Beni Mathar (SCET-SCOM, 2008). The zone is generally known for its predominant rearing of sheep and goats on large expanses of steppe rangelands: about 1,344,000 head of small ruminant animals (1,095,000 sheep and 249,000 goats).

Livestock production systems are generally pastoral and extensive to semi-extensive in type, with the following features:

- Major variations in the numbers of sheep, depending on variations in climate.
- Very low productivity of the livestock.

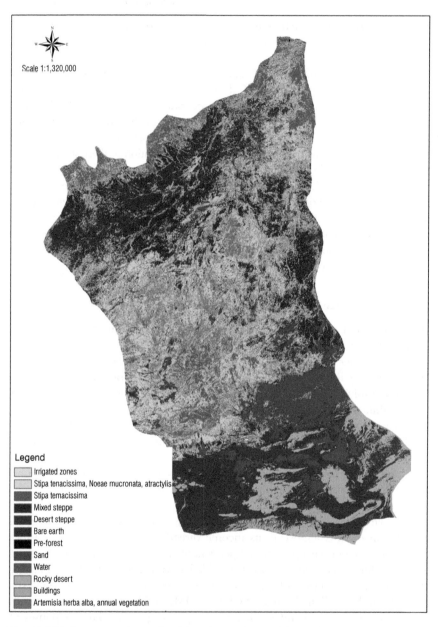

Figure 5.2 Various types of rangeland degradation in the highlands of the Eastern Region

Key: state of degradation: light grey – slight; medium grey – medium to severe; dark grey – very severe

- Major dependence of livestock on purchased feed.
- Variations in the roles attributed to the livestock (a source of wealth and/or social prestige etc.).
- Most of the herders in the region are considered poor: 77.5 per cent have a low to very low income, 19.2 per cent have a modest to medium income, and 3.3 per cent have an income that can be described as comfortable.

The sheep rearing systems distinguished on the basis of variables regarding the activity and its environment vary among zones as follows:

- *Livestock system 1.* This system is found in the far northeast and is marked by the small size of rangelands, providing insufficient food for the livestock, partly due to the increasing loss of rangeland vigour, particularly toward the south. This leads to major recourse to supplementary feed to meet the needs of flocks, and it is estimated that this supplementary feed covers roughly 50 per cent of these needs.
- *Livestock system 2.* This system is found in the centre-north, where rangelands are of medium size, with degraded pastoral resources. Relatively little supplementary feed is used in comparison with other regions, covering more than 45 per cent of needs. However, the percentage is constantly growing as a result of the inadequacy of rangelands and the stable or growing size of flocks.
- *Livestock system 3.* This system is found in the northwest, where rangelands are small to medium in size and in an advanced state of degradation. Inputs of supplementary feed are relatively low, due to the existence of sylvopastoral resources in the north and the low socio-economic level of farms.
- *Livestock system 4.* Rangelands are larger under this system, covering communes in the centre, and the food for flocks, which are purely breeding in type, is based essentially on pastoral resources. Parallel with pastoral resources under constant use, supplementary feed is currently based on purchases, due to the very low local production.
- *Livestock system 5.* Rangelands are very large under this system, but are in a mediocre state in almost all the southern and southeastern zones, and sheep rearing has been seriously affected by the sub-Saharan drought. Unlike the forms of adaptation found elsewhere, these herders do not take advantage of supplementary feed to cover the needs of their livestock, so that such additions remain relatively low.

Right of use and natural resource management methods

Rangelands in the highlands are divided between *esparto* grasslands, which are part of state forest land, and collectively-owned land. Collective rangelands – land belonging to the community of origin, which cannot be divided up and which all the descendants of the community can use – accounts for about 2 million hectares and falls under the charge of the Ministry of the Interior.

In the past, collective status supported a tribal type of organization based on collective ownership of pastoral resources recognized by the various tribes and marked by customary grazing areas used and respected by each tribe. These areas are already recognized in terms of demarcated collective lands.

Today, however, this status seems to be in contradiction with changes in the main components of pastoral society: the creation of administrative divisions, and a strong trend toward sedentarization and individualization in the use of resources and inputs. In the absence of a demarcation of collective lands, it is hard for the collective ownership of rangelands to withstand individual styles of behaviour marked by the private appropriation of land, clearing and conversion to agriculture. The project is based on the traditional collective structure in order to create cooperatives with an ethnic link, and thus a structure that will make the assumption of responsibility for the sustainable development of rangelands easier.

Intervention under the livestock and pastoral development project in the Eastern Region (PDPEO)

Aware of this state of affairs, the government departments in charge of the sector established various development programmes and projects for the zone, such as the PDPEO (phase I).[3] In collaboration with the Government of Morocco and the African Development Bank, IFAD financed the Livestock and Pastoral Development Project in the Eastern Region for US$45.2 million. The Fund played a major role in the design, implementation and monitoring of the project. When the project was being designed, its team carried out an in-depth study of the communities and their social organization. Then, on the basis of this study, the project team selected the following approaches to rangeland improvement: periodic temporary grazing bans, planting of fodder shrubs, reseeding and scarifying, all intended to increase the productivity of rangelands and the availability of fodder. With a view to improving livestock quality, the project team decided on improved health services for land races, fattening, and more flexible livestock management systems. Lastly, in order to ensure greater availability of water, the project decided to install or rehabilitate livestock watering points. The various monitoring and evaluation reports prepared by IFAD have proved vital in identifying the problems inherent in the project and formulating recommendations regarding support activities.

The importance of recognizing the collective rights of tribes has played a major role in the success of this model. Since 1919, Morocco has been the only country in western Asia and northern Africa to recognize the collective rights of tribes. The decentralization policies of the 1980s reorganized rural areas into communes, which were defined on the basis of tribal lands. These conditions facilitated the introduction of community-based range management (CBRM), an innovative approach, with the support of the local population, who saw the project as an opportunity to regain control of their resources. The PDPEO I demonstrated the existence of major potential to reverse the degradation process by implementing large-scale schemes for the institutional and administrative organization of herders, rehabilitation and improvement of rangeland and livestock productivity, and the training of herders and implementing officers. The organization of herders into ethno-lineage cooperatives created a space for training, consultation and negotiation in all the fields of rural activities, apart from the activities of planning, execution and supervision of grazing bans and plantations of fodder shrubs, and the improvement of livestock production.

Formation of pastoral cooperatives under the PDPEO I

In the 1970s and 1980s, the Moroccan government established pastoral improvement perimeters (PIPs), an institutional reform intended to improve rangeland management. PIPs were based on ecological and technological imperatives, with very little attention thus being given to existing tribal management systems, which had a very strong social, cultural and institutional dimension. Government technical bodies carried out the process without the participation of the communities concerned. In 1995, the World Bank estimated that 12.5 per cent of Moroccan rangelands were degraded (World Bank, 1995). There was general recognition that the PIP approach had failed and that if nothing appropriate was done, the trend to rangeland degradation would jeopardize the livelihood of millions of pastoral households for which livestock production was the main source of income and rangelands the main source of food for their livestock. It is in this context that IFAD intervened to develop the CBRM approach.

The CBRM approach is an innovative one based on five key principles:

1 Rural communes and tribal affiliation provide the basis for the creation of pastoral cooperatives.
2 Tribal institutions are reorganized into pastoral management cooperatives responsible for making technical decisions and administering resources.
3 Tribal members are required to purchase 'shares' in the cooperatives in order to become members and gain access to cooperative services and to better-quality pastures.
4 The project does not seek to settle herders, but promotes their mobility through new, more flexible livestock management systems.
5 The project promotes consensual decision-making processes with beneficiaries.

The risks and stakes were very high because of three major difficulties that could endanger the whole process:

1 The extent to which government technical bodies would support a process that reduced their control over rangeland development.
2 The communities' agreement to reorganize themselves into cooperatives and purchase shares to become members.
3 The respect that non-cooperative tribal members would have for the new situation brought about by the cooperatives.

The second and third points were particularly critical, given their equity implications, especially the risk that an elite would 'capture' project services and benefits, thus marginalizing poor households in cooperative decision-making processes.

The introduction of the idea of the participation of herders in the protection, conservation, improvement and sustainable management of the available resources led those designing the PDPEO I project to seek a form of organization for them that would, on the one hand, ensure their representation and, on the other, act as a dialogue partner for the government.

The selected form of organization for herders was that of 'pastoral cooperatives', which were established in application of law 1-83-226 of 9 Moharrem 1405 (5 October 1984), promulgating law 24-83 that established the general status of cooperatives and the mandate of the Office of Cooperation Development. The socio-tribal nature of pastoral society in the Eastern Region and the collective status of rangelands led to the constitution of ethno-lineage cooperatives on the basis of affinity among groups.

Ethno-lineage cooperatives were thus established, with the following as their main objectives:

- To be dialogue partners for the government with regard to rangeland rehabilitation and management (choice of pastoral improvement perimeters and zones to be rested, reporting of infringements and identification of those responsible etc.).
- To guarantee the sustainability of pastoral improvement work (grazing bans, rotation, planting, etc.).
- To supply cooperative-member herders with livestock feed and veterinary products.
- To manage infrastructure installed by the government (watering points, treatment and vaccination facilities, etc.).
- To assume eventual responsibility for cooperative staff, whose salaries should not be covered by the project after the end of 2004.
- To undertake joint actions with other institutions (rural communes, local government, agricultural and agro-industrial cooperatives, chamber of agriculture, associations and other groups of producers and herders, etc.).

The project zone had 43 pastoral cooperatives, with slightly over 9,000 members at the start of the second phase of the PDPEO in 2005.

These cooperatives were expected to act as intermediaries between their members and the government services intervening in the zone, manage rested rangeland areas, participate in the management of or directly manage watering points, and participate actively in livestock vaccination campaigns. They also sometimes provided their members with paid services, such as the use of trucks to transport water, livestock and feed. The cooperatives thus became vital dialogue partners on the ground. The most striking example of institutional capacity, and one that is often cited, is the Tendrara Union of Cooperatives, which has its own rules of procedure and negotiates directly with the local government. This union provided the space for discussions on the establishment of grazing bans and was also the channel for distribution of the compensation and feed anticipated under the National Drought Management Programme. It is also host to a nascent pastoral policing system and decides on rangeland opening and closing dates.

The conduct of the cooperative as a new space for affiliation is almost exemplary, although there are disparities in the levels of governance and the services provided. The majority of herders use these institutions to gain access to a certain number of resources and form partnerships. Before the cooperatives were created, the two spheres were the tribe and the rural commune. The slackening of tribal ties led to greater stress on administrative divisions – and particularly on *douars*, which are the professional cooperation structures that directly concern livestock production activities. The rural commune is increasingly seen as a new source of identity, although it has some difficulty in playing a greater role in contexts where material indicators of its presence are absent in the everyday life of herders on the move.

The most recent survey on the autonomy of the rural poor, carried out in 2005, shows that cooperatives are real focuses for the crystallization of affiliation and among the main structures looked to for the provision of services: 64.7 per cent of those surveyed said that the cooperative was the first place they turned to in order to obtain inputs and be represented as a profession (farmer/herder) and 76 per cent stated that the cooperative has an impact on the local economy and helps to solve conflicts.

One of the interesting aspects revealed by the survey is the transformation under way in a body of ethnic origin. One respondent out of three now states that membership of the tribe is not necessarily a condition for membership of the cooperative – and the lower the level, the more strongly the solidarity among the group members is expressed. This is seen in certain cooperatives by the lack of affinity among member lineages or the refusal to accept certain *douars* as members. The main differences existing between cooperatives and the traditional way of rangeland management generally lie in political conflicts caused by the administrative divisions that have thrown the tribal recognition of rangeland territories into question. This affects the operation of cooperatives, eventually leading to their blockage.

Another aspect should be stressed in order to show the potential of cooperatives as places for learning about democracy and democratic management. At the start of the PDPEO I project, certain evaluations criticized technicians for favouring traditional leaders as intermediaries, so that these leaders not only decided on the structure of the future cooperatives (the constituent lineages), but also occupied positions of responsibility. It must be observed that today, with the exception of certain cooperatives where the leaders have developed their leadership style and their skills, most of the cooperatives have changed chairpersons or seen new leaders appear. Some chairpersons have been dismissed from their positions because of their poor management or the appearance of people with better skills. These challenges to traditional leaders have also led to such dramatic events as the suicide of a chairman and the imprisonment of others. The results of the most recent survey on autonomization confirm these observations: 29 per cent of cooperatives have changed their officers more than five times, while only two have retained the same chairperson.

Herders laid major stress on leadership qualities as a vital element in the autonomous capital of cooperatives. The features of this leader are unusual: 76 per cent of respondents think the leader must have a broad network of relationships among government offices and defend the interests of the cooperative before those of his own ethnic group, while 88 per cent think he must be competent and be familiar with rules, regulations and procedures.

Since their creation, a number of cooperatives have undergone divisions, which sometimes solved situations of conflict (the case of the Ennahda, Elfath, Al Izdehar, Istitmar and Erreda cooperatives in the Beni Guil rural commune, which gave birth to five new cooperatives: Oulad Mouloud, Alhalloumia, Oulad Ali Ben Yassine, Ettadamoune and El Wafa respectively) and sometimes weakened the cooperatives due to the division of resources and goods, quarrels over grazing areas, etc. (the case of the Saada cooperative in Ain Beni Mathar).

Despite these limitations, the cooperatives are unanimously considered a success, and this success lies in:

- The involvement of pastoral cooperatives grafted onto ethnic groupings in the management of pastoral resources.
- The representation of livestock owners and herders with government bodies for the planning, choice of intervention sites and validation of land management actions in consultation with the government (for example, the Cooperative Development Plan, which is a planning document drawn up with the government and taken into account in the development plans of communes, and which has the force of law with regard to the planning of projects in partnership with the government).
- Good governance with regard to the management of rested range areas (opening and closing of grazing periods and fixing of the number of livestock to be introduced, and also penalization of cooperative members who violate grazing bans, through the payment of a fine to the cooperative).

There are currently (May 2013) 42 cooperatives. The cooperative graft seems to be holding firm for the moment, thanks to the efforts of extension workers and the support of provincial and local authorities on the one hand, and, on the other, the adherence of herders because of the substantial advantages they draw from the cooperatives (compensation for rested areas, subsidized livestock feed, veterinary care, etc.) and above all their growing awareness of the potential of this institution in terms of their identity and their institutional, economic and social representation at the local and regional levels.

Intervention of the PDPEO II and the Tripartite Partnership Agreement

Phase II of the PDPEO sought to meet the challenges identified below, particularly by stressing institution-building, the organizational and financial consolidation of cooperative institutions, and the boosting of local services, so that they can provide guidance and training, particularly:

- Drafting of a kind of regulatory tool, the Tripartite Partnership Agreement, which encourages good practices and penalizes poor practices with regard to sustainable resource management, signed by all the partners.
- Definition with the partners of the role the rural commune could play as a government institution, but one that is subject to the results of elections.
- Boosting of the local structures of the Ministry of Agriculture, Rural Development and Fisheries by establishing logistical and training facilities in order to support cooperatives in drawing up their development plans.
- Boosting of the local capacities of cooperatives with regard to grass-roots organization, technical training, accounting, management, marketing and project formulation.
- Help to cooperatives in assuming their role, including their incorporation into the tripartite agreement.

The Tripartite Partnership Agreement initiated under the PDPEO II project in 2006, was developed as a formal agreement among the Ministry of Agriculture, the Ministry of the Interior and the High Commission for Waters, Forests and Desertification Control in order to resolve juridical conflicts over the management and administration of collective lands in the highlands of the Eastern Region, while always ensuring the preservation of natural pastoral resources. The stated objective of the tripartite agreement is to establish close collaboration among the three signatory departments, while defining the roles and terms of reference of each partner with a view to ensuring the sustainable management of rangelands. It is based on three principles: (i) appropriate management and use in view of the potential of the ecosystem and the spatial integration of rangeland management through the various types of ownership status; (ii) consideration of the traditional uses and rights over rangelands within and between ethnic groups and tribes; and (iii) partnerships among and association of all the interested parties with a view to integrated, sustainable rangeland management.

A framework for rendering the tripartite agreement operational was defined under the PDPEO II project, and the GEF project offered to provide the institutional support necessary for implementation of the agreement and also to promote its extension to other concerned sectors, particularly the Ministry of Justice, an important partner in this connection, in drawing up a blueprint for integrated land-use planning in the PDPEO II zone. The intervention thrusts of the agreement concern:

- Implementation of land rehabilitation and management programmes based on promotion of a rational use of land in order to avoid practices that are destructive of pastoral resources: overgrazing, land clearing and conversion to agriculture, violation of rested or planted areas, unauthorized building on rangelands, unauthorized gathering of plant matter.
- Establishment of a monitoring and control system for land use.
- Guidance and training of beneficiaries, technical staff and other stakeholders.
- Juridical consolidation of rangelands.

- In the context of implementation of these two projects, various actions have been undertaken for implementation of the framework agreement:
  - A series of meetings of local committees was held in order to find solutions to the conflicts that had unfortunately remained at the local level. These meetings made it possible to try out the implementation process for the Tripartite Partnership Agreement in order to free up any blockage points.
  - Technical and juridical support was provided to prepare regulatory and institutional tools for implementation of the agreement. In this context, a number of proposed regulations and structures were developed: (i) a blueprint for nomination by government decision of those making up committees and proposed procedural rules for meetings of the committees; (ii) a proposal to promote the assumption of responsibility for rangeland management by cooperatives and local government through joint management with supervision of collective lands and *esparto* grasslands; and (iii) a model for the reorganization of the internal structure of cooperatives so that they can assume this responsibility for rangeland management.
  - Training sessions in techniques for sustainable land management and integrated water management have been held for cooperatives and local government in the context of capacity-building for stakeholders with regard to the planning of good rangeland management practices.
  - Studies regarding the Rangeland Master Plan and rehabilitation of *esparto* grasslands have enabled local government offices to plan action to improve rangelands in coordination with the users (cooperatives).

These actions are currently under way and it is still too early to evaluate the feasibility and results of the Tripartite Partnership Agreement.

Parallel with these guidance and training actions, the GEF desertification control project is currently adopting a participatory approach to the planning and implementation of rangeland development actions with cooperatives through the introduction of new tillage techniques (the Vallerani system) and new rangeland improvement strategies through the sowing of native pastoral species. This approach is intended to strengthen the bonds among cooperatives so that they can organize themselves into unions and in due course into federations.

Main lessons learnt

- Ethnic groupings and the law regulating them provided a framework for hosting and supporting modern pastoral cooperatives that incorporate traditional values, allowing them to organize themselves along tribal lines, which helps to reduce conflict.
- The cooperatives are based on existing socio-institutional systems managed by a structure trained and supervised by Moroccan government services (Ministry of the Interior, Ministry of Agriculture and Marine Fisheries, Office of Cooperation Development, etc.) with a view to facilitating collective action and the sustainable management of natural resources. This approach

enabled these highland cooperatives to become preferred dialogue partners of government bodies with regard to the collective management of rangelands and their infrastructure, the improvement of livestock production and the protection of natural resources.

- The method of organization into cooperatives made it possible to boost their management capacity, adopt appropriate technical measures to develop rangelands and establish a set of organizational and regulatory tools to manage rangelands in a responsible manner (the Tripartite Partnership Agreement).
- The adoption of appropriate technical measures and the creation of an appropriate juridical and institutional framework are essential for the success of innovative approaches.
- The innovation represented by community-based range management has become the keystone of the Moroccan approach to rangeland development and is being replicated in Syria and Tunisia.
- The formation of cooperatives has enabled herders in the highland zone to become the main dialogue partners of government bodies with regard to rangeland management and natural resource protection.

Notes

1 An Arabic word that refers to lands that are found in small depressions (called *sigas* in local language) and that are usually ploughed.
2 Arabic word that literally means 'scaring other people'. It refers to a single family that takes possession of a vast rangeland by clearing it and erecting buildings. This action forces the other herders to limit the mobility of their livestock to smaller areas causing extensive land degradation impacts.
3 Together with the Participatory Control of Desertification and Poverty Reduction in the Arid and Semi-Arid High Plateau Ecosystems of Eastern Morocco Project, financed by the Global Environment Facility and associated with the PDPEO.

6 Wetlands and drylands in the Sahel

The urgent need for good joint governance

Joost Brouwer

Overview

In dryland regions, wetlands stand out as areas where water and nutrients accumulate, plant and animal production potential is high, and production risk is low. Wetlands are therefore much sought after in dryland regions, by farmers, pastoralists, fishermen, collectors of natural products, and also wildlife. Economic data from reports on some of the 1,000 isolated wetlands in Niger demonstrate this importance, to people living at the isolated wetlands as well to people living further away, during 'normal' years as well as in times of drought. At the same time, the isolated wetlands are under threat of disappearing because of increasing human pressure, climate change, land use change in their catchments, etc. Descriptions of selected wetlands in Niger visited in the mid-1990s and again twelve years later show this, too. Good governance, i.e. integrated and participative management, of wetlands in dryland regions must be effectuated as soon as possible, so that these very important natural resources will be used wisely and sustainably and not used up. A case study from Lake Tabalak illustrates this.

Keywords: Sahel, isolated wetlands, economic value, threatened ecosystems, participatory integrated management

Introduction

Water is what makes life on Earth possible. It is no different in the arid and semi-arid regions of the world, where rainfall is notoriously unreliable. Wetlands are areas where water is concentrated and water supply dependable, thus reducing production risk. Nutrients from sediments and livestock manure are concentrated in wetlands as well, thus increasing ecological and agricultural production potential in comparison with the surrounding drylands. Because of this low production risk and high production potential, wetlands in arid and semi-arid regions are much sought after by people as well as animals. These wetlands also facilitate the utilization of the drylands surrounding them. In short, in dryland areas wetlands are extremely important resources.

Unfortunately wetlands in dryland areas are also under severe threat. These threats include conflicts of interests between different users and user groups, desertification, climate change, demographic change and socio-economic change, as well as lack of good governance.

In this chapter I use the isolated inland wetlands of Niger to illustrate the value of wetlands, and their importance for the functioning of the surrounding dryland ecosystems. First, the various types of wetlands that occur in Niger are discussed. This is followed by a description of their use for different purposes, during the wet season as well as the dry season, and during normal and dry years. Next some economic values of isolated wetlands in Niger to different user groups are quantified. After this, interactions between different types of wetland use, and between wetlands and surrounding uplands, are discussed. Recent trends and present and future threats to these wetlands are reviewed as well, followed by an illustrative case study from Lake Tabalak in west central Niger. In the final section conclusions are drawn, and governance recommendations made.

Wetland types in Niger

The few large floodplains

Niger contains a number of large floodplains. These occur along 550 km of the River Niger in the south-west of the country; along 180 km of the Komadougou-Yobé forming the border with Nigeria in the south-east of the country; and along some 100 km of the former shore of Lake Chad in the extreme south-east (MHE-Niger 1990a, 1991a). While these floodplains are very important ecologically and economically, also for the dryland regions that surround them, they are not the objective of this chapter.

The numerous smaller wetlands

In the north of Niger, there are a number of oases, with orchards, grape and date production (de Beaufort and Czajkowski 1986; MHE-Niger 1991d). Little information is available about these wetlands. Throughout the country there are also a number of dry, 'fossil' valleys, sometimes kilometres wide, dating from the time that the Sahara and Sahel were much wetter than now, approximately 6–10,000 years ago. Water has not flown for centuries in most of these valleys. Some still carry water from time to time, but in these ancient valleys groundwater is often close to the surface. (MHE-Niger 1990a–d, 1991b–c)

Most importantly, there are a large number of more or less isolated inland wetlands or lakes, called 'mares' in French. They are often located in depressions in the old drainage systems. There are more than 1,000 in Niger alone, varying in size between 10 and 2000 ha at maximum extent. Some are very temporary, and only hold water a couple of months each year. Others contain water much longer. A number are even permanent, and always, or almost always, have water (MHE-DRE-Niger 1993). These wetlands are enormously dynamic. Some disappear due to silting up (MHE-Niger 1992; Piaton and Puech 1992), but new ones appear as well. One such new wetland is at Dan Doutchi, in a depression that filled up as the drought broke in 1975: it now covers 1,800 ha when full (Mullié and Brouwer 1994). By far the greatest number of these isolated wetlands is to be found south of 15° N, in approximately the 300–600 mm rainfall zone, also called the Sahel zone. The northern limit is roughly the line from the SE corner of Mali across the departments of Tahoua, Zinder and Diffa to Lake Chad. The southern limit is more or less formed by the borders with Nigeria, Benin and Burkina Faso. In other countries of the Sahel zone, isolated wetland prevalence is without any doubt similar. In south-eastern Mauritania, for instance, there are at least 244 isolated wetlands of appreciable size (Cooper *et al.* 2006).

The use of isolated wetlands in Niger for various purposes: differences between the wet and the dry seasons, and from year to year

An overview of various uses of isolated wetlands in Niger at different times of year is given below. See Brouwer (2009, online) for more detailed information.

Cropping

During the rainy season there is little cropping activity or horticultural activity around isolated wetlands in Niger. Only crops like floating rice can cope with rising or permanently high water levels. During the rainy season, farmers with access to both wetland frontage and upland fields will be working on their upland fields, where they grow their staple food, pearl millet.

In agricultural statistics in Niger, a distinction is seldom made between *dry-season cropping* that is irrigated, and dry-season cropping that is dependent on residual moisture in the soil. In the latter, as the water in wetlands recedes, crops are sown in the emerging soil. As the water stored in the soil is used up by the crop, supplementary irrigation is sometimes applied. Dry-season cropping concerns crops like onions, tomatoes, beans, sweet potato, cabbage, lettuce and peppers (*pers. obs.*). These crops have a much higher nutritional value than the staple millet and are important to people living in the wetlands as well as to people living in the surrounding drylands. Much of the dry-season cropping is for (international) commercial purposes.

There is *inter-annual variation* in the area used in Niger for dry-season cropping. During the years 1984–1991 it varied between 42,000 ha and 64,000 ha, rice not included (MAE-Niger 1993). Dry-season cropping was most extensive during 1984 and 1989: 63–64,000 ha, vs. <54,000 ha in other years. These two years were respectively a drought year and a year with patchy rainfall and poor millet harvests in many parts of the country. This shows that the total area useable for e.g. recession agriculture cannot be reduced with impunity: areas not used during good rainfall years may be an essential safety net during years of poor rainfall (Brouwer and Ouattara 1995).

Livestock production

During the rainy season, wetlands can provide drinking water for livestock, although the availability in the uplands of green feed and surface pools makes that less necessary. In some wetlands, but mostly along the Niger River, the grass 'bourgou', *Echinochloa stagnina*, may be grown during the wet season on rising water levels. After the water level has dropped, it is harvested for hay.

During the dry season isolated wetlands can provide drinking water for livestock, and also grazing additional to the grazing in the surrounding drylands. Herders can bring in local cattle and small ruminants to drink every day, or every few days. Transhumant herders only use a particular wetland during a limited time of the year, as a part of their annual treks that sometimes cover thousands of kilometres.

No data could be found on inter-annual differences in utilization of isolated wetlands by livestock. With livestock numbers decreasing during drought periods, utilization by livestock of wetlands for drinking will also be lower in volume during droughts, but more important in terms of survival. It should be noted that a particular isolated wetland may be important for livestock only once every so many years, when that wetland can provide what the livestock and herders need while the other wetlands cannot. If wetland is not available that year because it is being used for other purposes, the whole associated livestock production system may collapse.

Fishing

During the rainy season, fishing activity is generally low. Measures to increase fish production, such as re-stocking and increasing aquatic vegetation for fish to spawn in, do take place during the rainy season (MHE-DFPP 1991).

Fishing mostly takes place during the dry season, when fish stocks have had time to grow and/or are driven closer together as the water level recedes. The main species caught are *Clarias gariepinus* (catfish), *Tilapia nilotica*, *T. zilii* and *Lates niloticus* (Nile perch). Also *Bagrus bayad*, *Protopterus annectens* (lungfish) and *Auchenoglanis sp.* (Mullié and Brouwer 1994).

Inter-annual variation in rainfall will lead to inter-annual variation in the maximum water level in isolated wetlands, and thus to variability in fish production in those wetlands. A nation-wide drought in 1984 did indeed lead to low fish production the following year, as mentioned in section 4.3. During drought years more aestivating lungfish *Protopterus annectens* may be dug out of the mud of dried out wetlands to serve as emergency food (Raverdeau 1991; Mahatan 1994; Mullié and Brouwer 1994a). Fish can be an important source of protein for people living in the wetlands as well as for people living in the surrounding drylands.

Hunting and tourism

Hunting other than traditional hunting was largely banned in Niger in 1974. In 1996, hunting was legalized again on a much larger scale (Brouwer *et al.* 2001). The *rainy season* is not the preferred season for hunting, except for the collecting of eggs of e.g. Comb Duck *Sarkidiornis melanotos*. These eggs may be incubated by chickens and the hatched ducklings raised for later consumption (*pers. obs.*). For tourism, too, the rainy season is not the preferred season. Although the landscape is beautifully green at that time of year, travel to isolated wetlands along un-metalled roads can be quite difficult. There are also many more mosquitoes than during the dry season.

The dry season is when most hunting in Niger takes place. Even before 1996, it was not uncommon for ducks and geese to be hunted with shotguns, at least along the River Niger. Live decoys and baited lines have been used as well (Giraudoux *et al.* 1988; Mullié *et al.* 1996). We have also seen little boys use catapults, as well as glue-sticks, to catch birds coming in to drink (Mullié and Brouwer 1994). Birds may also be caught as by-catch on fishing lines with hooks. In the local markets a multitude of animal species, including species found at isolated wetlands, are for sale for medicinal and magical purposes. To what extent these animals are caught in Niger itself is not clear (Brouwer and Mullié 1994a).

There are no data about *differences between years*, as there is as yet little or no hunting or tourism in the isolated wetlands of Niger. Note that hunters often do not live in the wetlands where they hunt. If the local population does not profit from the hunters, the hunters may not be welcome. The same applies to tourists, of course.

Collecting of natural products

Local people, from near the wetland and from surrounding drylands, collect natural products from their wetland *during the whole year*. These include wood for cooking; wood for construction (trees around wetlands are often larger than those growing further away from water); clay for brick making and pottery; water for domestic purposes, including the washing of clothes; plant and animal products for traditional medicinal and magical purposes (Mullié and Brouwer 1994). Products collected primarily during the dry season include the fruits and tubers of water lilies *Nymphaea sp.* for human consumption; bourgou *Echinochloa stagnina* to feed livestock; and water for agricultural purposes (Mullié and Brouwer 1994). Collectors may be local but may also come from further away.

Biodiversity

The vegetation of isolated wetlands in Niger, if present, often shows a concentric pattern, in which the dominating species varies with the depth and duration of inundation. Closest to the shore there is generally a zone dominated by the grass species *Veteveria nigritana* (shortest inundation time); then followed by *Oryza longistaminata* (wild rice), *Echinochloa stagnina* (bourgou), and finally *Nymphaea lotus* and *N. caerulaea* (waterlilies, where there is water a meter or more deep at least for four to five months of the year). In addition to these herbaceous species there may or may not be trees, sometimes in dense groups. These include various *Acacia* species, and *Mitragyna inermis* (Mullié *et al.* 1999).

During the rainy season most mammals as well as most birds are not very reliant on isolated wetlands, as there will be sufficient surface pools for drinking throughout the landscape. The wetlands in the Liptako-Gourma region north-west of Niamey harbour an important population of Black-crowned Cranes *Balearica pavonina*, a Sahelian species that is threatened by the disappearance of wetlands, disturbance and capture for the live bird trade (Meine and Archibald 1996; Brouwer and Mullié 2001).

During the dry season large mammals from the surrounding drylands, such as antelopes, buffalo, elephants, hyenas, jackals, foxes, and even lions, used to come to drink at isolated wetlands in Niger. However, other than foxes there are very few large mammals left in Niger, outside 'W' National in the south-west of the country. Waterbird counts were conducted in Niger during January–February every year between 1992 and 1997, along the River Niger as well as at isolated wetlands throughout the country. In total, more than 100 species of waterbird were observed during those counts, and almost 40 species of raptor. During the dry season, Niger is host to an estimated 1.8 million waterbirds. Most of these have been born in Europe or Asia, and some fly more than five thousand kilometres to spend the Eurasian winter in Niger. Niger's wetlands are therefore also important to the conservation of Europe's and Asia's biodiversity (Brouwer and Mullié 1994a; Mullié *et al.* 1999; Brouwer and Mullié 2001).

There is clear *inter-annual variation* in the importance of isolated wetlands in Niger for waterbirds. Two thirds of the waterbirds in Niger, on average about 1.2 million, use the isolated wetlands, depending on how much rain has fallen during the preceding rainy season. The River Niger becomes more important when the rains have been poor and the isolated wetlands only partly filled.

Economic values of isolated wetlands in Niger

An overview of the monetary values of isolated wetlands in Niger at different times of year is given in Table 6.1.

For some users, such as pastoralists, isolated wetlands are essential to their way of life. For other groups, having access to wetlands as well as drylands increases the range of crop and livestock production options, from which they can choose depending on how good the local rains and the flood levels of the wetland are or were. As many

Table 6.1 Some estimated economic values of isolated wetlands in Niger in the early 1990s. For details see Brouwer (2009), online

Product	Season	Year	Extent and value	Remarks
Cropping	Rainy		?	Value probably quite low; cropping priority is uplands
Cropping	Dry	1991	42–64,000 ha/yr $200–$4,300 per ha (uplands $70 per ha)	Area greater following poor rainy season in uplands; high nutrition, high value crops
Livestock keeping	Rainy and dry	1991	$35 million per year	Value of traded livestock that was dependent on wetlands for water
Fisheries	Rainy and dry	1978–1985	1,100–5,000 tons per year $0.9–4.2 million per year	Fish catch at all isolated wetlands in Niger, value to fishermen
Fisheries	Rainy and dry	1978–1985	$ 5–20(–40) million per year	Fish catch at all isolated wetlands in Niger, city prices
Fisheries	Rainy and dry	1989	430 ton, $250,000 per year	Region of Tahoua only; value in Niamey 5–10x greater; potential 2,000 ton
Hunting and tourism	Dry		?	Potential completely undeveloped
Collecting of natural products	Rainy and dry		?	Water, wood, clay; plant & animal products
Collecting of natural products	Dry	Drought years	?	Waterlily fruits and tubers, and lungfish, are emergency food in times of drought
Biodiversity	Rainy		?	Almost no information
Biodiversity	Dry		?	Average 1.2 million waterbirds in Jan–Feb; other species?

authors have reported, risk reduction is a major goal for resource-poor farmers in the Sahel (e.g. Ubels and Horst 1993, p.29; Mullié and Brouwer 1994).

Interactions between different types of wetland use and between wetlands and surrounding uplands

Values of isolated wetlands for a particular purpose also depend on interactions with utilization for other purposes. Sometimes such interactions are competitive and negative, sometimes they are positive. They can be local and intermittent, but also long-distance and permanent. Activities around wetlands can provide extra income that can be invested in uplands, and vice versa; but there can also be competition for resources, including labour. For additional information on links between isolated wetlands in the Sahel and associated uplands, and on interactions between different user groups at wetlands, see Brouwer (2009, available online) and Abdoul Kader (2012). Suffice it here to say:

- Catchment utilization
  - Uplands can provide water and nutrient-rich sediments to wetlands, but too much water and/or too much sediment is detrimental.
  - Too many dams and too much water off-take upstream will cause downstream wetlands to deteriorate or even die.
  - Raising the outflow level at a particular wetland will affect the water regime and the vegetation at the wetland and downstream.
- Cropping
  - Increased dry season cropping would make an isolated wetland less attractive for hunting and for tourism but providing employment opportunities may also lead to a reduction in seasonal outmigration in search of work.
  - Residues of the crops of the preceding dry season can provide places for fish to spawn.
  - Boundary markers between market gardens can trap sand and speed up silting up of a wetland. When the water level rises again and the garden plots are temporarily submerged, the boundary markers can impede the movement of fish as well as injure fishermen.
  - Increased dry-season cropping in a topographic depression can crowd out watering of livestock as well as their traditional grazing on the original wetland vegetation. Grazing on crop residues from the dry season cropping can be a partial substitute, but often needs to be paid for by the herders.
- Livestock raising
  - It is not clear to what extent transfer of nutrients by livestock to isolated wetlands is of benefit to dry-season cropping around those wetlands. It would be very interesting to investigate that, given the conflicts between farmers and pastoralists in wetlands, with pastoralists often having to give way to farmers and give up access to wetlands and grazing resources.
  - Livestock can cause damage to market gardens.
  - Isolated wetlands are linked to local grazing areas by local livestock and to more distant grazing areas and wetlands by transhumant livestock. The wetlands and grazing areas further south help make it possible to exploit the rainy-season livestock production potential of the northern Sahel. Without dry-season watering and grazing in the south, there can be no grazing in the north. Conversely, if transhumant livestock rearing becomes impossible in the north, nutrient transfer by livestock from grazing areas to wetlands and millet fields may be reduced in the south.
  - Browsing, grazing and trampling by livestock can destroy the vegetation in and around wetlands, leading to a disappearance of resources for people as well as increased erosion and silting up of the wetland.

– Livestock raising can benefit fishing and biodiversity in wetlands through the transfer of nutrients by livestock to isolated wetlands. The livestock watered at isolated wetlands in Niger have been estimated to contribute up to 10 tons of manure and associated urine per hectare per year, containing 300 kg N, 30 kg P and the associated energy of the organic matter for use by detritus-eating organisms (unpublished data). This has an enormous effect on plant and animal production in the wetlands, including fish production and waterbird presence: see Brouwer (2009).

• Fishing
– Abandoned fishing equipment can trap sand and accelerate the silting up of wetlands.
– Fishermen walking along the shore can damage market gardens.
– Disturbance of the wetland bed by fishermen can make the water more turbid and therefore less palatable to livestock.
– Isolated wetlands may be linked to other areas through fishermen that come from elsewhere to fish in the wetland.

• Collection of natural products
– Biodiversity at isolated wetlands is obviously important to collectors of natural plant and animal products.
– Harvesting of aquatic and fringing vegetation at wetlands, trees as well as herbs, by locals and by people from upland areas, is too often unsustainable and destructive, leading to a reduction of habitat for waterbirds and other animals, and also to a disappearance of resources for people.
– The introduction, accidental or otherwise, of plants such as Water Lettuce *Pistia stratiotes*, Water Hyacinth *Eichhornia crassipes*, and bulrush *Typha sp.*, may affect the functioning of the wetland as well as the collection of natural products.

• Biodiversity
– Biodiversity is likely to be negatively affected, immediately or eventually, by increases in dry-season cropping; degradation or destruction of aquatic and fringing vegetation by farmers, fishermen, herders and/or livestock; by an increase in disturbance by the same groups; by changes in the flooding regime through the raising of the outflow level of the wetland and/or increased retention of water upstream in the catchment; by too much hunting or hunting at too many wetlands; and by overcollection of natural products.
– Waterbirds at a particular wetland link that wetland with the other wetlands they frequent. These include wetlands in the same area with which the wetland forms a habitat system for all or part of the year; as well as all the other wetlands along the flyways of the birds concerned. Bird ringing and satellite tracking studies have shown that migratory birds link Niger to at least 83 other countries, from Guinea to NE Canada, across Scandinavia to Siberia, and down via the Caucasus and the Middle East to Madagascar and South Africa.

Recent trends and threats to isolated wetlands in the Sahel

A number of recent trends at, and changes to, isolated wetlands in the Sahel have already been mentioned in the previous section. Many of them are part of, or related to, world-wide demographic, climatic, environmental and socio-economic changes. The casual observer will say that whether these trends are seen as opportunities or threats will depend on one's point of view. However, that is not completely correct. For not overly large wetlands near Zinder, southern Niger, Framine (1994) already estimated that, without proper counter measures, it would take only 10–20 more years for a change from an aquatic to a marshy ecosystem to be completed. At the same time, it was said that 20–30 years after farmers move in, wetlands will be degraded for *all* kinds of use, including cropping. This degradation is confirmed by data in Table 6.2, where a comparison is made between the situation at a dozen isolated wetlands in southern Niger in 1992–1997 and in 2006–2008.

The importance of isolated wetlands to many user groups is not just limited to the Sahel. Scoones (1991) gives a similar but more wide-ranging evaluation of the importance of small wetlands in semi-arid areas of Africa. Other relevant publications include Dugan (1990), Claude *et al.* (1991), Hollis *et al.* (1993) and Sally *et al.* (1994).

Because of the continuing urbanization, the demand for rice in Niger, and elsewhere in West Africa, will continue to increase. There have been proposals to develop a further 70,000 ha of land for irrigation in Niger, out of 210,000 ha considered suitable, much of it around isolated wetlands. The market for various other crops grown around wetlands will no doubt increase as well. Note, however, that irrigation projects, too, have a finite life. For irrigated areas in SE Australia the period of usability is estimated at 150–200 years (Meyers 1994).

In addition there is the increasing pressure due to population growth, which in Niger is estimated at 3.1 per cent per annum. That growth percentage means a doubling of the population in less than 23 years, and a quadrupling in 45 years. Around wetlands the pressure will grow even faster, due to migration to wetlands from upland areas.

What effects climate change will have on all this is uncertain, but no-one appears willing to bet that the effects of climate change will be positive in the Sahel. This is in spite of the fact that the drought of 1973–1974 has led to the creation of quite sizeable (up to 1,800 ha), new isolated wetlands in Niger.

All in all, there is no doubt that the human pressure on wetlands in Niger will increase further, and enormously, during the years to come. It remains to be seen how the poorest people will fare under such conditions if they are not offered help. Under present conditions, in particular, poor people often still have considerable (traditional) access to wetlands and their resources. The danger is that those traditional access rights will be diminished further by new developments. Transhumant pastoralists, present at isolated wetlands only part of the year, are likely to lose out to farmers, present all year round. At the same time, conversion of upland grazing areas to millet fields has forced pastoralists to try their luck

Table 6.2 Examples of changes happening at isolated wetlands in Niger, from 1992–1997 to 2006–2008. 1992–1997 information collected by W.C. Mullié, J. Brouwer and colleagues; 2006–2008 information collected by J. Brouwer

Kobadié wetland, 50 km SW of Niamey along the road to Ouagadougou, *c.* 20 ha:
1992–1997: the wetland in October–November with presence of waterlilies;
2006: All large trees (*Khaya senegalensis*) and most medium size trees (*Mitragyna inermis*) were cut; more people are present, lots of disturbance, though few birds.

**IBA Kokoro wetland*, 30 km NE of Téra and 150 km NW of Niamey, max. 2,100 ha:
1992–1997: up to 13,108 water fowl of 44 species in a glorious setting of flooded grassland surrounded by patches of *Acacia nilotica* forest, red dunes, huge granite boulders and palm trees;
2008: large areas of fringing *Acacia nilotica* forest has been cleared; a lot more vegetable gardens has been constructed; and grazing pressure by livestock on the aquatic vegetation has increased enormously (perhaps in part because of the poor rains the preceding year, but most likely because of an increase in population and livestock size); birds are concentrated in a much smaller area of the original wetland and are fewer in number.

IBA Namga or Namaga wetland, 40 km NE of Téra and 150 km NW of Niamey, max. 500 ha:
1992–1997: up to 13,190 water fowl including 54 species of bird;
2008: the wetland has been mostly dried due to poor rains in 2007, but still quite a few birds are observed; the adjoining village, from which the wetland received its name, has grown significantly.

Mari wetland, 10 km NE of Tillabéri, 100 km NNW of Niamey, max. 270 ha:
1992–1997 up to 4,266 water fowl;
2006: no water fowl present because an earthen dam had been constructed to raise the level of the outflow of the wetland, while the (former?) wetland had been almost completely taken over by farmers.

Yaya wetland, 40 km W of Birni N'Konni:
1992–1997: a total of 122 water fowl was counted in this nice little wetland, next to a village;
2006: although still quite nice and with some water fowl, now there is an apparent increase in population and human activity when compared to the situation ten years earlier.

IBA Dan Doutchi wetland, 80 km NW of Birni N'Konni, max. 1800 ha; originated in 1975 after a huge rainfall event which followed the drought of 1973–1974:
1992–1997: up to 55 species of water fowl;
2006: an earth dam had been built to raise the level of the outflow of the wetland; still a lot of water present, with people, fishing activities and vegetable growing and some other human influence, but now with very few water birds present in the area.

IBA Tchérassa reservoir, 6 km NE of Birni N'Konni:
1992–1997: 15,000 Cattle Egrets and 3,000 other water fowl (mostly ducks) present in January 1994;
2006: large areas of *Acacia nilotica* were cut, especially in the areas where the Cattle Egrets used to roost; an increase in human population and activity is obvious.

Galmi reservoir, 60 km E of Birni N'Konni
1992–1997: up to 1,033 of water birds;
2006: few water fowl present, while the population pressure and fishing activities appear to have increased.

Table 6.2 continued

Tabalak wetland, 25 km NE of Tahoua along the road to Agadez, max. 1,150 ha:
1992–1997: up to 5,464 waterfowl of 48 species; Tabalak used to have quite a few trees
along its northern end (*Acacia nilotica, A. albida, Prosopis juliflora*, and *Balanites aegyptiaca*),
but in 1993 many of these were cut; in 1993–1994, about 20% of the perimeter was
covered by vegetable gardens, while 80% was accessed by livestock;
2007: much less water fowl, in combination with a big increase in human population
and human activities; now, it appears that 80% of the perimeter is covered by vegetable
gardens (with some narrow passages for livestock that want to reach the water, and
20% freely accessible to livestock).

The Liptako-Gourma region, where the countries of Niger, Burkina Faso and Mali meet
The Liptako-Gourma is an area with (still) lots of extensive wetlands, threatened
by population increases, migration and climate change. Some of the wetlands are
probably also threatened by the construction of a dam in the Niger River at Kandadji,
just south of Ayorou, about 80 km south of the Niger-Mali border. Dam construction
implies employment and (temporary) settlement of labourers; this condition attracts
people that provide goods and services to these labourers, causing, e.g.:
- construction of housing, for which timber is cut; in dry areas much of the timber
grows in drainage lines and around wetlands;
- provision of firewood, for which wood is cut;
- growing of vegetables, mostly around wetlands, which means less access to those
wetlands for pastoralists and destruction of the bordering vegetation;

*IBA = Important Bird Area according to BirdLife International (Fishpool and Evans 2001). Based on
Brouwer (2010), available online.

further north, where as yet there is less pressure from agriculture. This has caused
Peuhl, for instance, to graze their herds in former Touareg areas, again leading to
conflicts. Fishermen, collectors of natural products and biodiversity are also likely
to be affected.

What then is the best way to further manage and develop Sahelian wetlands?
Unfortunately, there is no simple answer. What is important is that it is realized
how things came to be as they are, and what side effects proposed changes may
have. Certainly, without creation and/or maintenance of the right infrastructure
and macro-economic climate, wetland management and development will
come to nought (cf. Breman 1992). What is also clear is that governance, that
is management and planning, will have to be participatory to be successful (cf.
Dugan 1990; Ubels and Horst 1993; Kouokam 1994). In addition, appropriate
attention will have to be paid to traditional techniques for utilizing the wetlands; to
possible trade-offs between the various types of wetland utilization for production
and conservation; and to the different roles of men and women in the traditional
production processes, with women often working smaller areas and growing
different crops (Ubels and Horst 1993; Mahatan 1994). Finally, governance
of Sahelian wetlands will without doubt have to take account of the intimate
relationships that exist between the use of wetlands; the use of the drylands that
surround them; and the use of other areas further away and at other times of
year by people and animals that use the isolated wetlands in the Sahel only during
particular seasons.

A management case study: Lake Tabalak and surrounding drylands

I use the example of Lake Tabalak and associated drylands to illustrate in more detail the developments over the past 40 years at quite a number of isolated wetlands in Niger, and the need for coordinated management of those wetlands and drylands. The case of Lake Tabalak is also illustrative of developments at many wetlands in other countries of the Sahel.

Wetland history and typology

Lake Tabalak, a Ramsar Wetland of International Importance since 2004 (Ramsar Bureau 2004), is located 50 km NE of Tahoua at 15.11 N 5.67 E, in the arrondisement of Tchin-Tabaraden, Région Tahoua. Average annual rainfall in this sandy and rocky part of Niger is only about 300 mm/yr, falling mostly during the short rainy season of July–September (Brouwer and Mullié 1993).

As recently as 1953, there was only a depression with *Acacia* and *Balanites* where Lake Tabalak is now. Torrential rains around 1970 led to an upsptream dam being ruptured, with the ensuing run-off creating Lake Tabalak. Local people as well as people from Birni N'Konni and Nigeria moved to the new lake, where the upgrading of the road to transport uranium from the mines in the north provided further work opportunities. Thus the village of Tabalak came into being (Ramsar Bureau 2004).

The maximum extent of the permanent lake formed in 1970 is, or was, about 1,200 ha. Its actual extent depends on the time of year, and on the rainfall of the preceding rainy season. Due to silting up of the lake basin and upstream off-take of water, the lake can nowadays be just about dried up by the end of the dry season. Similarly, its maximum depth has decreased from 5 m to less than 3 m (Abdoul Kader 2012).

Utilization, threats and management pre-2000

While still a wooded depression, Tabalak wetland was used by Bororo pastoralists to let their livestock feed on pods, leaves and branches, and perhaps also to water them while there was standing water among the trees. From 1974 on, after the depression had become a permanent lake in 1970, a number of pastoralists began to settle around the lake instead of only visiting it seasonally. Following the drought of 1983–1984, the government encouraged the settlement of Peulh, Haussa and Touareg at the lake so that they could practise market gardening and recover from their drought-related losses. A 50 hectare irrigation area was installed at the south-western end of the lake in 1986–1987 (Traoré 2010).

By the early 1990s an estimated 20 per cent of the lake's perimeter was taken up by market gardens. There was still ample access for the watering of livestock from the surrounding drylands, who also grazed and browsed the lake bed vegetation as well as crop residues remaining on the fields along the shores of the lake. Restocking Lake Tabalak with fish had taken place regularly since 1970 and by the early 1990s the estimated yield was 90–100 tonnes of fish per year. At that time, Tabalak wetland was also particularly favoured by waterbirds: an average of 4,000 Palaearctic and Afro-tropical waterbirds of up to 35 species was seen per count (Mullié and Brouwer 1993).

Threats to Lake Tabalak noted in the early 1990s included sedimentation and encroachment of sand dunes; salinization/alkalinization, and, for the waterbirds, serious disturbance by the local population, especially the fishermen. In addition, the trees the lake used to have at its northern end were mostly cut by local inhabitants in 1993, during a conflict with Department of Environment staff.

Management of Lake Tabalak and/or its surroundings did not appear to be coordinated in any way (Mullié and Brouwer 1993).

Utilization, threats and management by 2004

According to the site information sheet prepared for its designation as a Ramsar Wetland of International Importance (Ramsar Bureau 2004), by 2004 the height of the dam at the outlet of the lake had been increased, which also increased its storage capacity. Agricultural activities were said to occupy 600 ha, benefiting 5,400 people in 12 villages around the lake. All the arable land was deemed to be cultivated and agriculture was extending into marginal land on the surrounding plateaus (formerly grazing land). The significance of the lake for pastoralism was only mentioned in one sentence, in an off-hand way. Fish production was estimated at 100–300 tonnes per year, worth €50,000 to €150,000 locally. The remaining trees surrounding the wetland were used for construction and as firewood. Water from the lake was used for drinking and cooking. A decrease in the number of waterbirds counted seemed already apparent during the 1990s, from an average of 4,000 to an average of 1,350 per count in 1999–2000 (Département de la Faune, de la Pêche et de la Pisciculture, in Ramsar Bureau 2004).

The following *threats* to Lake Tabalak were mentioned: climate change, unsuitable agricultural practices leading to erosion, illegal cutting of trees and shrubs, the use of illegal means of fishing leading to depletion of the fish stock, and overgrazing, particularly on the sand dunes surrounding the lake.

Management was said to be shared by the state and local fishing, farming, women's organizations, preventing and managing of conflicts between the lake's users and organizing access to those resources together with the traditional leaders. At the same time, it was commented that agronomic development was only beginning to be realized and was not harmonized with other development actions (Ramsar Bureau 2004).

Utilization, threats and management by 2007

A mission for LUCOP (2007) noted strong agricultural and market gardening pressure round the lake. A second market gardening area, of 240 ha, had been established in 2006, including a pumping station, irrigation and drainage canals, and access roads (Traoré 2010; Abdoul Kader 2012). According to Brouwer (2010), by 2007, 80 per cent of the perimeter was taken up by market gardens, compared to 20 per cent in the early 1990s, and livestock access had diminished accordingly. Lake Tabalak was still quite important to livestock, however, as a source of water and fodder. Fodder was cut from the surrounding vegetation and there was also direct grazing of crop residues in the fields along the shoreline (LUCOP 2007). For birds, the most important sites were by then at the northern end of the lake, which still accommodated 70 Black-crowned Cranes (a threatened species) and 95 African Spoonbills, making the lake by far the most important site for this latter species in Niger (Niger Bird DataBase 2013).

Threats mentioned included cutting what remained of the *Acacia nilotica* groups, upstream erosion leading to silting up of the lake basin, and, most importantly, upstream off-take of 3 million m³ of water every year for the 240 ha market garden development, which increased the risk of the lake drying up during the dry season. Thousands of pastoralists and their families were negatively affected by this (Abdoul Kader 2012).

Regarding management, the mission noted that neither the local elected officials nor the users of Lake Tabalak appeared to be aware of Ramsar Wetland's status of International Importance, nor of the consequences of that status for management of the lake. Certainly the off-take of 3 million m³ of water at the upstream end would appear to be in conflict with the Ramsar status, as it was considered likely to lead to the drying up of (at least) the most southerly of the three basins of Lake Tabalak. The mission report included a proposal for (a start to) sustainable participatory integrated management of the natural resources of the lake and the surrounding uplands, including environmental education and eco-tourism (LUCOP 2007).

Utilization, threats and management by 2010

By 2009, the municipality of Tabalak had 35,000 inhabitants, with an average household size of 10.7 people. The total annual budget was €25,000 and the investment budget €5.335 (mayor's office of Tabalak, in Abdoul Kader 2012). Between 1975 and 2009, the area of upland agriculture in the municipality increased from 24,000 ha to 46,000 ha, while dry-season agriculture in depressions increased from 3,900 to 5,500 ha. During the same period, the area of grazing land decreased from 35,000 ha to 6,600 ha, including a severe loss of access to the resources of Lake Tabalak. As an example, in May 2010, when many herders practising transhumance were still at Lake Tabalak because the rains and the new pasture growth in the grasslands to the north had not started yet, only the smaller of the basins of Lake Tabalak still contained water. The entire depression was covered with market gardens. Only a couple of access routes to the water still existed for livestock. Market gardeners were selling access to crop residues for grazing in plots of 200–300 m², at a fee of 13,000–15,000 FCFA (€20–23) per 100 m², where formerly grazing in and around the wetland had been free. The transhumant pastoralists are generally at the lake from April till June and indicated that they had no choice but to accept this, and hope for an early start to the rainy season. If not, they might have to sell livestock at the time of year when prices were lowest and eventually abandon this livelihood altogether (Traoré 2010).

Similarly, 'cash for work' projects were converting surrounding upland traditional grazing areas into agricultural fields. It should be noted, however, that while an estimated 24 per cent of the population of the municipality only farmed, and 11 per cent only raised livestock, 29 per cent combined livestock with market gardening, 11 per cent combined market gardening with fishing, and 26 per cent practiced all three. There are no people who live solely by fishing and livestock raising and fishing are not combined. Because of this combination of activities, the local livestock numbers are also considerable. In 2010 there were 8,300 local cattle, 14,500 sheep, 11,500 goats, 12,400 donkeys, 11,500 camels (dromedaries) and 200 horses. This local livestock in part also goes north to graze for the rainy season, accompanied not by the entire family as in the case of transhumance but only by some youngsters. During the dry season, the agricultural fields are fertilized by the local livestock, and where possible, the transhumant livestock camp on them at night (Abdoul Kader 2012). Livestock also bring nutrients to the lake through their manure and urine when being watered. This increases the productivity of the lake and benefits farmers, and fishermen as well as waterbirds (Mullié and Brouwer 1994; Brouwer and Mullié *et al.* 1999 in Brouwer 2010).

Fishing continued to be a very important source of revenue to the community, bringing in €85,000 with only very simple equipment (SCE 2012 in Abdoul Kader 2012). It was also the best organized economic activity. Small fish were never put back, the size of fish caught being regulated only by mesh size of the nets. Regulations were enforced by the government and the presidents of the fishing cooperatives. During years of drought and towards the end of the fishing season, smaller mesh sizes were allowed. Fish prices per kg of each species were fixed at the start of the fishing season and income was divided between fishermen, merchants and the fishermen's cooperative.

Other uses of Lake Tabalak in 2010 included brick making, transporting water for construction purposes, and hunting birds (Abdoul Kader 2012).

In relation to threats, it should be noted that the return of immigrants from Ivory Coast and Libya, because of the upheaval in those countries since the turn of the century, has increased the human pressure on Lake Tabalak. Poor rainfall is also seen as a threat. More local threats include market gardening practices that are not suitable for the environment, such as using motor pumps for irrigation, inappropriate use of chemical fertilizers and pesticides, and the construction of field boundaries that trap wind-blown sand, can be an entry point for invasive plants, and can limit fish movement and injure fishermen when they are submerged when the water levels of the lake are higher. Other threats at Lake Tabalak are abandonment of fallowing and over-utilization of the vegetation to meet the needs of people and animals. Negative effects of fishing included abandoned fishing equipment catching sand, trampling of crops at the water's edge, and disturbance of the lake bed leading to increased turbidity of the water (Abdoul Kader 2012). See also the general section above, on interaction between different types of wetland utilization.

Regarding management, Abdoul Kader (2012) mentions the poor organization of, and frequent conflicts between, the various parties involved, in spite of there being organizations that represent the various user groups. Lake Tabalak is a clear example of 'the tragedy of the commons': most users see the lake as a resource for their own use, with which others interfere, rather than as a resource to be maintained by communal effort. Pastoralists tend to be the poorest and the least organized of the users of Lake Tabalak, and arguably the most easily squeezed out. Market gardeners-livestock raisers see themselves primarily as market gardeners and complain about the herders and their animals that damage their crops. As the water in the lake gets lower they take their animals to wells elsewhere to be watered, so that the market gardens will not suffer. They also feel that when the water in the lake is low, there are increased chances that their animals will pick up parasites and diseases if they drink from the lake.

Of the local inhabitants interviewed by Abdoul Kader (2012), 45 per cent recognized that there are conflicts between the different users, concerning fraud and damage by animals and the other interactions between different uses mentioned above. In 2010, 34 cattle died of unknown causes but presumably after drinking from the lake. Local representatives of the various ministries are responsible for enforcement of various regulations and for public awareness. Local inhabitants are also aware that the level of Lake Tabalak is now often much lower than it ever was before, and that there is a serious risk of it disappearing 'in 10 years' if no corrective action is undertaken. Most are willing to contribute labour towards such corrective action. All envisage expanding their activities around the lake at the same time, which is already over-used.

Steps proposed by some of the locals for more sustainable management of Lake Tabalak include

- Fewer single-issue solutions; in other words, an ecosystem approach to the management of the lake and associated dryland areas, with the various groups working together, giving as well as taking. Nothing will be achieved if villages and groups adopt a selfish attitude.
- More technical support for the various user groups.
- Capacity building of local user groups.
- Planting of trees in the catchment.
- Treatment of gullies to reduce the inflow of sediment.
- Digging of wells for irrigation so that the water in the lake itself can be reserved for livestock.
- Scooping out the lake bed to restore its storage capacity.

In addition, they see a need for

- Outside finance.
- The long-term cooperation and commitment to the lake by the government, development organizations and other non-users.
- Better access to outside markets and credit facilities.
- Better access to means of conserving their produce, including fish and meat.

Abdoul Kader (2012) added making more use of the Ramsar status of the lake to this list. He mentioned eco-tourism (e.g. to see migratory birds), development organizations, parties of interested people to the Ramsar Convention, levies on products from the lake, contributions by user organizations, and development of external markets as potential sources of finance of sustainable PINReM.

Conclusions and governance-oriented recommendations

From the above it will be clear that isolated wetlands in the Sahel, and arguably in other arid and semi-arid regions of the world, are first, natural resources that are very valuable to quite a number of user groups, second, natural resources that are intimately linked with the dryland areas that surround them, and third, natural resources that are under severe threat from a number of processes. Finally, they are poorly known in many instances. There is no recent synthesis of what is known about these isolated wetlands, and not even a good inventory of what wetlands there are, how they are utilized, what their value is, also to surrounding dryland systems, and how they might best be managed.

The following are urgently needed to be undertaken for isolated wetlands in the Sahel, and probably in other arid and semi-arid regions of the world:

1   An inventory and database of all wetlands larger than, for example, 10 ha when they are full (or perhaps less than 50 ha to start with) should be made.
2   Information on the physical characteristics of each wetland, its role in the functioning of the surrounding dryland systems, its utilization by people, its biodiversity, its economic value, and the threats to its functioning should be added to that database.
3   Reliable and coordinated governance of the wetlands and associated drylands should be encouraged, e.g. through the formulation and implementation of National Wetland Programmes that will in due course take over the coordination of the first two tasks, and that will promote and help implement wise use of all wetlands, through sustainable Participatory Integrated Natural Resource Management based on the Ecosystem Approach of the Convention on Biological Diversity, involving (valid representatives of) all stakeholders. Both the Convention on Combating Desertification and the Ramsar Convention should be included at international convention level, as well as the CBD, UNFCCC and CMS.

Acknowledgements

Thanks are due to Thomas Sommerhalter, formerly of DED and SNV in Niger, for his help with literature for the Tabalak case study.

7 Current situation and future patrimonializing perspectives for the governance of agro-pastoral resources in the Ait Ikis transhumants of the High Atlas (Morocco)

Pablo Domínguez

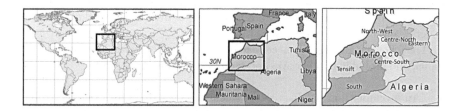

Briefing

Even if there is growing scientific evidence that Indigenous and Community Conserved Areas (ICCAs) created locally in specific cultural and ecological contexts are a positive management regime for the well-being of local populations and the conservation of the environment, in fact ICCAs are being strongly undermined worldwide. This chapter deals with this problem by focusing on a particular agro-pastoral ICCA in Morocco, the *agdal*. More concretely I will focus on the system of *tagdalts* (small *agdals*) of the Ait Ikis community, which consists of regulating seasonally the utilization of highland rangelands and agriculture through an assembly of users whose objective is to ensure a sustained use and egalitarian access to natural resources. As one of the key drivers of the undergoing *agdal* crisis in the Ait Ikis, I point to important shortcomings in the exchange interface between science and politics which imply the undervaluing of *agdals*. One of the ways for the necessary implication of the decision-makers and politicians that affect the socio-environmental problems of these systems could be the processes of patrimonialization, which seek to give a clear and public recognition to the natural and cultural values of these socio-ecological systems at a local, national and international level.

Keywords: governance, rangelands, patrimonialization, ICCAs, mountain, Morocco

Introduction

The alliance between the natural and social sciences has proven to be a worldwide successful analytical approach to understand and conserve ecosystems while seeing humans as a key agent within these (1971 Program Man and the Biosphere Program, 1972 Stockholm Declaration, 1992 Rio Conference). Consequently, authors from various areas of expertise have stressed the importance of Indigenous Peoples' and Community Conserved Territories and Areas, hereafter ICCAs (in the meaning given by Kothari *et al.*, 2012), vis-à-vis local communities' livelihoods, their socio-ecological resilience and the conservation of biodiversity (Agrawal, 2003; Baland and Platteau, 1999; Berkes, 2004; Auclair and Al Ifriqui, 2012; Gellner, 1969; Ostrom, 1990; Porter-Bolland *et al.*, 2012). It is well known that bottom-up approaches contribute to such goals (West *et al.*, 2006), and analysts have highlighted the need to integrate ICCAs into strategies of global environmental conservation and human development (Corrigan and Granziera, 2010). In fact, they have demonstrated ICCAs to be central in ensuring the well-being of millions of people and the conservation of about one-third of the global ecosystems (terrestrial and aquatic), which remain adaptable and highly resilient to various socio-ecological threats, for instance climate change, agro-business expansion or desertification (IUCN, 2012a). Nevertheless, ICCAs should not be regarded either as a universal panacea for conservation, nor as a strict developmental regime, because there are cases where ICCAs were unsuccessful (Ruiz-Mallen and Corbera, 2013). In an increasingly globalizing world, however, it has become obvious that multilevel participatory governance, which should combine local and state-level agencies, may secure a seamless connection between different actors and institutions. This seems to be the necessary approach in the future success of ICCAs (Berkes, 2007).

At the same time, the link between pastoralism and environmental degradation has been the source of fierce debate among researchers. Pastoralists are typically accused of degrading vegetation cover and causing desertification worldwide (Geist and Lambin, 2004: 818). Nevertheless, while this may be the case in many situations of unregulated rangelands, numerous studies have argued the reverse where institutions of community-based management of natural resources are well established (McCabe, 1990: 82; Banks *et al.*, 2003: 135). More importantly for this study, grazing has proved to be actively managed by local communities to relieve pressure on pastoral resources and to sustain forage production for the benefit of the communities themselves (Genin *et al.*, 2012: 412).

Despite such growing acknowledgements of ICCAs and pastoralism within scholarly circles and more than two decades of rising awareness from civil groups as well as interest within certain local administrations and international organizations, today pastoral ICCAs and the bio-cultural diversity they promote continue to experience a rapid process of degradation, particularly under the rules of the world's market system and forces of globalization (Jodha, 1985). It can be argued that on the basis of these processes of decline is a strong communication gap in the science-policy interface, which in effect encourages the undervaluing and undermining of ICCAs (Domínguez, 2010). Without appropriate intermediation and evaluation between these systems and state institutions, the facts established by scientists are too often translated by decision-makers into doubts and used as excuses to avoid action (Aumeeruddy-Thomas, 2013; Swyngedouw, 2010).

One of the ways to implicate decision-makers genuinely in the current socio-ecological problems of pastoral ICCAs is through *patrimonialization* procedures (Michon *et al.*, 2012; Auclair *et al.*, 2011. The concept of patrimony (heritage) is defined here as a set of tangible and intangible cultural and natural elements inherited from the past and focused on a stakeholder (an individual or a community), that helps to sustain the stakeholder while developing its identity and autonomy through adaptation in time and space (Ollagnon, 2000). Patrimonialization is thus regarded as a process through which these inherited but evolving natural and cultural values may be acknowledged at local, national and international levels (Cormier-Salem *et al.*, 2002).

To contribute to the better understanding of pastoralism and ICCAs under such an approach, this chapter will explore new patrimonial values of a set of agro-pastoral *agdals*. The *agdal* is the most paradigmatic case of ICCAs in Morocco. It can be defined as a seasonal prohibition that forbids access to an agro/sylvo/pastoral resources in order to allow them a resting period during their most sensitive period of growth (for example the three months of spring in the case of high mountain pastures). The spaces, dates and resources affected by this prohibition, as well as the processes by which they are established and applied, are enforced by the tribal assembly (*jmaa*) according to its own history, territorial heritage, political structure and economic strategies. Hence, while seeking to optimize the productivity of the resources, the *agdal* management system also assures the community of users a relatively fair access to local natural resources as all members of the community have equal rights to the common pool and together comprise its governance. More concretely, the chapter will look at the *tagdalts* (small *agdals*) of the Ait Ikis, a community of approximately 700 members belonging to the Mesioua tribe in the High Atlas of Marrakech (Morocco) where I have concentrated my researches during the last decade.

The hypothesis underlying this analysis is that the described patrimonial approach can contribute significantly to solve the current problems that Moroccan agro-pastoral ICCAs are facing and hence, the main goals of this chapter are:

1   To record and identify new natural and cultural patrimonial values of the Ait Ikis ICCAs.
2   To examine the opportunities of managing such values in the context of a patrimonializing procedure.

In order to undertake this new global analysis, I have completely reviewed some previous works, including my PhD thesis, to elaborate a new evolved and updated description of the agro-pastoral *agdal* governance system of the Ait Ikis group up to present, and to unveil their hidden patrimonial natural and social values. Second, I will show how the current governance regime interacts with the external world and some of the main causes of its degradation, at the same time as discussing a possible future patrimonializing perspective to face these challenges.

Context of the Ait Ikis agro-pastoral governance system

This study was carried out among the Ait Ikis group, the upland members of the Mesioua tribe (hereafter 'Mount Mesioui'), situated in the Moroccan High Atlas, less than 50km from Marrakesh as the crow flies (Figure 7.1). Like other high mountain areas, it is terraced in an altitudinal vegetation gradient. Between 1,000 and 2,500m, several types of ligneous vegetal structures (scrubs, bushes, and Mediterranean forests) occupy the mountain sides, being especially dense on the north slopes. From 2,500 to 3,600m (the Meltsene peak is the highest point in the region), high mountain plants and rich pastures appear, followed by steppe vegetal structures with a strong presence of cushion-shaped xerophytes, although some thick pastures still remain, combined with some resistant juniper bushes. The humid highland prairies that most importantly attract local agro-pastoralists' attention are in fact one of the rarest vegetal types. They occupy small and very specific biotopes of the high mountain spaces, such as the floors of small valleys, mall faults, the lower slopes or the proximity of water resurgences (Domínguez, 2005; Bellaoui, 1989).

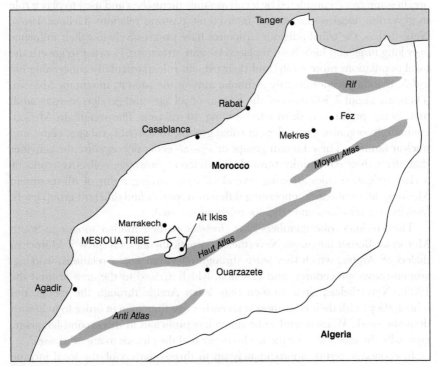

Figure 7.1 Location and borders of the Mesioua tribe with the Ait Ikis population in its interior (source: Domínguez, 2010)

The Yagour, a large territory of about 70km² located at the centre of the Mesioua highlands and on which pastoralism is forbidden by the *agdal* during three months in spring, is at the heart of our study site and hosts the most important fodder resources of Mount Mesioui (Figure 7.4). Nevertheless, the Yagour is just one of several territories in a larger and more complex agro-pastoral system, in which this rangeland is combined with the use of other *agdal* managed territories. Its importance lies in its large size (Yagour means 'bigger than' in the local language), determining the opening dates of many other *agdals* around, which allow access to their pastures before or after the Yagour does. Each year, herding in the Yagour is prohibited by the *agdal* system from approximately 28 March to the end of June/beginning of July, mainly according to the annual rainfall (the higher the annual rainfall the later the start date). These dates on which herding is banned are established every year by an assembly of herders using the Yagour, the locally so-called *jmaa*, that constitutes the most fundamental institution of their autonomous political control. As with the other smaller local *agdals*, the maintenance of the prohibition of access is overseen by individuals elected by the community of users as guardians, the *Ait Rbain*, who communicate any infraction to the tribal assembly, which applies the appropriate sanction or resolution for each type of infraction.

The different *agdal* prohibitions were traditionally legitimized and supported by long-observed cults of local saints. The descendants of these saints were (and still are, in some cases) considered by locals as saints themselves and used to play a role in governing local resources and inter-ethnic pastoral relations (Gellner, 1969). Nevertheless, the tribal religious structures have progressively lost their influence over long time, and have been replaced by state structures, in order to govern the local populations more easily, and their present role, particularly concerning big *agdals*, is today predominantly symbolic among the present mountain Mesioui. There are about 7,500 users of the Yagour of all ages and genders, despite adult men being prominent, distributed among 40 villages. The mountain Mesioui continue to organize themselves in tribal groups, sub-groups, villages, clans, and nuclear families. These human groups or *segments* generally organize the activities that affect their community through the different *jmaas* (i.e. collective works of a clan, irrigation rules affecting several villages, herding rights of all mountain Mesioui, different *agdals* concerning different resources and different group levels, festivity organizations and religious celebrations, etc.).

The Mesioua tribe members have *Tachelhit* as their mother tongue, a South Moroccan Berber language. Nevertheless, practically all men speak a Moroccan dialect of Arabic, which they learn through television, social relations, working, administrative procedures, and at school which arrived to the area around the 1980s. Nevertheless, since women only learn Arabic through the media and school, they finish their education at an earlier age than men in order to help with domestic work. Women tend to be much less proficient in this second language, especially the oldest among them who never had the chance to attend classes.

In economic terms, approximately up to three-quarters of the local income can come from the agro-pastoral sector, which is usually combined with seasonal emigration or some specialized local works such as masonry, smithing or other similar occupations (Bellaoui, 1989). Animal-rearing consists mainly of cows, sheep and goats. The mountain Mesioui are patrilineal, and like other Berber societies, all decisions regarding the household use of the agro-pastoral resources are made by the male head of the household, and in his absence, by the eldest adult male of the family (depending on the family situation it may be a brother, the eldest son, etc.).

The importance of the different *agdals* within the local economy is attested through the way in which prohibitions facilitate the regeneration of large quantities of high quality and diverse agro-pastoral resources, which is greatly sought after by farmers during the different periods of scarcity on other lands (e.g. winter in the highlands and summer in the lowlands). For example, in the case of the Ait Ikis on which I will focus most concretely, the contribution of the *agdal* managed summer pasture of the Yagour highlands was estimated at 12 per cent of the overall family income, including migrant remittances, approximately 18 per cent of the overall agro-pastoral income and over 24 per cent of the overall pastoral income (Domínguez, 2010). From this study one can deduce the importance of certain *agdal* managements as they correlate directly with the quantitative importance of the local economic resources that these *agdals* manage. Nevertheless, it is fundamental to not only focus on the quantitative level, but also to analyse the strategic place that *agdals* occupy within the animal food calendar as for example the Yagour's pastures protected by the *agdal* prohibition during the three months of spring are consumed in situ during the summer, a period of the year when the animal food resources of the lower pastures have run out. Indeed, local stockbreeders insist that 'pastoralism and the *agdals* are our means of survival' (Domínguez *et al.*, 2012).

The governance of Ait Ikis agro-pastoral diversity: the tagdalts

The Ait Ikis community occupies four different habitats (Figure 7.2) according to the following altitudinal sequence: Azgour/Tifni, Ikis, Warzazt and Yagour n'Ikis (the portion of the greater Yagour territory that belongs to this group). In proportion to their number, the Ait Ikis use a larger part of the Yagour than the other mountain Mesioui communities. To explain this situation, they refer to a historical or legendary heroic event that entitled them to a larger land area in the Yagour. The diverse and steep topography and the climate variations of Ait Ikis result in periods of scarcity for herds, particularly in summer, as a result of the drought, and partially in winter as a result of the harsh cold and the snow covering most of the high altitude pastures, rendering them physically inaccessible. Thus, these agro-shepherds must think through the use of their territory in terms of time and space, in order to address the food needs of the herds and to ensure enough transfer of fertility through animal manure, to areas under cultivation. To achieve this, they have implemented a complex and fine transhumance system, controlled by the application of different *agdals* (locally called *tagdalts*, small *agdals*) whose rules (particularly people entitled to access them, dates on which access is

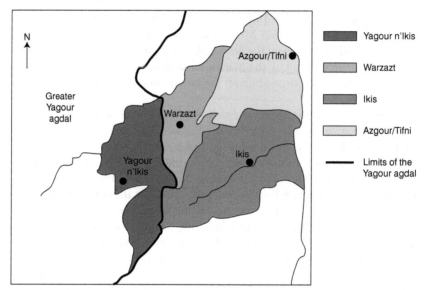

Figure 7.2 Territory of the Ait Ikis and their four habitats (based on Domínguez, 2010)

prohibited, spaces and resources concerned, penalties to be paid by infringers, etc.) are reviewed each year by the *jmaa*, the village assembly.

In this section, I will attempt to highlight the social and natural values, which are implicit in the Ait Ikis territorial governance, permitting them to develop their own identity and autonomy inherited from the past but in constant readaptation, and hence, instituting this system in the category of a socio-ecological patrimony as defined by Ollagnon (2000). I will explain the different prohibition choices governing the rhythm of transhumance of the herds and the movement of the families, paying particular interest to the evolution of fodder, agricultural and fruit resources throughout the year and how this has been changing throughout the last decades. This will enable us to gain a better understanding of this highly dynamic and complex mobile agro-pastoral system. Through a series of explanations, all of which have been updated from my PhD thesis, expanded and newly reformulated for this chapter, I will explain the system of opening and closing of the different *tagdalts* in the four habitats on which the Ait Ikis transhumance is modelled. At the same time I will also show in an expanded manner vis-à-vis my previous works, its strong imbrications within the agricultural and ritual calendars.

From 28 September to 28 March (based on Domínguez, 2010)

On 28 September (15th in the local Julian calendar) the *agdal* prohibitions that are imposed upon the territory of Ikis are strict, meaning that herding as well as the harvesting of walnuts and gathering fruit were forbidden before this date. Until this date, most people were settled in the higher lands of Warzazt, but at the end of September the majority of them transhume with their animals and possessions back to Ikis. Ikis is in fact the home village of the entire group (the reason why the local group is called Ait Ikis, meaning 'those from Ikis'). It is located at a height of almost 1,700 masl, over 300 metres lower than Warzazt, and geographically speaking it is better protected from the cold winter winds flowing downwards from the highest peaks. People here have better insulated houses made of local granite where they can spend the winter in contrast to the less effective sandstone of Warzazt. It is also here where 90 per cent of the walnut trees of the Ait Ikis grow. In fact, at this altitude walnut trees find their climactic environment within the whole Zat river basin and this is important as walnuts are a key complementary income for the households. They are able to reach relatively high prices in the local market, even equal to the price of barley, and walnuts are even used for bartering while they are being gathered. The arrival of such an important economic event for locals and the fact that it coincides with the return from the summer pastures to the winter habitat, is cause for celebration. The Ait Ikis population make a sacrifice of animals (a *maarouf*) at their oldest settlement, Ikis, and hold a communal meal close to the tomb of the local female saint, Afoud, in her honour. Through this ritual, they make pledges to guarantee a prosperous and safe winter in their lowland habitat where all members of the group work closer together to get through the hard winter. At this point, all spaces of the Ait Ikis are open to herding and throughout autumn and winter the free movement of the animals is permitted in all spaces. Nevertheless, during this period, farmers and shepherds tend to stay more or less within the boundaries of the space they inhabit (Warzazt, Ikis or Azgour). Without major competition for natural resources during this period as all has been collected in advance, the *agdal* prohibitions do not need to be reimposed until spring returns, and there is a chance to compete for higher rates of productivity. Hence, *agdals* can be seen as a cooperative system motivated by individual competition for natural resources in order to avoid collective over-grazing or over-harvesting by free-riders.

From 28 March to approximately 20 April (based on Domínguez, 2010)

On 28 March (the 15th in the local Julian calendar), the entire Yagour including those from Ait Ikis (Yagour n'Ikis in the figure) are under the global tribal herding prohibition of the *agdal* to encourage the growth of pastoral vegetatation. This affects especially the herbaceous ones which, at the end of June, can be more than one metre high in a rainy year in the most favourable soils if the herding prohibition is fully observed. At the same time, during the three months of the herding prohibition, the flowering, pollination and consequent production of seeds that are central to the continuity of these ecosystems are also guaranteed giving an extraordinary aesthetic appearance that attracts an increasingly great number of trekking tourists at this time of the year. One or two hundred shepherds from the whole Mesioua tribe, some of whom are members of the Ait Ikis and use the Yagour at the end of winter (February–March), but only when snow is not present, hence varying from year to year, must leave the Yagour and search for new spring pastures at lower altitudes. The Yagour is thus emptied of all its users for three months, and generally thought to be occupied by spirits and devils, locally called *djins*, at the service of the different local saints, determined to assure that the *agdal* prohibition is respected. Hence, and even if such beliefs have been in decline for some decades now (Domínguez *et al.*, 2010), it is still generally thought that one is at risk in the Yagour while the *agdal* prohibition is in place, particularly if herding animals. More or less at the same time, another small very particular *agdal* is decreed regarding the herbaceous strips dividing the different agricultural plots, in the 'open' space of Warzazt. Hence, this agdal is not applied in a spatial homogenous manner but in a reticular way, over the different lines dividing private terraces. This prohibition is also applied the presence of the same diabolic spirits described for the Yagour and even if it is considered a more domesticated space, withdrawing grass from the common grass strips between private fields can be equally punished by these supernatural beings.

Approximately from 20 April to 20 May[1] (based on Domínguez, 2010)

At the beginning of spring, on a date based on each year's rainfall and availability of pastoral resources, Warzazt, the second highest settlement of the Ait Ikis, also closes its entire pasture to allow the grass to grow on the slopes and the small plains beyond the cultivated fields. The month of May is in fact, according to the local breeders and shepherds, the most sensitive time for the growth of herbaceous plants in Warzazt. Hence, 20 out of the almost 100 Ait Ikis families whose main home is in Warzazt (especially sheep-breeding families), are obliged to migrate to the valley of Ikis, with the exception of some shepherds who with their animals at the sheepfolds of Tifni (on the road to the hamlet of Azgour). Since it only affects a small part of all Ait Ikis, this movement of people does not seem to inspire major communal ritual celebrations. Nevertheless, it does assure that the barley that is currently growing at its maximal rate on Warzazt's fields, is well protected from possible animal damage. This is especially important for Warzazt field owners living at this time of the year in Ikis and having great difficulty in restricting access to their fields at such a critical period of growth for their crops. Hence, the decision of the Ait Ikis assembly forces 20 families out of Warzazt, assuring both the recovery of the pastures and unproblematic growth of the barley.

Approximately from 20 May to June–July (based on Domínguez, 2010)

After a month, around the 20 May, the space of Warzazt lifts its *agdal* and pasture is open again to herding and living. This creates an inverse migration: people come up from Ikis and Tifni to Warzazt, and even from Azgour, where less than a month later (towards the end of June), the barley harvest begins. The difference between this upward movement and the previous downward one relies not only on the fact that they have opposite directions, but also on the number of people that move. In fact, in this case, almost all families of the Ait Ikis, nearly 90, move towards higher lands in this transhumance. Also, the two shops in Warzazt that have been closed since September are now open and even the *fqih* moves with the group from Ikis to Warzazt. This movement to the higher lands symbolizes the beginning of the summer for the Ait Ikis and iradiates a general feeling of happiness and joy. It is also the end of the academic year for children and it is always preceded, just a few days before this upward transhumance, by the celebration of another ritual *maarouf* in Ikis again, similar to the one celebrated after their return on 28 September, but this time in the hope of obtaining the blessing of Allah for a good summer in the highlands. Hence, through these two key ritual offerings, one before the winter season and one before the summer season, which included cattle sacrifices but also bags of grain, butter, couscous, and other local products, these products are distributed equally among all members of the community, irrespective of who gave more or less. Symbolically, the most important feature of the ritual is that it is performed before the 'eyes' of the saint and of God, as the saint's tomb is also considered to be a gateway to Allah. The idea is that after having meticulously followed the ritual and proved to the saint and God their piety with the most poor of their community, Allah would reward his devout Muslim observants. After this one-day ritual, the participants, all males of the village, children included, go home calmly confident that they had left the old season behind and entered a safe and hopefully prosperous new season with divine will and protection on their side.

Approximately from June–July to 28 September (based on Domínguez, 2010)

After implementing the *agdal* prohibition on the high altitude territories of Mount Mesioui for approximately three months, the Yagour reopens. This opening occurs earlier or later, again depending on the annual ecological conditions (mainly gross annual rainfall), according to the decision made by the *jmaa* of Mount Mesioui. Nevertheless, today this role is somewhat lifted or bootlegged by the state's intervention who reclaim their new role as referees and pacificators in the place of the saints' descendants that used to be in charge of this. The transhumant shepherds, Ait Ikis and other groups from all the territories bordering the Yagour, move upwards bringing in a great number of herds (up to 45,000 animals according to the numbers estimated in Domínguez 2010) and people (over 7,000 persons including men, women, adults and children). Here many of them meet again after one year's separation and new *maaroufs* and other celebratory events, rituals, sacrifices and even marriages are held at this time. However, in those areas that encourage highland agriculture (for example Warzazt), the *jmaa* also imposes small *agdals* to protect the crop fields, especially since the harvesting of cereals in the Yagour always takes place a few days before its opening. In fact, there is a local rule that states that nobody from the Ait Ikis may enter or cross its territories of Warzazt and Yagour n'Ikis with animals during the three days before the closure of the great *agdal* of Yagour, in order to allow them to harvest all their crops if they are ripe enough, before the remaining local shepherds from other villages have to cross their own lands to reach the Yagour. Moreover, towards the middle of July, the floor of the Ikis valley is put in *agdal* and people can no longer graze their animals there, neither locals nor people from outside, so that the fruit growing in this area is allowed to fully ripen and not be open to theft of animal damage. Towards the end of July, another *agdal* is imposed on the entire Ikis valley, as a way of reducing pressure on the pastures during the critical summer period. Finally, towards mid-August the cornfields of Warzazt are also submitted to an *agdal* and people can no longer gather freely in the fields, not even in their own lands except when irrigating them. Only every 15 days or so, the cornfield *agdal* at Warzazt and the fruit tree *agdal* at Ikis are lifted to prevent the rotting of certain corncobs and fruits that ripen before these two *agdals* expire, respectively around 15 September and the 28 September, so reaching the end of the cycle and starting a new year.

The agdals in environmental conservation

In terms of conservation output, the *agdal* system has proved to have additional beneficial effects: on first, vegetation cover and second local biodiversity (Hammi *et al.*, 2007; Alaoui-Haroni, 2009; Montes *et al.*, 2005). Analyses of aerial and satellite photographs by Hammi *et al.* (2007) have shown how forest vegetation in the Ait Bougmez persists, or has even increased, since 1964 in areas subjected to *agdal* regulations, whereas in *non-agdal* areas where natural resources are freely harvested, there is a net reduction in vegetal formations. In fact, almost the entire deforested areas in this site (21.5 per cent of the forest surface in 1964), concern only *non-agdal* areas. In addition, Montes *et al.* (2005) have demonstrated how *agdal* management of the Ait Bougmez forests has contributed to the conservation of plant coverage and soils as well as a certain biodiversity in terms of insects. Moreover, in her work, Alaoui-Haroni (2009) has demonstrated the proactive conservation of certain plant species through the *agdal* prohibition, in pastures such as the Oukaimeden, which are close and very similar to Mount Mesioui summer pastures, particularly the Yagour. Like everywhere in the High Atlas, the Mount Mesioui *agdal* areas contain different types of resources, mainly pastoral, but also forest, fruit, and cereal crops, and even concern cemeteries where any extraction of vegetation is strictly forbidden for spiritual reasons (Figure 7.3). These different types of *agdal* generally have more abundant vegetation than surrounding *non-agdal* environments. But most important for biodiversity is that such specialized and differentiated land use patterns (Figure 7.4) – different *agdal* opening dates, different spaces, different kinds of access, different kinds of *agdal* within wider *agdals*, and so on – create an ecological mosaic with different vegetation patches and biodiversity pools throughout the territory, also serving as seed distribution points (Auclair and Al Ifriqui, 2012).

In this context, a parallel botanical study of the Yagour (Domínguez and Hammi, 2010) was undertaken in order to find evidence of the capacities of local pastoralists to conserve their resources through the local governance system. This study consisted of comparing sites grazed by a similar number of livestock (same pastoral pressure) but subjected to different human uses following a degree of

Figure 7.3 Ait Inzal cemetery under agdal prohibition with an obvious result on the herbaceous and Juniperus oxycedrus (pool of biodiversity and seed distribution point) (based on Domínguez, 2010)

intensity in the application of the *agdal* prohibition from areas with more human pressure to areas with less human pressure, always within the *agdal* of Yagour. Moreover, these sites following the gradient of anthropic pressure also coincide with another degree, from the most 'peripheral' site of the *agdal* just beside the boundary (Assagoul, shown by a dotted line in in Figure 7.5) to the most 'central' site (Zguigui, shown by a continuous line in Figure 7.5), via another intermediary site (Tamadout, shown by a broken line in Figure 7.5).

The central area of the Yagour (Zguigui) reflects the most traditional *agdal* model, in which the shepherds' permanent housing is far from their pastures, generally more than half a day's walk. Hence, this area is only used for traditional pastoralism, no agriculture is present and it remains uninhabited for approximately six months of the year: the three months usually covered by snow and the three months comprising the *agdal* prohibition, which is largely respected in this case because of the aforementioned distance problem. The 'peripheral' area (Assagoul) reflects the least traditional *agdal* model, in which combined agro-pastoral and semi-sedentary uses have been increasing for the last half century or more. Moreover, in Assagoul the shepherds' permanent housing is very close (just a 30-minute walk away). But, this situation is associated with the fact that the *agdal* prohibition imposed over the whole mountain Mesioui is easier to break, and the area can be more frequently used because shepherds can quickly go up and down every day when there is no snow and no watchmen from other tribal segments. Breaching the *agdal* grazing prohibition under these conditions is easier, as well as the fact that their use of this part of the Yagour is more frequent due

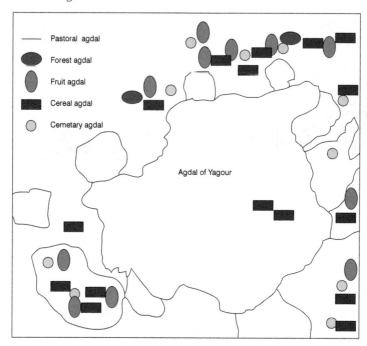

Figure 7.4 Schematized map of the different mountain Mesioui agdals including the big central Yagour agdal, the whole comprising a biodiversity pool and a seed distribution point depending on their different uses (based on Domínguez, 2010)

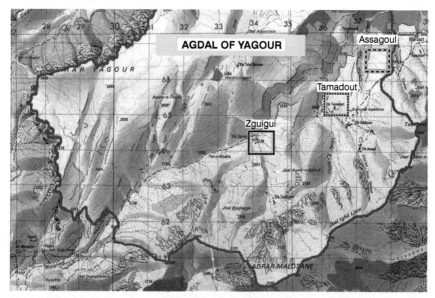

Figure 7.5 Map with the three study sites: Assagoul, Tamadout and Zguigui. The border Yagour's agdal border is indicated by a thick line (based on Domínguez, 2010)

to its proximity to the relatively recently settled village of Warzazt (in the last five decades its quasi-sedentary population has constantly increased). At the intermediary site (Tamadout), agro-pastoralism is already well established, but the sedentarization process is not as advanced as in Assagoul-Warzazt. Here the shepherds' permanent housing is still relatively remote (for some almost a four-hour walk). No agro-shepherds stay all year, especially during the winter, and they stay only sporadically during the *agdal* prohibition period.

Data were collected by analysing in two subsequent years (2005 and 2006) series of three plots measuring $9m^2$ per site, thus making nine plots per year (three plots times three sites) and 18 plots over the two years. The three plots in each site were distributed along a gradient from 'humid' areas (generally the lowest points of each site), to 'intermediary' and 'dry' areas (generally the highest points of each site) within the most fertile lands of the Yagour (mainly the sedimentary micro-plateaus at around 2,100 m). I reveal here the data collected from the three sites which were taken at approximately similar altitudes, gradients and orientations. Hammi pre-identified many of the different species of plants in the field. This was the most practical way to organize the samples in the different plots because it was necessary to distinguish these from the non-recognized species that were later identified in the laboratory (Plant Ecology Laboratory at the Cadi Ayad University, Marrakech).

As a result, these three sites within the *agdal* of Yagour demonstrated to be the reservoir of 117 species and 24 different families that were identified within its most fertile lands. At the most central site with the most traditional *agdal* management system (Zguigui), there were 66 species and 21 families identified, while at the most peripheral site with the least traditional *agdal* management system (Assagoul), there were only 54 species and 16 families. Thus, the hypothesis of the most traditional *agdal* as a better conserver of the pastoral environment appears to be initially corroborated by these results. Not only erosion seems lighter on site in this more traditionally *agdal* managed part of the Yagour, but a tendency towards greater botanical diversity is indicated by these numerical data as we move from the more 'modern' to the more 'traditional' *agdal* management. This hypothesis is also validated by the intermediary site, since 64 species were found in Tamadout, showing greater species diversity than at Assagoul and less than at Zguigui, the two 'extremes' in terms of the number of species and management types. At a family level, it presents 17 families, one more than Assagoul (16), and a much lower number of families than the most traditional *agdal* management area with 21 families (Figure 7.6).

Discussion on the challenges and future patrimonializing perspectives for local agdal rangeland governance

In this part, I will focus on the strong transformations and challenges that the system that I have described is undergoing as a whole and will discuss the possible future attempts to overcome these from the point of view of patrimonialization procedures. I will do so through the concrete analysis of the Ait Ikis community

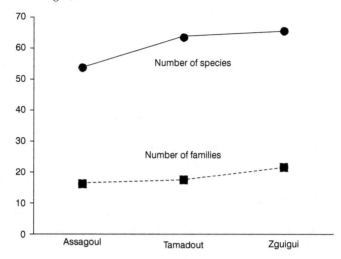

Figure 7.6 Number of species and families at each of the three sites in the Yagour used to measure botanical diversity (based on Domínguez, 2010)

which I have studied most in depth. Starting from agricultural expansion observations, Demay (2004) as well as Domínguez and Hammi (2010) noted seasonal over-grazing on the flatter lands of the Ait Ikis part of the Yagour, the most peripheral one under the great *agdal*. This is mainly due to the gradual spread of mono-specific cereal fields (mainly barley but also wheat) over the richest high mountain pastures, leaving increasingly less land for pastoral species and hence for herding activity. This derives, especially in years of drought, from a premature opening of the Ait Ikis' small surrounding *agdals*[2] or diminished observance of the great *agdal* of Yagour, often encouraging the invasion of other villages' neighbouring rangelands. Therefore, at present there are strong tensions, between villages and particularly between the richest agro-shepherds and the rest of the Ait Ikis people, since everyone is finding it difficult to meet the food requirements of their own herds and families. However, these difficulties are being lived in different degrees depending on each social class. In fact, only the most important landowners, who generally have more livestock and consequently make the most of the available fodder if the prohibition is lifted early. They make a greater profit from these earlier openings and thus, they push for them. Therefore, the smaller owners (however the majority) generally vigorously oppose the intentions of the higher class. Thus, as is evident from from different life stories and tensions regarding the transhumace rules, and based on the *agdals'* governance and the access to pastoral resources seems to be much more vigorous now than in the last hundred years (Domínguez, 2010).

An apparent intensification of droughts in the last decades, perhaps due to climate change, as well as a rise in demography, has further fuelled these tensions. Nowadays agricultural production is locally said to be always more reliable than pastoralism in a year with scarce rainfall. But one of the main explanations of this cereal field expansion and the consequent *agdal* crises is the improvement in livestock of recent decades implemented by the central state, which together with investments from emigration, also relatively recent and linked to the globalization of economy, are putting much pressure on the old governance system of the Ait Ikis. Even certain sheep-breeders are beginning not to move seasonally but put their livestock in permanent sheepfolds at the Yagour. In fact, since the 1960s, some Ait Ikis inhabitants migrated to France, mainly to work in the coal mines of coal and iron foundries of the north, saving enough money to quickly become a new local elite who started investing in agro-pastoral activity and innovation as soon as they returned. This change in the social hierarchy coincided with the improvement of sheep breeds promoted by the Moroccan state. A selected breed, the Sardi, was introduced into the region and today, even the sheep that intensely transhume with the Ait Ikis have been crossed with it. This breed is more productive when it is in a restricted space and well-nourished with grain, but unsuitable because of its slow gait and constant stalling for transhumance, the traditional way of production so linked to *agdal* management. Thus, large areas of pasture, once believed by most locals to be protected and preserved by local saints, are now being used for intensive agriculture to feed the Sardi sheep, which as we have seen, if fattened up with grain, they fetch a higher market price than the free-range Beldi breed (Demay, 2004). This is possible thanks to the expanding demand for red meat for the growing tourist industry of neighbouring Marrakesh. This causes negative ecological and socio-economic consequences such as the loss of pastures and their consequent soil loss, as well as increasing socio-economic inequalities within the local community (Domínguez, 2010).

In fact, it is no coincidence that once this breed of sheep was introduced, and that cheap wheat flour coming from the industrialized plains of the Haouz province for bread consumption was being increasingly subsidized by the central state, the production of barley was boosted on the lands of the Yagour, as human feeding was no longer the problem and feeding the newly introduced Sardi brought about higher incomes. Hence, using the savings that these emigrants had accumulated, the new elite was able to hire local labour and in buy mules and agricultural machinery. This was done in order to further work on the new lands of the Yagour, with the crops now serving mainly to feed Sardi of the higher social class rather than the rest of the people. In fact, the Sardi's maximum weight levels require a strong supply of cereals. In the Yagour of Ikis, the local elite's example was followed during the 1980s by a number of agro-shepherds, intending to feed their new and growing Sardi herds more nutritiously (Demay, 2004), and doubling the amount of cultivated soil in 20 years, a trend which is still growing today (Domínguez, 2010). Such agricultural expansion and shift in herding land use along with new globalizing influences such as emerging state structures and ideologies, mass media, new agro-zootechnical advances, migrations, market integration, tourism, NGOs and global Islamic movements, seem to be contributing to the demise of *agdal* governance systems and tradition as a whole. In fact, these systems generally remind non-indigenous actors and policy-makers of an inferior tribal past which must be (for policy-makers and other external actors) entirely overcome, even if such criticism of traditional localism is a politically given value that has been repeatedly challenged, both from the natural and the social sciences.

Despite the increasing scientific recognition of local governance systems and at least two decades of increasing awareness by civil society and policy-makers, I observed in the High Atlas mountains that these systems were being rapidly eroded in the course of the progressive interconnection of people and ecosystems under the rules and forces of global markets (Domínguez, 2010) like elsewhere around the globe (Byrne and Glover, 2002; Jodha, 1985). On the basis of such failure it can be argued that there has been misunderstanding at the science-policy interface (Swyngedouw, 2010). Such a communicative failure implies that the facts established by the scientists in this arena, are not translated by the decision-makers, and do not incorporate the most pressing concerns and priorities pointed out by scientists.

In light of the present work, it seems more likely that the crisis of the communal management regime of the Ait Ikis *agdals* and its consequent environmental degradations have been brought about not just by locals' ignorance on the management of their own natural resources, but through external socio-economic stimuli poorly planned by the administrative and political persons in charge. One of the ways to achieve the mentioned necessary implications of decision-makers and politicians that affect the socio-ecological problems of the *agdals*, are through patrimonialization, which seeks to give a clear public recognition to the natural and cultural values of these socio-ecological systems of governance at a local, national and international level. As exposed in the introductory section, this concept of patrimony can be defined as the whole material and symbolic elements centred on a stakeholder (an individual or a community), that struggles to maintain and develop its identity and autonomy by socio-ecological adaptation through time and space in a dynamic universe (Ollagnon, 2000). In this sense, different figures exist that give a public recognition to this status and protect/reinforce the different ways in which these patrimonies exist. These figures have been established in cooperation with experts, administrations and local actors.

In the case of the *agdals*, given that they generally concern very specific local communities, somewhat isolated and with strong cultural particularities, the follow-up of such a patrimonialization procedure must be based on an especially participative approach. These approaches may combine cycles of reflection and action in a way that can merge the theoretical knowledge of the external actors and the practical wisdom of the local populations to achieve real solutions that answer to the pressing problems of the latter and the environment upon which they rely (Reason and Bradbury, 2008; Robinson, 2008). In this type of action-research patrimonializing approach, the scientists work closely with the local communities to produce the knowledge and follow the procedures that value a unique natural and cultural heritage. This way of working facilitates the possible governance transformations in agreement with the local populations, at the same time as they are tested and shared through international scientific literature and respectful dialogue with the public administrations. By opposition to the dominant way of linking science, conservation and development, this approach is relatively new, and is a highly valued source of original research today and has a recognized future development ahead in terms of innovation and applied science (Ruiz-Mallen *et al.*, 2012). Contrary to the dominant way of scientific thought, this relatively new and innovative method does not consider itself free of values or being morally neutral. Nor is it part of a framework of undisputed or undisputable paradigms. On the opposite, it seeks to make local actors participate, thereby facilitating a degree of integration and in-depth learning about local and scientific knowledge, rarely attained by other methods which are more distant from or less sensitive to the local populations (Funtowicz and Ravetz, 1991; Ravetz and Funtowicz, 1999).

Thus, a training network of students and researchers composed partially by local community members together with scientists, local entrepreneurs, NGOs and state actors, inspired by an action-research approach and seeking to reinforce the values and local institutions that are gradually being replaced by public administrations, could be a potential channel to combat the communicative failure between local populations, scientists and policy-makers. In fact, combining ideas and proposals made in accordance with the local community can promote and reinforce these local modes of governance in the future. In the specific case of small communities such as the Ait Ikis or more generally those of Mount Mesioui, such an action-research training network should attract at the same time autochthonous and foreign development actors, capable of participating on a continuous and long-term basis in the creation of initiatives to support these *agdal* systems of governance that have a proven interest in conserving the environment and local equity. Of course, such a project would have to be designed for the long term (5–10 years), in several stages, and on a well-targeted site. For example, addressing the whole valley of the Zat where the Ait Ikis lies and the *agdals* of many other settlements too (Figure 7.4), composing a holistic coherent system of great interest to the knowledge transfer question exposed here. It seems to me that only on this space-temporal scale could we apply, in a more effective way than top-down approaches, the scientific knowledge obtained about of *agdal* governance. The main objectives of such a network should therefore be:

1   To train students and researchers, autochthonous and foreigners, in the patrimonialization action-reseach arena around *agdals*, concerning conservation and development, focusing on a small and well-targeted group and territory such as the Ait Ikis or Mount Mesioui, and bringing about real interaction that should last over time.

2   To create 'activist' synergies between the actors related to governance, both shepherds and breeders, as well as researchers, universities, public administrations and other development actors (international NGOs, companies, cooperatives, local associations, etc.).

3   To explore new ways of transmitting and sharing knowledge about governance between local populations and actors external to local communities.

Conclusion

By the data presented here, I can conclude that: first, the traditional *agdal* governance system assures continuous vegetal cover, and hence no soil erosion, thanks to its collectively agreed rotatory use of space; second, it also assures relatively equal access to local natural resources as all members of the community have the same rights to the common pool and decide on their rules and management processes together, according to the majority of the community's interests and local traditional ecological knowledge. Finally, it promotes the conservation of a certain pastoral biodiversity, particularly that which is of most interest to the local community. Nevertheless, a communicative failure in the science-policy interface is observed and the local *agdal* systems, like other traditional community-based governance systems around the globe, seems to be in a deep crisis. I consider that a participative patrimonializing action-research approach could be one of the means to better promote the *agdals* as a socio-culturally resilient, economically sustainable and ecologically enriching land use system, having been demonstrated by the local populations through the centuries to be a key element of resilient governance to promote local livelihoods and environmental conservation.

Acknowledgements

This research was funded by the Marie Curie Grant (MIRG-CT-2006-036532) and the Programme AGDAL ('biodiversité et gestion communautaire de l'accès aux ressources sylvopastorales'/Institut Françis de la Biodiversité – Institut de Recherche pour le Développement: financement n° 2886). Pablo Domínguez was also funded by the 'Formation à la recherche' scholarship from the Agence Universitaire de la Francophonie, the 'Field work' scholarship from the UNESCO Fellowship Program and the 'BECAS MAE-AECID' from the Spanish Agency of International Cooperation and Development. The revision of the English in this chapter was funded by the group Antropologia i Historia de les Identitats Socials I Politiques of the Universitat Autònoma de Barcelona. The author also thanks Mohamed Mahdi and Anne-Marie Brisebarre, the organizers of the congress 'La transhumance, est-elleuneactivité durable?' (Meknes, Morocco), in which a previous version of this chapter was presented. I would also like to thank Simohamed Ait Bella, Taoufik El-Khalili and Mjid Mourad for their excellent work as translators and researchers, all the members of the local NGO Association des amis du Zat and especially its president Ahmed Bellaoui, for having provided us with so many human resources and infrastructure to take us to the local communities, and all the Mesioua and Ait Ikis informers without which this work would have simply not been possible.

Notes

1   These dates vary each year according to each year's negotiations at the village's assembly (*jmaa*).
2   As we saw in the section 'The governance of ait ikis agro-pastoral diversity', apart from the big Yagour *agdal*, the Ait Ikis base their agro-pastoral territorial governance on nearly ten other small *agdals* concerning different resources.

8 Rangeland management in Lebanon

Cases from northern Lebanon and Bekaa

Elsa Sattout

Briefing

Lebanon is located at the heart of a mega-diverse area of Crop Wild Relative species, important food crops and pasture species, and landraces of high genetic diversity. Pastoralism which has been an integral part of communal livelihoods in rural and remote areas is fading away with the new farming system. Rangeland management, governed by the Lebanese Ministry of Agriculture, follow a centralized governance with regulatory measures which need to be upgraded with evolved farming systems and lifestyles. Guidelines to preserve the pastoral system integrate the institutionalization of collaborative management in forest and rangelands and mobilize human capacities towards this end; initiate applied research studies on carrying capacities of rangelands and valuation of rangelands ecosystem services, strengthening national stakeholders' capacity, and lobby for rights over the lands of herders to protect cultural aspects of ecological and social landscapes.

Keywords: governance, arid and semi-arid lands, DPSIR, pastoralism, regulatory framework

Introduction

Lebanon is located at the cross-roads of three continents on the eastern shore of the Mediterranean basin. It extends over 10,452 km² with an average width of only 48 km and a length of 225 km. The country is recognized as a hotspot for Eastern Mediterranean plants of various origins (Myers *et al.*, 2000; Heywood, 1998; Mittermeier *et al.*, 2004). It is at the heart of a mega-diverse area of wild relative species such as wheat, barley, lentils, almonds, pistachio, etc. (Sattout *et al.*, 2005; Heywood, 2008; Davies *et al.*, 2012), important food crops and pasture species, and landraces of high genetic diversity (Assi 2005; Sattout and Abboud, 2007).

Historically, the country was once covered by forests. Imprints of centuries of cedar grove (*Cedrus libani* A. Rich) exploitation, culminating in their use by the Turks as railroad fuel, during World War I, show eroded mountains with very little potential for afforestation (Fish, 1944). Systematic woodcutting over several millennia, followed by the expansion of agro-pastoral activities and subsequent urbanization, has left Lebanon with nothing more than relict forest patches and scrub vegetation. At present, the forest cover and woodlands expanding, mostly on the Mount Lebanon chain, occupy approximately 13 percent (139,000 ha) and 10 percent (108,000 ha) respectively of the country's surface area (FAO, 2005a; ELARD, 2010). Arid and semi-arid habitats are typical of the Anti-Lebanon foothills, occupied by a heavily degraded garrigue or batha (Abi Saleh *et al.*, 1996). Occupying 40 percent of the land surface areas, arid and semi-arid habitats are shelter to important food grains – wheat, barley, millet and sorghum as well as economic plants. The soil in these barren areas supports poor overgrazed rangelands.

Semi-arid regions, subject to very low mean annual rainfall with flash floods during winters, are predominantly used for grazing. Even though these regions are characterized by low population density, they have fast population growth rates. This growth tends to extend and intensify in cultivated land and squeeze out nomadic groups (FAO, 2010; Sattout and Abboud, 2007; Ministry of Agriculture, 2003).

Pastoral systems have been an integral part of communal livelihoods, particularly in villages lying on the eastern slopes of the Lebanon Mountain chain and the Anti-Lebanon especially in northern villages in Akkar, Dunniyeh, and Bsharre as well as the Hermel and Bekaa regions where soil fertility is relatively low (Figure 8.1).

Most of the small ruminant herds are found in the Bekaa valley and its adjacent steppic areas. Seasonal movements of local shepherds and their herds are made to Syria during winter, while during the summer Lebanese rangelands receive semi-nomadic herds coming from the Syrian Desert to the Bekaa. Local migration, from low altitude to high peaks in the Western Mountain chain, occurs during summer season. In past decades, a major shift has taken place from mobile grazing to sedentary animal production where goats and sheep production relies increasingly on feed blocks and feed supplements.

While bovines and dairy production are becoming increasingly popular, the size of goat flocks has decreased over a 10-year-period from 417,000 heads (2000) to 400,000 (2011) while culminating at 494,700 heads in 2005. Similarly, sheep herds decreased from 354,000 heads (2000) to 255,000 (2011) with culminating in a number of 370,400 heads in 2006 (FAOSTAT, 2013). In the previous decade, this was mainly due to the expansion of dairy products manufactured by farmers as a result of grants and loans (Ministry of Agriculture, 2003). The decrease in grazing practices in some villages is indirectly improving the quality of the green cover and witnessing an improved growth of the vegetation formations.

Figure 8.1 Overgrazed highlands in northern Lebanon

Rights to the lands and environmental resources management

Governance and regulatory frameworks

The forestry service at the Ministry of Agriculture (MOA) is the national competent authority responsible for the development of national strategy for forests and rangeland management. The present national regulations set forth a framework for herdsmen's rights over forestlands and rangelands whether these are governmental lands, communal or private lands. The Lebanese forestry law which dates back to the Ottoman Empire is still applied and herdsmen are given the rights over common lands (Ministry of Agriculture, 2003). Rights over governmental land are usually given to municipalities and neighboring villages. Grazing practices are defined based on a series of criteria whereby grazing is banned in degraded sites protected for reforestation purposes. Nevertheless, each municipality has to coordinate all decisions with the MOA, as well as land owners when they want to lease their fields for grazing. A consortium, formed by the Minister of Agriculture, member of the committee of the communal lands and representative of the district governor, is established to manage the parcels. Grazing on private property depends on the land owners, who have the right to ban transit of any herds through their field after submitting a request to the local forestry department unit. Accordingly, the parcel is declared protected by ministerial decision (MOE, 2003).

The mechanism of implementation is led by the forest guards, who are the government agent following up the implementation of the terms and conditions

148 *Elsa Sattout*

Figure 8.2 Nomadic herders during summer in northern rangelands coming from Arsal in the Bekaa

set by either the municipality or the MOA. The implementation mechanism involves local "forestry units" in the villages, members of the General Security and local police.

Rangeland use and management

Pastoral societies have been given rights over lands to secure seasonal movement of these societies with their herds. These rights of passage and use are applicable, within a set of terms of conditions, on all types of lands except protected forests and nature reserves as well as private lands designated by a ministerial decision and communal and *Emiri* lands falling under compulsory protection (burned areas and young forests/woodlands). The terms and conditions, set by the MOA, define the period of permitted grazing practices, including size of herds, tagging the animals and respecting the rangelands' boundaries. Those forests are leased either by auction or through a three-year long-term agreement. Marginal lands and parcels of forests can be leased for a maximum period of 15 years.

The restriction of transhumance on private lands is conditional on the approval of a request to ban the passage of livestock by 75 percent of private land owners. In such cases, herd movements are diverted and herders are given an alternative: to own only six goats each with grazing rights only in their own farm (Mr. G. Kassar, Personal communication, President of the Directorate of Rural Development and Natural Resources in the north, Lebanon). In Northern Lebanon, this has resulted in a decrease in the size of flocks. A ministerial decision has been issued concerning the region of Koura to ban the passage of flocks in private fields (Mr. G. Kassar, Personal communication, President of the DRDNR in the North, Tripoli, Lebanon, 2013).

The impact of the private landowners' decisions on the livelihoods of herders and pastoral systems can be mitigated through decentralization and governance reform to ensure best rangeland management practices on *Emiri* lands in order to compensate for the scarcity of lands; and through overseeing the use of marginal lands as rangelands. *Emiri* lands constitute 30 to 35 percent of the forests and woodlands.

Land ownership defines the administrative procedures for permits. There are four types of land ownership[1] in Lebanon. The shorter path is the one where herders lease private lands, named "Waqf" or "Mulk.".The venture is agreed solely between two agents whereby the forestry service provides technical support in terms of size of flocks and period of grazing (Figure 8.3).

The administrative procedure for getting a grazing permit on Emiri land has to reach directly the department of rural development in the district (Mouhafaza), which in its turn sends the request to the forestry service. The agreement on pastoralism on communal lands is made between herders and the municipality. In this case, the administrative procedure follows the regular chain of passing through the RDRDNR, the forestry service, the DRDNR and ending in the Directorate General of the Ministry of Agriculture. Exceptionally, nowadays the administrative procedures are following the hierarchy presented in Figure 8.4 where the requests for grazing are communicated to the general director (Mrs. Z. Tamim, Personal communication, Chief Department of Rangelands, Reserves and Parks-per interim, 2013). According to the forestry law, the forestry service under the Directorate of Rural Development and Natural Resources is responsible for issuing the grazing permits. The provision of forestry service support is required for all types of land ownership in terms of size of flocks, plot borders and any other issues.

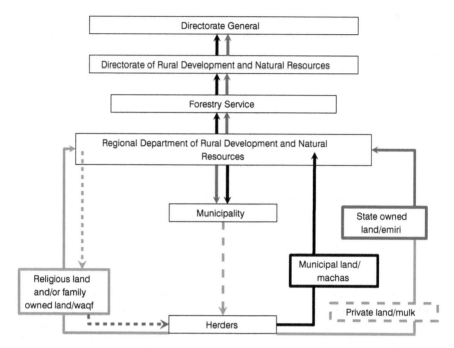

Figure 8.3 Administrative procedures for acquiring rights over the lands for grazing

Figure 8.4 Summer pastoralism

DPSIR analysis on rangeland management

Overgrazing is the result of many factors among which we may point out the following: overstocking and absence of adjustment of herd size to year-to-year condition change, inappropriate management of grazing relevant to timing and intensity, limited alternative fodder sources and poor herders' management skills (Ministry of Agriculture, 2003). Nevertheless, underlying causes are defined based on a rapid analysis of the main drivers of rangeland degradation and the identification of pressure put on parcels of land and experienced by herdsmen and government. The analysis presented in this chapter is based on three decades of national conservation practices in Lebanon, a review of existing regulatory measures, and personal communications with government officials, local community members, and herders (Figure 8.5). Nevertheless, this chapter highlights specific topics to be thoroughly studied in order to validate a first insight into rangeland management problems and solutions.

It is evident that the state of rangelands in Lebanon does not only depend on the centralized administrative structure. Other factors play a major role including the dynamic of the relationship between local authorities, central agencies, land owners and shepherds, as well as some gaps identified in the scientific and technical support in relation to rangeland carrying capacities.

The governance system is flawed because it is not properly accountable in an unstable country, which is leading to simpler processes up to down as opposed to the bottom-up approach in terms of decision-making process linked to particular interests. The shortage of representation and negotiation capacities addressed by herders pushes them away from sustainable land management processes causing a lack of democracy and weakening local governance.

One of the essential pillars of improving rangeland management is empowering local governance and pastoralist communities through capacity building (Figure 8.5). Nevertheless, strengthening local governance is hindered by political conflicts and the interference of political groups and their interests. But the gradual rise of local awareness on the importance of supporting initiatives for better rangeland and natural resource management will improve governance structure. It will imply a drastic change in the dynamic relationship between governance agents at local and national level as well as with herder communities. Mutation in the structural dynamic can be induced through the incorporation of herders on the board of the Hima system where they are subject to regular capacity development activities. Herding communities can be part of an established consortium with a clear organizational scheme and terms of reference allowing them to participate in operational processes of rangeland management.

The Hima system revived in 2004 can be the platform where lessons learned can lead towards better management of rangelands. Its revival as part of a community based approach and the reclamation of marginal fields for the production of forage might protect the pastoral system (and the rangelands themselves) instead of fostering the establishment of a static farming system. The initiative to revive the Hima system was launched by the Society for the Protection of Nature (SPNL) in Ebel El Saqi in the Southern part of Lebanon.

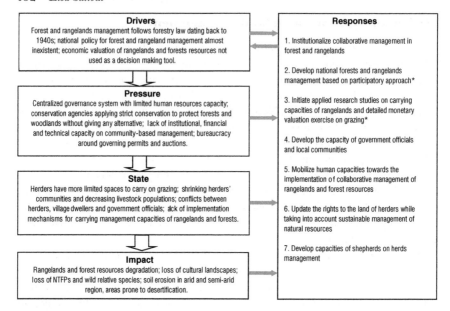

Figure 8.5 The driving forces and their impact on rangeland management in Lebanon and some solutions

*MOA has been granted an international fund to implement starting this year to revive and strengthen traditional and CBM system such as Hima

Case study of Hima system in Lebanon

Hima is the governance system of an area protected by a local authority for public interest and natural habitat conservation. It was developed even before Islam. It originated in the Arabian peninsula more than 1,500 years ago. During the life of the Prophet Mohammed, the Protected Areas were well established and managed to reduce overgrazing. The Prophet changed the ancient private Hima system, which belonged to selected powerful individuals, into a legal system that protected natural areas for more communal benefits, and subsequently caliphs followed the same system (Sing, n.d.). The Hima system insured rangeland protection during the vegetation regeneration season and would have foreseen indirectly the carrying capacity of grazing parcels through the definition of the size of flocks.

SPNL Himas are established on communal land. They apply a community-based management (CBM) system while establishing collaborative platforms between local authorities and community members such as farmers and shepherds and empowering women in rural areas. Adopting sustainability as the sole principle, the CBM system is embedded within the revival of the Hima.

Ebel El Saqi was the first site witnessing the revival of the Hima system by SPNL in collaboration with the municipality. At a later stage, Hima Kfar Zabad was established in the Bekaa to protect the wetlands and their surroundings from degradation. SPNL interventions in both Himas boosted community empowerment through their involvement in sustainable management systems of natural resources. Nevertheless, the survival of Hima Ebel El Saqi has been overwhelmed by prevailing political conflicts between members of the municipal council and struggled over individual benefits diverted from internationally funded projects. Political influences in the villages and the role played by political parties in the election (or hindering the election) of municipal officials and mayor were main obstacles for rethinking this Hima system in the context of a war-torn country such as Lebanon.

In contrast to Hima Ebel El Saqi, Hima Kfar Zabad is still standing and has overcome conflicts through the formation of a committee constituting a buffer mediator for gathering conflicting parties. The situation in Kfar Zabad favored cooperation between SPNL and the Anjar municipality to work on the IBA in Anjar (Anjar-Kfar Zabad wetlands). This cooperation was sort of a bridge to link again with Kfar Zabad and to work on a management plan and ecotourism strategy for Hima Anjar-Kfar Zabad. This approach revived the Hima Kfar Zabad and facilitated the negotiation process to resolve conflicts and resumed activities in Hima Kfar Zabad during 2012. Through these experiences, SPNL emphasizes the CBM system in Himas where grazing and management plans would be based on a participatory approach (SPNL, 2013).

Towards better management of rangelands in Lebanon

The National Physical Master Plan developed in 2004 foresees the encouragement of concerned municipalities to create a series of Regional Natural Parks, with the main objective of combining the economic and social development of the cities and villages with the proper use and respect of their natural wealth including silvopastoral systems (CDR, 2004). Even though provisions for silvopastoral systems have been included in the planning and zoning of lands, still there is no clear-cut policy reinforced bylaws or any interim regulatory measures for institutional reform, and neither implementation mechanisms have been put in place.

Economic valuation of grazing practices and rangeland management is a useful tool that allows us to revisit and analyze the rangeland management system. It may also lead to induce changes in management practices and governance of rangelands. Monetary value of grazing practices in forests and woodlands was estimated at €960,000 for 9.6 million forage units in a study performed in 2005. This value constitutes 0.97 percent of the total economic value of Lebanese forests (Sattout *et al.*, 2005). An ongoing study on the monetary value of rangeland management and other forest resources is underway (Sattout, unpublished). This study will constitute one of the major pillars for the development of national strategy for forest resources and rangeland management.

As visionaries on the importance of CBM in rangeland management, many people are joining in efforts to ensure the sustainability of the Hima system in Lebanon and the infusion of the cosmovision on sustainability as developed by Ríos Osario *et al.* (2005). This vision has a series of principles including the "preservation and promotion of lands, protection of non-renewable resources, protection of human consumption products in order to improve the community's standard of living, and promotion of the community so that it takes care of its environment, its socialization at the level of organization to better understand environmental protection as a guarantee for a life full of dignity for generation living and to come" (Río Osario *et al.*, 2005). This is translated by the navigation of SPNL on a long journey to promote sustainable grazing through various activities including internationally funded regional and national projects, applied research programs and national/regional workshops. On the other hand, the Lebanese Ministry of Agriculture is more aware of the importance of the decentralization process of administrative procedures for rangeland management as well as the need to establish relationship dynamics with herders to leverage their socio-economic livelihood and to preserve the resilience of rangelands in Lebanon.

Conclusion

Independently of land ownership, the administrative structure for rangeland management is still centralized and it is solely guided by the Ministry of Agriculture. Collaborative forest resources and rangeland management is still in its infancy in Lebanon. In the early 1990s, biodiversity protection and management approaches adopted strict conservation principles with a centralized governance system marginalizing local communities. The shift of this approach towards participatory practices was possible through the evolution of a conservation concept ensured through internationally funded conservation ventures applied in Lebanese Protected Areas (PAs) (Sattout *et al.*, forthcoming). The approach involved the establishment of close partnerships between the MOE, Government Appointed Committees (GACs), Non-governmental Organizations (NGOs), and the private sector. This approach can be adapted to rangelands, whereby the revival of the Hima system could be fostering collaborative natural resources management.

In conclusion, the tipping points towards best practices in rangeland management are:

• Institutionalizing CBM and sustainable management of rangelands.
• Defining the carrying capacities of rangelands and forestlands.
• Assessing the socio-economic profile and livelihood of shepherds.
• Participatory mapping of herders' paths in the lowlands and highlands.
• Drawing a road map for institutional reform which would be based on collaborative management of rangelands.
• Bridging the gaps between government agencies and pastoralist communities.

Improved governance involving decentralization and institutional reform at the regional level set the path for better environmental resources management, as the local government knows more about the carrying capacity of their lands and the drawbacks of the "grazing ecological footprint." The reclamation of marginal lands and their conversion to rangelands is one of the proposed solutions, but still the government must oversee laws allowing collective pastoral management . The revival of the Hima system has been restricted to environmental protection until now and it did not take into account strictly and effectively rangelands and herders' livelihoods. Nevertheless, it may constitute a good starting point to combine both ecological protection and sustainability of pastoralist communities.

The present chapter was developed based on rapid assessments of existing regulatory measures, current administrative structures and communications with relevant stakeholders. It constitutes a starting point for primary thoughts on rangeland management in Lebanon and emits a wakeup call for improving rangeland management in Lebanon based on future research studies.

Note

1 Emiri: state-owned land/managed by the MOA. Sometimes their management is referred to the communities. Macha'a: communal lands/municipality owned/managed by municipal council. Waqf: land owned by religious communities or families/managed by representatives of the religious community or family. Mulk: private land.

9 Legal and policy aspects of rangeland management – Mongolia

Ian Hannam

Overview

One of the greatest challenges Mongolia faces now and into the future is the responsible use and sustainable management of its rangeland resources, in particular with changing circumstances from climate change. Effective environmental law and policy can ensure that a balance is maintained between economic development and environmental protection, particularly given the high dependence of people's livelihoods on rangeland natural resources.

Keywords: governance, rangelands, land management, environmental laws

Introduction

Since the 1950s, Mongolia had been transformed by rapid economic development and industrialization from what was predominantly an agricultural economy based on nomadic animal husbandry, towards an industrial economy. Today over half the population lives in urban areas. As was the case with many rapidly industrializing countries, environmental and resource management considerations were generally absent from land planning and utilization. With an area of 1.56 million square km, and a population of around only 2 million, Mongolia is the seventeenth largest country in the world territorially but much of the land is not productive. Under the Mongolian Constitution 1992 all land is State-owned. Land that is productive is under developmental pressures that are leading to environmental deterioration. Land available for agricultural production is decreasing: grazing land was 141 million hectares in the 1960s but has now dropped to 117 million hectares while the number of livestock has risen to 43 million head. This number has increased in recent years because Mongolia has not had a *dzud* for several years.[1] Like many developing countries, Mongolia's economy is raw-material oriented, where raw materials from the agricultural and mining sectors and semi-finished products provide the main export items. Many environmental, social, economic, political and legislative factors interact in Mongolia that affects its ability to achieve sustainable rangeland management. Mongolia was a socialist state with a centrally planned economy until 1990 when it became independent of the USSR and adopted a democratic form of government and free market economy (UNDP 2005).

Under the Mongolian Land Law 2002, 'pastureland' (which equates with rangeland) means 'rural agricultural land covered with natural and cultivated vegetation for grazing of livestock and animals' (Article 3.1.6). The rangeland cover a large proportion of the country (112 million ha or 71 per cent) but around 122 million ha of Mongolia is devoted to nomadic pastoralism: 4.6 per cent of this lies in the alpine zone, 22.9 per cent in the forest-steppe zone, 28 per cent in the steppe zone, 23.3 per cent in the semi-desert zone and 16.2 per cent in the desert. The climate is harsh with extremes of heat and cold. Availability of water and other renewable natural resources is very limited, and rangeland ecosystems are fragile, highly susceptible to degradation and slow to recover. Low precipitation is unequally distributed both temporally (the majority occurs during the three-month period in the summer) and geographically (the north of the country receives most of the precipitation; the southern part is semi-arid or desert). Climatological data indicate that the Mongolian climate is gradually growing drier, which signals changes to the way it must manage its rangeland resources. The rates of humus production, vegetative regeneration and growth, and livestock productivity are very low in comparison to other countries in the region. A significant portion of the land resources are degraded from overgrazing, deforestation, erosion and desertification. Crop cultivation is an important cause of soil erosion. Climatic conditions make high levels of soil loss associated with tilling of the soil almost inevitable, aggravated by the inadequate use of soil protection techniques. From the 1960s to the 1990s the area under cultivation increased greatly, mostly in the form of wheat fields, many of which (>60 percent) have since been abandoned and subject to wind and water erosion. Climate change is a contributing factor to desertification and wind erosion (Mongolian Government 2008).

The rangeland is degraded because herders are unable to apply sustainable grazing practices. The rangeland is not valued so its regulation and management has been avoided in the past. Herders continue to graze their livestock unrestrained on public land, where there is high competition for good pasture. They use public pasture and water free of charge and without initiative to protect and properly use it (Swift 2007). As relatively intact terrestrial ecosystems, the Mongolian rangelands play a significant role in sequestrating atmospheric carbon dioxide, conserving biodiversity, and especially in providing livelihood benefits to local herders. However, over the past 50 years, rangeland degradation has undermined the ecosystem services they generate.

Existing legal and policy situation

An investigation into the environmental law of Mongolia reports that during the last 20 years Mongolian legislation has developed within the legal framework for a new market economy-based society and in this regard the existing environmental law system is reasonably well founded. The regulations, procedures and programs accompanying the *Environmental Protection Law 1995* have advanced to the stage where it is intended the environmental laws achieve the objectives of major national environmental policies – as defined in the Principles of National Security, Universal Sustainable Development Policy, Principles of Sustainable Development of Mongolia in twenty-first century, Government Policy on Ecology and the Millennium Development Goals of Mongolia. However, the Mongolian environmental law system does not have the capability to effectively manage the main environmental problems experienced by the country, which is a function of: structural and procedural deficiencies and poor quality of legislation; poor government administration of the environment, inadequate institutions; lack of effective community participation; failure to prepare environmental law around the sensitive ecological environment – which is in decline from: increasing degradation of water, soils and vegetation; expanding desertification; increased water, air and land pollution; loss of biodiversity, species decline and ecosystem dysfunction.

Under the market economy concept, the numerous environmental laws adopted have provided a reasonable general legal framework. However, the legal assessment shows that they lack many essential elements considered necessary for them to attain their stated objective. Moreover, law-makers had developed the law without fully considering the principles for long-term sustainable use of natural resources – instead focusing on managing the current situation. Many essential elements are missing from the laws (especially for education and training, developing information, dispute resolution) (Hannam 2009).

Since the mid-1990s, under a special provision of the Environmental Protection Law 1995, and various individual natural resource 'use fee' laws that followed, citizens have had access to many natural resources (forest, water, land, natural plants and hunting native animals) for the payment of a fee. Although this system is similar in concept to the worldwide 'principle of user pays', it has been very limited in the way it has been applied for all land but rangeland in particular because it does not apply to grassland, where the fee amount is very low (and not indexed), is poorly administered, is not accompanied by natural resource incentives and support schemes. Further, a substantial amount of fee collected is siphoned off by the central budget and only a small amount of revenue is reinvested locally for conservation and land improvement purposes – which was its principal object. Recently, the government has been investigating the application of the user pays system over the grassland where it is proposed to charge a fee on livestock based on sheep head equivalent. Herders would receive various inducements to improve their land stewardship under this scheme (Hannam and Borjigdkhan 2009). This scheme would be backed by the

2009 Policy on Herders and Herding Households which identifies 36 priority areas to improve management of rangelands, including such issues as: valuation and pricing of grassland and establishing a market mechanism for grassland; studies into the economics of grazing; investigating national and international markets and trade of pastureland products; development of a Resettlement Plan for herders displaced by financial constraints and natural disasters, and for those who voluntarily seek an alternative livelihood. Given the high incidence of poverty among the herder community there is some scepticism over the ability of people to pay and of the overall financial viability of the scheme (Mongolian Government 2009).

In Mongolia, traditionally, organizations have been based on sectors of agriculture, infrastructure, and energy and little attention has been paid to natural resource management which cuts across all sectors of government. Rangeland degradation impacts on a large number of ministries ranging from finance and planning to agriculture and health, and improved coordination between ministries is required for effective management to be attained. Moreover, many critical barriers exist to the effective administration of the rangeland environment, though the limitations imposed by the current organizational system of Ministries and Departments, have been identified (Tortell *et al.* 2008). A critical limitation for rangeland management is the significant imbalance between the Ministry/ Departmental organizational system and the distribution of individual laws and administrative functions and duties across respective organizations. The Ministry for Nature, Environment and Tourism is responsible for a number of primary environmental laws, including laws for mining, pollution control, water resources, air quality, wildlife, forestry, and geological resources – a situation it has no hope of administering effectively due to significant human and financial resource restraints. This problem is also reflected in Mongolia's system of Parliamentary Committees, where, for example, the Parliamentary Standing Committee on Agriculture and the Environment has responsibility for a diverse range of environmental issues, including agricultural production, safety and control of food and agriculture products, rural development policy, regulation of grants and loans from international organizations and donor countries related to rural development policies, livestock management, land and mineral resources, forests, water, flora and fauna, atmosphere and other natural resources, protected areas, pasture and crop lands, environmental monitoring, air pollution, toxic chemicals, environmental protection, water policy, resources, and water pollution, solid waste, recycling, environmental policy, environmental research and development, and hunting. Given the pressures placed on the administration to manage its environmental responsibilities, and the fact that few other agencies have a role in managing the environment, it indicates that Mongolia must develop an alternative administrative system and legislative system to the ones currently in place if it is to have any chance of controlling the serious environmental problems confronting the country in general but rangeland specifically. Thus, the existing environmental organizational system that affects rangelands is characterized as (Tortell *et al.* 2008):

- Inadequate level of staff and lack of support resources.
- Incomplete mandate and responsibilities curtailed.
- Weak human capacity at all levels.
- Inadequate facility to train and keep good staff.
- Lack of identifiable career structure, adequate working conditions, leadership, feedback and incentives for excellence.
- Absence of a corporate plan to identify accountability to the Mongolian people.

Reform approach

Recent investigations initiated by the Mongolian Government have established legislative, policy and institutional reforms to improve natural resources management including rangelands (Hannam 2009). The reforms focus on the institutional structure at central and local levels and six elements were specified as the basis of the reform, including: reorganizing the system for managing legislation; using an ecological approach as the basis for environmental law and to restructure institutional arrangements; introducing new administrations that identify with the major environmental problems and which focus on coordinated management; introducing a management system with specialized institutions/agencies to manage 'clusters' of legislation associated with principal problem areas and which identify with the institutions/agencies; reforming many existing natural resources laws and developing new types of environmental law; and accepting a long-term plan to undertake and implement the legal, policy and institutional reforms.

Mongolia commenced an environmental law reform program in 2011. The Environmental Protection Law 1995, the Environmental Impact Assessment Law 1998, Water Law 2004 and the Law on Reinvestment of Natural Resource Fees for Conservation and Restoration of Natural Resources 2000 have already been improved by amendment and a Law for Soil Protection and Desertification Control has been drafted. All of these laws are relevant to rangeland management.

An outcome of the 2008 environmental law investigations was the identification of a new 'Natural Resources Management' legislative and institutional administration as the primary agency to manage ecological and natural resources. It is regarded that this type of system would be potentially more effective to manage the rangeland resources than that are currently in place. This administration would be responsible for developing a national strategy for rangeland management, rangeland policy and associated management guidelines (Hannam 2009).

Pastureland law

Mongolia has drafted a Pastureland Law (Mongolian Government 2007) which would be the principal law for managing the rangelands. The aim was to develop a legal framework to provide land tenure for livestock producers, herder groups, cooperatives and herding households, to establish remote pasture reserves, and for the operation of pasture use committees as a basis to overcome many of the problems that stem from lack of land ownership. It also aims to develop a legal framework to exempt herding households from individual income tax and to introduce pasture use fees differentially based on economic and ecological assessments and to consider a livestock husbandry risk fund. The State Policy on Herders and Herding Households 2009 would provide strategic support to the Pastureland Law. The policy aims to create a favourable legal, economic and business environment and produce better living conditions for herders, prevention of poverty in herders and employment and social security (Mongolian Government 2009).

The draft Pastureland Law has been through extensive public and parliamentary discussion processes since 2007. Although at the time of writing this chapter it had still not been promulgated, these sectors are working through a complex set of issues to ensure effective legislation finally results. The main purpose is to provide a legal method for the transition from an unplanned and unregulated pastureland user system to a system characterized by: secure possession of pastureland for herders and legal entities; a pastureland planning and management system; the development and management of pastureland information; distinguishing the functions, duties and responsibilities between the different levels of administration; and mechanisms to improve the identification and management of problems associated with land degradation and the effects of global climate change. Importantly, the draft law includes procedures to classify pastureland on an ecological basis and provide for the agricultural and economic needs of traditional herding communities and the livestock husbandry industry. In this regard, the new administrative, implementation and operational procedures of the Pastureland Law will support economically productive pastoral agriculture while managing pressures on the ecological environment from climate change, desertification and natural disasters (Mongolian Government 2007 and 2010).

Importantly, the draft Pastureland Law includes a procedure to allocate land for grazing and for its management and protection, which constitutes the basis of land tenure and this will help overcome many problems that stem from the traditional pasture usage system (Fernández-Giménez 2006). The procedure includes the identification and classification of pastureland, a request (application) for pastureland possession for the purpose of livestock husbandry and the issue of a certificate for possession. It will also engage the communities in the land tenure process. Global experience shows that land-use systems that enable stakeholders to formally participate in the decision-making process generally provide a more satisfactory and balanced outcome for all parties. This procedure will help promote the sustainable use of pastureland and development of a stewardship ethic which is important for a stable long-term tenure system. These are important procedures and should increase the capability of Mongolia to manage its rangeland resources more effectively in the face of the increasing effects of climate change and other natural events (Batima 2006).

The draft Pastureland Law contains many legal elements considered essential for a successful rangeland law but it is accepted that additional support systems will be required to enable herder communities and legal entities to achieve a sustainable livelihood and for the State to achieve its national goals for pastureland management (Hannam 2007; Mongolian Government 2009). Some areas identified include: development of operational policy; development of a 'national strategy for grassland management'; development of land management plans; formation of local stakeholder advisory committees; providing access to finance and credit; developing a comprehensive education and training program; and ensuring stakeholders have access to information and knowledge.

Rangeland conservation and climate change

In an effort to improve its management of the climate change effects on rangeland ecosystems, the Mongolian Government is following the procedure established under the UNFCCC to develop a Nationally Appropriate Mitigation Action (NAMA) for grassland and livestock management (Mongolian Government 2010; Asian Development Bank 2011). Under these procedures a NAMA is defined as 'any kind of activity that reduces greenhouse gas emissions'. For Mongolia, the specific grassland and livestock management activities developed under the NAMA procedure would be nationally appropriate and tailored to its national circumstances and in line with the UNFCCC principle of common but differentiated responsibilities. In following the UNFCCC procedure, the NAMA will be embedded within Mongolia's national sustainable development strategy. The mitigating activities will be measurable, reportable and verifiable and supported. Importantly, by following the procedures set down in the UNFCCC process and satisfying the standards for national and international registration, this would open up the potential for Mongolia to access climate change funding to implement the NAMA (KPMG 2011). One of the essential requirements for the effective implementation of the grassland/livestock NAMA is a legal and policy framework that in Mongolia's case would include a Pastureland Law along the lines of that originally drafted in 2007.

A 'national grassland mitigation strategy' has been promoted under the reforms proposed. It could be formulated from the objectives and elements of relevant international treaties and strategies and integrating these with Mongolian national climate change mitigation protocols, and the national policy for grassland. The strategy could be enshrined within the Pastureland Law – to give it a statutory basis. The challenge will be to balance the required environmental outcomes of a grassland strategy and the objectives for a NAMA within the overall climate change framework of Mongolia (Hannam 2012). A national grassland mitigation strategy could:

- Set out the relationship between the strategy, international treaties and national legislation and policy in relation to grassland and livestock management.
- Outline the relationship between the principal national policy areas.

- Outline a coordination and cooperative mechanism to properly operationalize rangeland management.
- Specify the changes required in the agricultural land-use sector.
- Outline the procedures for a grassland carbon accounting and forecasting system and specifying areas where mitigation activities can be applied.
- Outline the procedures for establishing local-level Pasture User Groups and their role in grassland management.
- Outline the procedure for establishing local-level voluntary carbon markets and carbon accounting standards.
- Outline a plan for ongoing research into climate change impacts on grassland and livestock herding – as a basis for ongoing legislative, policy and reform action.
- Outline the specific financial mechanisms to support rangeland management.

It is considered that the NAMA approach adopted by Mongolia would also be suitable for other developing countries which have extensive rangeland areas, to follow.

Improving grassland use

Two principal limitations to effective implementation of a sustainable rangeland program are the lack of pasture ownership (possession), and a lack of incentive to use grassland sustainably because pasture use does not attract a fee. With regard to grassland possession, although this has been addressed in the draft Pastureland Law, it, along with the proposal to charge a fee for grassland use, have been very controversial. Introducing procedures to enable pastureland possession with incentives to regulate stocking density would potentially lead to sustainable use of pastures and the incentive to improve the livestock quality and industry productivity (Mongolian Centre for Policy Research 2010). The proposal to introduce pastureland possession consists of creating the appropriate legal environment and actions for its implementation. The grazing of grassland in Mongolia without any fee encourages the misuse of pasture and contradicts the long-term interest for securing herders' livelihoods by ensuring a sustainable livestock sector development. The use of a Livestock Risk Management (Protection) Fund (under the Law on Government Special Funds 2006) is promoted as a suitable basis to introduce a fee on livestock for the use of pasture. Revenues raised through this system would be spent on sustainable pastureland activities and risk management with both herders and local governments being beneficiaries. Many of the risk management activities are sustainable activities and would help to increase carbon storage in grassland and manage climate change impacts. This process could provide for such activities as: (Mongolian Centre for Policy Research 2010)

- Repair of animal shelters.
- Building or repairing sheds for calves and lambs.

- Repairing small storages for fodder and grass.
- Reserving manure.
- Making a small-scale snow breaker.
- Preparing animal fodder and salt marsh.
- Fencing and protecting springs.
- Establishing hand wells.
- Cleaning and restoring wells.
- Restoring a pump and generator of deep wells.
- Controlling pasture rodents.
- Restoring water reservoirs.
- Planting fruit and other trees near wells.
- Improving grassland and hay fields.
- Making animal shelters.
- Restoring hay field fencing.
- Fertilizing hay fields with manure.
- Building inter-group fodder points.

Local herder organizations

Local pasture user organizations have been promoted as an important part of the process to achieve sustainable use of rangelands (Blattler 2012). It is recognized that the role of herder organizations would also play a critical role in implementation of a livestock/grassland NAMA (Hannam 2012). Over time, herders in Mongolia have been organized into different institutions, both formally and informally (Fernández-Giménez 2006). Moreover, since 1999 Mongolia has seen a number of community-based grassland management projects aimed to improve herders' livelihoods and pasture-management practices. This is also facilitated by a number of different donor pasture-management programs and international NGOs. In recent years, special attention has been given to two donor-funded projects which take a different approach to herder organization, namely herder groups (through a UNDP/Sustainable Grasslands Project) and Pasture User Groups (PUGs). Since 2004, the Swiss-Government funded Green Gold project has facilitated the formation of hundreds of such groups and will, in the years to come continue to do so by scaling up this collective action approach and broadening its geographical reach (MSRM 2012). Herder Groups are usually fairly small with up to 20 households, are organized primarily on the basis of a combination of kinship and shared use of key resources (e.g. wells, winter pastures). By contrast, PUGs involve up to over 150 households and are organized on the basis of territory where local areas are divided into a number of territorial units.

Under the two main laws concerning herders' relations to rangeland management in Mongolia, namely the Land Law 2002 (Art. 52.2) and the Civil Code of Mongolia 2002, grassland can be managed by groups of people for a specific period of time. As a form of organization, PUGs are entitled to enter into a 'pastureland management contract' or 'pasture use agreement' with a local government organization. The relationship between a local government and the herders is regulated through a Contract on Utilization of Pastureland for Pasture User Group. As a tool to apply rangeland management at the local level, the Contract provides for a range of objectives and can establish the general management requirements for a defined area of land. Each PUG is thus covered by the Contract for pasture use which is signed by the Soum and Bagh governors, the head of the PUG and the PUG leader.

Despite the PUG system having the benefit of the combination of a given territory and a contract system which regulates relations within that territory, the issue of pasture use rights still has to be resolved to ensure all legal and practical aspects of the contractual arrangements can be properly realized, in particular: (1) roles, rights and responsibilities; (2) access/use and flexibility; (3) boundaries, flexibility and permeability/leakage; (4) monitoring, control and enforcement; and (5) security of tenure. The contract system can form the centrepiece in linking the legal, policy and institutional framework in the management of pastureland at the local level (Blattler 2012).

In some PUGs, pasture utilization is covered all year round with the pastures of all the four seasons being registered on maps which form a part of the contract. The contracts are made in a similar legislative format to that provided for in the Land Law 2002, and can specify the size of the grassland area, its location, seasonal use, and stock carrying capacity, procedures for dispute settlement and conflict resolution, and specific tasks for the PUG. In this regard, the contract specifies the limit on animal numbers in a prescribed area and in this form it becomes an integrated instrument for grassland management which would also be beneficial for operationalizing various mitigation aspects of a livestock/grassland NAMA (Hannam 2012).

The establishment of PUGs generally works from a bottom-up approach in an attempt to reach out and involve all herders in a given area in the decision-making process. Experience shows that land-use systems that enable stakeholders to formally participate in the decision-making process generally provide more satisfactory and balanced outcomes to all parties and will help promote the sustainable use of grassland and development of a grassland stewardship ethic which is important for a stable long-term tenure system.

Relationship between PUG and local government

For the PUG concept to be successful there needs to be a good relationship between PUGs and local government. In this regard, the draft Pastureland Law provides an appropriate framework to formally establish PUGs in consideration of the role of local government. The PUGs would need to be established with a distinct and complementary role to play in livestock and grassland management. Potentially, the PUGs could have a wider role extending beyond grassland management and include herding issues related to veterinary services, breeding, livestock inspection, and connecting with herders scattered over a wide area.

PUGs can be developed as an outreach mechanism as a link to herders and with prescribed financial support.

Ecological approach

One of the main impediments to improvement of the condition of rangeland resources is that the current environmental law system does not identify closely with the principal ecological characteristics of the country. Few environmental laws effectively identify with the physical environmental elements they are supposed to be protecting and the legislation lacks detailed planning and decision-making provisions for assessment, evaluation and understanding ecological limitations. In particular, Mongolian environmental law does not express a 'connection' with the Mongolian environment, which, as documented in various environmental studies, contains a rich and diverse ecology that requires special management (UNDP 2005; Hannam 2009). During reform, including the promulgation of the *Pastureland Law*, opportunity should be taken to adopt an 'ecological' approach (e.g. ecological zones, landscape regions, and river basins – see Saandar and Gunin 1993) as a fundamental basis of the reform of the environmental law, policy and institutional system, and in particular to restructure the law to give it a strong focus on ecosystems and their constituent parts, including people and communities, natural resources, and the heritage qualities and characteristics of locations, places and areas. Such an approach would be consistent with modern international environmental law reform practices and recognize the obligations of humans in managing the environment (Hannam 2009).

Future challenges

One of the greatest challenges Mongolia faces now and into the future is the responsible use and sustainable management of its rangeland resources, in particular with changing circumstances from climate change. It must ensure that balance is maintained between economic development and environmental protection, particularly given the high dependence of people's livelihoods on nature and natural resources, and the vulnerability of Mongolia's rangeland to natural and human induced disasters. Engaging and empowering people and local communities through knowledge is a vital component of this process. Many citizens and government officials, particularly those at local and provincial levels, are under-informed about the rights and obligations that are set down in Mongolian environmental legislation. It is hard to see that improvement can be made without promulgation of the Pastureland Law, or a law similar to it. Raising awareness of the country's legal provisions and the rights and obligations of citizens and the government will go a long way towards promoting responsible use of rangeland, and ensuring the variety of economic, social, environmental and other interests are best-served. In particular, the main challenges faced by Mongolia include improving the capacity and performance of central government organizations responsible for rangeland management, especially water, soil and biodiversity; development of new institutional structures and mechanisms for natural resource management; improving coordination of central government organizations and local governments on natural resources; creating new enabling conditions for civil society to participate in natural resources governance; strengthening partnerships with non-government organizations and the private sector to promote natural resources awareness, ecological education of the public and enforcing environment standards for rangeland conservation. In this regard, the most recent investigations into rangeland management in Mongolia have established the following immediate and short-term priorities, and they make reasonable suggestions as to how these priorities may be achieved:

- Empowering communities – it is difficult to envisage any real progress in management of rangeland in Mongolia without a significant improvement in the ability for local communities to fully participate in decision-making processes and exercise an equal say in the long-term use of resources, including access to resources and land management processes.
- Reforms to land user rights – this should include immediate resolution of land and pasture usage fees and land-use contracts that ensure security of tenure and long-term access to these critical resources by the herding community and other legitimate users.
- Institutional reform – recent studies provide substantial information and ideas to help the Mongolian Government reform its natural resource management institutions. Current inefficiencies in administration and development of accountabilities are a major limitation to rangeland management and represent an immediate priority for attention.
- Environmental awareness education – there is an immediate priority to improve the level of understanding of management of rural environmental issues through a comprehensive national environmental education program. A program should address all levels, including school and university education, herders, government officials and members of parliament. It is advocated that the current system of NGOs in Mongolia is well placed to have a major role in environmental education and appropriate legislation should be amended to enable this activity.

Note

1 A *dzud* is a winter disaster that covers pastures with ice and causes mass livestock starvation. *Dzuds* affected Mongolia in 1996–1997, 1999–2000 and 2000–2001 – the last of which killed 13 per cent of the country's total livestock.

10 Rangeland governance in an open system

Protecting transhumance corridors in the Far North Province of Cameroon

Mark Moritz, Catherine Larissa Bebisse, Albert K. Drent, Saïdou Kari, Mouhaman Arabi and Paul Scholte

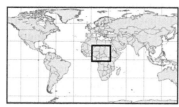

Overview

The mobile pastoral system in the far north region of Cameroon is an excellent example of the paradox of pastoral land tenure, in that pastoralists need secure access to pasture and water, but also flexibility in resource use, i.e., the ability to move elsewhere because of spatio-temporal variation in resource availability. In this chapter we draw from our collective research and development experience with mobile pastoralists, and discuss how non-governmental organizations have used ordinances and bureaucratic procedures to protect pastoral resources, in particular transhumance corridors that connect seasonal grazing lands in the far north region. We argue that the mobile pastoral system is best understood as an open system and explain what the implications are for the protection of pastoral resources. We argue that delimiting and protecting transhumance corridors is not the panacea and we conclude with a discussion of the advantages and disadvantages of this approach.

Keywords: pastoral systems, rangeland governance, common-pool resources, transhumance corridors, non-governmental organizations

Introduction

The mobile pastoral system in the Far North Province of Cameroon is an excellent example of what Fernández-Giménez has referred to as the 'paradox of pastoral land tenure' (2002), in that pastoralists need secure access to pasture and water, but also flexibility in resource use, i.e., the ability to move elsewhere because of spatio-temporal variation in resource availability (Niamir-Fuller 1999, Turner 1999). Longitudinal, interdisciplinary studies of pastoral systems have shown that mobility is a key adaptation in pastoral systems (Behnke *et al.* 1993, Ellis and Swift 1988, McCabe 2004, Niamir-Fuller 1999) and that limitations on mobility often have disastrous consequences (Shahrani 2002).

In the Chad Basin, mobile pastoralists have the freedom to move within and between states and the pastoral system is best described as an open system in which there are no social or natural boundaries (Moritz *et al.* 2013). Pastoralists share an ethos of open access, which prescribes that all pastoralists, regardless of class, ethnicity, or nationality, have free access to common-pool grazing resources. Contrary to expectations there is no evidence of a tragedy of the commons (Moritz *et al.* 2014, Moritz *et al.* 2013, Scholte *et al.* 2006). We have found indications that the system we describe for the Chad Basin is common in other pastoral systems in West Africa (Niamir-Fuller 1999), even when it is not labelled as such (Frantz 1986, Horowitz 1986, Stenning 1957, Swallow 1990) and it has also been described for pastoralists outside Africa (e.g., in Iran; Bradburd 1992).

One of the major threats to the common-pool grazing resources does not come from the pastoral system of open access, but from agricultural expansion onto seasonal grazing lands and the transhumance corridors connecting them (Galvin 2009, Moritz 2006a). One of the most common ways to protect pastoral resources and pastoralists' user rights of these resources from agricultural expansion is to designate agricultural and pastoral zones and delimit transhumance corridors. These solutions have been implemented at local as well as national levels in the forms of rural or pastoral codes (Hesse 2000). Niger's Rural Code is one example of national legislation that formally secured existing corridors and recognized pastoralists' user rights of grazing resources (IUCN 2011b). While the focus in the literature has been on problems of implementation and governance of these rural codes (Flintan 2012, Hesse 2000, Tielkes *et al.* 2001), there has been less discussion of the conflict between the flexibility and openness of the pastoral system and the fixing and delimitation of resources and resource use through the delimitation of pastoral zones and transhumance corridors. In his discussion of governance of rangelands in West Africa, Turner (1999), however, has argued that there is a risk in formalizing pastoral tenure institutions into rural codes where flexibility is more appropriate in terms of managing access to common-pool grazing resources in situations where there is considerable spatio-temporal variation in the distribution of these resources. The danger is that if tenure institutions become more formal and rigid, it will limit mobility with potentially negative consequences for the resilience of the social-ecological system.

Here we discuss the conceptual framework of open systems that we have used to describe and explain pastoral management of open access to common-pool grazing resources (Moritz *et al.* 2013) and its implications for the governance of rangelands and pastoral infrastructure in West Africa and beyond, with a particular focus on the protection of transhumance corridors that allow mobile pastoralists to move between seasonal grazing areas.

We have been conducting research on different pastoral systems in the Chad Basin for the last 20 years (Moritz 2008, Moritz *et al.* 2013, Moritz *et al.* 2010, Scholte *et al.* 2006), and our discussion draws here from our involvement in pastoral development in the far north region in different capacities. Two of the authors worked for the Waza Logone Project in the 1990s (PS, SK), two others are currently members of Centre d'Appui à la Recherche et au Pastoralisme (CARPA) (SK, AM), one studied the process of delimiting the transhumance corridor as an intern at CARPA (LBC), and two others have studied different pastoral systems in the Far North Province, including pastoral development (MM, AKD).

Study area

Mobile pastoralists in the Far North Province of Cameroon

The Far North Province of Cameroon has one of the highest population densities in the country and is characterized by a great diversity in ethno-linguistic groups and a mosaic of different agricultural and pastoral systems, which have been integrated at household, community, and regional level for centuries (Moritz 2010, Seignobos and Iyébi-Mandjek 2000). One could describe the grazing lands as fragmented (Galvin *et al.* 2008), but the grazing lands have historically always been part of a mosaic of different forms of land use in the far north region (Seignobos and Iyébi-Mandjek 2000). Moreover, there is considerable spatial variation in population densities and forms of land use (see also Raynaut 2001). Pastoralists have been able to exploit common-pool grazing resources across the region by using transhumance corridors to move between areas with lower population densities, including the key resource area of the Logone floodplain. However, in the last decades there has been increasing pressure on grazing lands as well as on the corridors linking the seasonal grazing areas due to demographic pressures and economic development (Moritz 2008).

The cattle population in the Far North Province is significant and has been estimated at 2.1 million and the small stock population at 2.8 million (Ziébé *et al,* 2005). Animal husbandry provides subsistence and a significant source of income for a large part of the rural population, including peri-urban pastoralists, agro-pastoralists, and mobile pastoralists (Moritz 2012). The population of mobile pastoralists consists of different groups of Suwa Arabs and FulBe, in which the latter consists of different sub-ethnic groups like the Jamaare, Mare, Uuda, Alijam, Adanko, and Anagamba, which are more or less endogamous and have their own dialect, cattle breed, house types, and marriage system. Pastoralists in the region have been incorporated in the market economy for centuries and are linked to extensive livestock trade networks that cross the Chad Basin (Kerven 1992, Moritz 2003). However, pastoral systems have remained primarily subsistence-orientated rather than capitalist-orientated. Pastoralists sell animals when they have a need; their production goal is not to maximize profits (Moritz 2012).

Pastoral mobility is driven by seasonal variations in rainfall, which results in spatio-temporal variation in pastoral resources: forage and water. FulBe pastoralists in the far north region talk about four distinct seasons when they discuss their mobility patterns. The rainy season (duumol) runs from July through September with the main rains in July and August (loDDo). It is followed by the cold dry season, (daBBunde) from October to January and the hot dry season (ceedu) from March to May. June is a transition season (seeto) from dry to rainy season. One of the key resource areas in the region is the Logone floodplain (Scholte and Brouwer 2008), called Yaayre in Fulfulde, which is flooded by the Logone River and its branches from September until November (see Figure 10.1). After the water recedes in December, thousands of Arab and FulBe pastoralists from Cameroon, Nigeria and Niger move with more than 200,000 cattle into the floodplain making it one of the most important dry season grazing lands in the Chad Basin (Seignobos and Iyébi-Mandjek 2000). Many pastoralists remain there until the start of the rainy season, while most move either further north into the floodplain or south to the grazing lands that surround Lake Maga. Pastoralists find nutritious regrowth and surface water in the floodplain far into the dry season, when surrounding pastures have dried up. At the start of the rainy season, pastoralists return to the higher elevated dunes of the Diamaré or their respective countries. In the far north region, there is an extensive network of 'invisible' pastoral infrastructure that includes campsites, watering points, and transhumance corridors and allows mobile pastoralists to exploit the spatio-temporal variation in resources.

Pastoral infrastructure

Pastoral infrastructure is critical for supporting pastoral mobility in this open system, in particular transhumance corridors that allow pastoralists to move between seasonal grazing areas and exploit the spatio-temporal variation in forage throughout the Chad Basin. However, one of the problems is that the infrastructure of mobile pastoralists is often 'invisible' because they do not remain in one location throughout the year and do not leave many traces. For example, despite decades of geographic research (Boutrais 1984, Frechou 1966, Seignobos and Iyébi-Mandjek 2000), there are no traces of mobile pastoralists on maps or atlases. Instead their movements are indicated with broad arrows (as in example Figure 10.1). This invisibility is problematic because the existing pastoral infrastructure is often not recognized or protected, which allows farmers to convert campsites and transhumance routes into fields.

As part of a longitudinal, interdisciplinary study that examines how mobile pastoralists manage common-pool grazing resources, we have used GPS/GIS technology to document pastoral mobility as well as the infrastructure used to

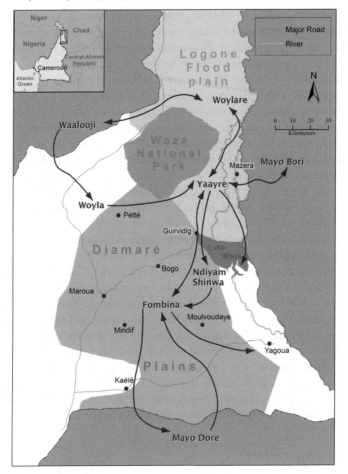

Figure 10.1 The Far North province of Cameroon. The arrows broadly indicate the general direction of the transhumance orbits of mobile pastoralists in our study area of the Logone Floodplain and the Diamaré Plains. There are currently no maps showing the pastoral infrastructure of campsites, watering points, and transhumance corridors (even though they are visible on satellite images, including Google Earth)

move within and between seasonal grazing areas, such as campsites, watering points, and transhumance corridors (Moritz *et al.* 2010).

> *Campsites.* Mobile pastoralists often return to the same campsite in a particular seasonal grazing area year after year. They set up their houses and corrals in these sites and their herds forage the surrounding pastures. The campsites are often slightly elevated and cleared from vegetation to protect humans and animals and close to a permanent water source for the young calves that stay behind in the camp during the day. Because pastoralists return to the same campsites over the years, cattle dung accumulates in the corrals, which makes

them attractive sites for farmers who seek to clear new fields for their crops. There are two kinds of campsites: transit and sojourn campsites. Transit campsites are found along transhumance corridors and used to move from one seasonal grazing area to another. Pastoralists only stay for one to three days in these campsites. Sojourn campsites are located in seasonal grazing areas and pastoralists spend up to three to six months in these sites.

Watering points. Access to water is critical for livestock in the dry season in arid and semi-arid rangelands. In the floodplain most watering places are natural and thus open for all – rivers, depressions, lakes – and located throughout the floodplain, while the artificial lakes dug by the Lake Chad Basin Commission (LCBC) are explicitly open for all pastoralists from the member states (Moritz *et al.* 2013). During the rainy season when mobile pastoralists are outside the floodplain, they find water in small, natural ponds throughout their grazing areas.

Transhumance corridors. When mobile pastoralists move with their animals to the Logone floodplain in October, they use a network of transhumance corridors that connect their rainy season grazing areas in the Diamaré to the dry season grazing areas of the floodplain (see Figure 10.1). Along these corridors there are watering points and transit campsites where pastoralists overnight for a day or two, before they move on. The corridors transect densely populated agricultural areas and one of the main threats to pastoral mobility has been the expansion of agricultural fields onto these corridors.

These campsites, watering points, and transhumance corridors are critical for sustainable management of rangelands because they allow pastoralists to move between and camp within seasonal grazing areas in the far north region of Cameroon as well as the larger Chad Basin. Below we will discuss how development organizations have attempted to delimit and protect these infrastructures in the far north region of Cameroon. But first we will describe pastoralists' use of these infrastructures and how they support the open pastoral system in the Chad Basin.

Open access, open systems in the Chad Basin

Mobile pastoralists in the region share a strong ethos of open access to common-pool grazing resources. They believe that every pastoralist has the same rights to use grazing lands, regardless of ethnicity, nationality, seniority, or socio-economic status. Pastoralists emphatically argue that access is free and open for everyone; it does not matter whether pastoralists are coming from Cameroon or Nigeria, whether they are newcomers or old-timers or whether they are FulBe or Arab. When asked about open access, pastoralists would say as a matter of fact, *na'i non, naa yimBe* 'it's [about] cattle, not [about] people', or *nagge nyaamataa nagge* 'cattle do not eat [other] cattle', meaning all cattle are equal and have equal access to the pastures (Moritz *et al.* 2013). For mobile pastoralists, keeping cattle is not only a way of making a living and a way of life, but one could argue that cattle are life because without them people cannot live as pastoralists. In this sense, to deny cattle access to grazing resources is to deny pastoralists life. This ethos of open access, which is shared among all mobile pastoralists in our study area, including absentee owners and their hired herders, informs how pastoralists coordinate their movements and use of common-pool grazing resources (Moritz *et al.* 2013).

Although pastoralists gain customary rights over campsites after two or three years of consecutive seasonal occupation, these rights do not give pastoralists exclusive access over the common-pool grazing resources surrounding the campsite. Thus, access to grazing lands is open, even when pastoralists have customary rights to campsites within these grazing lands. No one is obliged to ask for permission from traditional or governmental authorities or other pastoralists to set up camp near established campsites. This applies to all pastoralists, including newcomers from other groups or countries. Pastoralists may ask fellow pastoralists whether they can set up camp close by but this request cannot be refused. Moreover, many pastoralists do not ask out of principle or inform their neighbours about site decisions, not even when they set up camp 250 metres from another campsite. These rules are not limited to the floodplain; they also apply to the rainy season grazing areas in the Diamaré.

We have referred to this system as management of open access (Moritz *et al.* 2013), which we argue is not an oxymoron because there are clear rules about who has access to the common-pool grazing resources (all pastoralists) and who can be excluded (no one). The rules are reaffirmed in everyday practice every time pastoralists set up camps in new sites without asking. The ethos and practice of open access is a form of everyday management that regulates the use of common-pool resources in that there are two important outcomes: the emergence of an ideal-free distribution of mobile pastoralists in which the distribution of grazing pressure matches the distribution of grazing resources (Moritz *et al.* 2014), and the lack of major conflict among pastoralists (Scholte *et al.* 2006). These outcomes require the everyday commitment of pastoralists to the ethos and practice of open access. Pastoralists themselves talk about open access not in terms of an absence of rules, but in terms of rights for all. Moreover, these rules are meaningful to mobile pastoralists – without access to common-pool grazing resources they cannot survive in this semi-arid environment (Moritz *et al.* 2013).

In addition, the pastoral system in the far north region is also an open system in the sense that there are no social or ethnic boundaries. All who are committed to mobile pastoralism, in which the needs of animals are central, are members of the user group. And while there are distinct ethnic groups among pastoralists, these groups are not territorial, and the ethnic boundaries are permeable as people 'enter' ethnic groups that they share transhumance routes with (see also Bradburd 1992).

Legal and institutional context of rangeland governance

Central governments in the Chad Basin have generally been supportive of pastoralists' mobility and have guaranteed their open access to common-pool grazing resources. First, current laws support open access to common-pool grazing resources. Second, national and international policies protect transhumance corridors that allow pastoralists to move between seasonal grazing areas in the Chad Basin.

Grazing lands in Cameroon are legally state property (Ordinance N° 74-1 of 1974). However, the law explicitly gives all pastoralists the right to use these common-pool resources, unless the state uses these grazing lands for other purposes such as wildlife conservation or agricultural development projects. National laws thus support pastoralists' open access to grazing lands; provided pastoralists vaccinate their animals and pay their taxes, they cannot be denied access to these common-pool grazing resources.

In addition, the Lake Chad Basin Commission (LCBC) has been supporting the system of open access to common-pool grazing resources since its creation in the 1960s, by the four countries bordering Lake Chad: Cameroon, Chad, Niger, and Nigeria. The member countries recognize the importance of the livestock for the economy in the Chad Basin and its primary concerns are coordination of veterinary controls and facilitating livestock trade (and thus livestock movements) between countries. In addition, the commission aims to regulate and control the use of water and other natural resources in the basin and to initiate, promote, and coordinate natural resource development projects and research. International agreements between Lake Chad Basin Commission member countries enable freedom of movement for pastoralists in the Chad Basin, provided they have vaccinated their animals and paid the local and national taxes. This allows pastoralists from Chad, Niger, Nigeria, Cameroon, and more recently the Central African Republic and Sudan which joined the LCBC, to travel freely within the Chad Basin if they can show their certificate of vaccination and tax receipts.

While there are no specific laws concerning pastoralists' use of grazing lands in Cameroon, there are a number of decrees and ordinances that are currently used by organizations working with mobile pastoralists to protect grazing lands and transhumance corridors within the far north region. The most important and most widely used decree concerns the resolution of conflicts between agricultural and pastoral uses of land (n° 78-263). The decree specifies the procedures for settling agro-pastoral disputes at the local or district level, as well as how the committee works that is in charge of organizing the agricultural and pastoral spaces. A number of the activities of these local committees are: delimiting agricultural and pastoral zones, enforcing the boundaries of these zones, designating transhumance corridors, taking measures to avoid land-use conflicts, and resolving conflicts between agricultural and pastoral uses of land.

There are some indications that Cameroon is moving towards a comprehensive 'pastoral code' that would describe and regulate pastoral use of grazing lands, but this new law has not been voted on yet, and so most organizations working to protect pastoral infrastructure have used the decree concerning the resolution of agro-pastoral conflicts (n° 78-263) to achieve their goals.

Protection of transhumance corridors

In the last 20 years, development and other non-government organizations have used the decree for settling agro-pastoral conflicts (n° 78-263) to delimit and protect the pastoral infrastructure in the far north region of Cameroon. For example, at the end of the 1990s, an international development organization, the Waza Logone Project (IUCN), designated pastoral and agricultural zones and delimited transhumance corridors that pastoralists use to enter to the Logone floodplain at the beginning of the dry season (Kari and Scholte 2001). The Waza Logone Project's main role was to motivate and organize the different stakeholders including: pastoralists, agriculturalists, and traditional and governmental authorities, to delimit and protect (through consensus) transhumance corridors, overnight campsites, and pastoral zones. The protection of the pastoral infrastructure was critical because it concerned an important bottleneck in the network that was used by between 50,000 and 100,000 cattle every year. Since then, the same process has been used by a number of Cameroonian non-governmental organizations advocating for pastoralists to protect other transhumance corridors and pastoral zones, in particular the Fédération des Eleveurs des Bovins (FEB) and the Centre d'Appui à la Recherche et au Pastoralisme (CARPA). Today about 150 kilometres of transhumance corridors have been protected through this process, although this is still less than 10 per cent of the transhumance corridors in the region.

Most recently, CARPA led the effort to protect another critical transhumance corridor that mobile pastoralists take to move to the Logone floodplain (Bebisse 2011). The corridor was blocked by a forest created by the Cameroonian government. CARPA brought all the stakeholders together, i.e., everyone with an interest in agro-pastoral conflicts, which included representatives from the agricultural and pastoral communities, representatives of the different government services (e.g., veterinary services, police), traditional authorities of all the villages along the corridor, municipal authorities (e.g., mayor and council members), and the government authorities (e.g., district head or sous-préfet). The process involved surveying the corridor, identifying conflicts along the corridor, signing an agreement, delimiting the corridor with cement markers, and the creation of a local oversight (or management) committee to continue dialogue between the different user groups and support the participatory management of the corridors (Bebisse 2011).

As there are various conflicts of interest between the different stakeholders – the most important ones being political conflicts between the traditional and governmental authorities (Moritz 2006b) – the process takes considerable time and negotiation. Part of the problem is the situation of legal pluralism in which national laws are often trumped by traditional practices. For example, while the district chief (sous-préfet) is officially in charge of land rights, in practice traditional authorities are the ones allocating land rights and adjudicating in conflicts over land in the far north region (Teyssier *et al.* 2003). This adds to the challenges of bringing the stakeholders together and getting them to agree on the delimitation of the corridors.

The process is also relatively expensive; not so much because of the hundreds of cement markers but because of the costs of getting everyone to the field, which includes a daily rate for the different officials as well as transportation costs (often a euphemism for informal payments). While local non-governmental organizations have been responsible for the organization of the process and the negotiations between the different stakeholders, the financial support has primarily come from outsiders, in particular research and development organizations interested in protecting pastoral mobility (including our own research projects). The reliance on external funds also raises questions about the sustainability of these interventions. Due to the nature of the development funding cycle – e.g., limited funds, short duration, pressure for immediate and tangible results, uncertainty of renewal – there is often no meaningful participation and investment of the local stakeholders (Igoe 2004). What then remains of these projects are the physical cement markers, but no sustainable solution to the problem of conflicting land uses (Catley *et al.* 2013).

However, pastoralists have also initiated the process and raised funds themselves. For example, mobile pastoralists have approached the traditional chief of Kolora, someone who has advocated often on behalf of mobile pastoralists, and CARPA to help them protect the corridor Kolora-Kobo-Horlong, which is a 16-kilometre track in the overall network of transhumance corridors and used by relatively small number of camps and households. The pastoralists also succeeded in securing access to an artificial lake for watering cattle near Kobo and a prohibition of cultivation within a 1.5-kilometre radius of the lake. In the agreement, the parties also designated agricultural and pastoral zones in order to prevent encroachment of farms and fields into grazing lands. The total costs were 2.5 million FCFA or about $5,000, of which 80 per cent came from pastoralists themselves, with 20 per cent of matching funds from our research project.

The protection of transhumance corridors described above is no panacea. The process is not finished with the delimitation of the corridors and the creation of oversight committees. Despite the protection, oversight committees and cement markers, there continues to be encroachment of fields onto the grazing areas, campsites, and transhumance corridors. One of the reasons why the delimitation of corridors currently does not offer a permanent solution is that the use of the decree for settling agro-pastoral conflicts (n° 78-263) to delimit the corridors and pastoral zones does not give them legal protection. This is only achieved when the governor or the divisional officer (préfet) signs an administrative act (arrêté) that specifies that the delimited grazing lands or corridors be exclusively reserved for pastoral use. With an administrative act, trespassers can be taken to court; without an administrative act, the only recourse is arbitration between the parties by the agro-pastoral committee. This means that continuous follow up by advocates of mobile pastoralists, e.g., CARPA and FEB, is necessary to prod the authorities into action when there are problems along the corridors. The transhumance corridor delimited by the Waza Logone Project in the 1990s, for example, is still there but fields have slowly expanded and now there is no longer the legally required clearance of 25 metres on each side. The cement markers have disappeared or are located in sorghum fields.

Local organizations like CARPA, FEB, and the Observatoire du Pastoralisme dans l'Extrême-Nord (OPEN) are focusing their efforts on educating stakeholders and other authorities about pastoral systems and the importance of mobility, developing and promoting new laws and policies for sustainable management of pastoral resources. In addition, they encourage the participation of pastoralists in the management of pastoral resources and infrastructure. The limitations of the current approach are that it is primarily driven by the organizations that work on behalf of mobile pastoralists. Pastoralists attend the process, but they are not taking an active role. One of the main reasons is that very few mobile pastoralists in the far north region have any formal education. They do not speak the official languages (French, English) and do not have a good understanding of the laws and bureaucratic processes. The situation in the far north is very different from the northwest of Cameroon, which has a long tradition of pastoralists receiving formal education and pastoralists organizing themselves in advocacy groups like the Mbororo Social and Cultural Development Association (MBOSCUDA) (Davis 1995, Pelican 2008). The problem is not limited to pastoralists attending the process; farmers were also not well represented and implicated in the process of delimiting the corridors. We observed heated discussions between farmers and the authorities during their visits to the field, as the former felt excluded from the process (Bebisse 2011). The limited involvement of both pastoralists and farmers in the process has implications for the sustainability of the existing infrastructures.

Discussion: governance of open systems

What are the implications of management of open systems (Moritz *et al.* 2013) for the governance of pastoral infrastructure, and in particular the protection and delimitation of transhumance corridors?

First, because we are dealing with an open system in which mobile pastoralists are not bounded to one particular place, the protection of pastoral resources and infrastructure should be for all pastoralists (and not just for current users) and all pastoralists should have the right to use the associated infrastructure of campsites, watering points, and transhumance corridors. Because mobile pastoralists in the Chad Basin operate in an open system, it is critical that mobility is supported at the supra-national level of the Lake Chad Basin Commission as well as national, regional and local levels. However, currently there is a tension between laws and policies at the national and supra-national level, which support pastoral mobility in an open system, and its implementation at the local and regional levels. The interests at the national and supra-national level, in support of pastoral mobility, are often not aligned with those at the regional and local levels, where there are governmental as well as traditional authorities with primarily agricultural constituencies. For example, at the national level, authorities benefit from the free movement of cattle because of taxes and other levies on pastoralists and livestock traders, whereas at the local level, authorities derive most of their income from agricultural populations.

Second, the delimitation of corridors has the potential to reduce pastoralists' flexibility in mobility. The annual transhumance movements between the rainy season grazing lands in the Diamaré plains and the dry season grazing lands in the Logone floodplain have a long history, going back at least 60 years (Mouchet 1960). But the routes that pastoralists took to reach the floodplain have changed considerably in that period (and continue to change) following major land-use changes along these routes. For pastoralists it is most critical to be able to move from one seasonal grazing area to another, and the corridors are primarily a means to an end. The recent history of transhumance corridors shows that while some corridors are being closed off, new ones are opening up. Transhumance orbits change over time because of social and ecological reasons and so do the transhumance corridors that take pastoralists to different seasonal grazing areas in the Chad Basin.

The infrastructure of transhumance corridors in the far north region of Cameroon, where we conduct our research, reflects the openness and flexibility of this pastoral system as it facilitates the movements within and between seasonal grazing areas. Recognizing the importance of mobility for sustainable development of pastoral systems, development organizations working with mobile pastoralists have engaged in several projects in which transhumance corridors were delimited and demarcated, as we described above. However, the protected status has not prevented encroachment on these routes; cement markers delimiting the corridors are now located in sorghum fields. In response, pastoralists are using new routes, which they claim are sometimes better than the ones that they lost.

Third, it is also important to realize that the delimitation of corridors has its own set of problems because it fixes not only the infrastructure, but also the institutions that govern these infrastructures. In some ways, the process of delimitation of corridors and pastoral zones gives pastoralists a sense of entitlement to particular corridors or grazing areas, which makes them more likely to appeal to the authorities and the oversight committees to resolve conflicts, whereas they used to be more flexible in their resolution of conflicts in the past (Drent forthcoming). The appeal to authorities often has the opposite effect and leads to permanent conflict that is perpetuated by the authorities seeking rents from both herders and farmers (Moritz 2006b). More importantly, the involvement of authorities reduces the options for local user groups of herders and farmers to find their own negotiated and flexible low-stakes solutions for the conflicts that are inherent to the mosaic of land use characteristic of the Sahelian and Sudanian zones of West and Central Africa. In their comparison of herder-farmer conflicts in northwest Cameroon and Burkina Faso, Dafinger and Pelican (2006) observed a similar phenomenon. After the creation of agricultural and pastoral zones in northwest Cameroon the number of disputes decreased but their intensity increased and they tended to escalate in larger conflicts. Dafinger and Pelican argued that the creation of land-use zones reduced daily negotiations between herders and farmers and their ability to resolve them without involvement of the authorities (2006). We see similar developments in the far north region of Cameroon, with the protection of transhumance corridors.

We have argued that while it is important to protect pastoralists' rights of access to grazing resources in an open system, this is not the same as delimiting pastoral infrastructures. This is one of the key lessons of the 'paradox of pastoral land tenure' – pastoralists' need for secure access to pasture and water but also flexibility in resource use (Fernández-Giménez 2002). The critical lesson here is that governance should be focused on supporting the flexibility of pastoral mobility in an open system, and this is not achieved by mapping, fixing and delimiting the corridors, which may even have the opposite effect. The desire to map, fix and delimit the 'invisible pastoral infrastructure' is an example of what the political scientist James Scott has described as a modernist legibility project in his book *Seeing like a State* (1998). One of the assumptions guiding development projects, including our own previous efforts, is that the invisibility is a problem, and that by mapping and delimiting the infrastructure – making it visible and legible – transhumance corridors can be protected. However, we argue that these legibility projects have their own limitations because it fixes infrastructures and institutions where flexibility in movements and conflict resolution are more appropriate.

Conclusion

What is then our proposed approach? How to protect pastoralists' rights to resources as well as their freedom to move? The protection of seasonal grazing areas and transhumance corridors is still important. But rather than thinking about the delimitation of zones and corridors as the end of the process (or conversation), it may be more useful to think of the delimitation as the means of the process, or the start of a conversation about the management of common-pool resources. In this view, the protection and delimitation of one particular transhumance corridor is not a permanent solution; it is an argument for pastoralists' user rights in a broader conversation about the management of common-pool resources. In this conversation, there will be counter-arguments and the likely result is that the path of the corridor will likely change. However, the end goal for pastoralists in this conversation is not to protect particular resources, but to protect their general user rights and their freedom to move.

11 Strengthening communal governance of rangeland in Northern Kenya

Guyo Roba

Overview

Garba Tula District of Isiolo County is a mainly pastoralist area based on extensive livestock keeping across communally managed rangelands. Boran pastoralists maintain a pastoral livelihood as well as conserve the land for use by large wildlife populations. Change in governance arrangements have led to several degradation processes which are largely derived from bad decision making, like appearance of elite capture or the misappropriation of key resources. These processes are collectively weakening the traditional governance system disturbing production, infrastructure, grazing routes and land access. All this leads to land degradation and associated impacts on livelihoods dependent on that resource.

IUCN, in collaboration with local actors like the Resource Advocacy Programme (RAP), government agencies and international institutions, such as the International Institute for Environment and Development (IIED), and with the involvement of local government and institutions are conducting a participatory approach with two goals: first to legalize traditional governance systems and second to develop participatory tools for rangeland planning. The result is a way to enable the strength of traditional grazing management and formal endorsement of the traditional rules and regulations. The complicity and involvement of both local pastoralists population and local authorities should support the sustainability of the process.

Keywords: governance, rangelands, land management, pastoralism, participatory approaches

Background

Garba Tula District of Isiolo County, like many other arid and semi-arid districts of Northern Kenya, is populated by a majority pastoralist population who practise extensive livestock keeping across communally managed rangelands. These rangelands are home to approximately 40,000 predominantly Boran pastoralists who maintain a pastoral livelihood as well as conserve the land for use by large wildlife populations, in this important area between Meru and Kora national parks and Bisan Adi game reserve (Davies and Roba, 2010). Land in Garba Tula District, like many other communally managed resources, has been held in trust by the county council since the introduction of the Trust Land Act in 1963. Despite the intention that county councils would be accountable to the communities and make decisions based on traditional values, the Trust Land system has in reality allowed elite capture, and misappropriation of key resource areas for individual benefit, with local communities poorly informed of their rights within this system (Davies and Roba, 2010). The resultant impact on communally managed rangelands of Garba Tula has been negative, with a weakening of the traditional governance system, promotion of individual tenure systems, disruption of grazing routes and resource access and resultant reduction of pasture available for grazing and intensification of land use. All this leads to land degradation and severe impacts on livelihood dependent on that resource.

Despite the importance of the Boran customary rangeland management system to the sustainable management of this areas and its resources these traditional systems are rarely recognized by the State or the temporary users who access some shared resources during the dry seasons to make seasonal use of the resources. This lack of recognition and the increasing influence of the State are weakening these institutions and the leadership they provide in terms of rangeland management. The ultimate weakening of the traditional governance systems, as well as changes in land use, promotion of individualization of land and inappropriate resource development have caused damage to the way in which resources have been managed in Garba Tula and the rangelands are now increasingly affected by a range of threats such as deforestation, unmanaged fires, overgrazing and invasive alien species (IUCN, 2011b). In addition, communities are often excluded from planning and decision-making processes on natural resources, as more varied and influential interest groups seek to utilize and appropriate the land (Hesse and Pattison, 2013).

Despite the above current and historical challenges, changes are occurring in the governance system in Kenya that provide important opportunities for pastoralists and other communities who rely on communally managed landscapes. The evolving governance system in Kenya has provided additional strength to improve natural resource governance in Garba Tula. Given the focus on the devolution of responsibilities for natural resource management to local communities in the constitution, the local government were open and facilitative to processes like development of bylaws based on customary rules and norms.

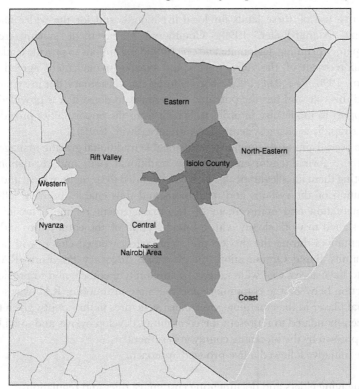

Figure 11.1 Location of Isiolo County on a map of Kenya

Underpinning this shift in Kenya's governance arrangements is the empowerment of grassroots institutions to enable them to take greater responsibility for management of natural resources and to position them squarely within the devolved governance architecture. The initiative outlined here sought to improve natural resource governance to support better livelihood security and ecosystem management in the drylands of Garba Tula.[1] It focused on multiple objectives:

1 Decision makers and stakeholders have increased awareness and policy guidance for dryland management.
2 Improved capacity of local communities, institutions and government for more effective participatory decision making in natural resources.
3 More participatory collaborative arrangements and institutions to manage dryland ecosystem resources.

Approach

The approach is based on the fundamental importance of communal management systems to the sustainable management of arid rangeland resources and the productive use of these lands for local livelihoods, and for the wider national economy (Niamir-Fuller, 1999). Communal management systems require participatory planning, legitimate and recognized institutions to provide leadership and enforcement of the rules, norms and grazing management agreed upon (Ostrom, 1990; Roe *et al.*, 2009). For centuries the Customary Boran system has fulfilled this role and has the potential to continue to do so if it is provided with the support to modernize in order to benefit from the opportunities provided by Kenya's rapidly evolving systems of governance (Swift, 1991).

The overall aim of the initiative was to enable traditional grazing management and secure formal endorsement of the traditional rules and regulations, by translating them into 'legal speak'. This was intended to strengthen local and State recognition of the systems and institutions and thus enable the more effective implementation and enforcement of the management regime. The initiative was designed to work closely with a broad section of the community and their representatives during the process and deliberately worked closely with a local Community Based Organization, the Resource Advocacy Program[2] (RAP), in order to have access to a wide range of community members and to provide the connection between the community and the State institutions. RAP was seen as a crucial player in the emerging governance structures in the county, given that it had been mandated to represent the community, develop bylaws and to lobby for their approval by the incoming county government.

The initiative followed a five-pronged approach:

1   Engaging elders and documenting customary rules and regulations.
2   Negotiating and drafting bylaws based on customary rules and regulations.
3   Adoption of bylaws by the county government.
4   Participatory resource mapping and planning between government and the community.
5   Promotion of community-based management plans to investors and development partners.

The work of developing bylaws was designed to go hand in hand with the work on rangeland planning, which would provide a mechanism for implementing many aspects of the bylaws, and a delineated landscape for which the rules and regulations would apply. The steps in bylaw development and rangeland planning are outlined here in more detail.

Bylaw development: this is a multiple stage iterative process of dialogue, collecting, and distilling information for developing the bylaw. The initial documentation was done through discussion with elders at different grazing unit levels. This information was validated through an extensive discussion process until a zero draft was developed which was then fed back to selected, respected elders in an initial validation workshop, based on which amendments were made. Subsequent drafts, along with an accompanying political opinion document have been peer reviewed among knowledgeable legal and political experts. The process of developing the Act and Regulations have greatly increased the awareness among local communities of the value and potential of their customary system and the opportunities they have for playing a more active role in the management of the natural resources they sustain. The communities involved in the process now have a good appreciation of the provisions in the new constitution and the strength that a community bylaw would give them in managing the use of and access to resources in Garba Tula, with or without a recognized tenure system. The process of establishing community land tenure systems in Kenya has enabled the learning from the Garba Tula process to be taken further within the debates on how to operationalize such a system in terms of systems, institutions and areas. It has also encouraged communities in Garba Tula to consider how the process of developing a community bylaw can position them to be able to pilot a community Land tenure model in the district, having considered some of the fundamental issues around who governs what, and how.

Rangeland mapping and planning: these exercises were initially completed in all five *Dhedas* (traditional grazing units), through participatory community workshops and later, with the support of additional partners, rangeland mapping and planning were conducted in all *Dhedas* in Isiolo County.[3] This enabled communities and development practitioners to have a solid, shared understanding of the landscape use and dynamics and its management at a broad scale. These maps have been used as base information for the development of the GIS maps under the IIED initiative. The rangeland plans were developed with the participation of local traditional elders, local natural resources institutions, members of the government planning department, as well as local line ministries. These plans are informing water infrastructure development and it is hoped that these plans will be adopted by the county government as recognized natural resource plans for the county against which future investments and development will be delivered. In addition, the process has helped communities to assess multiple resource users and created avenues to improve collaboration and co-existence among competing user groups.

The fundamental approach used is that of effective participation. The initiative sought to give communities the skills to engage in decision-making processes, through the endorsement of their own legitimate systems of management and use, as well as building their capacities in new skills of management and planning. The approach is couched in the tenets of participatory approaches that result in:

- More durable solutions.
- Ownership of decision made.
- More contextual analysis and responses.
- Quality decision making.
- Systems of accountability.

It also sought to model more appropriate methods for planning within drylands, adopting landscape-level approaches to analysis and mapping that a) fit with the traditional management arrangements and b) supported the continued need for mobility and seasonal use of resources.

Significant change

Owing to the participatory approaches modelled through this initiative there has been a general improvement in awareness among decision makers and local people on the value of community engagement and the benefit of linking traditional and modern approaches to planning. Relationships between local people and government have improved, and there is a much greater appreciation of the indigenous knowledge and practice. The rangeland planning processes not only highlighted the vast array of knowledge held by the local communities but also the fundamental logic behind the way resources have been traditionally managed.

Participatory environmental planning

As part of efforts to improve natural resource management, the initiative has helped bridge the gap between State and customary institutions modelling and institutionalizing participatory approaches to natural resource planning and implementation that build on the knowledge of the indigenous system and operate at a landscape level: something which is imperative within these dryland ecosystems. The project has conducted rangeland planning and mapping processes with community members, government officials, representatives of indigenous institutions, NGOs in the areas and representatives of women and youth groups in five Dedhas.

These five Dhedas were chosen to ensure full coverage within the Isiolo County and thus contribution to county-wide planning. In total, close to 100 people directly benefited from this training with over 40,000 indirect beneficiaries. The

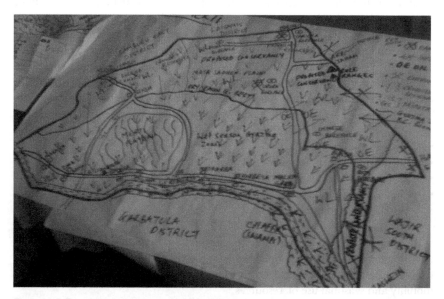

Figure 11.2 Rangeland vision map for Merti Dheda

participatory mapping processes enable communities to think broadly about the status of the resources they utilize, to consider the multiple priorities and needs of different user groups and the challenges they are currently facing in ensuring their sustainable management. Plans were then developed for each of the five sites, identifying clear activities, and responsible parties for improving the management of natural resources in the area. Issues such as institutional systems and financial accountability measures are also identified, which are often lacking in community-based institutions and which are crucial for legitimacy and accountability.

Through participatory natural resource mapping and planning processes, local communities have understood and enacted their rights to engage in decision-making processes that determine how natural resources will be utilized and managed in the future. The engagement of the district and county-level government in the processes has given the process legitimacy beyond previous 'project-focused' community plans. Communities have been given a voice in the design of a government-recognized planning process and have been able to express their opinions on future interventions. It is these communities, and their representatives that will now be active in the devolved systems of NR management being established in the area, and these communities who are giving endorsement for planned development activities in the area by a range of different actors.

The maps and plans resulting from this work are also guiding future discussions on natural resource and land use in the county. Through collaboration with the IIED, the maps have been digitized and will be utilized within the county planning units, and will be available to the upcoming County Climate Change committees to guide decisions on public investments and support to community proposals to improve resilience and adaptive capacities. Outside the county government the products and methodologies from these planning and managing dryland natural resources are also being taken up by donors and partners alike within Kenya and the region: the plans have been used to guide the work of others working in Isiolo, and the approaches and tools used have been adopted in Garissa County and in the Karamoja region of neighbouring Uganda.

The engagement of the district and county-level government in the processes, through training of trainers in the participatory methodology, has given the process legitimacy beyond previous 'project-focused' community plans. Communities have been given a voice in the design of a government-recognized planning process and have been able to express their opinions on future interventions. It is these communities, and their representatives that will now be active in the devolved systems of natural resource management being established in the area through the bylaw development, and these communities who are giving endorsement for planned development activities in the area by a range of different actors.

These participatory methods for promoting community consultation, as well as the landscape-level approaches to planning, have also been noticeably taken up by others working in the area. IIED have utilized the maps and plans developed in this programme during their engagement and are essentially building on the foundation of the work achieved. Others, including the international NGOs Action Contre la Faim and FH-Kenya, have changed their focus due to the content of the plans. The donor agency the Swiss Development Corporation, through their new 'Water for Livestock' project, have borrowed heavily from rangeland plans to identify suitable water infrastructure development sites and actively sought to ensure their processes are more consultative, that final decisions are validated by government and communities, and that activities are based on priorities identified within already developed rangeland maps and plans. This change put communities and community institutions at the centre of decision making in natural resource use and infrastructural development.

The long-term, consultative process of bylaw development, not only highlighted the robustness of the traditional system, but also the provisions within the new legislation for local communities, and their traditional institutions to engage more effectively in decision making and governance processes. The dialogues held at county and the national levels were an opportunity for community members to further this understanding, as debates were held on the opportunities and progress being made in the devolution process and the establishment of community land tenure. Yet those same community members were also able to share their experiences, and their opinions on the approach used within this project thereby disseminating the lessons further, to partners, and visiting groups from other ASAL areas, and raising the credibility of the community representatives. This provides evidence of a general increase in awareness of rights among communities.

Finally, despite the bylaw not having yet been passed by county government, the initiative has managed to draft a piece of legislation that is owned and endorsed by communities, and which government has also played an active role in developing. If and when this is passed by the county assembly it will be an important step forward for both community rights in decision making, as well as the promotion of more appropriate governance mechanisms for dryland environments.

Lessons and sustainability

Responding to the needs expressed by communities: one of the key reasons that this project succeeded in achieving change in attitudes and behaviours among local people and government, and that progress has been made towards developing clear legislations and systems for improved governance, is because the project was responding to a clear request from the communities. This whole initiative began with discussions with community elders on how to strengthen their rights in decision making on how their land and resources are managed and utilized, independent of any project implementation. As such, these communities and their representatives remained active participants in the initiative, promoting the processes and outputs throughout.

Working through legitimate community organizations/institutions: these communities elected Resource Advocacy Programme (RAP) as their clear representative for the project. While this has had some limitations in terms of capacity and effectiveness, it has ensured easy communication between IUCN and communities, and also between communities and the government. The outstanding challenge is around the capacity of RAP to be an effective interlocutor for the community. RAP being a nascent institution has a number of operational capacities which at times undermine the process. Thus a lot of support needed to be dedicated to building their capacity.

Timely response to the evolving governance situation: the project responded to the evolving governance situation within Kenya, and sought to position communities to be able to take up the opportunities provided for by the new constitution and land law. Again while this posed some challenges, due to changing county structures, delays with elections and loss of key project champions within government, it also provided a fertile ground for testing governance approaches and engaging in broader debates on appropriate governance models for the drylands of Kenya.

Constant engagement and consultation with the communities and government: this was enabled by partnership with RAP which operates among the communities and is effectively part of the community. This constant engagement and promotion of participatory approaches in decision making and planning is more effective in achieving attitudinal change and also enabled partners to be responsive to changing circumstances and opportunities.

Lessons on evidence: governance processes often require a long time and the impacts of multiple processes may be felt in the far distant future. Therefore tracking evidence in the short term is invariably complex and difficult, while monitoring for long-term evidence is often beyond the scope of donor-funded projects.

Sustainability

To ensure sustainability of service, the initiative is implemented through an existing local partner RAP. RAP is a locally based natural resource management institution that got its mandate directly from the local elders and communities. The capacity that RAP has gained through the project will enable it to continue to work on governance issues in the area and push forward the processes that require finalisation.

In addition, the training of government staff and partners on participatory rangeland planning and resource management ensured that learning was being taken up within sustainable government institutions that could roll out the approach on a broader scale. Through the use of the plans within the newly formed Climate Change Adaptation Committees it is also hoped that they will go on to influence government planning within the larger county.

The decision to work towards developing a new Act and set of rules and regulations is in itself an effort to ensure sustainability of impact as it sought to put in place a system that would ensure continued community engagement in decision making and management. The Garba Tula model will also continue to play an important role in the debate around the Customary Institutions Bill. Several laws are currently proposed for community land and the role of traditional institutions/customary law in the new legal dispensation over natural resources remains crucial. Many institutions have expressed an interest in using

Isiolo County, and Garba Tula District more specifically, as a pilot for the new community land law system, given all the work that has already been done on identifying and strengthening community institutions and systems, and linking this to clearly defined rangelands and resources. There is a strong possibility that the county government, and the new county governor (who in fact reviewed the bylaws in a different capacity before his appointment) will be in support of such future ventures in order to put Garba Tula and Isiolo County on the devolved governance map.

Conclusion

Natural resource governance work requires a long gestation period to produce required impacts and often requires high levels of skills and human resource input compared to infrastructural interventions and such investments. The process requires more patience than donor projects can typically exercise and requires a high degree of community leadership that also proves challenging for typical project-driven approaches. It is critical to devolve power to the community and this effectively disempowers the external agent: where the agent exercises too much influence they may compromise the essence of the initiative. Although project funds can make a valuable contribution, they must remain subordinate to the overall process.

Governance processes are very hard to monitor and this invariably creates a barrier or disincentive to investment from donors. However, if the governance arrangement is previously identified and space is created for adequate dialogue at various levels, the subsequent processes tend to be easier and much faster. Although long-term impacts may not be felt for several years, when such results do begin to manifest, they can grow exponentially, based on community-wide trust in an improved governance system.

Notes

1 The initiative was implemented by IUCN, the International Union for the Conservation of Nature.
2 RAP is a community trust established through a mandate of elders to spearhead natural resource governance initiatives.
3 Main support was provided by the International Institute for Environment and Development (IIED).

12 Searching for extensive livestock governance in inland northwest of Spain

Achievements of two case studies in Castile-León

Pedro M. Herrera

Briefing

The centre of Spain, like the whole Iberian Peninsula, holds a wide pastoralist heritage, as a result of the strong economic influence pastoralism has had in its history and the mix of cultures that contributed to develop highly efficient models of husbandry and land management based on extensive grazing. The influence has been so intense that the current processes of abandonment of rural environments and the loss of traditional activity, furthermore than generating unemployment and migration from livestock linked communities, is also leading to a lack of valuable habitats and ecosystems dependent on pastoralist practices.

Starting from this historical perspective (evoking the times of the Islamic occupation and the 'Mesta'), this chapter unravels the actual state of extensive livestock production in northern central Spain, describing the drivers of a deep crisis that is affecting both the traditional rural way of life and the ecosystems supporting it.

Finally, it focuses on the developing groundswell (partially the inheritance of the transhumance recovery groups from the early 1980s) that is trying to mobilize social, ecological and economic support for pastoralists and extensive farmers. The report also describes some initiatives and new proposals geared by this supporting movement to allow and promote pastoralism and extensive livestock production to improve pastoralists' livelihoods and their role in land governance, sustainable development and conservation.

The northwestern Iberian pastoralist culture: the extensive livestock farming tradition in Spain

Pastoralism has been anchored in Iberian culture since prehistoric times. The Iberian Peninsula shows a remarkable ecological background where movements and seasonal migrations are boosted by climatic and geological issues. Two key aspects reinforce this statement, the first being the Mediterranean climate forcing animals to move seasonally, looking for better feeding areas. The second is the transverse disposition of mountain chains interrupting the North-South paths but allowing up-down movements along altitudinal gradients.

Many pastoralism experts refer its historical origins to people from the Palaeolithic era following the great herds of wild herbivores along those seasonal migrations (Garzón, 1992). Palaeolithic people followed the great herbivore movements, using the same shelters and surveillance spots over and over, like those found in Atapuerca related to these migratory ways (Santos *et al.,*, 2011). Transition to the Neolithic age might have preserved the same ways and infrastructure (shelters, springs, ponds, mountain passes) lying in the origin of the actual network of livestock tracks (Ibarrola, 2008).

Some Celtic/Gaelic tribes present in the North Iberian Peninsula around the fall of the Roman Empire were mobile herders (Montserrat and Fillat, 1990). Thus, the tension between pastoralists and farmers, symbolized by the Celtic and Iberian tribes' contact, developed a complex mix of production systems (Montserrat, 2007). After the Arab invasion of the eighth century, the cold lands of the north were briefly assigned to Berber tribes; they left behind a deep footprint in the region after heading back to Africa, including land tenure systems that have survived for centuries. Some of those regulations (e.g. the *sistema de hojas* or 'patch system') established the basis for transhumance and transterminance.[1]

After the Reconquest, Alfonso X, known as *El Sabio* (the Wise) founded *La Mesta* in 1276, which introduced a key organization for the development of herding in Spain. *La Mesta* was a core organization of the Castilian Crown (Klein, 1979), that lasted over six centuries and rose to extraordinary levels of power and influence until its dissolution in the nineteenth century. Spanish pastoralism, including transhumance and the network of livestock corridors, was deeply rooted in society under *La Mesta*'s command. However, it was not a social institution but a powerful tool of political and economic influence. As such, it was controlled by nobility and they forced kings to act at their will and imposed a privilege system that energized conflict throughout the country. Transhumant shepherds were the elite of this system, acquiring several privileges with royal support that made them admired, envied and hated (Valdivielso, 1998).

After the fall of *La Mesta* in the nineteenth century, the politicians of the Enlightenment Age started to develop agricultural policies to boost agriculture through livestock production (García Sanz, 1994 and 1978).The system of livestock production changed to a more settled one to profit from animal power, until the twentieth century. In the meantime, pastoralists kept on moving their herds following the ancient ways with only a portion of their former influence.

During the 1960s, Spain started to industrialize farming, which significantly changed the agricultural sector by concentrating and intensifying production. Also, intensive livestock production based on external inputs and breeds started to substitute extensive systems (Banco Mundial/FAO, 1966). That also started the process of abandonment and migration (Domínguez, 2001). In 1986, Spain became a member of the European Union and thus joined the Common Agricultural Policy, which is currently the main driver of agriculture and livestock in the country. The consolidation of the new industrial system has brought about a huge increase in production and livestock numbers, providing for the demands of the expanding urban society (Lasanta, 2010) while driving traditional farming to a deep crisis and to the loss of prestige, legitimacy and influence. From the 1960s to the 1990s the extensive livestock breeding sector moved from being highly respected and influential to being a marginal part of the agricultural sector. Extensive farmers were considered to be troublemakers by the newly constituted forest and environmental administration and were accused by environmentalists of being a significant source of land degradation.

Nevertheless, extensive livestock production survived all of these changes and kept its heritage and culture, remaining in the marginal rural areas of the Iberian Peninsula. However, the low costs and marginal distribution contributed to their survival, skipping some of the greatest problems of industrial livestock and keeping active extensive models adapted to local conditions, landscape friendly and able to provide valuable ecosystem services.

Most European countries embody remnants of traditional land-management system, including transhumant shepherds and other extensive farming structures, but Spain hosts a great variety of systems with several species, land-management tools, tenure rights and cultural heritage, which confers this country a special significance in the European context.

Current challenges for extensive livestock farmers and pastoralists

Extensive farming models promote sustainable livestock management while maintaining high natural value areas, contributing to biodiversity, conserving habitats of interest, preventing wildfires, conserving infrastructures, restoring ecosystems, improving rangeland richness and maturity, and providing other environmental services that extensive farmers are not actually being rewarded for (García and Entretantos Foundation, 2012). Numerous high natural value habitats, ecosystems and corridors in Spain, widely distributed throughout the country, are sustained by extensive farming (Oppermann *et al.*, 2012). Moreover, research during the last decade has shown a significant relationship between extensive livestock farming, biodiversity and environmental quality (Lasanta, 2010). Herding activities such as grazing, irrigating meadows and mowing have developed a mosaic landscape, contributed to maintaining woods or preventing wildfires. Moreover, this extensive livestock produces healthy food, raw materials and manure that contribute to agricultural soils' fertility.

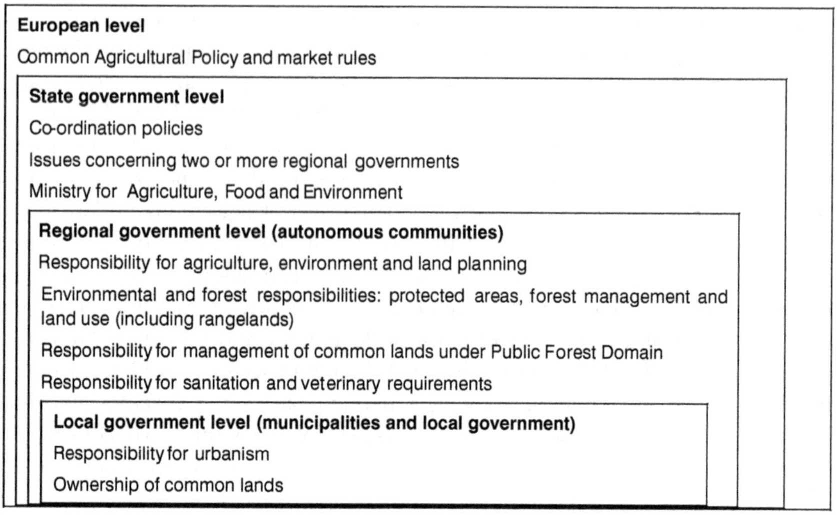

European level
Common Agricultural Policy and market rules

State government level
Co-ordination policies
Issues concerning two or more regional governments
Ministry for Agriculture, Food and Environment

Regional government level (autonomous communities)
Responsibility for agriculture, environment and land planning
Environmental and forest responsibilities: protected areas, forest management and land use (including rangelands)
Responsibility for management of common lands under Public Forest Domain
Responsibility for sanitation and veterinary requirements

Local government level (municipalities and local government)
Responsibility for urbanism
Ownership of common lands

Figure 12.1 Distribution of powers related to livestock among different levels of government in Spain

Extensive livestock farming in Spain shows a complex mix of different systems and orientations (Mantecón *et al.*, 1994), including sheep systems (transhumants, transterminants and stubble fields grazing,), cattle systems (meat, dairy, semi-extensive, *dehesa*[2]), and mixed species systems (with goats, horses, pigs, etc.). Northern regions, such as Catalonia, the Basque Country, the Pyrenees, Cantabria and Asturias, practise mountain-based pastoralism and southern regions like Andalusia, Murcia, Extremadura and the Canary Islands also use the *dehesa* and other semi-arid systems, along with mountain rangelands (Ferrer *et al.*, 2001). Most systems actually use semi-extensive tools adapted to local conditions, feeding livestock in barns temporarily during scarcity seasons when livestock is not able to graze directly. These periods are also variable and are getting shorter to reduce costs. The feed supplied during the indoor season may also vary from locally collected hay to fodder bought in markets.

Challenges and problems livestock farmers currently face are similar to those confronting the entire country, but territorial characteristics individualize each Spanish region. Both political distribution of territorial power across the different levels of government and diverse systems of land ownership have led to territorial variability. To help interpret the case studies at the end of this chapter, the challenges and problems described hereafter are examined at the national level and contextualized to Northwest Spain and specifically the Castile-León Autonomous Community, since in Spain Autonomous Communities (regional governments) hold most of the territorial, agricultural and environmental powers.

Governance: between nature conservation and abandonment

In recent years many factors have strongly affected land governance in Spain, but, in relation to livestock production two of them need to be highlighted. The first is nature conservation policies, especially those applied between the 1980s and 1990s. The lack of legitimacy experienced by herders and the perception of livestock as a negative agent in conservation led the environmental administration to consider livestock as an enemy and ban their activity in the most valued protected lands. This policy is currently under revision, but it has strongly affected citizens' perception of livestock and contributed to marginalization of this activity. In terms of governance, the rights of land use moved from local farming communities to the environmental administration which was more interested in reforestation or fire-fighting than in preserving traditional land uses that are often seen as harmful to conservation.

The second driving factor is abandonment and depopulation. The crisis, which has been affecting the traditional rural environment from the second half of the twentieth century, has shown a progressive lack of population and the loss of traditional agricultural activities that used to maintain rural environments. Abandonment is also related to a loss of governance due to the lack of capacity of local institutions to manage their own lands, the lack of political power in poorly populated municipalities in regional and national politics, the low capacity of performing communal work, masculinization and especially in those lands where property is small and fragmented, ownership is also abandoned by migrants leading to difficulties in land management.

The environmental consequences of declining rural activity are changes to the vegetation cover composition and structure (Corbelle and Crecente, 2008). Once abandoned, the former agricultural lands are colonized by spontaneous vegetation following a process of succession that leads, in the absence of disturbance from poor pastures, to woodlands (Prévosto et al., 2006). However, if disturbance continues, the ecosystem keeps degrading, even if exploitation stops. The speed of such successional processes depends on soil characteristics, climate, neighbouring seed sources and the kind of agricultural activity formerly developed (Sluiter, 2005). Sometimes, this process has been accelerated by seeding forest species directly on agricultural lands with similar results. The growing vegetation cover increases habitat availability, species richness and landscape quality, but the effects may strongly differ from the structural pattern of previous activity. The loss of extensive farming landscape is considered to be globally negative because it implies the loss of semi-natural habitats of high ecological value and linked to human land use. The elimination of livestock leaves landscapes under-grazed (Lasanta, 2010) allowing dense shrub colonization, homogenization of landscape structure, retiring primary production, loss of diversity and increasing wildfire risks (Naveh and Kutiel, 1990; Lasanta et al., 2005; Beguería et al., 2003; Laiolo et al., 2004). When wildfires make their appearance the degradation intensifies, the ecosystem simplifies and water cycle regulation diminishes, thereby damaging the support capacity. Some authors have stated that the consequences of under-grazing are significantly more serious than those of over-grazing (Ferrer and Broca 1999).

Two key ecological consequences of abandonment are erosion and wildfires. The intensification of erosive processes depends on geographical characteristics (e.g. slope and climate). Abandonment of moderate slope landscapes and Atlantic climates should reduce erosive processes and protect soils (Cammeraat and Imeson, 1999; Tasser, 2007) while in Mediterranean climates, with lower rates of vegetation growth, abandonment usually leads to an increase in erosive processes, especially in steeply sloped areas where infrastructures like walls and terraces built up to retain soils are also abandoned (Cerdá, 2003; Beguería, 2006). Even if some areas are regenerating after abandonment, this argument cannot contradict the fact that rich semi-natural habitats, which are ecologically diverse and able to shelter uncommon species, are disappearing driven by the loss of extensive production (Corbelle and Crecente, 2008). Landscape quality is also affected, with complex cultural landscapes built throughout centuries being substituted by younger forest ecosystems.

Finally, abandonment is not only about economy or ecology. The hardest consequence of this situation is a general feeling of lack of future expectations constraining the whole rural society. Women were the first to feel this, and masculinization of rural areas has also become a great issue linked to depopulation and abandonment.

Wildfires, abandonment and governance

Forest fires are a major problem in Castilian mountains and other Spanish and Mediterranean regions. There is a strong link between abandonment and the prevalence of wildfires in Spain (Reinhardt *et al.*, 2008). This relationship is not only due to accumulation of biomass after abandonment, but also to the simplification of landscape structure and the lack of discontinuities, allowing fire to affect large surfaces of uniform shrub lands (Moreira *et al.*, 2001; Romero and Perry, 2004; FAO, 2006a; Millington, 2007).

The incidence of fires involving human activities is much higher in some regions of the Castile-León Community than in others, highly increasing in the peripheral mountainous areas in the northwest (the provinces of León and Zamora) and in the South. These areas share the same socioeconomic problems and environmental management questions over the causes and where solutions should be sought.

An initial analysis suggests that a strong tradition of using fire as a scrubland management tool remains in these areas (Molinero, 2008). This widespread use of fire prevents the development of new economic activities based on the exploitation of natural resources, boosting degradation linked to the abandonment of unprofitable activities (Izquierdo, 2005; Rey-Benayas *et al.*, 2007). Among other reasons, the use of fire to regenerate pasture for use by livestock is the first and foremost frequent cause (GEA, 2005). Elderly people remember cleared areas near villages as a defence against other potentially threatening wildfires and the preservation of a classic cultivated and exploited landscape.

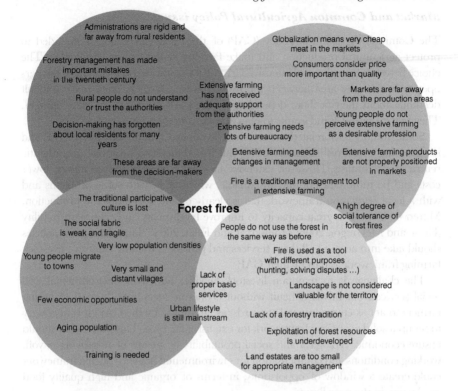

Administrations are rigid and far away from rural residents

Globalization means very cheap meat in the markets

Forestry management has made important mistakes in the twentieth century

Consumers consider price more important than quality

Rural people do not understand or trust the authorities

Extensive farming has not received adequate support from the authorities

Markets are far away from the production areas

Decision-making has forgotten about local residents for many years

Extensive farming needs lots of bureaucracy

Young people do not perceive extensive farming as a desirable profession

These areas are far away from the decision-makers

Extensive farming needs changes in management

Extensive farming products are not properly positioned in markets

Fire is a traditional management tool in extensive farming

The traditional participative culture is lost

Forest fires

A high degree of social tolerance of forest fires

The social fabric is weak and fragile

People do not use the forest in the same way as before

Very low population densities

Fire is used as a tool with different purposes (hunting, solving disputes ...)

Young people migrate to towns

Very small and distant villages

Lack of proper basic services

Landscape is not considered valuable for the territory

Few economic opportunities

Urban lifestyle is still mainstream

Lack of a forestry tradition

Aging population

Exploitation of forest resources is underdeveloped

Training is needed

Land estates are too small for appropriate management

Figure 12.2 Wildfires and local governance(García and Entretantos Foundation, 2011)

Moreover, the 'need for cleaning' is one of the key subjective factors about human causality of wildfires. Local people feel the landscape is 'dirty' when invaded by scrub, and try to 'clean' it in the traditional way; discontinuities and infrastructure that allowed their ancestors to control and use fire as an agricultural tool are no longer available. It is significant that local people do not consider the the burning of scrub as causing wildfires, but as a means of cleansing. Traditional use of fire has become a serious problem for these territories that are progressively impoverished, not only in terms of landscape or biodiversity, but also from an economic, social and cultural point of view (García and Entretantos Foundation, 2011).

Figure 12.2 represents some details of the diagnosis in a cloud of concepts trying to reflect some of the most outstanding and widespread ideas involving the issue of wildfires and their close relationship to land governance. Each component is related to the others and, therefore, influences and is influenced by other components of the situation. The organization of the chart has grouped most governance related issues in the upper left-hand circle, but there are other related topics. Wildfires are located in the centre of the diagram (according to their original purpose), but any of the other items displayed could be occupying this position.

Market and Common Agricultural Policy issues

The Common Agricultural Policy (CAP) of the European Union is intended to protect agricultural production and make farming systems more sustainable. The choice between extensive and intensive farming is not always clear, and most farmers operate in the grey area between the two. However, farmers often make difficult decisions about their facilities depending on the CAP measures and development. They rely on subsides and grants to plan and execute their business activities.

Some authors have related the return of livestock to mountains to the CAP and its 'greening measures' (Lasanta, 2010) but it is difficult to promote an authentic return of pastoralists. However, extensive farming is able to reduce inputs, lower costs and be more efficient and sustainable, which deals with some problems and with a legal regulation framework that is clearly oriented to industrial production. Moreover, it shows a great capacity to improve biodiversity and ecosystem stability (Hesse and McGregor, 2006; Montserrat and Fillat, 2004). Thus, European policies should take into account all these services and provide a friendly extensive livestock farming framework as part of their CAP.

The challenge is to maintain livestock facilities and their environmental and social services, but this is difficult without economic incentives. Instead of asking farmers to act as environmental stewards (as attempted by the CAP) it is necessary to set up a solid economic framework for extensive farming. This framework should ensure economic, ecological and social profitability by means of improving payoff, working conditions and compensation for environmental benefits. Such a framework could create a window of opportunity, in terms of organic and high quality food production in the near future.

Many farmers believe that a specific strategy to support pastoralism and extensive farming is still needed. CAP grants are oriented to compensate rents but they need to focus on the entire contribution of extensive livestock. Nevertheless, agro-environmental measures and animal welfare subsidies are converging as a powerful tool to enhance livestock sustainability to improve both environmental conditions and competitiveness, but they are used below their potential. Farmers should help to develop a new model of high quality production. Until now, however, the rigidity of CAP rules has interfered with the ability of farmers to market their products by imposing high costs and requirements.

In summary, extensive farmers feel that they are not properly acknowledged in the new CAP and they demand an explicit recognition of extensive livestock farming and rangelands and a specific set of rules to develop this activity, clearly differentiated from intensive livestock production. The CAP should adjust to land managed, ecosystem services provided, and high natural value areas conserved, analysing and considering regional and local features.

Other problems with rangeland governance

The best way to summarize the big picture about extensive livestock and pastoralism in Spain is the loss of land control, including its ability to support livelihoods.

The mountains and rangelands of Northwest Spain have experienced a land-management focus which has been derived from a local level (linked to widespread small-scale agricultural activity supporting a lot of people) to a regional level (linked to forest and environment management developed by regional governments). The main role in this change has been held by environmental and forest policies that used to regard any traditional uses as counter to conservation. Protected areas have demonstrated that the point of conservation policies is to show improvements both in nature conservation and in local welfare, but they always need local support from people and municipalities. Regional governments are recently trying to incorporate local institutions and population in the planning and management tools of protected areas, but environmental budgets have suffered severe cuts from the start of the crisis and nowadays most of these policies have been abandoned.

Mountain livestock farming is closely related to this kind of protected area in the Spanish inland north. The first form of political support extensive farmers have experienced came from civil servants and politicians linked to forest and environmental management, changing the way herders were regarded. Nevertheless, this political support is an incipient movement inside the regional administration and it is not enough to really change the role of extensive livestock farming.

According to farmers and supporters, the trend in extensive livestock production and pastoralism shows a regressive scenario driven by several socioeconomic, market and technical causes, including agricultural policies, environmental issues and rural development projects that are not properly addressing extensive livestock issues. This scenario means that the first lands to be abandoned are isolated and marginalized territories hosting high natural value areas.

The main governance and management problems were difficulties in accessing and managing rangelands in these areas. Market issues and progressive narrowing of profits are preventing herders from investing and developing essential infrastructures (e.g. access, water sources, paths and fences). However, if there is a lack of infrastructure exploitation, costs increase affecting efficiency and profit, creating a negative feedback loop. Some abandoned lands are also unavailable for grazing due to ownership issues and *cañadas y vías pecuarias* (livestock tracks) are fragmented and in poor condition.

Recovering governance in extensive farming: the background of pastoral and extensive livestock supporting in Spain

The severity of the scenario for pastoralism and extensive farming has mobilized support within Spanish society particularly from environmental related institutions and NGOs. Aware of the dramatic consequences of abandonment of extensive livestock activity, ecology researchers, universities, environmentalists and other concerned stakeholders have publicly supported extensive farmers as a key to maintaining natural heritage and rural society. However, there are some conflicts between pastoralists and environmentalists that need to be addressed.

Supporters of extensive livestock have emerged throughout Spain but have not yet constituted a true lobby platform. In the past 10 years, some pastoralists and farmers' organizations are increasing and developing an incipient network of extensive farming, led by national organizations, like the Spanish Federation of Pastoralist Associations. It is currently unclear how this situation may evolve to a supporting network with two types of organizations involved: one focusing on advocacy and the other giving more technical and professional support. Professional organizations should be led by and consist of farmers, defending their interests and conditions while the rest visualize the social support and try to improve the ecological, social and cultural benefits of pastoralism and extensive livestock, helping professional organizations to enhance their capacities by providing technical assistance when needed.

The transhumant movement

One of the most significant supportive movements for pastoralism has been established to sustain transhumance. It is not main the aim of this report, but its current influence in support of pastoralism demands a brief commentary. It is also the first example of a state-level support movement and also shows an interesting role played by government, transhumance being the pastoralist activity that suffers most from limitations imposed by the transfer of powers to regional governments.

By the third quarter of the twentieth century transhumance in Spain still existed while undergoing profound changes: abandonment of wool production, breeding intensification, crossing local breeds with meat producing ones, use of transport to move herds and substitution of sheep for cattle. The changes imposed by the CAP and the intensification of farming make it more difficult to maintain mobility and the 'Transhumance and Pastoralism Symposium' held during EXPO 92, concluded that Spanish transhumance was fading.

Nevertheless, there were still resistant pastoralists in some Spanish regions. In 1993, Jesús Garzón organized his first demonstration of transhumance, in collaboration with the Spanish Merino Breeders Association, and mobilized more than 2,600 sheep along 1,000 km of the vías pecuarias network from Extremadura to Zamora in Castile-León. This demonstration of transhumance recovered the annual movement of livestock, mostly sheep, up and down Spain. Herds crossed big cities following the ancient paths and awakened a social interest in transhumance that had been lost over the past years.

The Vías Pecuarias Act was updated in 1995, being one of the most significant laws protecting livestock tracks in the world. This law safeguards up to 125,000 km of paths covering 400,000 ha and gives support to the most important framework of public lands in Spain, providing the infrastructure needed to recover transhumant ways (Hernández, 1996). In 2005, the first National Congress on Vías Pecuarias (Manzano, 2006) opened the debate about their conservation among politicians, environmentalists, livestock breeders and researchers. The second National Congress took place in 2010. Pastoralists and environmentalists, nevertheless, are still complaining about the state of some of these ways and the illegitimate appropriation by private and public interests.

The Transhumance and Extensive Livestock Working Group held at the Agriculture and Environment Ministry was created in 2009, with the participation of several directorates of the Ministry, regional governments and organizations linked to extensive livestock. That group has held several meetings and activities trying to diagnose the actual situation of transhumance in Spain and has promoted the drafting and approval of the 'White Paper on Transhumance in Spain', published in the Boletín Oficial del Estado in 2012 (SGAA, 2011), establishing the actual strategic framework to protect and develop transhumance in Spain. This book marks a turning point in Spanish transhumance.

One thing about this support movement is the low profile kept by pastoralists, who have remained hidden while all these achievements were attained and sometimes they had been forgotten by the same people supporting them. In July 2013, the National Association of Transhumant Pastoralists gathered in León to introduce their new association and claim a more active role for pastoralists. This association intends to make visible the problems and difficulties experienced by transhumants, trying to become genuine interlocutors with government agencies and to give transhumance a higher profile.

Transhumant support has not been the only state-wide movement supporting pastoralists. There have been greater efforts in research and management of the *dehesa* system, uniting several universities and regional governments in western Spain and other projects related to extensive farming. Transhumance is the most significant and the only system outside regional power. There are people and organizations linking transhumant pastoralists with social support, but there needs to be a stronger social network and more committed consultation and assistance for transhumants and pastoralists.

Linking pastoralism with environmental protection

As stated, most environmental responsibilities (including rangelands and forestry) are under the aegis of regional governments. Accordingly, most projects supporting extensive livestock are also managed at a regional level. Andalusia has been in the vanguard with supported extensive livestock, with some people within the regional government sensitive to pastoralist issues. Also, Andulusia has a stimulating intellectual climate with public universities and research centres, a lively social network and a set of well-funded projects. This has resulted in offering a degree of support to pastoralists uncommon in Spain, with the possible exceptions of Catalonia (before the crisis), the Basque Country (with very different population and land-use conditions) and some of the Canary Islands.

Since 2003, the regional government of Andalusia has funded much research on possibilities and managing extensive livestock related to fire prevention. Livestock grazing was considered to be a powerful tool to maintain fuel breaks (RCC, 2006) and contribute to improving benefits derived from the correct management of extensive livestock breeding. In 2006, the government of Andalusia extended this fire prevention system from trial areas to many other Natural Parks in the region resulting in the Grazed Fuel Break Network of Andalusia (RAPCA). This network has expanded progressively and currently encompasses over 200 livestock farmers grazing their animals in more than 15,000 acres of fuel breaks (Ruiz-Mirazo, 2011). The more interesting goal of this project in relation to local governance is the change in the relationship between environmental administration and extensive farmers. Extensive farmers have regained access to prohibited forest and rangelands and have become part of wildfire prevention actions so they feel supported by the administration as positive contributors to the prevention of wildfires.

In addition to being the region with one the most advanced land management and environmentally focused programs for pastoralists, Andalusia is credited with the foundation of a school for shepherds 2010. The pastoralist schools are now spreading and have formed a pastoralist school network co-ordinated by the local development group *Altiplano* in Granada, but with a nationwide range of activities. Several groups of rural developments are involved in this project, including pastoralist schools in Asturias, Castile-León, Catalonia and Basque Country. Andalusia also held the last stakeholder meeting to agree on a global pastoralist position regarding the new Common Agricultural Policy and has started to develop a regional supporting network, following the previously described system.

Castile-León: two case studies

The Castile-León region occupies the inland area of northwestern Spain. Geographically, this region includes the central plateau (from 700 to 1,000 metres high), mostly under cultivation, surrounded by a mountainous belt, where extensive farming is distributed. The region experiences a Mediterranean climate, with an Atlantic influence higher in the northern mountains that maintains hydration during summer, establishing a high variability of local and regional microclimates. The social and economic weight of rural areas of Castile-León has been decreasing due to abandonment, depopulation and urban polarization with some devastating consequences (Molina, 2012). Castile-León has a population of 2.5 million people, 670,000 of whom live in each of the 2,500 municipalities with less than 2,000 inhabitants. Towns have increased their population five times in the twentieth century, while rural areas show a very low population density and lack considerable political influence.

Abandonment is key to understanding landscape changes (García de Celis, 2011). The lack of livestock production in rangelands has lowered the grazing load and allowed a woodland recovery process with landscapes evolving from agricultural to forestry land covers (Corbelle and Crecente, 2008). Also, abandonment is leading to a significant loss of biodiversity (formerly associated with the mosaic of rangelands, meadows, orchards, pastures and hedges that is now suffering a deep homogenization). Moreover, inhabitants have expressed a feeling of powerlessness in dealing with problems such as wildfires (Montserrat and Villar, 1999; Aldezabal *et al.*, 2002; García Trujillo, 2004; Molinero, 2008; Cassinello, 2012).

Some of the highest natural value areas of the region have been able to maintain a high rate of biodiversity characteristic of the region (Gómez, 2008) and they are trying to develop a sustainable economy model based on quality products and tourism. However, these areas are experiencing almost the same difficulties as the rest of rural Castile (Junta de Castilla y León, 2000). Rural culture harmed and deprived of social consideration and legitimacy has been diminishing throughout the twentieth century and is currently facing extinction (Izquierdo, 2005).

Extensive livestock in Castile-León

Castile-León is also an important extensive farming region (Ciria, 2008), showing one of the most interesting heritages in terms of pastoralism and livestock production (Sal and Pascual, 1992). The most common pastoralist management system in Castile-León is valley-mountains, with herds kept in the lowlands during the hardest part of the winter and migrating locally up to high altitude pastures (Montserrat, 2004) staying there until winter starts.

Ruminants, especially cattle and sheep are the main stock of Castile-León extensive farming. The evolution of livestock in Castile-León is showing a significant reduction over the past few years, more noticeable in sheep. This situation is not exclusive to Castile-León, but given the importance this sector has in the local economy, it is critical (Rodríguez Ruiz, 2013).

Experts point to several technical causes including decreasing consumption of lamb (MARM, 2011). Transhumant shepherds also cite low-profile conflicts for access to and control of the mountain rangelands. Cattle owners maintain the idea of 'one village-one farmer' to improve their capacity to claim enough land surface for CAP subsidies. The consequence is to use rangeland surface area for sheep and goats, which are better managers of mountain rangelands. In these kinds of conflicts, mobile pastoralists tend to be worse of, unable to compete with economic power and social relationships of locally settled farmers.

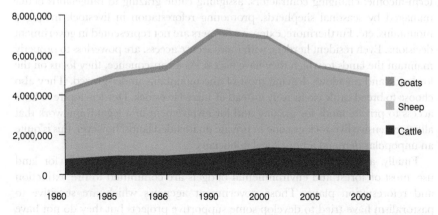

Figure 12.3 Evolution of main livestock in Castile-León in numbers of animals (Junta de Castilla y León, 2005 and 2009)

There are enough rangelands for all active extensive farmers and the impact of under-grazing is more damaging than overgrazing (Ferrer and Broca, 1999). Moreover, many territories of the mountainous belt of Castile-León are composed of communal lands, legally owned by local councils[3] and protected by Public Domain status.[4] The opportunity to set communally managed systems to improve pastoralism and extensive farming in those areas is evident, while these lands are being abandoned (Agencia de Gestión Agraria y Pesquera de Andalucía, 2011a).

Finally, it is necessary to address the role played by women in extensive farming. Masculinization of the rural world is having also consequences for farming work, not only for the traditional related roles of women but also depriving extensive farming of professional capacity, initiative and knowledge.

Governance and land-management aspects

The nature conservation administration and farmers coincide over wide territories, in Protected and High Value Natural Areas. Some declarations of protected areas (showing a lack of participation, severe deficiencies in planning and management tools and diminished resources), have created local confrontations between farmers and the regional government, generating land-use conflicts. Even if the role of pastoralists is improved, the challenge is how to engage their contribution to land planning and management. This engagement is proving to be difficult, even when the regional government supervises land uses, including grazing. Farmers' communication with government is actually channelled through environmental institutions instead of agricultural ones which are more concerned with industrial meat production. In the current situation, there are too few professional farmers in the field and many villages do not own sufficient livestock to properly maintain their territory, even the lowland pastures.

Transhumant, mobile or non-resident herders find themselves in an uncertain situation and are reluctant to make proper investments in rangelands, losing influence and capacity. Often landowners make bad decisions about livestock driven by short term-income: changing contractors, assigning cattle grazing to rangelands better managed by seasonal shepherds, promoting reforestation in livestock managed mountains, etc. Furthermore, extensive farmers are not represented in government decisions. Even resident herders, with more secure access, are powerless to properly maintain the lands to which they have access. As a consequence, they focus on the lowlands and meadows, leaving most of the mountains under-grazed. They also choose to breed cattle exclusively instead of mixed livestock. Herders aspire to have access to private lands for grazing and for involvement in a legal framework that allows extensive livestock grazing in private unattended lands; however, this is quite an unpopular demand among local politicians.

Finally, as forest and environmental administration is responsible for land use, most of forest and environmental budgets are committed to fire extinction and reforestation plans. Those government agencies which are sensitive to pastoralism have tried to develop some supportive projects but they do not have the influence to promote wide-ranging measures to improve extensive farming.

Thus, the situation has evolved to a conscious precariousness where a weak but persistent social fabric linked to extensive farming tries to survive in very difficult circumstances.

The 42 Plan and the organization of an extensive farmers network

The regional government of Castile-León, set up Plan 42 in 2002, a broad strategy of intervention formally designed to address the wildfire problem in the most affected districts. Plan 42 meant, from the very beginning, a shift in perspective about preventing wildfires.

While using a large set of measures related to classic or indirect prevention techniques – such as firebreaks, infrastructure and preventive silviculture, Plan 42 was focused on the use of social tools as instruments to change habits. They also introduced approaches to intervention in rural areas, including the relationships between professionals and the population, restoring sentimental links between people and their environment, networking, a long-term focus and the role of local activists (Junta de Castilla y León, 2006).

The participatory work with local people typified by Plan 42 allowed a wildfire prevention approach that focused on governance, development and sustainability. Those factors were shown to be inseparable from the social context where wildfires spread.[5] As a result of these works a great number of proposals were gathered from participatory activities.

Figure 12.4 shows how these proposals were clearly oriented to reclaiming the role of citizens in land management and recovering their control over territory. Wildfires, and by extension rural degradation, demand the improvement of local governance by empowered people interacting wisely with their territory. The proposed lines of work drew intervention options from a variety of cultural, structural, economic and social issues linked to complex scenarios such as land ownership, markets, administrative organization and social fabric.

The use of participatory tools led to a better understanding between professional and herders. When they began to meet, herders envisaged a more active role in fire prevention and professional developed a better understanding of the herders' background. An unexpected benefit of Plan 42 was its influence on the organization of extensive livestock farmers. Early in the participatory processes, some groups of extensive livestock farmers started to ask for separate meetings and social organization began to emerge.

The first works with local herders started with clearing. Herders and professionals negotiated funding from the regional government to clear scrub and create new rangelands in exchange for farmers' explicit renunciation of fire to control land. That embryonic relationship between herders and the regional government started to cement a sense of shared responsibility in rangeland management. Herders felt that they were listened to by the administration for possibly the first time.

Though, the most interesting work of Plan 42 regarding local governance was developed by the central governance of the Aravalle (in the province of Ávila), where

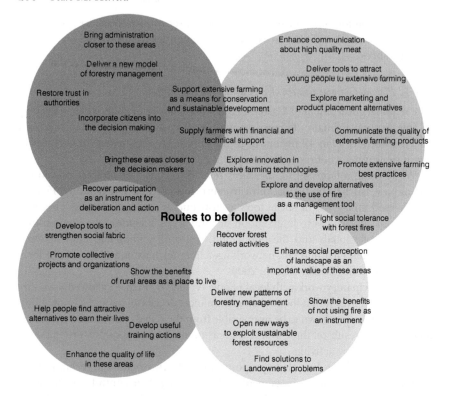

Figure 12.4 Restoring people's active role in preventing wildfires (García and Entretantos Foundation, 2011)

participatory land planning for grazing sites was agreed to between landowners and herders. Figure 12.5 shows the participatory map that led to signing the arrangement where up to 500 people were involved (Picardo, 2011). That was the first time participation was used in Castile-León to form a public arrangement between herders and landowners, resulting in extensive work on both public and private land.

Extensive farmers also realized that they were not being consulted about their role in conservation and land use. They felt unable to talk directly to government agencies and powerless in negotiations and lobbying. Therefore, farmers started to strengthen social links and create new local associations to represent them. Under by Plan 42 they started occasional 'Herder's Meetings' that helped to establish contact with related national and international networks and organizations. These associations led a regional federation and were incorporated to the nationwide organization. They established workshops and debates focusing on building capacities to improve communication. As a result, local associations initiated some governance proposals (e.g. rangeland use plans, clearing or common infrastructure). Plan 42 was in force through the entire process, providing farmers with specialized consultation, establishing contacts, networking with government agencies, encouraging communcation and helping them to improve social skills and group dynamics.

Figure 12.5 Participatory map of grazing sites undertaken in Aravalle (Picardo, 2011)

Plan 42 ended on 31 December 2011, but its decline had begun years before with a lack of political support and resource assignment. Its prolonged downfall involved people (technicians, professionals and participants) who were in conflict. In 2010 all contracts involving technical assistance were interrupted and in 2011 all staff were dismissed and the program was unofficially closed. However, some new groups, like the Entretantos Foundation, have resulted from Plan 42. Focused on social participation as a tool for land management, that entity is trying to preserve the participatory processes from Plan 42 and continue supporting and advocating the farmers' network.

The Ancares Leoneses Biosphere Reserve (ALEBR) work with extensive livestock

Ancares Leoneses is a mountainous area in the northwest of Spain, recognized as a biosphere reserve in 2006. Their municipalities (Candín, Peranzanes, Vega de Espinareda and Villafranca del Bierzo, are all part of the province of León) manage this reserve along with the CIUDEN Foundation. The biosphere reserve focuses on participatory planning and management, which have become one of its main assets.[6]

Participation in Ancares Leoneses Biosphere Reserve

The participatory process envisaged the local population obtaining a key role in the development of diagnostic and planning tools for the biosphere reserve. The main result of this process was the set up and and approval of two key documents, the Strategic Plan and the Action Plan 2011-2013 (RBALE, 2011).

Social participation also led to the establishment of a Council of Participation with representatives of local stakeholders. The ruling, representation and composition of this group were also established by participation, being agreed within the decision-making process of the reserve. It is now working with rotating quarterly meetings acting as a representative for local population, both advising and being involved in the management and specific actions of the biosphere reserve.

Another key group inside the reserve is the Scientific Committee. This consists of six researchers from three universities in the region that voluntarily advise the reserve. The Scientific Committee is not only leading projects and acting as a consultant but also enforcing the way the reserve deals with local people, from peer to peer, sharing wisdom and decision-making capacity (Alonso and Herrera, 2013).

Therefore, the reserve has already begun to 'plant' synergies between those groups which collaborate with each other in various projects and commissions. The idea is to develop networking and social cohesion among interested sectors and progressively incorporate them into the working of the reserve, encouraging interested groups to run sectorial projects and initiate ideas (always accomplishing principles).

The position of AGARBALE in the biosphere reserve

The formation extensive livestock farming association (AGARBALE) was a significant milestone in the participatory dynamics of ALEBR. The need for an extensive farmers' organization led to the establishment of a farming group to demand help in establishing permanent support. Their first objectives were to improve extensive livestock activity, to dignify the profession and to enhance their role over territory, thereby making visible the environmental services they provide to society (Alonso and Herrera, 2013).

Cattle are the most important livestock in the biosphere reserve. The composition of livestock means that grazing is essentially homogeneous, requiring good pastures and playing an incomplete role in land management. The exploitation system of cattle is extensive, with the mountains being cattle free for almost the entire year. If there is little or no snow, even during the winter, cattle remain outdoors, supplemented when fodder is scarce or for fattening. Mountain and under-canopy rangelands demand a diversified livestock grazing, but there are no goat or sheep herders in Ancares, so most slopes and scrublands remain ungrazed. This results in heathland scrub invasion (boosted by wildfires) and wood colonization from the lowlands to the slopes. Herders experience this landscape change as a significant patrimonial and cultural loss.

Nowadays extensive farmers are important agents in land management but are not the only ones.[7] The biosphere reserve is under the protection of several conservation bodies: it is a protected area under the Castilla y León Act, but without leadership, planning or management tools; it also belongs to Natura 2000 network under the same conditions. The situation may be described as the superimposition of several figures and agents un-coordinated and without a common framework. Thus, local governance is complicated but, to be fair, this negative picture is balanced by the support of the public system and the viability of some activities developed in the area, especially hunting and extensive farming.

The ALEBR work with extensive farmers is attempting to improve, via local participation, their governance and land-management activities. However, business must be profitable, so farmers can invest in and promote better practices. Herders need to appreciate that their involvement implies improvements in their livelihood, not only in land management. The work with specialists included in the Scientific Committee of ALEBR, assessing with farmers directly the reproduction, feeding and management situation has clearly reinforced the process and kept farmers involved.

The second step has always been to strengthen social links. Extensive farmers created their association and linked it to the reserve territory. The role of reserve has always been to connect local farmers with other herders and their networks. They started to visit other farmers and encourage them to go to meetings and to think about being joining the networks. They also established links to other herder organizations and organized the 2012 'Herders' Meeting'.

One other way to involve herders in local governance is to establish synergies among them and other activities. The ALEBR collaborates with an association of tourism professionals, so both organizations gain from strengthening links. For example, tourist facilities could sell high quality fresh meat produced in the reserve and farmers could acquire new clients sharing a common interest. That also could be the first step to new opportunities. The marketable organoleptic characteristics of extensive meat could be offered to highly demanding consumers and proximity to markets (Aldai and Mantecón, 2012) boosted by an exclusive biosphere reserve label.

The reserve has attempted to empower herders but it has proven to be indirect and slow, even though some steps in the right direction have been taken. Recently, the farmer's association AGARBALE has been incorporated into a new land stewardship project linked to a project conserving the habitat of capercaillie (*Tetrao urogallus cantabricus*).[8] The reserve and AGARBALE are entering into land stewardship contracts with local councils to address some habitat improvements maintained by extensive farmers. This is the first land-management project led by this association and it is important because the final objective is not to improve farming but to preserve the capercailzie's habitat. Overall, herders confirm the important role they play in land management and how their activity could be used as a tool for improving land, recovering habitats and ecosystems and conserving natural heritage by sending a clear message not only to government agencies in charge but also to themselves.

This is an on-going pilot project, but its development and first results are encouraging. Herders are interested and they have moved from their first reluctant positions to a more active role, even when forest work has been scheduled for late 2013.

Needs, trends and lines of future

Spain is currently undergoing a profound change in local administration, recentralizing and concentrating decision-making. In addition, social and economic indicators show how the factors that had led to abandonment and depopulation are still active, heading toward a breaking point. Therefore, new models of rural intervention are needed, especially in rangelands, forests and mountains. Castile-León is a good site to explore new ways to manage extensive territories and extensive production is proved to be one of the most efficient tools of intervention (Serrano and Mantecón, 2003).

Projects related to governance and participatory land uses are just beginning, but are already producing good results. It is important to continue strengthening networks and social fabric among extensive farmers to gain communication and lobbying capacity. Furthermore, it essential to establish a common strategy to develop pastoralism and extensive farming, through the consensus and participation of all agents involved, in order to create a participatory legal framework. Social support for pastoralism and extensive livestock is emerging, and it is necessary to organize and co-ordinate it by boosting its visibility and influencing dialogue without interfering in pastoralists' social organization.

Another line of work has begun to focus on high calibre products generated by pastoralists that explains their quality and health properties to consumers. It is necessary to differentiate extensive production and to offer their products to new and conscientious markets that will be able to provide funding.

Pastoralism and extensive farming are experiencing real improvements in their production methods to face new challenges, but they need to incorporate sustainability and efficiency issues to target those new markets. This strategy implies reducing external dependence and improving the use of local resources. Farmers should enhance control over their entire production process in order to sell their products directly. They are unlikely to remain farmers once they begin to sell and market their products. This would be much more difficult for mobile pastoralists than for settled ones, so the challenge is to articulate those markets and adjust to specific transhumants and mobile characteristics.

Transhumance has been addressed to solve some critical problems in their development (Rodríguez Pascual, 2011), including the need to improve professionalization and generational renewal, training, developing of social structure, improvement of scientific and technical basis, more control over productive processes, more focus on elaboration and transformation and incorporation of extensive farming to research, innovation and development projects. Their representatives also demand the establishment of better co-ordination mechanisms among administrations involved in pastoralism, rescue the main role played by pastoralist women and to improve the protection of livestock corridors (Casas, 2013).

However, extensive farmers are trying to develop these goals in hostile environments and with little support from public institutions that consider pastoralists as marginal in rural policies. Despite the stability and protection provided by the social system and Common Agricultural Policy, extensive farmers and pastoralists have great difficulties making a living from an activity that is valuable for everybody.

Additionally, there are territorial issues that should be solved. Pastoralism and extensive farming are necessary to manage rangelands, shrublands and woodlands in a way to favour ecosystem services. The experiences developed until now show good results, but more ambitious designs and approaches are needed. Land management is an immediate challenge for environmental and agricultural policies and pastoralists are a critical part of this. Arrangements must be made to improve governance in rangelands and marginal areas but they have to be addressed from consensus and a participatory basis that incorporates local populations from the beginning. Participatory planning tools should be established to adjust grazing and ecosystem needs. Traditional breeds and land-use systems need to be recovered and upgraded and the only way to arrange that is from a wide social consensus about how and at what cost society should manage and conserve their valuable natural lands.

Conclusions and lessons

The above case studies show the beginning of a huge task shared with pastoralists and extensive farmers. The overall aim implies the need for citizens to regain control over territory as a way to improve the sustainability of rural areas, especially in commonly owned lands. This sustainability requires improved governance of rural lands to enhance both natural heritage and livelihoods of local populations.

The first steps taken show hopeful results and validate the participative approach with rural populations, particularly in terms of governance and initiative. Herders and farmers have demonstrated an immediate interest in participating in land-use projects and a latent demand for consulting and assessment of their activity. The active incorporation of extensive farmers into these projects has led to the assumption of new responsibilities and the beginning of self-developing social processes that, when adequately promoted, obtained effective results using available resources.

Some projects show how pastoralists and extensive farmers could manage land for fire prevention or ecosystem management with the support of minimal investments and resources, in a way more efficient than traditional land intervention related to nature and forest management.

Local groups of pastoralists and extensive farmers have started, with the help of professional and academics, to develop social and political structures and organizations to improve their interlocution and relevance in governance. They are trying to fight for their interests and profitability, but they are also accounting for their usefulness facing new models of land management, especially in rangelands and marginal ecosystems. They are developing an incipient social support network willing to preserve the positive effects pastoralists have providing ecological services and conserving biodiversity and ecosystem functionality. Most of these projects have tried to empower pastoralists and extensive farmers in terms of governance, but also to enhance their business in terms of efficiency and sustainability, being aware of the ecological and social services lent by pastoralism. This is a complex task demanding more active involvement of society, which should be the next challenge for Spanish pastoralists.

The case studies show advances in developing farmer networks as a way to improve their influence and visibility and their active role in land planning. Land management is a major challenge in terms of global change but many of the intervention strategies are actually failing. The use of extensive livestock production as a land-management tool suitable to intervene in nature conservation, ecosystem restoration, fire prevention and biodiversity improvement is showing hopeful results. This strategy, however, demands that pastoralists and extensive farmers take a prominent role, which requires that pastoralists reach better levels of knowledge and capacity and the deployment of better human and financial resources.

Notes

1   Small-scale mobility up and down a mountainous area maintaining the same residence.
2   An agrosylvopastoral system typical of the Iberian Peninsula consisting of a mix of oak species and pastures and used primarily for grazing with cattle, pigs, goats and sheep.
3   Local councils (*juntas vecinales*) are the political bodies in municipalities of Castile-León that encompass more than one village. Each of the villages forms a local council with participation of all neighbours. Local councils have one representative elected to the municipality (the President of the Local Council) who also represent the council's property, including common forest lands.
4   Spain has an influential 'Forest Act' that regulates forest heritage. Among other regulations, this Act establishes the Forest Public Domain that includes the areas categorized as Public Utility Forests. The Catalogue of Public Utility Forests is held by Regional Governments and protects large swathes of common land. The uses of these lands are subject to administrative discretion and to land management plans undertaken by regional forest agencies. Regional governments, with the participation of local owners (usually municipalities or local councils) are in charge of improvement, protection and exploitation of those forests, including grazing regulations.
5   Participatory works with people on Plan 42 were formerly begun by professional strying to mobilize local population into fire prevention. Coordinators of the program started to hire a little cluster of small companies with experience in mediation and facilitation of participatory processes. The collaborative work between participation professionals and local professionals was successful in terms of social involvement, developing some new ideas (e.g. participatory-designed clearance cutting around populations). However, even if these projects were, at the beginning just for wildfire prevention, participatory processes determined that wildfires were not the disease, but just a symptom of a deeper sickness related to the way land is used.
6   The improvements made at this point by the CIUDEN Foundation incorporated a technical staff (consisting of a Head Manager and an environmentalist) and the

consultation of a small technical assistance, GAMA SL, with wide experience in participation) to develop ALEBR planning tools. That team agreed to use participatory methodologies as a basis for reserve decision-making, following the main principles and documents governing the reserve. They built up a powerful dynamic process based on stakeholder participation to develop the main instruments governing the reserve and involving local population in the decision-making process.

7 Hunting, for example, is organized by a Regional Hunting Reserve that co-ordinates game in the whole reserve distributing hunting fees between municipalities through a reserve council integrating municipalities and government that has not met lately. Forest management is also undertaken by the Regional Government Environmental Department, with the participation of local councils.

8 The Spanish government is leading a Capercaillie Conservation Project founded by EU's LIFE Program with participation of several national and regional governments and institutions. This project holds a Land Stewardship line of work that is granting habitat improvements for this species.

13 Strengthening communal rangelands management in Botswana

Legal and policy opportunities and constraints

Lael Buckham-Walsh and Cathrine Chipo Mutambirwa

Overview

This chapter explores the management of communal rangelands in Botswana. The approach links national analysis with local observations from case studies in published literature and the International Union for Conservation of Nature's (IUCN's) work on participatory planning and community engagement in natural resource management in the Kgalagadi District, where the legal and policy opportunities and constraints to achieving sustainable land management are examined. Kgalagadi District is the southernmost district of Botswana and lies within the Kalahari Desert.

Despite Botswana's progressive approach to developing the robust land administration and land tenure systems that contribute to good governance and economic progress, in reality land management is still confronted by the need to connect a traditional communal rangeland management system with a growing urban economy and an increasing land market.

Background information

Botswana is a semi-arid, sparsely populated country centrally located in the interior of Southern Africa. Officially known as the Republic of Botswana, the country has a total area of 582,000 km^2 and a population of 2.004 million people (World Bank, 2013). Botswana's economy is closely linked to that of South Africa. Since independence, Botswana has experienced one of the fastest growth rates in per capita income in the world, transforming itself from one of the poorest countries in the world to a middle-income country (UN-Habitat, 2010). Due to its record of good economic governance, Botswana was ranked as Africa's least corrupt country by Transparency International in 2004 and is still regarded today to be ahead of many European and Asian countries (UN-Habitat, 2010).

Botswana is characterized by arid to semi-arid conditions. Rainfall estimates vary from 150 to 250 mm per annum (Tyson, 1986; van Rooyen and Brendenkamp, 1996 cited in Haddon, 2005) to 100–600 mm annually (International Fund for Agricultural Development, 2000). Most of Botswana is flat, arid land with unreliable, low rainfall. Roughly 46 per cent of the total land area is classified as agricultural land, although only 5 per cent is suitable for cultivation and only 1 per cent was cultivated in 2002. Approximately 0.3 per cent of cropland was irrigated in 2003. The Kalahari Desert, much of which is savannah grassland and sparse woodland, covers two-thirds of the land area and supports large herds of cattle, goats, and wildlife. Twenty-one per cent of the total land area is forest land and 31 per cent is designated as nationally-protected areas. Deforestation is occurring at a rate of 1 per cent per year (World Bank, 2009; FAO, 2005b cited in USAID, 2010).

Low rates of surface runoff and groundwater recharge are common due to a combination of low rainfall, high potential evaporation rates, flat topography and deep sandy soils. The main rivers only register flow for between 10 and 70 days a year, on average, and similarly during the wet season, a continuous stream flow is not visible (Mazvimavi and Motsholapheko, 2008). Mean annual rates of surface runoff generally do not exceed 50 mm. No surface runoff is recorded over the whole of the west and centre of the country. The fact that the country's main river systems do not originate from within the country raises the need for transboundary negotiations to tap into steady, more reliable water resources (Swatuk, 2008).

Groundwater provides about 80 per cent of the country's water requirements for domestic use, mining, livestock, and power generation. Approximately 64 per cent of the water used in urban areas is from groundwater sources, with the exception of major urban centres such as Gaborone, Lobatse, Francistown, and Selebi-Phikwe, which are supplied from surface water sources. The estimated mean annual aquifer recharge from rainfall is about 3 mm but rises to over 40 mm in the extreme north, while much of the central and western part of the country records close to zero. Only a small percentage of the annual groundwater recharge can be utilized because of the extremely large number of boreholes that would be needed, as well as the poor-quality of the water and high development costs (Manzungu *et al.*, 2009).

Agricultural activities accounted for a high percentage of the Gross Domestic Product (GDP) at the time of independence but this has dwindled as diamond mining and tourism have flourished. Agriculture includes commercial and traditional farms with commercial enterprises primarily devoted to the production of cattle, with some cultivation of cereals and pulses. Most of Botswana's farms (about 63,000) average roughly 5 hectares and employ rain-fed farming methods. The country has about 112 farms larger than 150 hectares. Commercial farms represent less than 1 per cent of all farms in the country and use 8 per cent of the total land area. These enterprises are responsible for 20 per cent of cattle production and 40 per cent of the cereals and pulses produced (USAID, 2010).

Approximately 39 per cent of Botswana's human population resides in rural areas where communal land ownership is most prevalent. In sub-Saharan Africa, most livestock are grazed on communal rangeland either under open access or rather loosely controlled common property tenure. Herds are owned and managed by individuals and families (ILRI, 1995). However, there have been varying perspectives on the importance and value of communal rangelands. One perspective is that their yields tend to be roughly one-third of the yields of commercial farms because the owners lack the ability to invest in inputs, and because the quality of some of the communal land is below average (Taylor, 2007 cited in USAID, 2010). However, recent evidence informs us that Botswana's cattle population stood at 2.55 million in 2011, where grazing in communal rangelands accounted for 86 per cent of the cattle and 71 per cent of farmers in Botswana, while private grazing in ranches accounted for 14 per cent of the national cattle herd and 5 per cent of the land area (GoB, 2013 cited in Mosalagae and Mogotsi, 2013). Many urban people also have land rights (residences, ploughed fields, livestock, and water rights) in tribal areas to supplement their incomes (UN-Habitat, 2010).

Traditional farming systems have been constrained in certain places by the fencing and privatization of large areas for commercial production, supported by a series of national agricultural policies and international trade agreements that have improved access to international markets for beef (Dougill *et al.*, 2010). This has intensified the development of commercialized privately-owned ranch farming systems, owned by absentee farmers who employ a few local residents to manage their land and livestock, with former communal rangeland being privatized, fenced and restricted from the local community (Adams *et al.*, 2002). This has created a shift from collective community-based natural resource management approaches to more intensive production based approaches and has further restricted the land available to communal systems that support residents of settlements across the Kalahari where few other livelihood options exist (Ringrose *et al.*, 1996; Hitchcock, 2002). The existence of dual grazing rights has put added pressure on communal rangelands which are grazed by both commercial and communal farmers.

Kalahari Desert

The Kalahari is the widespread elevated, flat, sand-covered plain that occupies part of Southern Africa (Thomas, 2002). It occupies almost all of Botswana, the eastern third of Namibia, and the northernmost part of the Northern Cape province in South Africa (Silberbauer, 2013) (Figure 13,1). The geological unit of the Kalahari Sands covers 2.5 million km^2 (Thomas and Shaw, 1991). Kgalagadi is a district in southwest Botswana, lying along the country's border with Namibia and South Africa. International Union for Conservation of Nature's (IUCN's) work on participatory planning and community engagement in natural resource management focuses on the Kgalagadi District.

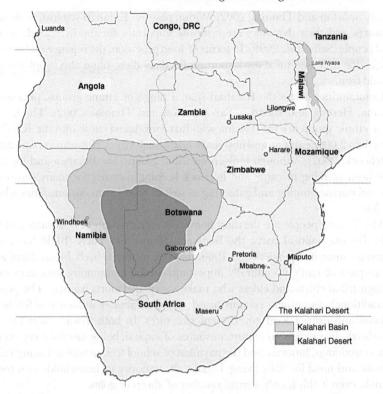

Figure 13.1 Location of the Kalahari Desert in Southern Africa

Lying in the semi-arid interior of Southern Africa, approximately 80 per cent of Botswana is covered with Kalahari sand soils and savannah ecosystems that support both commercial and communal livestock systems, as well as National Parks and Wildlife Management Areas. The climate is typified by a mean annual rainfall varying from less than 200 mm per annum in the South-West to 650 mm per annum in the North-East with an inter-annual variability of about 40 per cent (Bhalotra, 1987). Despite significant economic growth based largely on diamonds, 47 per cent of Botswana's population lives below the UN's two US dollars per day poverty line (CIA, 2009). In Botswana, pastoral agriculture represents the chief source of livelihood for more than 40 per cent of the nation's residents (FAO, 2006a), and cattle represent an important source of status and well-being for the vast majority of Kalahari residents (White, 1993).

The food production and livelihood system of the Kalahari remains predominantly a pastoral one. These savannah ecosystems are utilized for both cattle and small stock, mainly goats and sheep, in proportions dependent on the land tenure system (i.e. communal or private) and on the environmental characteristics of forage availability, notably the ratio of bush to grass and the availability of palatable grass species. Traditional systems are transhumant, with a high degree of herd mobility which respond to the patchy nature of rainfall and forage (Sporton and Thomas, 2002). Within pastoral Kalahari systems, ecological resources and their dynamics are critically important for the livelihoods of the local people (Sallu *et al.*, 2009). In terms of food provision, the reliance on livestock means that milk and meat are important for daily diets, often also supplemented by wild fruit.

Communities across the Kalahari span a range of ethnic groups, principally Tswana, Herero, and Basarwa/San (Sporton and Thomas, 2002). The largest single ethnic group are the Tswana who first introduced cattle into the Kalahari more than 2,000 years ago and now make up the majority of Botswana's population (Hitchcock, 2002). Although indigenous tribal groups, the Basarwa and the San have been working in cattle and livestock keeping societies for many centuries; they still pursue hunting and gathering as well as ecotourism opportunities where possible.

The Tswana people are the most dominant ethnic group in Botswana and the main Tswana political party, the Botswana Democracy Party (BDP) has ruled Botswana since independence in 1966. Tswana society is itself hierarchical and the keeping of cattle is culturally important. Strong community structures exist through tribal chiefs and elders who make up village courts (kgotla). The power of traditional community systems has declined as greater influence is felt from national and district level government structures. In both Tswana and Herero households, livestock is an important source of capital, being saved for key events such as weddings, funerals, and the payment of school fees, as well as having value for milk and meat for daily living. Usually the majority of households own some animals, even if this is only a small number of sheep or goats.

Livestock rearing is the mainstay of Botswana's rural economy with a large proportion of the national herd grazed on communal land. A large percentage of the population draws its livelihood from livestock and the government has traditionally pursued policies that strongly support the growth of livestock production in the form of high prices for meat and livestock input subsidies (Arntzen and Fidzani, 1997). Government programs have provided support for small stock rearing as a route to help poorer households through times of drought. With increasing national wealth, there is a growing divide between rich and poor. Despite measures to boost rural economies and livelihood opportunities, international measures still show that Namibia, South Africa, and Botswana have a very high level of income inequality among countries calculated by the Gini index (CIA, 2009). This divide is thought to be responsible for driving increasing pressures for private land ownership (Hitchcock, 2002). Other factors like out-migration from rural areas and increased mortality rates because of the HIV-AIDS pandemic are also affecting rural community structures. Many communities in Botswana are dealing with a lack of fit, working-age people, leaving grandparents to run households with young children and significant numbers of orphans. The strength of extended family and ethnic groups still remains a strong binding agent, however continued out-migration is likely to threaten and reduce system resilience associated with the ability to move livestock across an area, which is also curtailed by disease related controls.

Land tenure and land management policies

The management of rangelands is governed by a number of land tenure policies and laws in Botswana. The legal framework governing Botswana's land is a mixture of formal and customary laws, with much of the formal law reflecting longstanding principles of customary law. The six major pieces of formal legislation include: (1) The State Land Act, 1966; (2) The Tribal Land Act, 1968; (3) The Tribal Grazing Lands Policy, 1975; (4) The Town and Country Planning Act, 1977; (5) The National Agricultural Development Policy, 1991; and (6) The Sectional Titles Act, 1999 (Adams *et al.*, 2003; Taylor, 2007).

At independence, Botswana adopted four national principles:

- self-reliance
- democracy
- development
- unity.

Land administration was immediately identified as key to assisting in the attainment of the four national principles and government set out to effectively implement land reforms on the ground (Mathuba, 2003). Land tenure has undergone changes since Botswana's independence with the promulgation of a new legal framework, policies, institutions, and governance mechanisms. Today Botswana has three principal forms of land tenure, namely Customary (Tribal) Land, State Land and Freehold Land (Mathuba, 2003). These modern day land tenure systems mirror tenure under the British Rule, viz. Native Land, Crown Land and Freehold Land (Mathuba, 2003).

At independence, about 49 per cent of the national land area was tribal land, less than 4 per cent was freehold and the balance state land. Between independence in 1966 and 1972, a further 15,000 square kilometres of state land were demarcated and sold as freehold land both to Europeans and Batswana (Adams *et al.*, 2003). By 1980, the conversion of state land to tribal land and the purchase and conversion of freehold land in congested areas had caused tribal land to increase to 69 per cent, freehold land to fall to 5.7 per cent and state land to fall to 25 per cent. Today, tribal land comprises 71 per cent of the land area (Clover and Eriksen, 2009), freehold about 4 per cent and state land 25 per cent (UN-Habitat, 2010).

Customary law in Botswana provides tribe members with a right of avail, which is the right to be allocated residential (urban or rural), arable and grazing land based on tribal membership. Tribal members receive land at no cost and have continuing rights to the land as long as they use it in accordance with the purpose of the allocation. Rights to residential land are permanent and continuous, while individually-cultivated lands may revert to community land after the harvest. Customary law permits the transfer of land among tribe members. The Tribal Land Act is almost wholly consistent with customary law but transfers the traditional authority held by chiefs and headmen over land to the Land Boards (Adams *et al.*, 2003; GoB, 2002 cited in USAID, 2010).

State Land Act, 1966

The State Land Act was introduced in 1966 to address the mismanagement and disputed occupation of state land. The Act was instrumental in defining the state land of Botswana and turning Crown land into state land (Adams *et al.*, 2003). It provided presidential powers over state land conferring on the President the power to provide for its disposal. The Act provided for management of state land (urban land, parks and forest reserves) by the central government and local government councils.

Tribal Land Act, 1968

The Tribal Land Act was introduced in 1968, two years after independence. The Act brought about three main changes to land governance (Mathuba, 2003; Centre on Housing Rights and Evictions (COHRE), 2004; Adams *et al.*, 2003; Taylor, 2007):

- The introduction of the principle of leases under common law for commercial uses of tribal land.
- Grants of rights to wells, borehole drilling, and individual residential plots to Batswana.
- The establishment of Land Boards which transferred the chiefs' powers over tribal (customary) land to the Land Boards.

This brought about changes in the way rangelands were managed as land management and allocation was no longer at a local level and under the administration of chiefs. This also led to fragmentation of rangelands as fenced commercial ranches in communal rangelands were now recognized and individuals were granted the exclusive use of areas surrounding boreholes.

The Act vests tribal land in the citizens of Botswana and grants administrative power (formerly held by chiefs and headmen) over the land to one of the 12 district Land Boards. The Board then holds the land in trust for the socio-economic benefit of the citizens. The Act also empowers the Board, after due consultation with the District Council to determine land use zones for the entire tribal land and subsequently to create management plans for the guidance of land use and the development of tribal land. The Land Boards can allocate land, cancel customary rights, and rezone agricultural land for commercial, residential, and industrial uses.

The Act vested

All the rights and title to land in each tribal area ... in the land board ... in trust for the benefit and advantage of the tribesmen of that area and for the purpose of promoting the economic and social development of all the peoples of Botswana.

(Adams *et al.*, 2003)

Tribal Grazing Lands Policy (TGLP), 1975

During the early 1970s, the government became increasingly concerned with the growth in cattle numbers in Botswana, particularly in relation to the serious dangers that they posed to the environment. As livestock numbers grew, more pressure was put on livestock owners to sink more boreholes for livestock watering resulting in increased pressure for land in areas with good water sources. In order to arrest this trend, the Tribal Grazing Lands Policy (TGLP) was introduced (Frimpong, 1995).

Under the traditional system of land tenure, land was always regarded as communal and tribal chiefs allocated the land for arable and/or grazing use. The traditional system was replaced in 1968 by the Tribal Land Act which introduced decentralized Land Boards to administer land, removing the authority from chiefs. The passing of the Tribal Land Act and the establishment of Land Boards did not fundamentally change the concepts of land tenure (Greenhow, 1978). However with time, the traditional communally-owned rangelands in the eastern Kalahari were perceived by the government to be overstocked and overgrazed by livestock and thus degraded. Buying into the 'tragedy of the commons' chronicle popularized by Hardin (1968), the Tribal Grazing Land Policy (TGLP) advocated structural reforms to the country's livestock industry in order to ultimately enhance national economic and social development (GoB, 1975). Subsequently, part of the tribal grazing land was demarcated into ranches. The TGLP encouraged development further west into the more arid Kalahari Desert, aided by borehole installations. The specific objectives of the TGLP were to (Mosalagae and Mogotsi, 2013):

- Improve range management by preventing overgrazing and further degradation through paddocking and rotational grazing. Individual owners or syndicates of large herds (>400 animals) were to be moved off communal lands into fenced, borehole focused ranches of uniform size.
- Increase livestock productivity and farmers' income by promoting better management practices such as daily watering, selective breeding and early weaning.
- Promote social equity by retaining only small-scale farmers on communal lands and thus allowing them room to improve their livelihoods.
- Secure the interest of future generations and/or those who were not livestock farmers by reserving some land through the creation of reserves, later used as Wildlife Management Areas for hunting purposes.

This resulted in some key changes and the re-zoning of tribal land into three categories: Commercial Grazing Areas, Communal Grazing Areas, and Reserved Grazing Areas (Frimpong, 1995). The idea behind the policy was to reduce pressure on the communal areas by relocating large cattle owners to the demarcated ranches leaving smallholder farmers in the communal areas. Exclusive rights to specific areas of grazing land were also given to individuals and groups for commercial ranches together with boreholes and fencing. Leases were granted and rents paid to the Land Boards with the rationale to pool resources to the Land Board for assistance to all the areas under their jurisdiction. This privatization policy was expanded under the National Policy on Agricultural Development.

National Policy on Agricultural Development (NPAD), 1991

Upon realizing the shortcomings of TGLP, the government introduced the National Policy on Agricultural Development (NPAD) in 1991 (Mosalagae and Mogotsi, 2013). The aim of NPAD was to provide subsidies to improve productivity in the livestock sub-sector by promoting the sustainable use of rangeland resources through fencing of communal grazing areas (GoB, 1991). The National Agricultural Development Policy also permits owners of boreholes to apply for 50-year leases to an area of 6,400 square hectares around their boreholes. Leaseholders are permitted to fence the area and have exclusive rights to all natural resources within the area. Provision was made under the policy to reserve land demarcated into Wildlife Management Areas (WMAs) in an attempt to balance the scales. WMAs are multiple use areas, combining wildlife conservation with the creation of economic opportunities for the rural population (GoB, 1999). Intense developments within WMAs such as borehole drilling are prohibited, while hunting is controlled through permits or total bans. Botswana also developed complementary polices and pieces of legislation founded on sustainable utilization of natural resources which also influence WMAs. These include the Wildlife Conservation Policy (1986), Tourism Policy (1990), National Conservation Strategy (1990), Wildlife Conservation and National Parks Act (1992), Tourism Act (1992) and the Community Based Natural Resource Management (CBNRM) Policy.

Community-based Natural Resource Management (CBNRM) Policy, 2007

The Community Based Natural Resource Management (CBNRM) Policy was developed in Botswana to guide and facilitate the strengthening of, and support to, existing and future CBNRM activities, while safeguarding the interest of communities and attracting investment in natural resource enterprises. Arntzen *et al.* (2003) have summarized the CBNRM policy which improves and builds on earlier policies in specifying land tenure and natural resource user rights for communities. One of the key objectives of the CBNRM policy is to specify land tenure and natural resource user rights, which may be devolved to communities. Under this policy:

- Communities may obtain a 15-year Community Natural Resource Management lease for the commercial use of natural resources, subject to an approved Land Use and Management Plan, and payment of annual land rental and resource utilization royalties to the Ministry of Environment and Tourism.

- Communities are also permitted to sublease the land or natural resource to joint venture partners subject to approval by the Land Authority.

Kgalagadi Land Board management policy, 2006

This policy was developed in 2005 and adopted by the District Council in December 2006. The policy has the specific objectives of ensuring sustainable use of land and economic diversification, equitable distribution of land, harmonizing land allocation with ecosystems and guiding the Land Board in decision-making, and therefore only allows for one plot per applicant.

Complementary policies

Other complementary national policies include:

- The Wetlands Policy which is a guide to protecting water bodies. Water bodies and pans are recognized as important in the Kalahari as they hold surface water during wet seasons. However most pans face a risk of degradation as they are used as sources of quarry raw material.
- The Wildlife Conservation Policy (1986) which ensures sustainable wildlife resource utilization in various land uses such as communal areas, freehold land, leasehold land, Wildlife Management Areas (WMAs), national parks, game reserves and sanctuaries.

The village of Khawa is located in Kgalagadi District along the south-eastern border of the Kgalagadi Transfrontier Park. The community has been allocated the use of the KD/15 wildlife management area (WMA) managed through the community trust, the Khawa Kopanelo Development Trust (KKDT). The community has 'user rights' but not 'ownership rights' and engages in wildlife photography, hunting (managed through a hunting quota from the Wildlife Department) and fixed safari camps for game viewing and photography (KD/15 LUMP, 2005). Human-wildlife conflict is often a problem as livestock wander into WMAs where grazing conditions are often more favourable compared to the surrounding rangelands. Livestock is specifically excluded from WMAs which are reserved for wildlife conservation with the creation of alternative economic opportunities for the rural people. There is a problem of encroachment of livestock into WMAs due to the lack of recognition of WMAs by members of the community, although this is likely to be addressed in the review of the National Land Use Map which is currently underway.

District level policies also govern land management at the local level:

- The Kgalagadi Integrated Land Use Plan which has the intention to categorize land into various uses.
- The District and Western Region Masterplan identifies communal areas suitable for livestock, tourism, and community or services development.

- The Kgalagadi Communal Area Management Plans (KCAMP 2005–2020) which falls within the framework of the Western Region Master Plan has as its overall objective the management of land in the communal areas in the Kgalagadi District to enhance rural livelihoods, and facilitate the implementation of government policies. This plan has been used as a working document, but it has not yet been gazetted due to amendments that need to be done before its adoption. It is to be noted that the Bokspits, Rappelspan, Vaalhoek and Struizendum (BORAVAST) village Plan that has been commissioned by the Ministry of Agriculture is a subsidiary to implementation of KCAMP. The District Land Use Planning Unit has been involved in helping the communities prepare Land Use Plans and Resource Management Plans.

The Dam and Haffir Building Policy, 1974 and revised in 1993

The Dam and Haffir Building Policy stipulates certain conditions regarding the construction and maintenance of small earth dams that provide water for livestock, irrigation, and fishing (Mpho, 2005; Fortmann and Roe, 1986). This policy aimed to devolve greater management responsibilities to groups of people organized as borehole syndicates (BS) or dam management groups (DMGs) and represents an attempt to address perceived mismanagement of small dams by farmers. Under the scheme, government-constructed small dams were to be handed over free of charge to groups of people who agreed to abide by stipulated management rules. Critical management requirements included members paying stipulated fees, observance of standard stock limitations set at 400 livestock units (LSU) per year per water source, and commitment to collective maintenance and repair of the dams. The revised policy of 1993 allowed multipurpose agricultural use of dams which was consistent with the land use zoning policy and the stipulated operational rules.

The rules relating to community mobilization and general management were premised on a strong state role in how resources were used, probably on the grounds that the state provided capital for the dams and boreholes. Government extension staff were required to take the initiative in organizing groups who wanted dams, while district councils could choose to take complete or partial administrative control of dams. Each dam or borehole management group was to be formed before the water facility was constructed and would consist of farmers who wanted the dam and were willing to control their grazing. Prior to dam construction, each group was obliged to sign a standard form, abide by the terms of agreement to signify willingness to maintain and repair the dam, and pay a specific fee per adult beast per year. Dam or borehole management groups in a community grazing area were to consist of approximately 5–20 members. Average herd size was stipulated at 20–80 LSU at the time of application with a possible maximum of 400 LSU. No single person was allowed to water more than 50 head of cattle.

The Livestock Water Development Programme, 1988

The Livestock Water Development Programme was started in 1988 and is open to farmers with herds of between 60 and 500 cattle as well as syndicates with a minimum herd of 60. Both leasehold and communal farmers were eligible for support and the programme provided 40–60 per cent funding or grants for drilling or equipping boreholes in drought-prone areas, or where water development is considered to be expensive. Since 1989, two-thirds of the approved applications have been from syndicates (CAR, 2006).

Pre-colonial land management

Pre-colonial institutions focused on grazing management although individuals also relied on communal rangelands for other resources. Access to land, grazing pastures and water was based on membership in the community or tribe and was managed by the chief and his headmen (Baland and Platteau, 1996). Rights to access grazing pastures could be gained by outsiders with the permission of the chief, who would only grant access if there was adequate land. The chief had the overall authority to evict trespassers or individuals not complying with the management regimes of the area.

Although citizens could establish private rights to water through developing a water point (White, 1993), the distance between water points was controlled to ensure sufficient grazing and was also based on the quality of the land. Wells and dams were considered individual or family properties while all citizens had a right to the water that collected in natural pans and rivers falling within their tribal territory (Poteete, 1999).

The success of the traditional system in managing communal rangelands is credited to:

- The structure of the political system giving the chief the ultimate authority and legitimacy needed to enforce the rules governing access to, and use of, the range.
- The delegation of specific management responsibilities to headmen and overseers decentralized the system, allowing those with an intimate knowledge of the range and its users more powers to decide how it was to be used. Headmen and overseers were able to monitor and enforce rules pertaining to the use of grazing areas (Hitchcock, 1980).
- Neighbours monitored each other's actions and those who deviated from the expectations of the group were reported to the overseer who would inform the chief. In return, the economic reward and status the headmen and overseers received from their positions as range managers reinforced their allegiance to the chief as custodians of the range. All matters and disputes pertaining to land allocation were settled by the chief at the kgotla, the traditional meeting place and court.

This arrangement cultivated a mutual trust in authority and also built a sense of community and readiness to protect collective welfare. It also enhanced community cohesiveness and vigilance in guarding the use of resources. Citizens were loyal to the chief and shared the same values and beliefs regarding range preservation because it was critical for the well-being of the tribe.

Institutional assessment

Current legislation makes provision for institutions to support communal rangeland management and three key local level institutions have been sanctioned by the different pieces of legislation in Botswana to support communal land management, and provide an opportunity for better land management.

Land Boards

Together with local councils, tribal administration and district administration, Land Boards are one of the four local government bodies in Botswana. Land Boards are governed under an autonomous 'body corporate' structure responsible for all matters related to the allocation of land in tribal areas (UN-Habitat, 2010). Each main Land Board is composed of 12 members selected and/or democratically elected in the community meeting held at the Kgotla. While the Land Boards have sole authority over land, they work closely with other local authorities and relevant departments. The Land Boards fall under the Ministry of Local Government (and have recently been relocated to the relevant Ministry of Lands and Housing), which controls and coordinates their activities and other parts of the local administration. Tribal (Customary) Land is wholly administered, governed and allocated by the Land Boards who give permission for the sinking of a borehole or digging of a well. Certain rules have been formulated by the Land Boards to manage overcrowding of boreholes by settlements and cattle-posts. A general rule of eight kilometres between new boreholes or watering points applies throughout the country. Borehole sinking is a complex task, which has to merge the wishes of the applicant to drill in a certain place, the technical feasibility of finding potable water at a reasonable depth, the presence of sufficient unutilized land, to allow the 8 km rule to be applied, and the absence of counter claims to that land (Adams *et al.*, 2003).

The Land Boards were made more effective through the creation of resolution mechanisms with amendments to the Tribal Land Act in 1993. These resolution mechanisms took the form of the power to cancel a grant of any land rights and the hearing of appeals from the public, confirming or setting aside any decision of any subordinate land authority, and the imposition of restriction on the use of tribal land as well as the introduction of penalties for offences (Adams *et al.*, 2003; Mathuba, 2003).

Borehole syndicates

The formation of borehole syndicates and dam management groups are both supported under policies in Botswana. These address the mismanagement of small dams by farmers and ensure dam users abide by stipulated management rules. Critical management requirements that were identified included members paying stipulated fees, observance of standard stock limitations set at 400 livestock units (LSU) per year per water source, and commitment to collective maintenance and repair of the dams. Dam or borehole management groups in a community grazing area were to consist of approximately 5–20 members. Average herd size was stipulated at 20–80 LSU at the time of application with a possible maximum of 400 LSU. No single person was allowed to water more than 50 head of cattle. Government extension staff were required to take initiative in organizing groups who wanted dams, while district councils could choose to take complete or partial administrative control of dams. Each dam or borehole management group was to be formed before the water facility was constructed and would consist of farmers who wanted the dam and were willing to control their grazing (Manzungu *et al.*, 2009).

Community-based organizations

In Botswana there are corporate organizations formed by all residents or rights holders within a designated area (sometimes spanning several villages). These Trusts, Conservancies, or Communal Property Associations, respectively, elect their own management committees and are governed by legally recognized constitutions. Membership, physical boundaries and accountability mechanisms must be defined by the constitutions (Campbell and Shackleton, 2001).

The CBNRM policy makes provision for community-based organizations or trusts formed by local community members, governed by a formal constitution and an organizational structure that is legally registered. In these cases, local residents or resource users have received user or proprietary rights over resources. This provides them with the authority, through their elected executives or boards, to make rules, approve developments, enter in partnerships with the private sector, receive revenues, and distribute benefits. Most to all of the cash benefits are returned to the community (Campbell and Shackleton, 2001).

The community-based organizations (CBOs) are the key to CBNRM projects in Botswana with clear benefits through the sustainable use, protection and conservation of natural resources, promotion of community-based tourism activities, sustainable use and marketing of veld products for community benefit, promotion of craft production and marketing, community education on the wise and correct management of natural resources and safeguarding the cultural heritage. Most activities are wildlife based, and CBOs are supported by the Department of Wildlife and operate under the umbrella organization BOCOBONET which represents the interest of CBOs and provides support through training and advice (Arntzen *et al.*, 2003).

Analysis of current institutional arrangements

The evolution of Botswana's legislation from a traditional system of resource management to more formalized laws and institutions has met some challenges around commitment and implementation at the local level and the lack of incentives and institutional mechanisms to keep animal herd numbers at a recommended size (Makepe, 2006).

Overstocking on Botswana's communal rangelands has been associated with the failure of existing institutions to coordinate herders' actions in ways that can substantially reduce the uncertainty each herder has over the actions of other herders (Rappoport, 1985; Runge, 1984, 1986). Owing to this, herders keep larger animal numbers than they would otherwise keep if every member of the community was forced to adhere to the recommended herd size (Makepe, 2006)

This uncertainty together with a culture where livestock are kept primarily as a store of wealth and a means of intergenerational wealth transfer (Doran *et al.,* 1979) and with free access to communal rangelands, supported by customary land tenure systems, has led to severe overstocking, overgrazing and land degradation (Merafe, 1992).

Land degradation

Land degradation has a broad range of definitions that essentially describe circumstances of reduced biological productivity of the land (UNCCD, 1994; Reynolds and Stafford Smith, 2002). According to the United Nations Convention to Combat Desertification (UNCCD) definition, land degradation can be caused by both human and climate factors (UNCCD, 1994). Although climate and rainfall variability play a big role in the Kalahari (Washington *et al.,* 2005), 'overstocking' is one of the main human induced drivers of degradation in communal rangelands across Southern Africa, causing rangeland degradation and severe soil erosion in certain places (Merafe, 1992).

Degradation is most prevalent around water points, kraals and settlements mainly in the form of bush encroachment, the reduction in the cover of perennial, palatable species and their replacement by annual less palatable grasses, the presence of alien invasive species, bare soils and mobile dunes (Allen, 1996; Ringrose, 1996; Thomas *et al.,* 2000; Moleele *et al.,* 2002; Muzila *et al.,* 2011; Reed *et al.,* 2008).

Real concerns exist over land degradation which directly impacts the livelihoods of pastoralists in the Kalahari, increases their vulnerability to environmental change and reduces the resilience of the rangeland ecosystem (Thomas and Twyman 2004; Thomas *et al.,* 2000). In some parts of Botswana, land degradation has led to extensive areas of thorny bush encroachment, which cannot be accessed by cattle (Moleele *et al.,* 2002), therefore reducing the economic returns from rangelands and leading to the mobilization of dune fields (Reed *et al.,* 2008).

Efforts in the Kalahari have focused on addressing land degradation and improving the livelihoods of rural people who depend so heavily on communal rangelands and natural resources. There are various examples of engagements, participatory approaches and dialogues to promote learning among local communities, to improve accountability for rangeland management and to understand the drivers of land degradation from community perspectives (Reed *et al.*, 2008; Mosalagae and Mogotsi, 2013; Manzungu *et al.*, 2009).

The recent work by the International Union for Conservation of Nature (IUCN) on enhancing decision-making for interactive environmental learning and action in the Molopo-Nossob River Basin aims to build on the efforts of previous initiatives like the Indigenous Vegetation Project (IVP) funded by the Global Environmental Facility through the United Nations Environmental Programme (UNEP) in order to pin point and address the cause of continued rangeland degradation in the BORAVAST villages of Bokspits, Rappelspan, Vaalhoek, and Struizendam.

Feedback from consultations with pastoralists and range users from 2011–2013, revealed that rangeland degradation is still a serious challenge. These observations are supported in published literature by Dougill *et al.* (1999), Berkeley *et al.* (2005), Reed *et al.* (2008), Thomas *et al.* (2005) and Moleele *et al.* (2002). Signs of degradation are evident by (1) the increasingly high levels of bush encroachment by 'three thorn' (*Rhigozum trichotomum*) across wide areas and around water points, as a result of fire suppression and the maintenance of intensive grazing throughout drought periods (Dougill *et al.*, 1999), (2) poorly spaced boreholes (barely 2 km apart) (Davies, unpublished) and increasing borehole depths in South-West Botswana (Thomas *et al.*, 2005), (3) patchy coverage of vegetation in rangelands, (4) the presence and increasing density of alien invasive species around settlements and water points and (5) clear patches of bare ground around villages observed on satellite imagery. This demonstrates that rangeland management practises and mechanisms are still not put into use effectively in the Kalahari (Davies, unpublished; Moleele *et al.*, 2002).

Case study of the BORAVAST villages in Kgalagadi District

The BORAVAST Trust was formed in 1996 and consists of 12 representatives. The trust represents the interests of communities relating to CBNRM activities in the four villages of Bokspits, Rappelspan, Vaalhoek, and Struizendam in Kgalagadi District. The functioning of the trust has been problematic with capacity challenges and internal disputes and it has failed to support rangeland management activities within the BORAVAST community. There is an over reliance on projects and government support and little opportunity to engage in tourism and CBNRM despite its close location to the Kgalagadi Transfrontier Park.

Research conducted through the Indigenous Vegetation Project (IVP) investigated livestock management practices and constraints in the villages of Bokspits and Vaalhoek. Livestock management is categorized as village-based communal grazing and borehole-based cattle-posts owned by individuals or syndicates (Darkoh, 2000). This revealed that animals are allowed to move freely around boreholes and wells which are the only consistent sources of water in the dry Kalahari, and are therefore used as mechanisms to control livestock mobility without being herded (Perkins, 1996). Goats and calves are only kraaled at night to protect them from predators.

This livestock mobility is considered to be a key strategy to cope with drought and utilize heterogeneous areas (Hitchcock, 1978). Herd mobility used to be practised in BORAVAST, relying on seasonal availability of wild melons to provide moisture for animals. However, the practice is much less common now and herding tends to be static around a given water point. Nevertheless, there is scope for herd management using rotational grazing around water points and there is plenty of opportunity to widen and improve this practice. The IVP research revealed that herd management is only practised to some degree in Bokspits and Vaalhoek where farmers have access to a community ranch, cattle post or 'other grazing areas' but there was no rotational grazing system per se in communal areas. Recent consultations with range users have confirmed this absence of livestock herd management and have revealed that rangeland degradation is also the result of close spacing of water points and the lack of access to grazing areas. The IVP research concurs and highlights the lack of funds, lack of grazing pasture, poor animal condition, and lack of access to markets and to some extent lack of water as driving forces behind land degradation (Olaotswe, 2006).

Five Dunes Farm which lies in the vicinity of the BORAVAST villages is an example of a farm that has some rangeland management mechanisms in practice. The farmer uses hired labour to move the herds and has a contract to sell animals to the Botswana Meat Commission (BMC). He took a loan to install a borehole and this gives effective control of a radius of approximately 8 km. His herd management appears to be very simple, with stock taken in one direction for a given period of time. It seems that the farm is effectively managed in two zones with fairly limited herd management within those zones. However, the farm was in noticeably better condition than other communal land visited, with an abundance of small termite mounds and a diversity of productive grasses and other flora. The good management appears to be the result of the enthusiasm and knowledge of the farmer. The farmer had been trained in farm management and this was reflected in his business planning. However, he showed an inherent knowledge of the environment, of rangeland plants and livestock management practices. The key to his enterprise was managing the farm as a family-based syndicate. The syndicate was set up to access loans for boreholes and is the main vehicle for governance on the farm.

This suggests that successful rangeland management, although not prevalent in the area, is possible without the use of fencing. Boreholes appear to dictate control over rangelands, but this works effectively only in conjunction with strategic herd management.

Case study of Mogojogojo Village in the Ngwaketsi territory

The Lekgwathi borehole drilled in 1957, located in Mogojogojo Village is an example of a well-functioning syndicate. From the onset, the community supported the borehole's construction as a way to mitigate the effects of drought and males from the community volunteered their labour for construction. The borehole was handed over to a local syndicate whose current membership is estimated at over 30 community members. Syndicate members and non-members sell their cattle to the Botswana Meat Commission (BMC), butcheries and traders although they seem to share the same sentiments as the BORAVAST community, complaining that the BMC does not pay well enough. The syndicate has a management committee composed of nine members and the positions are elected by the general membership every five years. The committee meets regularly to discuss all issues pertaining to the status of the borehole, and meetings are a platform for raising complaints and solving conflicts, mediated by the local chief resident. The borehole is operated according to a constitution that stipulates the regulations of use and punitive actions. The secretary keeps a record of all the borehole events (e.g. when it breaks down and the cost of repair). The involvement of the chief is strong and every new management committee is introduced and sanctioned by the chief (Manzungu *et al.*, 2009).

The borehole is mainly used for watering livestock in conjunction with water from other natural and man-made water impounding structures. As in the case of the BORAVAST villages where domestic water is provided mainly from a government constructed desalination plant, a government-constructed borehole not far from Lekgwathi borehole supplies water for domestic use. Syndicate members are restricted in the amount of water they can access for livestock watering, and farmers make use of surface water where possible during the rainy season.

It is estimated that 7,601 cattle are watered from the borehole which serves 11 settlements (Manzungu *et al.*, 2009). The borehole is well maintained and well managed with a gatekeeper regulating livestock entry into the drinking area. Periodic conflicts that do arise relate to disputes involving paying the livestock drinking charges but issues are resolved collectively during general syndicate meetings. The enforcement of rules is very strict and farmers refusing to pay their contributions are swiftly expelled from the syndicate, forfeiting the right to water their livestock. Difficult cases are referred to the village chief for arbitration. This system has effectively ensured that conflicts are easily resolved, largely without the chief's intervention (Manzungu *et al.*, 2009).

The syndicate can be said to be independent of the state and the local villages as it operates independently of village institutions. Syndicate members rarely interact with village institutions except when obtaining information from the Village Development Committee (VDC) on how to run their syndicate. The VDC, a local government development initiative, has provided support in the formation of the syndicate constitution, ensuring the syndicate acts strategically and in providing a platform to table issues to the village councillor and the Member of Parliament.

Challenges to confront

Despite the Government of Botswana taking a progressive approach in adapting its legislation to accelerate the rates of land privatization in order to increase the overall value of cattle regionally, and buffer some of the effects of climate change and degradation much concern has been expressed over the degradation of communal rangelands as a result of overstocking (Arntzen, 1990; Allen, 1996; Ringrose, 1996).

Researchers have come out heavily in criticism of Botswana's policies which are thought to be in favour of economic principles. This legislation has been highlighted as the key reason for continued rangeland degradation in communal areas. As far as implementation of the policies and legislation is concerned, the problem lies in the weak institutional arrangements. This includes institutional inconsistencies as illustrated by problems relating to legal registration of dam management groups or borehole syndicates, the institutional challenges around commitment and implementation at the local level, the lack of incentives and institutional mechanisms to implement best practices, contradictory land uses and limited opportunities to market animals separately of the Botswana Meat Corporation (among others). This has been attributed to the replacement of the custom of traditional leaders with less viable institutional arrangements.

Researchers such as Makepe (2006) and Sporton and Thomas (2002) have supported the idea that the move away from traditional tribal and village institutional systems and away from local decision-making and control is the root cause of degradation in Botswana and even at a wider regional level (Rohde *et al.*, 2006). Manzungu *et al.* (2009) and Moench *et al.* (1999) have highlighted that the top-down approach to policy development and the development of linear policy models places users at the bottom and managers at the top. This disconnection between the realities of the users on the ground and the policy development at a higher level results in contradictions between stated objectives and the practices that emerge, as in the case with the TGLP. The collective capacity of pastoral communities to respond to droughts is based on the nature and effectiveness of formal or informal institutions, including social networks (Twyman *et al.*, 2002) which are not valued in current policies and practices.

Adopting best practices on communal lands requires community-based management at a village level to provide wider social, cultural, and economic benefits in other dryland pastoral regions (Klintenberg *et al.*, 2007; Oba *et al.*, 2008). Empowering village level committees thus should be a priority to enable benefits and success across environmental, economic, and societal aspects of the dryland pastoral system. This idea is supported by Makepe (2006) as this system worked well in pre-colonial times.

Given that droughts tend to occur at a district or national scale devolving accountability to district and national institutions will offer a better capacity to respond. The enhanced support of local extension services, and their ability to outline the long-term benefits of improvements in agricultural management practices, such as those in locally-developed management guides, is essential in improving rangeland management and is supported in research by Dougill *et al.* (2010).

Botswana's land policies have been heavily criticized as being unfavourable to the communal grazing situation in Botswana. The TGLP led to a change in land tenure and a reduction in the size of communal grazing lands. It is widely believed to favour wealthy farmers or ranch owners who are allocated land in communal areas, fragmenting and shrinking the remaining communal land, therefore increasing pressure on this land and aggravating the overgrazing problem rather than alleviating it (Carl Bro International, 1982; Tsimako, 1991; Segosebe, 1997).

The TGLP has received some criticism that its objectives were based on false principles and that it failed to address its objectives (Mosalagae and Mogotsi, 2013; Tsimako, 1991; White, 1993; Frimpong, 1995). First, there was not enough land to demarcate into viable livestock ranches as previously assumed. Second, overriding abiotic factors like rainfall, fire and drought, characteristic of the non-equilibrium nature of semi-arid and arid environments, called into question the coupling of plant-livestock relations, emphasized by the equilibrium theory in grazing systems (Behnke *et al.*, 1993; Scoones, 1995). The TGLP assumed that farmers' allocated ranches would stay on the ranches. To the contrary, ranch owners employed dual grazing rights, where they let their herds onto the commons during wet grazing periods and retreated to their ranches during dry seasons.

Another criticism is the lack of incentives to reduce herd sizes. At present, there is no appropriate institutional mechanism in place to assure herders that if they keep to the recommended herd size, others will follow suit. Hence, each herder has the incentive to take what they require out of the rangeland without any consideration for the future state of the land (Runge, 1981). For this reason, overstocking on Botswana's communal rangelands can be associated with the failure of existing institutions and rules to coordinate herders' actions in ways that can substantially reduce the uncertainty each herder has over the actions of other herders (Rappoport, 1985; Runge, 1984; Runge, 1986). It also relates not only to the number of animals, but to their distribution and mobility and the amount of time spent grazing in one place. Where this is the case, fences, boreholes, and other constraints to distribution will continue to contribute to land degradation.

As a result of continued implementation of privatization policies which favour ranching and further land fragmentation as well as fencing and borehole grazing rights, it is expected that pressure on remaining communal rangelands will continue to increase and both environmental and societal resilience to natural environmental variability will be reduced leading to the inevitable destruction of the natural resource base unless the tenure system is changed (Taylor, 2007).

Opportunities for improved rangelands management

The promotion of social organization and individualism is imperative to be applied as customary institutions for collective action in herding, water, and rangeland management is sorely needed in the Kalahari communities of Botswana. Opportunities exist within existing structures such as the syndicates, as rangeland management in many cases appears to revolve around syndicates, which own and manage boreholes and therefore dictate grazing use in surrounding areas. Manzungu *et al.* (2009) demonstrate that despite flaws in policies and a top-down approach in their development, strong syndicates are a method of organizing groups, holding individuals accountable and effectively managing grazing areas around boreholes. In certain parts of Botswana (e.g. Kgatleng district), cattle owners are already organized in borehole syndicates. Its organization, which is a hierarchical but inclusive structure, is a home-grown institution through which collective action over grazing management (as it is already the case with water) can be entrenched. Considerable research has been devoted to determining the conditions necessary for successful collective action (Wade, 1987; Baland and Platteau, 1996; Ostrom, 1999). Drawing from these lessons the borehole syndicate structure can be strengthened and empowered as an instrument to achieve improved rangeland management.

There is greater need to increase access to markets and improve the access and empowerment of poorer communal farmers, through community-based management committees or formal syndicates. This can reduce system vulnerability much more than programs designed to improve land management within loose communal land management structures. Greater sharing of management knowledge and practices between private and communal land owners offers an opportunity for improved rangeland management, for reduced system vulnerability and to redress some of the inequalities in poverty and livelihood status across the Kalahari. It is evident there are local experts in the community operating under the same conditions and constraints, yet who are demonstrating effective management, and who can act as valuable resource people for further expansion of improved rangelands management.

There remains a need for greater encouragement of, and support for, improved rangeland management approaches, notably in sharing lessons between the management practices on private ranches with communal rangelands. Improved rangeland management involves better matching of grazing intensities with fodder availability, which is extremely variable in such arid areas (Joubert *et al.*, 2008). This could result in the future from either local-scale rotational grazing practices or district level schemes to support landscape scale movement of cattle in response to changes in fodder availability. Such regional movements have long characterized the Kalahari pastoralist's drought coping strategies, formalized traditionally through the mafisa livestock movement system in which friends and family exchange livestock over hundreds of kilometres enabling herds to track forage resources at a landscape scale. This would require the introduction of improved national marketing systems to facilitate rapid destocking at the onset of drought as seen in Namibia (Katjiua and Ward, 2007). Barriers include the increasing numbers of absentee livestock owners (Perkins, 1996) and continued privatization of communal areas that reduce the extent of traditional grazing reserves during drought (Twyman *et al.*, 2002).

Makepe (2006) identifies the dismantling and de-legitimization of traditional resource management institutions in favour of privatization as the root cause of resource overuse and rangeland degradation in Botswana. She supports the premise that collective action can play a big role in correcting poor ecological conditions.

Rangeland management practices can be achieved through better under-standing and monitoring of rangeland management. The potential for learning about management practices, e.g. mix of cattle breeds, rotational grazing, controlled burning and drought feed supplements offers a route to improving livestock yields from communal lands and enhancing system resilience (Reed *et al.*, 2007; Sallu *et al.*, 2009).

Cattle herds and associated incomes from this are likely to continue declining in communal lands under most scenarios. This is due to the effects of ongoing land degradation which will be exacerbated by climate change and fast rates of land tenure conversion to private ownership. Improvements in rangeland management practices are, as yet, only making small improvements to the income that can be derived from communal herds.

Conclusion

The conclusions of this analysis reinforce the findings of earlier researchers in the Kalahari and indicate that the government land privatization policy has helped wealthier ranchers, but has increased the vulnerability of poorer communal pastoralists. However, privatization does remain a route to enhance resilience at a national and district scale as the wealthier, private land-owning group has become less vulnerable to drought, because of this group's ability to purchase food and leverage help from institutions and to undertake a wider range of management options (Chanda *et al.*, 2003).

The analysis also suggests that increasing access to markets and improving the access and empowerment of poorer communal farmers, through community-based management committees or formal syndicates, can reduce system vulnerability more than programs designed to improve land management within 'loose' communal land management structures (Dougill *et al.*, 2010). The achievement of this will involve formalization of management structures at a village level, community engagement in developing and using locally appropriate rangeland monitoring and evaluation tools, and institutional support to empower community groups to function both for their own community and among other communities. This would allow community groups to share knowledge and allow livestock movements in response to fodder availability patterns as required for efficient use of dryland fodder resources.

14 Rebuilding pastoral governance

Lessons learnt and conclusions

*Pedro M. Herrera, Jonathan Davies and
Pablo Manzano Baena*

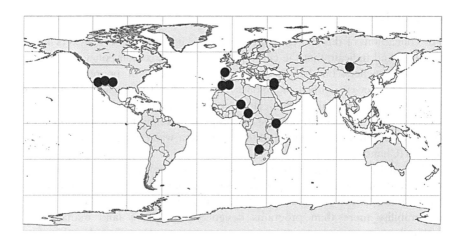

The case studies presented in the previous chapters show a strong effort to recover pastoralist governance around the world. The 11 cases represent global work regarding new models of managing rangelands and other grass related ecosystems. The chapters describe varying situations, including the organization of land use and infrastructures of open-access nomadic pastoralism in Central Africa – with special attention to its relationship with wetlands and drylands, the bylaws of traditional land management systems in Kenya and the recovery of traditional land management systems. Elsewhere in Africa, case studies address modern co-operative systems in Morocco and the adaptation of land tenure systems to extensive cattle production in Botswana. Pastoralism in the Middle East is addressed in two chapters that cover different visions of the recovery the Hima system of land tenure in Lebanon and Jordan. An Asian perspective is analysed with the incorporation of Mongolia, one of the hotspots of pastoralism, with millions of hectares of state land dedicated to mobile pastoralism and facing a great challenge and transformation related both to political and climate change experienced in the last decades.

The case studies are not just centred on developing countries. Three cases, grouped in the chapter on the United States, show how pastoralists and ranchers deal with ecological, economic and social constraints in three North American states (California, Arizona and Texas). Pastoralists there face different challenges from those of Africa and Asia, but they express the same needs for the proper governance of rangelands to ensure the services they provide for society. The Spanish case reveals an interesting pastoralist cultural heritage and addresses the question of how abandonment and under-grazing may actually expand severe ecological problems like wildfires or diversity loss.

The collected case studies focus on recovering and enhancing pastoral governance as an important way to properly manage wide expanses of rangelands. The tools to achieve this aim are community-based management (CBM) of rangelands and using participatory land use governance to upgrade and adapt traditional systems of land use and land access rights to increase sustainability while conserving the wisdom and perspective that are already part of the system. The goal is not only to manage rangelands better, but also to prevent ecological problems from unsuitable practices like poor grazing adjustment, to fight against global change and biodiversity loss and to provide sustainable livelihoods to the people living in those systems. There are voids in the map that we would like to have filled such as in Australia, the Horn of Africa and South America. Recovering governance is a long-term project and there will be more opportunities to learn from pastoralism around the world.

The basis of recovering governance

This chapter aims to synthesize the lessons learnt from the case studies and organize them into a common framework in order to share the solutions adopted in each particular case and to reflect on their potential applications across the globe. The overall objective is to provide good examples of pastoral governance recovery, unravelling the path to success for such projects. Also, there is a special focus on the constraints that have been experienced, and the failures and errors identified through the work presented. We provide methodological and practical guidelines to design, implement, and assess pastoral governance initiatives.

Recovering governance is a complex task based on three main aspects, as defined in the IUCN Social Policy (IUCN, 2000) and highlighted by the Jordan case study:

1   Rules, norms, institutions and processes that determine how power and responsibilities are exercised.
2   Decision-making.
3   Citizens' participation.

Governance can be defined as the expression of the relationship among citizens, leaders and public institutions for managing land and other resources (DFID, 2006). The three main factors to consider from the side of government (Kaufmann *et al.*, 1999) are as follows:

1   Government's capability to get things done.
2   Responsiveness of public policies and institutions to the needs of citizens.
3   Accountability.

From the perspective of citizens the factors under consideration are their participation in decision-making and how society addresses compliance with established laws and accounts for government actions.

This book focuses on one particular aspect of governance, which is how pastoralist (or extensive livestock) rangelands are managed. Many rangelands are experiencing degradation, driven by changes to the way rangelands are managed and failure to understand and maintain, or otherwise adapt, customary governance practices. Failures in pastoralism are often attributable to the weakening of traditional management systems that until recently were able to effectively manage those ecosystems. The effects of this governance loss are both the maladjustment of grazing load and the appropriation of rangelands for other purposes (e.g., intensive agriculture or livestock production, 'ranchetting', mining, urbanization or tourism), driving processes of rangeland degradation.

We examine the consequences of rangeland degradation, in terms of natural heritage (e.g., desertification, biodiversity loss or wildfire incidence) and social and economic considerations that include low productivity and the reduced ability of rangelands to support the livelihoods of their often poor and marginalized populations. The solution to these problems cannot be properly addressed without taking into account local populations. IUCN Social Policy (IUCN, 2000) establishes that sustainable use of natural resources cannot be achieved unless local people have fair access to them and have control of natural resources, without discrimination based on gender, class, ethnicity, age or other social variables. Accordingly, the starting point of any solution proposed to improve rangelands and decelerate their degradation should empower communities and local users by recognizing their rights and responsibilities and ensuring their means to sustainable livelihoods and human development. This empowerment points to several achievements that need to be considered while planning any kind of development project:

•   Fair and safe land tenure and access systems.
•   Participation in land planning and decision-making.
•   Capacity building and support of local communities to develop their participation.
•   Establishment of legal and institutional frameworks adapted to allow community management of natural resources.

To address rangeland degradation requires the restoration of prudent management systems by recovering pastoralist culture, livelihoods and governance along with the benefits and services they provide. The recovery of pastoralism demands the re-establishment of traditional management systems while introducing a governance framework able to support and secure such a system. Simply recovering traditional systems and making them work in the context of global change, economics and communications is inconceivable. However, maintenance, upgrading, adaptation and development can lead to a recovery of pastoral governance in the twenty-first century. The only way to ensure such reclamation is to ensure that pastoralists and local populations are involved in and participating in the management processes from the beginning.

A participatory approach to rangelands governance

There are two complementary approaches indicated among the case studies to recover rangelands governance: participatory approaches and community-based management (CBM). CBM is closely related to community-based natural resource management (CBNRM), which is an emerging model for sustainable natural resource management that addresses environmental protection and social justice (Gruber, 2010). The principles leading this approach are participative democracy, networking between active agents involved, and integration of decision-making levels. Several institutions devoted to sustainable development are adopting this approach in order to improve the sustainability and capacity to provide livelihoods for local people (Bond *et al.*, 2006; IFAD, 2006). Such management models are applied to a range of managed ecosystems including forests (Molnar *et al.*, 2011; Bowler *et al.*, 2010), coastal ecosystems (Samarakoon *et al.*, 2011) and, of course rangelands.

Some chapters argue that CBNRM is the best tool to improve forest and rangeland governance. The Botswana chapter in this book outlines the adoption of a CBNRM Policy by the government to safeguard the interest of communities and attract investment in natural resource enterprises. In this case, CBNRM helped to build and improve land tenure and natural resource user rights for local communities. The Botswana chapter also demonstrates the central role played by community-based organizations in the development of CBNRM projects.

All of the case studies demonstrate that a participatory approach is needed and most of them have tried to reach their goals through thorough participatory processes based on similar approaches. The central role of local populations and stakeholders are established as a key for success. Many authors have defined effective local participatory processes that rely on a set of considerations emphasizing the correct role of stakeholders. The following list compiles the most important of these considerations (Reed, 2008):

1   Stakeholder participation needs to be underpinned by a philosophy that emphasizes empowerment, equity, trust and learning.
2   Stakeholder participation should be considered as early as possible and throughout the process.
3   Relevant stakeholders need to be analysed and represented systematically.
4   Clear objectives for the participatory process need to be agreed among stakeholders at the outset.

5   Methods should be selected and tailored to the decision-making context, considering the objectives, type of participants and appropriate level of engagement.
6   Highly skilled facilitation is essential.
7   Local and scientific knowledge should be integrated.
8   Participation needs to be institutionalized.

The Kenya case study, for example, clearly addressed these considerations, displaying an appropriate methodological approach for the recovery of the traditional rangeland governance system in the Kenyan drylands. The project aims to improve natural resource governance in an attempt to support better livelihood security and ecosystem management in the drylands of Garba Tula. The main objectives include policy guidance for dryland management, improved capacity of participation in decision-making for local communities, institutions and government, and participatory collaborative arrangements and institutions to manage dryland ecosystem resources.

The methodological approach proposed in the Kenya case study could serve as a guideline for designing projects with similar aims. Effective participation is at the heart of this approach; by teaching local communities the skills to engage in decision-making processes people can participate in local systems of governance. Participatory tools can improve people's capacities in management and planning.

The strengthening of traditional grazing management sought in the Kenyan case study was developed by translating the customary *Boran* system into a legal framework that could be adopted by the local authorities and state government. This complex task had to be performed upon the demand of and with the authentic participation of the local population. The logical sequence of such a project, are as follows, although in this case phases 2 and 3 were implemented in parallel:

First phase: reparation:
1   Engage community leaders.
2   Incorporate local organizations and institutions.
3   Document customary rules and regulations.

Second phase: establishment of bylaws:
4   Negotiate and draft bylaws based on customary rules and regulations.
5   Adopt these bylaws on a county/local level.

Third phase: participatory planning:
6   Create a participatory resource map.
7   Negotiate land planning between government and the community.

Fourth phase: implementation of plans:
8   Promote the community-based management plans to investors and development partners.

The Jordan case shows a clear path to success using a participatory approach to governance, supported by local accomplishments. The four major goals are building capacity, empowering people, opening access to decision-making and engaging under-privileged groups. Capacity building, according to the Jordan chapter, is represented by five keystones: focused vision and clearly identified problems and long-term solutions; reliable and thorough information; acknowledgement of political choices from various proposed solutions; risk assessment and risk reduction both in the short and long-term; and advocating for local and under-privileged people.

The empowerment of people – including women – is highlighted in the Jordan example as a foundation to success, allowing local communities to develop the management system they choose. The chapter lists five factors influencing success in empowerment: authentic local participation; networks and communication mechanisms between participants and stakeholders; shared strategies with participants; early achievements from pilot projects; and a gender-sensitive approach that enhances the voices and capacities of women for participation and promotes their role within the community governance structures.

The background to successful governance developments

Many chapters in this book highlight concerns that could be added to the previous checklist in order to improve the approach for strengthening governance. The Jordanian example of reviving the traditional Hima system lists some of these concerns and orientations, starting from the community participatory approach already established as a common framework. They overlap with the previous checklist on several points but also point to some important considerations that facilitate the design of successful projects, such as the incorporation of minority and more vulnerable groups, the development of gender-sensitive approaches and the search for consensus over shared strategies for the development of local land resources. The work highlights an effective practice in the participatory approach, which is to design pilot projects early on, with measurable milestones, in order to generate tangible evidence of the value of community planning and to provide local leadership with early success, which serves to encourage and empower participants.

Political decentralization

The case studies show two main ways for government to take responsibility in developing rangeland governance processes: decentralization and co-ordination, which, if well implemented, will ensure the implementation of the regulations developed and guarantee the continuation of the use and access rights adopted.

Decentralization can be broadly defined as local governments exercising authority over local resources and governance systems. Decentralization can in some cases lead to greater transparency and accountability for local government actions, including legal guardianship of the agreements reached, and the capacity of participants to defend the process in the face of challenges.

Political decentralization is a major condition demanded in several governance projects. As stated in the Lebanon case study, decentralization implies that a local government must have both the authority and resources to plan and co-ordinate local-level strategic plans and provide frontline services. Local governments need to be open to development and legal support of rules, bylaws, contracts or plans obtained as a result of participatory processes. The need for decentralization is made clear in the Jordan case as well as in the background of other chapters (e.g., Spain, Morocco and Mongolia); it can be considered to be of interest globally.

Co-ordination and integration of government responsibility

Co-ordination implies that decisions made by a branch of government about land tenure rights will not be violated by any other branch of government, guaranteeing the security of agreements reached during participatory processes. This co-ordination can be implemented by several mechanisms, for example by including all agencies and administrations with responsibilities in the participatory process, appointing transversal committees representing the whole administration or delegating power in specific institutions, but they all present significant challenges to establish. One solution, as explained in the North American chapter about Arizona Comprehensive Fire Plans, consists of developing high-level land planning tools, supported by a nation-wide legal framework for all government agencies. This way relevant government branches are compelled to participate in the process or at least to accept its results.

The lack of co-ordination between government branches is one of the most important challenges to governance and it occupies a prominent position among the common constraints and difficulties. As a result, an important focus of governance projects should be on ensuring government co-ordination before attempting to develop planning tools that could be undermined by the administration itself.

Finally, rangelands (and mobile pastoralists too) are often transnational, which means that co-ordination can involve the governments of two or more countries that must agree to shared regulations in an area. The Cameroon case analyses government involvement in the maintenance of open access to common-pool grazing resource systems, as supported by the Lake Chad Basin Commission (LCBC) since its creation in the 1960s. The LCBC was formed by the four countries bordering Lake Chad – Cameroon, Chad, Niger and Nigeria – and recently it added the Central African Republic and Sudan. The LCBC has been co-ordinating veterinary controls, facilitating livestock trade, allowing pastoralists to travel freely (after addressing health and tax issues) and promoting conservation and development projects in the Chad Basin.

In the same way, it is important to develop an international framework to support community rights and traditional land tenure and access systems. The importance of such international agreements is to support transnational systems and the enforcement and capacity of local initiatives to develop long-term agreements respected by their own governments. The support of international institutions has a key role in the relationship with governments by pressuring them to abide by their promises.

The need for tenure security

Many of the case studies highlight the need to establish close relationships with local governments that are clearly committed to the results of the processes and the insistence on decentralization for long-term success of rangeland governance. The security of rights is one approach to maintain their positive effects over time. The Mongolian chapter assesses the success of land management reforms as a means to ensure security of tenure and long-term access to resources by the herding community and other legitimate users are essential to long-term success. Without security in land rights, pastoralists have been shown to reject the responsibility for rangelands management and have been discouraged from investing the time and resources required for long-term sustainability of the resources managed.

The security of land use and land access rights promoted by the case studies constitutes a major constraint in the viability of land management projects. Long-term rangeland governance issues, which depend on long-term investments and actions, also imply long-term security of use and access rights for people in charge. It must be noted that securing rights is a great challenge, especially in conflict zones, where the viability of whole projects can be threatened by disputes.

The way to secure rights starts with the visibility of pastoralist communities and the establishment of a clear position in land management. The first step is to build up a network of relationships that supports herders' interests. As stated in both the United States and the Spanish case studies, pastoralists need a network of social and political relations to secure their role in land rights management. The existence of a strong pastoralist social fabric is a requirement to stand up for their rights and defend the achievements gained.

One source of conflict is the perception that secure ownership rights are needed to allow economic agents to develop markets and production, and the belief that this is how most developed countries manage their land. However, even in industrialized countries there are wide tracts of public or common land (mostly rangelands, drylands and woodlands) that governments own and are responsible for. The claim for private ownership of some of these lands can lead to intensification, encroachment, abandonment and improper uses that end in degrading those lands.

In practice, outright ownership is not necessarily a pre-condition for sustainable management of rangelands, and in many cases has been a factor in desertification. It is necessary to see resource rights on a continuum, from the most universal open-access rights at one extreme, to individual private property rights at the other. Along this continuum, the right to manage and the right to exclude others, even periodically, are the crucial factors in enabling sustainable rangelands management.

The continuum of property rights[1]

The keystone for security is the commitment and involvement of government in the models of participatory processes that should be established. A significant challenge is to incorporate local and regional government agencies as co-

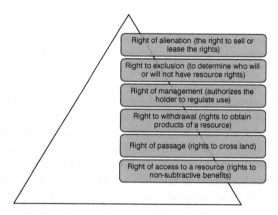

Figure 14.1 The continuum of property rights

operative agents in the commitment to approve, validate and secure the resultant instruments. The Kenya case study clearly demonstrates this process with regional and local government involved in the participatory creation of bylaws for customary land tenure rights. Moreover, the involvement of government is vital for the development of bylaws into land planning tools that are obtained from participatory processes.

Strategic vision

A number of chapters in this book consider the importance of addressing land management projects from a strategic planning point of view, which is referred to as the strategic planning cycle for sustainable land management (SLM). Strategic planning introduces a logical framework based on a sequential progression that includes performing diagnostics, formulating objectives, programming and executing actions, evaluating the process and feedback. The importance of a strategic vision comes from the use of evaluable objectives as a starting point, allowing participants to evaluate results and propose changes and feedback to the whole project, while enhancing the active role of participants (Jain and Polman, 2007).

Improving sustainability, efficiency, profitability and welfare of herders means improving rangelands

Most of the case studies conclude that the improvement of rangelands implies greater profitability for pastoralism. As stated in the North American case study, the encouragement of profitable pastoralism and other traditional livelihoods can emerge from traditional land practices. The effort to maintain rich, mature rangelands requires pastoralist intervention, and in order to guarantee this intervention, pastoralists need to profit from rangelands and maintain economic benefits over time. Such profitability needs to be adequate to preserve their activity and compensate for hardships and economic insecurity that can accompany herding.

Accordingly, actions to improve efficiency, sustainability and profitability of pastoralism can engender positive development in rangeland management. However, there is a risk in making improvements that increase profitability by intensifying production but which make the area more dependent upon external inputs and accordingly, more vulnerable to external influences. As explained in the previous chapter, one approach to mitigating that risk is to let pastoralists operate in the way they know and focus efforts on facilitating marketing, selling and social acceptance of their products as a priority.

Strengthening project implementation for rangelands governance

Several community-based management (CBM) projects have provided a description of the conditions needed to develop good management systems based on community participation. A number of concerns deserve mention:[2]

- *Scale.* Projects need to be addressed at an appropriate scale, considering that ecological relationships are wider than land planning units, so external links need to be accounted for. The Garba Tula case study, for example, highlights the adoption of landscape level approaches to analysis and mapping, which is more appropriate for that level of land planning because it fits with traditional management arrangements and is able to accomplish the need for mobility and seasonal use of resources.
- *Time.* Regaining control of and establishing adequate management systems requires a long-term focus even though livelihoods and market issues demand short-term achievements. All of the case studies show evolving projects, with open temporary horizons. The Spanish chapter states clearly that participatory projects are intended for the long-term and eventually they would evolve following unexpected paths.
- *Complexity/difficulty.* Natural and social systems are complex, so CBM projects need to manage extremely diverse interests and relationship among all agents involved. The Cameroon chapter shows how a complex pastoral system that involves tremendously diverse people and livestock was able to profit from a common open system.
- *Human resources.* It is not easy to implement a CBM project; they often need resources and skills that can be difficult to obtain. The case studies from West Morocco and Kenya show exemplary paths leading to the successful implementation of projects in demanding conditions. However, identifying suitable skills and allocating adequate resources for them has proven challenging in a number of initiatives.
- *Land tenure.* Community management needs to modify the ownership and control over natural resources demanding a secure legal and community framework to establish those rights. Most cases show different systems of land tenure and the efforts to adapt them to current circumstances strengthening and updating traditional land tenure systems, as the Hima system (e.g., Lebanon, Jordan), the Agdals (Morocco) and others.

- *Partnerships.* The establishment of adequate partnerships among the agents involved (stakeholders, government, private sector, NGO and community agents) constitutes a basis for successful change. Most case studies focus on partnerships among involved agents, both in developed and developing countries.
- *Ecological status of the resources.* Finally, the viability of such management systems depends on the quality of the natural resources to be managed. It is necessary to correctly assess this status prior to developing new management systems and to be aware of their genuine capacity to support the livelihoods involved. The Mongolian case study, for example, addresses several ecological factors and their role in global change.

Those topics could be used as a checklist to refine the methodological approach adopted for each target site in order to achieve high quality processes.

Rebuilding pastoral governance: investing in human, social and political capital

While the considerations above are important to the success of participatory approaches, the specific pastoralist requirements of any system should be sustained and improved upon over time. The development of projects designed to recover traditional governance systems need to address several technical elements. In the case of Eastern Morocco, the role of fledgling co-operatives, created out of traditional institutions, describes some of the conditions needed to ensure the performance of pastoral activities:

- Lead role of pastoralist organizations (e.g., professional associations, co-operatives or pasture users groups) participating with their peers, with ethnic institutions, and with other public or private institutions, always ensuring adequate representation of pastoralists.
- Special consideration of pastoralist interests during the process, which may include adequate interlocution with the administration, presence in land planning, and improvements in terms of profitability. If pastoralism is not profitable the whole governance of rangelands will be at stake.

However, the recovery of traditional pastoralist governance involves complex, ecologically-oriented systems that regulate the agro-silvo-pastoral production system and demand deep knowledge of social and ecological relationships. These systems have deeper roots than land management. As the project of Western Morocco shows, traditional systems often emerge from a religious and cultural basis, thereby possessing heritage and spiritual considerations that need to be included in the big picture. Misunderstanding of the spiritual, cultural and religious processes behind traditional institutions can potentially lead to the misdiagnosis of local situations in rural societies.

Elements of good practice in strengthening pastoral governance

Good practices highlight topics that have been considered in the case studies such as the institutionalization of CBNRM and bridging the gaps between government agencies and pastoralist communities. The case studies provide an overview of activities and approaches that can be helpful to design new projects and to assess and evaluate performance in current ones. Being mostly participatory projects, the case studies are long-term, locally driven and dynamic projects, which engender capacity change and adaptation driven by the involvement of their participants. Accordingly, their objectives, actions and achievements vary over time as situations change.

Compilation of basic information

Baseline information has been shown to be essential for developing and monitoring good governance. The Sahel-Niger paper, for example, reveals the need for adequate background analysis to develop appropriate management systems, especially when wetlands are involved. The communities prepared an inventory of natural resources and biodiversity information about the land that includes its physical description, utilization by people, its biodiversity, economic value and the threats to its functioning. Moreover, such a compilation, based on local people's knowledge, may constitute the basis for further governance developments.

Recovering ancestral knowledge

The case studies largely show that the key to strengthening rangeland governance is not to invent a new management system, but rather to update successful traditional mechanisms. Good management practices are often based on a deep ancestral knowledge of ecological and social dynamics that have survived until the present and have been transmitted from herder to herder. As stated in the first part of the book, pastoralist practices have proven to manage complex ecosystems such as rangelands, keeping them in good health.

All studies reviewed here relied to some degree on recovering traditional systems and tools, some of them quite well known and described: the Agdal in Morocco; the Hima in Jordan and Lebanon; the Boran system in Kenya. Some of them, like the open-access system described in the Logone Floodplain in Cameroon, are even more complex in their regulations due to the lack of a clearly stated mechanism or authorities in charge, in apparent contradiction with a well-managed system that groups 200,000 cattle driven by thousands of pastoralists from different countries and ethnicities.

Even the most modern systems of rangeland management among the case studies show a clear dependence upon traditional knowledge. An example is the chapter from North America, where traditional knowledge – like fire used as a management tool – has been reinstated in order to preserve rangelands. The same is shown in the Spanish case, which demonstrates an attempt to recover the ancient uses of mountain pastures as a way to preserve biologically diverse grassland habitats.

Moreover, when modernized legal frameworks ignore traditional knowledge, constraints and failures in the application of management are observed. For example, the Mongolian study reveals that contemporary environmental laws show a lack of coherence in terms of relationships between those laws and the ecological processes and limitations. In such a case the recovery of traditional knowledge could constitute a powerful basis to develop effective new tools.

Restoring the influence of traditional and tribal leadership

Several case studies show the importance of restoring ancestral governance mechanisms as a preliminary step to regain local control over territory. The East Morocco case highlights some key conclusions about the importance of ancestral rights recovery. The Moroccan case states that the acknowledgement of tribal rights has been a keystone to their success; the reorganization of countryside in rural communes has been based on tribal criteria, which eased the common management of rangelands. Importantly, local people have perceived an opportunity to regain control of their own resources and actively responded by getting deeply involved in the process. The Kenya case study also shows deep involvement of tribal institutions in the development of new management systems, highlighting the role of the Boran institutions through a local community-based organization, the Resource Advocacy Program.

The challenge to restoring community rights is how communities can adapt them to the rapidly changing conditions of the world. The West Moroccan case also provides a roadmap for reforming ethnic and tribal institutions. The first step is to develop a legal framework for hosting and supporting modern organizations based on existing socio-institutional traditional systems that incorporate traditional values and organize themselves along tribal lines while improving the organizations with management structures in conjunction with government institutions with a view to facilitating collective action and the sustainable management of natural resources. A benefit of such an approach is that government support boosts management capacity, adopts appropriate technical measures to develop rangelands and establishes a set of organizational and regulatory tools to manage rangelands in a responsible manner. The adoption of appropriate technical measures and the creation of an appropriate juridical and institutional framework are essential for the success of innovative approaches.

Updating traditional systems

The presence of well-established traditional governance mechanisms – like the Agdal in Morocco, Hima in Lebanon and Jordan, and the Boran system in Kenya – provides a good starting point for recovering pastoralist approaches to land management. The East Moroccan study describes an ecological framework and process, which collectively decides on space rotation and collaboratively provides equal access to local natural resources for all members of the community.

The case studies examine various ways of modernizing these systems. The simplest is recognition of traditional systems without interfering in their functioning. This may be the only option in complex scenarios involving various countries and territories, as proposed in the Chad Basin and described by the Cameroon chapter. Another way could be the 'revival' of traditional systems with strong effort in developing governance using participatory tools, as shown in Jordan. A third way is to completely transform and update traditional systems towards a collaborative and participatory approach. Examples of this approach are seen in the legal framework that was developed with grassroots organizations in the Kenya case and aspects of the Mongolian case and the West Moroccan cases.

Empowering women through rangeland governance

Explicit attention to the role of women pastoralists receives inadequate attention in the case studies in this book, and would be worthy of a unique volume. Nevertheless, important lessons have be learnt regarding the roles women play in governing communal rangelands, and the risks that strengthening governance could place on pastoralist women's rights. Demographic changes and urbanization affect men and women pastoralists differently and there is a growing phenomenon of pastoralist-women headed households. These women may play the principle role in the pastoral economy, but their authority over the management of rangelands is not guaranteed. The Jordanian chapter shows that it is possible to strengthen rangeland governance through explicit focus on the role of women as resource managers. This not only has led to re-establishment of effective management regimes, but has rapidly led to broad-based women's empowerment.

A common feature in many case studies has been the restoration and legitimization of customary institutions. While this clearly leads to more effective management of rangelands, it cannot be assumed that this leads to greater equity in resource use. Great care must be taken to avoid transferring unprecedented power to a few male community leaders at the expense of women. It is appropriate, although challenging, to talk about reforming customary institutions and behaviours through dialogue and empowerment of women as well as men. Indeed, as the Jordan example shows, governance may be an excellent entry-point for work on more general women's empowerment.

Enhancing social fabric and grassroots organizations among pastoralists

Pastoralist grassroots organizations are needed as a basis for developing governance projects. Governance demands empowerment, voice, accountability and capacity and none of these can be developed without a supportive social network. Accordingly, one of the first tasks in developing governance projects is to evaluate the social fabric in the target communities and assess the attributes of good governance that exist already.

The way to develop social fabric is unique for each project, as shown in the case studies. If there are empowered pastoralist organizations, as in the United States, such grassroots organizations assume leadership in developing governance projects. Otherwise, one of the first steps must be to develop a strong social fabric that enables pastoralists to strengthen their capacity, voice, empowerment and interlocution. As the North American case reports, creating social connections is one way to maintain access to, and the ability to benefit from, rangelands in a changing ecological, economic and social environment.

The first way to do this, as already explained, is to work from traditional institutions, adapting them to participation and governance. The Garba Tula case study explains how the contact in terms of partnership with active customary organizations played a leading role in the whole developing project. The East Morocco case promotes the transformation of tribal organizations into new co-operatives that transcend their origins to play a key role in rangeland governance.

In the absence of traditional organizations it is possible to help herders to support and assess emerging organizations or platforms, as proposed by the Lebanon case study. Likewise, the Spanish case also promotes the birth of new farmers' associations, independent from the unions and professional organizations that (in farmers' words) do not represent properly their interests. In this case, the Castile-León examples focus on developing local social fabric among pastoralists as a way to empower them and promote better representation to deal with local and regional government. Fledgling farmers' associations are intended to develop pastoralists' public voice and image.

Another way is to empower and give voice to local community-based organizations, as suggested in the Jordan project. The Botswana case study states that CBNRM relies mostly on CBOs that formalize the needs of management structures at a village level from the point of view of farmers' social fabric. Finally, even when dealing with the more complex and open situations – like the exposed open-access system in the Logone Floodplain in Cameroon – grassroots organizations should participate as interlocutors for governments and the private sector in order to preserve the integrity of the open system during local crisis.

However, not all grassroots organizations are suitable for leading governance projects. Many of them lack the capacity for governance work (e.g., accountability and transparency, equity, representativeness or gender balance). Support to these CBOs is often necessary to ensure a sound participatory approach. However, most of those organizations evolve within governance projects and experience deep transformations. The East Morocco case, for example, shows the change of pastoralist co-operatives from tribal based organizations to more open and specialized bodies, representing transversal interests and empowered enough to deal with governance issues.

The Mongolian case demonstrates how local organizations champion rangeland management. Their approach is based on local pasture user organizations – pasture user groups and herder groups – that play a critical role in implementing community-based grassland management projects. The aim of these projects, some of them supplemented by international funds, has been to facilitate the formation of hundreds of these associations, to develop capacity to establish participatory plans and to sign contracts on rangeland utilization with local government agencies. The contract system can form the centrepiece in linking the legal, policy and institutional framework for the management of pastureland at the local level. These associations allow herders to participate in decision-making, promote the sustainable use of grasslands, and address other aspects of livestock management through relationship-building among herders and between them and other stakeholders.

Open access, ethos driven management

The most complex systems included in the chapters are managed by open access and open rights systems, e.g., mobile pastoralism in the Chad Basin in the Cameroon chapter. The difficulty of managing open access and open use systems is overridden by pastoralists' strong ethos about common rights for all that is embodied in the 'It is about cattle, not about people.' Those mechanisms also show two good practices in rangeland management: to focus on livestock needs more than people's issues and to rely on strong ethical systems that guarantee equal rights for people involved.

Developing bylaws out of pastoralist traditional rules and regulations

Most case studies illustrate the need for an adequate legal framework protecting sustainable use and access rights to natural resources. The Kenya case study shows the most advanced effort to develop bylaws out of customary rules and regulations, although other cases, like those from Morocco, Lebanon or Cameroon also point to the need for good translation between customary rules and the legal framework established in each country. This is the critical lesson: to work with government brings its own challenges. One solution is for NGOs to position themselves as government partners in implementing policies, either with the executive arm of government or, as in the case of Kenya, in relationship with members of the legislature, which was critical for achieving political integration.

Approving specific pastoralist laws

Some of the case studies, especially those located in countries with tight legal frameworks (e.g., Mongolia or Spain), advocate for specific laws protecting pastoralists and extensive farming. The Mongolian study explains the role of Mongolian 'Pastureland act' in rangeland governance while the Spanish case illustrates a state-wide 'Rangelands act', which follows the example of some regional governments that have developed similar laws.

Promoting land reform approaches

Globalization is driving major governmental changes throughout the world, making governments more actively involved in land management, especially in developing countries. These changes also demand new land planning tools that need to take into account pastoralism as a keystone for governing rangelands. The Mongolian case shows a land reform approach for addressing those changes. This reform approach could be suitable for other countries to enhance the role of rangelands and natural resources in environmental and productive policies that address the following factors: reorganizing the legal framework; using an ecological approach; decentralizing and co-ordinating the administration; specialist institutions or agencies in charge; unifying the aim of environmental laws; and accepting a long-term plan to develop legal, policy and institutional reforms. A number of the case studies illustrate the need for reviewing land use policies, laws, regulations and bylaws in order to reform effective community-based resource management.

Building on pastoralist professionalism

Pastoralism governance projects usually go better if their promoters are aware that most pastoralists are true specialists in their jobs. They have been making a living from their livestock since birth, receiving training from their elders and learning from the tradition they wish to preserve. Given certain basic enabling factors, including access to fair markets for their goods and environmental services, it is reasonable to assume that pastoralists are competent rangeland managers. Land degradation does not arise from an internal lack of pastoralist capacity but from external drivers, involving global change. The technical basis of pastoral governance (and rangeland management) should assume this knowledge. The changes experienced in pastoralist production generally relate to new market conditions, new rules and regulations about health, feed or mobility, or the application of new technologies, all of which are matters in which pastoralists may need support and training.

Several chapters reveal the importance of properly addressing the needs of pastoralists for training when developing governance projects. For example, the North American study shows the pastoralists' preference for learning from their peers, highlighting a common error of pastoralism development projects: to offer unsolicited technical assessment instead of working within the bounds proposed by pastoralists themselves. Pastoralists are aware of their needs, in terms of technical assessment, but also in terms of what is more important to them, which the case studies show: self-organization, business management, accountancy, marketing, planning, networking, lobbying and government relationships. Pastoralist governance projects will likely improve their probabilities of success if they follow the lead of pastoralists in livestock and rangeland management while focusing on enhancing their social, economic and networking outcomes.

Improving the image of pastoralists

The high quality production of pastoralism, while not strictly a governance consideration, could generate better prices and higher incomes for pastoralists if that quality is marketed. Pastoralism needs to become competitive in relation to industrial livestock production, which tends to sell at cheaper prices and to address better health and legal requirements. Pastoralists need to make visible the higher quality products they sell, the environmental services they provide for the whole society and the cultural heritage they keep. In many cases, to achieve this they need to improve their public image and help the general public appreciate their value.

Both the North American and Spanish case studies highlight the weight of pastoralist's public image when developing land planning and management. Moreover, the Spanish study shows that the improvement of pastoralists' image is a nation-wide task to be embraced by the entire pastoralist movement. A better image is one way to enhance pastoralists' business and lobbying capacity.

Collaborative perspective of rangeland management

Pastoralists and governments usually have the same objectives for rangeland management, which are higher production, sustainable management of resources, prevention of erosive processes and desertification, and improved livelihoods for local population. Pastoralists possess the tools for managing rangelands and governments have the power to secure the best management system. A collaborative arrangement between government and pastoralists – with stakeholders and population affected – would be the best way to improve rangeland governance. All case studies reflected an active wish for collusion with local, regional and state governments and several of them have accomplished it.

The revival of the Hima system, as developed in Jordan or Lebanon, and the Agdal in Morocco shows how land management can provide governance for a whole set of natural resources and productive lands. Both the Spanish and North American cases highlight the valuable position of ranchers and farmers in other issues not directly related to livestock, such as fire prevention, hunting or water management. Pastoralists already have a broad vision of land management and their involvement enriches the big picture of land management.

Multi-functional rangelands

Rangelands are managed by pastoralists and extensive livestock keepers, but livestock is not the only profitable outcome obtained from judicious management. The Botswana, Morocco, Spain and North America case studies reveal that when profitability of pastoralism and extensive livestock production is not enough to maintain high levels of investment and pastoralist livelihoods are at stake, it could be necessary to balance herders' rents with complementary activities such as tourism, hunting, fishing or other sustainable rangeland activities.

The planning and management of this production relies on modelling land governance that could be assigned to the same institutions and tools governing pastoralist management. However, it demands more knowledge and skills, which are sometimes beyond herders' capacity. Consequently, it could be necessary to incorporate new technical assessment and new participants in rangeland governance.

Preserving pastoral infrastructure

Pastoralism, especially mobile and nomadic pastoralism, depends on the good condition of infrastructure needed to ensure mobility, including water points, livestock tracks, resting places and campsites. The Cameroon chapter describes the pastoralists' main infrastructure, which is frequently hidden, around the Logone floodplain, highlighting its importance and pointing to the difficulty of preserving it. The chapter analyses the way government is attempting to develop regulations that protect livestock corridors. Several local committees have been proposed to delineate agricultural and pastoral zones and designate transhumance corridors. One goal has been to motivate and organize stakeholders to delimit and preserve, by means of consensus, this infrastructure and some 150 km of transhumance corridors have now been protected. However, protection starts with delimitation. Government has to include those boundaries in an appropriate legal framework that is able to prevent encroachment and land conflicts, but the participatory processes that provide consensus are lengthy, expensive and dependent on external funds. Sometimes relevant stakeholders such as mobile pastoralists and farmers remain out of the processes and do not effectively represent their own interests.

Another topic revealed in the Cameroon case study is the need for flexibility in the delimitation, mapping and legal protection of pastoralists' infrastructure. Livestock corridors that are not clearly delineated can be used by pastoralists in a flexible way, depending on temporal conditions. Sometimes, delimitating and making permanent structures leads to the disappearance of others, reducing flexibility and interfering with pastoralist movements. Other times, the delimitation of corridors fixes not only the infrastructure, but also the governance of this infrastructure, creating fixed rights that interfere with open-access mechanisms.

Spain's advanced legal framework to protect livestock tracks is the 'Vías Pecuarias Act', which was updated in 1995 and backed up by a complete set of regional laws and council plans. It is one of the most significant laws protecting livestock tracks in the world. This law safeguards up to 125,000 km of tracks covering 400,000 ha and supports the largest network of public lands in Spain.

Future challenges and perspectives for pastoralist governance

Fighting poverty and vulnerability of traditional pastoralist systems

Pastoralist governance systems are under pressure, particularly when they are related to customary frameworks that are barely accepted by legal systems. They also come under pressure from internal changes, such as the profound changes in demography and power relations that many communities are undergoing. Nevertheless, these systems support the livelihoods of millions of people, including many poor rural populations. Pastoral governance systems are vital for the effective management of rangelands, but they need major support to not only resume their role in stewardship of the rangelands, but to adjust to the profound implications of poverty and past development failures. Immediate progress is possible by connecting pastoralists to markets and empowering pastoralists, through community-based organizations and updating traditional institutions.

Building alliances and extending pastoral networks

Restoring pastoralist governance requires broad-based co-operation. Various chapters propose networking and enhancing social relationships among pastoralists and the formation of partnerships with international development and conservation institutions to improve interactions with local governments and institutions. New opportunities for strengthening alliances in support of pastoralism are arising as pastoralist under-development is recognized as a failure of human rights rather than failure of pastoralism itself.

Pastoral governance, biodiversity and nature conservation

The main axis of this work is the assumption that good rangeland management promotes conservation of rangelands, including biodiversity and ecological services. Most pastoralist organizations have engaged in this discourse and are spreading it, but some issues need to be properly addressed in the relationships between pastoralists and conservationists, particularly where compromises are needed. Some aspects like predator control, the use of fire, and efficient resource consumption demand an open dialogue and collaborative approach in order to enable concessions on both sides.

Economically valuing pastoralist practices and other economic tools

The Lebanon case points directly to the need for a good economic valuation of services provided by pastoralists as a tool for improving rangeland management. According to this chapter, economic valuation of grazing practices and rangelands management is among the best tools to support revisiting and analysing the actual rangelands management system. They may also lead to induce changes in management practices and governance. Methodologies have been developed and applied which clearly show the value of pastoralism, particularly using a 'total economic valuation' approach, which includes forgotten and indirect values (including environmental services). While these arguments have been effective in raising appreciation of and support for pastoralism, there remains a significant gap in market access to further incentivize the sustainable management of the diverse goods and services of pastoralism. The Mongolian chapter clearly states the economic and cultural need for incentives to promote sustainable use of rangelands, encouraging this kind of use against more intensive or degrading ones.

Developing training and educational networks

Pastoralism needs to adapt to a changing world with plenty of challenges. Several chapters propose mechanisms to develop an educational model that weaves together traditional knowledge with scientific research while preserving pastoralist technical heritage, taking inspiration from an action-research approach. The North Moroccan chapter proposes a training network for pastoralists, students and researchers to reinforce the values and local institutions that are gradually being replaced by public administrations. Combining ideas and proposals made in accordance with the local population can promote and reinforce these local modes of governance in the future. The Spanish chapter also shows how the synergy between traditional and scientific knowledge can be expressed in educational tools in the Ancares Leoneses Biosphere Reserve. The Mongolian chapter meanwhile demonstrates that future educational challenges are an immediate priority in order to improve the level of understanding of management of rural environmental issues through comprehensive national environmental education programs. Those programs should address all actors, including school and university educators, herders, government officials and politicians.

Role of pastoralism in addressing and adapting to climate change

The first chapters of this book show the consequences of global change for rangelands and other grazing-dependent ecosystems and illustrate how pastoralism can contribute to the prevention of degradation processes that are driven by climate and global change. Some of the chapters, especially the Mongolian one, highlight the importance of addressing global change in rangeland policies. The Mongolian government has exercised the approach of the United Nations Framework Convention on Climate Change to develop a Nationally Appropriate Mitigation Action (NAMA) for grassland and livestock management. This NAMA should hold specific grassland and livestock management activities embedded within Mongolia's national sustainable development strategy. Other chapters, like the West Morocco case study, also point to the fight against climate change as a challenge for pastoralism.

A new model of relationship between urban populations and pastoralists

The world is urbanizing at an increasing rate that will result in a vast urban population by the middle of the twenty-first century. The world urban population is expected to increase by 72 per cent 2050, up to 6.3 billion: the same size as the world's entire population in 2002. Virtually all of the expected growth in the world population will be concentrated in the urban areas of the less developed regions (United Nations, 2012).

Urban and rural populations by development group, 1950–2050[3]

This situation constitutes a major driver of the intensification of rangeland use in developing countries with deep impact on several conditions affecting pastoralism and governance. The food demand from new urban populations is driving unsustainable land use, leading to encroachment of rangelands. Such land use changes are favoured by the absence of accurate cost-benefit analyses, which leads to ignoring the environmental benefits of pastoralism. The dominant paradigm of intensification of agricultural inputs seldom considers gross production in return for the use of limiting resources, such as water, leading to inefficient uses of those resources (see for example Behnke and Kerven, 2011). Urban demands could finally lead to a situation with an industrial model of agriculture and livestock production, highly dependent on external inputs (such as water, fodder and oil) and the abandonment of less productive lands and the resultant loss of traditional management.

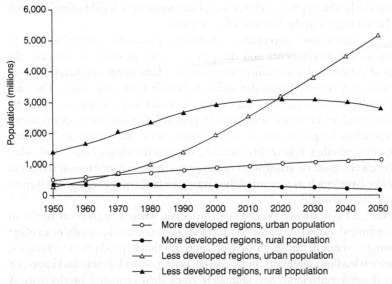

Figure 14.2 Urban and rural populations by development group, 1950–2050

Conclusion

Traditional rangeland management practices by pastoralists demonstrate deep wisdom applied through elaborate institutions and a rich culture. This cumulative body of knowledge, practice and belief has evolved through adaptive processes and has been handed down the generations by cultural transmission: it is about the relationships among people, livestock and the environment. The establishment of local governance systems to protect rangeland ecosystems and prevent their degradation needs to be put in pastoralists' hands because they have the resources, capacity, knowledge and motivation to manage rangelands. Thus, their ability to maintain livelihoods from this way of life also needs to be ensured. Traditional pastoralist management systems are a good starting point to strengthen governance of the commons. The systems work under customary rules guaranteeing rights and access to common resources. Of course they need to adapt to the modern world, including the challenges of economic globalization and global change.

The recovery of pastoralist governance relies mainly on strengthening the social fabric to allow pastoral communities to participate in managing their own territory. The basis for this social fabric is the strengthening of grassroots organizations that pastoralists are developing to defend their interests. The way to strengthen social fabric is context-specific and can include starting new farmers' associations, helping herders to join such groups, assessing emerging organizations or platforms, empowering and giving voice to local community-based organizations (CBOs), and promoting the transformation of community organizations into new structures that transcend their origins to play a key role in governance. The development of working governance systems depends to a large degree on the health, representativeness and involvement of local institutions such as CBOs that represent the interests of pastoralists.

Effective rangeland governance demands grassroots organizations as interlocutors for governments and the private sector in order to preserve the integrity of established governance arrangements. Grassroots organizations help to maintain and increase pastoralist ability to benefit from rangelands. They are a collaborative effort to manage large land areas and foster a network of social and institutional relationships demanded by pastoralists. Grassroots organizations help pastoralists to go further in land management, allowing transboundary management, whether it is of fire, wildlife, or co-ordinating grazing and other uses. The involvement of grassroots organizations in governance means having to tackle some issues such as accountability, transparency, equity, representativeness and gender inclusiveness.

Conflict and governance breakdown can occur when governments prefer to allocate delimited ownership rights over formerly common lands, usually in an effort to encourage economic agents to develop more profitable production techniques. This choice is leading to intensification, encroachment, abandonment and improper uses that degrade rangelands and ultimately erode their economic productivity. A viable alternative is to allocate or strengthen use, management and exclusionary rights for communities. Long-term involvement in rangeland governance also means long-term security of rights, which is one of the greatest challenges, particularly in contested lands. One way to secure rights is to strengthen the visibility of pastoralist communities and establish a clear position in land management by building up a network of relationships that support herders' interests.

A foundation for security is the commitment of governments to create models and legal tools supporting the empowerment and increased capacity of pastoralists. The challenge is to ensure authentic involvement of local and regional governments in the development of legal systems. Regional and local government agencies should be active in participatory processes that establish communal management plans and bylaws; their involvement is vital for the development of those systems into legally supported land planning tools. Political decentralization and co-ordination among public sector agencies and ministries are important enabling factors for improved rangelands governance.

Persistent market failures in pastoral areas continue to be a major impediment to progress, and yet are relatively easily overcome. To provide appropriate incentives, access to markets must be strengthened to capitalize on the diversity of pastoral production. Markets are needed for the direct products of pastoralism, such as milk, fibre and meat, as well as for rangeland products that abound in well-managed environments, such as gums, fruit and medicinal plants. Markets are also needed for the indirect values of pastoralism, including a range of environmental services such as conserving biodiversity, protecting water sheds, and sequestering atmospheric carbon. Innovative approaches are proving valuable, such as selling direct products at a premium to reflect the underlying indirect values (e.g., trademark products) or trading on the biodiversity benefits of pastoralism through ecotourism.

To thrive, pastoralism must be recognized as both a supplier of high quality livestock products and as a protector of natural and cultural heritage. Such recognition can lead to long-term territorial contracts that ensure land rights for pastoralists in exchange for maintaining the ecosystem and landscape services demanded by urban societies. Additional opportunities for pastoralists exist that are linked to peri-urban land stewardship, for example, fire management for urban areas. This strategic perspective should be addressed by a new model for relationships between urban and rural communities starting with the acceptance of the active role pastoralists play in land management and the need to secure this activity as a way to protect urban surroundings.

The conservation sector already collaborates closely with pastoralists in a number of countries, recognizing the value of pastoralism as a land use that is fundamentally sympathetic to the conservation of biological diversity. In these countries, pastoral lands are one form of protected area in a mosaic of different protected area types. Meanwhile, many other countries appear implacably opposed to pastoralism and their conservation strategies are centred on appropriating pastoral lands and excluding pastoralism. The Aichi targets of the Convention on Biological Diversity and the IUCN Governance Matrix for Protected Area Management both lend legitimacy and credibility to what are termed 'Indigenous and Community Conserved Areas': a term that applies to the majority of pastoral lands. A great deal more can be done to translate these standards into greater worldwide respect for pastoral land management.

Finally, one of the most significant changes for pastoralists in recent decades, and the cause for most optimism, is the increasing acceptance that pastoral poverty and rangelands degradation are the outcome of failure to respect basic human rights. This is emerging in parallel with a growing global pastoralist lobby, which gains legitimacy from the recognition of pastoralism by the United Nations Permanent Forum on Indigenous Issues, and is gaining voice through the work of groups like the World Alliance of Mobile Indigenous Peoples and their regional pastoral networks. While the secret to strengthening the social fabric of pastoralism is through grassroots, bottom-up approaches, as pastoralists become more organized at a local level they can take confidence from and contribute to the emergence of a global alliance for pastoralism and mobile indigenous peoples.

Notes

1 Schlager and Ostrom, 1992.
2 This list draws on the work of Bond *et al.*, 2006.
3 United Nations, 2012.

References

Abdoul Kader, H.A. (2012). Gestion de la mare de Tabalak/Niger, analyse des interactions entre acteurs. Mémoire présenté en vue de l'obtention du diplôme de Master complémentaire en gestion des ressources animales et végétales en milieux tropicaux, filière production animale, Universités de Liège et de Gembloux.

Abi-Saleh, B., Nazih, N., Hanna, R., Safi, N., and Tohme, H. (1996). *Etude de la Diversité Biologique du Liban*, Vol. 3. Beyrouth: MOA/PNUE.

Abu-Zanat, M.M., Abu-Settah, M., and Tadros, K. (1993). Maintenance and development of rangelands in Jordan and their role to compact desertification. In proceeding workshop of maintenance and development of rangeland in the Arab world and their role to compact desertification, Amman, Jordan, 3–6 April 1993.

Adams, M., Kalabamu, F., and White, R. (2003). Land tenure policy and practice in Botswana: governance lessons for southern Africa. *Austrian Journal of Development Studies* 19(1): 55–74.

Adams, M., White, R., Raditloaneng, N., Aliber, M., Stracey, G., Mcvey, C., Kalabamu, F., Mcauslan, P., Kgengwenyane, N., Sharp, C., and Egner, B. (2002). National land policy: issues report. Republic of Botswana, Ministry of Lands, Housing and Environment, Department of Lands, Natural Resource Services (Pty) Ltd, Gaborone, Republic of Botswana.

Adb Asian Development Bank. (2011). Inception Report, ADB R-CDTA 7534, Strengthening carbon financing for regional grassland management in Northeast Asia.

Adler, P.B., Raff, D.A., and Lauenroth, W.K. (2001). The effect of grazing on the spatial heterogeneity of vegetation. *Oecologia* 128: 465–479.

Adriansen, H.K. (2005). Pastoral mobility: a review. *Nomadic Peoples* 9: 207–214.

Agencia de Gestión Agraria y Pesquera ae Andalucía. (2011a). Diagnóstico Global. Proyecto de Cooperación R.R.N 'Escuelas de Pastores en Red'.

Agencia de Gestión Agraria y Pesquera de Andalucía. (2011b). Programa formativo modelo y banco de recursos pedagógicos. Proyecto de Cooperación R.R.N 'Escuelas de Pastores en Red'.

Agrawal, A. (2003). Sustainable governance of common-pool resources: context, methods, and politics. *Annual Review of Anthropology* 32: 243–262.

Al Alaoui, M. (1997). Les coopératives pastorales 'ethno-lignagères' du Maroc oriental: présupposés et attendus d'une 'greffe' coopérative. In: Bourbouze, A., Msika, B., Nasri, N and Sghaier Zaafouri, M. (eds). *Pastoralisme et foncier: impact du régime foncier sur la gestion de l'espace pastoral et la conduite des troupeaux en régions arides et semi-arides* Montpellier : CIHEAM (Options Méditerranéennes: Série A. Séminaires Méditerranéens; no. 32.), pp. 129–139.

Alaoui-Haroni, S. (2009). Les pelouses humides dans le haut Atlas: biodiversité végétale, dynamique spatiale et pratiques de gestion coutumière. PhD Dissertation, University of Cadi Ayyad, Laboratoire d'Écologie végétale, Marrakech.

Aldai, N. and Mantecón, A.R. (2012). Perfil de ácidos grasos totales de la carne de ternera producida en el valle del Nansa (Cantabria). *XVII Congreso Internacional ANEMBE de Medicina Bovina.* Santander: ANEMBE, pp. 189–191.

Aldézabal, A., García González, R., Gómez, D., and Fillat, F. (2002). El papel de los herbívoros en la conservación de los pastos. *Ecosistemas* 2002/3. http://www. revistaecosistemas.net/index.php/ecosistemas/article/view/254

Allen, J. (1996). A study of the spatial distribution of livestock pressure in the Oliphants drift area, South East Botswana using Landsat TM. Unpublished minor field studies, no. 6. Swedish University of Agricultural Sciences, Uppsala.

Allen, L.S. (2006). Collaboration in the borderlands: the Malpai Borderlands Group. *Rangelands* 27(1): 18–23.

Allred, B.W., Fuhlendorf, S.D., and Hamilton, R.G. (2011). The role of herbivores in Great Plains conservation: comparative ecology of bison and cattle. *Ecosphere*, 2, art. 26.

Allred, B.W., Fuhlendorf, S.D., Smeins, F.E., and Taylor, C.A. (2012). Herbivore species and grazing intensity regulate community composition and an encroaching woody plant in semi-arid rangeland. *Basic and Applied Ecology* 13: 149–158, http://dx.doi. org/10.1016/j.baae.2012.02.007.

Alonso, N. and Herrera, P. (2013). Reserva de la Biosfera Ancares Leoneses: laboratorio de participación social en la gestión del patrimonio. Bienes, paisajes e itinerarios/revista PH. Instituto Andaluz del Patrimonio Histórico n° 84. October 2013.

Al-Oun, S. (2008). In remediation and restoration projects regarding the terrestrial ecosystems in Jordan, roadmap (Overview and Phase I), United Nations Compensation Commission (UNCC), May 2008.

Arnstein, S.R. (1969). A ladder of citizen participation. *Journal of the American Institute of Planners* 35(4): 216–224. doi:10.1080/01944366908977225.

Arntzen, J.W. (1990). Economic policies and range and degradation in Botswana. *Journal of International Development* 2(4): 471–499.

Arntzen, J.W. and Fidzani, N.H. (1997). Incentives for sustainable natural resource management and economic diversification in Botswana. Draft report to the National Conservation Strategy Agency, University of Botswana.

Arntzen, J.W., Molokomme, D.L., Terry, E.M, Moleele, N., Tshosa, O., and Mazambani, D. (2003). Main Findings of the Review of CBNRM in Botswana.

Asner, G.P., Elmore, A.J., Olander, L.P., Martin, R.E., and Harris, A.T. (2004). Grazing systems, ecosystem responses, and global change. *Annual Review of Environment and Resources* 29: 261–299.

Assi, R. (2005). Conservation and sustainable use of dryland agrobiodiversity of the near east – Lebanese components. Final report, Lebanon: UNDP/GEF, LARI.

Auclair, L. and Al Ifriqui, M. (2005). Les agdal du Haut Atlas marocain, enjeux d'une recherche pluridisciplinaire. Actes des 2èmes Rencontres d'Anthropologie du Maghreb. Centre Jacques Berque, Rabat, 60–7.

Auclair, L. and Alifriqui, M. (eds) (2012). Agdals. Société et gestion des ressources dans l'Atlas marocain, Institut Royal de la Culture Amazighe – Institut de Recherche pour le Développement, Rabat, Morocco.

Auclair, L., Baudot, P., Genin, D., Romagny, B., and Simenel, R. (2011). Patrimony for resilience: evidence from the Forest Agdal in the Moroccan High Atlas Mountains.

Ecology and Society 16(4): article 24. http://www.ecologyandsociety.org/vol16/iss4/art24/

Augustine, D.J. and Mcnaughton, S.J. (1998). Ungulate effects on the functional species composition of plant communities: herbivore selectivity and plant tolerance. *Journal of Wildlife Management* 62: 1165–1183.

Aumeeruddy-Thomas, Y. (2013). Savoirs locaux et biodiversité: interactions sociétés et aires protégées. In Juhé-Beaulaton, D., Cormier-Salem, M.-C., de Robert, P. and Roussel, B. (eds) *Effervescence patrimoniale au Sud. Enjeux, questions, limites*, IRD, pp. 55–75.

Azcárate, F.M., Robleño, I., Seoane, J., Manzano, P., and Peco, B. (2013). Drove roads as local biodiversity reservoirs: effects on landscape pattern and plant communities in a Mediterranean region. *Applied Vegetation Science* 16: 480–490.

Bailey, L.R. (1980). *If You Take My Sheep: The Evolution and Conflicts of Navajo Pastoralism, 1630–1868*. Pasadena, CA: Westernlore Publications.

Baland, J.P. and Platteau, J.P. (1996). *Halting Degradation of Natural Resources: Is there a Role for Communities?* Oxford: Oxford University Press.

Baland, J.P. and Platteau, J.P. (1999). The ambiguous impact of inequality on local resource management. *World Development* 27(5): 773–788.

Balcells, E. (1985). Reciente transformación de la cabaña ganadera. III Coloquio Nacional de Geografía Agraria. Asociación de Geógrafos Españoles, Cáceres, 163–237.

Banco Mundial/FAO. (1966). Informe. El desarrollo de la agricultura en España. Ministerio de Hacienda, Madrid.

Banks, T., Richard, C., Ping, L., and Zhaoli, Y. (2003). Community-based grassland management in western China: rationale, pilot project experience, and policy implications. *Mountain Research and Development* 2(2): 132–140.

Barry, S.J. (2011). Current findings on grazing impacts: California's special status species benefit from grazing. *California Cattlemen's Association Magazine*, June, pp. 18–20.

Batima, P. (2006). Climate change vulnerability and adaptation in the livestock sector of Mongolia, Final Report Project AS06. Assessments of Impact and Adaptation to Climate Change, International START Secretariat, Washington DC.

Bebisse, L. (2011). Gestion des conflits fonciers, mobilité patorale et securisation des pistes de transhumance: cas du projet de securisation de la piste de transhumance de bogo dans l'extreme-nord du Cameroun. MA thesis, University of Maroua.

Beguería, S. (2006). Changes in land cover and shallow landslide activity: a case study in the Spanish Pyrenees. *Geomorphology* 74,196–206.

Beguería, S., López-Moreno, J.I., Lorente, A., Seeger, M., and García-Ruiz, J.M. (2003). Assessing the effects of climate oscillations and land-use changes on stream flow in the Central Spanish Pyrenees. *Ambio* 32(4): 283–286.

Behnke, R. and Kerven, C. (2011). Replacing pastoralism with irrigated agriculture in the Awash Valley, North-Eastern Ethiopia: counting the costs. Paper presented at the International Conference on the Future of Pastoralism. Institute of Development Studies, University of Sussex and the Feinstein International Center of Tufts University.

Behnke, R.H., Scoones, I., and Kerven, C. (eds). (1993). *Range Ecology at Disequilibrium: New Models of Natural Variability and Pastoral Adaptation in African Savannas*. Overseas Development Institute. London: ODI.

Bellaoui, A. (1989). Les pays de l'Adrar-n-Dern. Etude géographique du Haut Atlas de Marrakech. PhD dissertation, Université de Tours, Département de Géographie, Tours.

Bellaoui, A. (2005). La vallée du Zat. Un pays d'accueil touristique émergeant dans l'arrière-pays montagneux de Marrakech, *Revue Téoros* 24(1): 42–47.

Belsky, J.A. (1992). Effects of grazing, competition, disturbance and fire on species composition and diversity in grassland communities. *Journal of Vegetation Science* 3: 187–200.

Berkes, F. (2004) Rethinking community-based conservation. *Conservation Biology* 18: 621–630.

Berkes, F. (2007) Community-based conservation in a globalized world. *Proceedings of the National Academy of Sciences*, 104: 15188–15193.

Berkes, F., Colding, J., and Folke, C. (2000). Rediscovery of traditional ecological knowledge as adaptive management. *Ecological Applications* 10: 1251–1262.

Berkeley, A., Thomas, A.D., and Dougill, A.J. (2005). Spatial dynamics of biological soil crusts: bush canopies, litter and burial in Kalahari rangelands. *African Journal of Ecology* 43: 137–145.

Bhalotra, Y.P.R. (1987). Climate of Botswana. Part II, Elements of climate, 1. Rainfall. Department of Meteorological Services, Republic of Botswana.

Blattler, D. (2012). Draft sub-study on policy of the SDC-supported project – linking herders to carbon markets. Bern University of Applied Sciences, School of Agriculture, Forest and Food Sciences HAFL, Zollikofen, Switzerland.

Blench, R. (2001). *You Can't go Home Again: Pastoralism in the New Millennium*, Overseas Development Institute/FAO, London.

Blewett, R.A. (1995). Property rights as a cause of the tragedy of the commons: institutional change and the pastoral Maasai of Kenya. *Eastern Economic Journal* 21: 477–490.

BOE 279 (1997). Catálogo de razas de ganado en España. Real Decreto 1682/1997.

Bocco, R. (1987). La notion de dirah chez les tribus bédouines en Jordanie: Le Cas De Bani Sakhr. In *Terroires Et Sociétés Au Maghreb Et Au Moyen-Orient. Série Etudes Sur Le Monde Arabe*, No. 2, Maison De L'orient, Lyon, pp.195–215.

Bond I., Davis, C., Nott, K., Nott C., and Stuart-Hill, C. (2006). *Community-based natural resource management manual*, Johannesburg: WWF.

Botes, L. and Van Rensburg, D. (2000). Community participation in development: nine plagues and twelve commandments. *Community Development Journal* 35: 41–58.

Boutrais, J. (ed.) (1984). *Le Nord du Cameroun: des hommes, une région*. Paris: ORSTOM.

Bowler, D., Buyung-Ali, L., Healey, J.R., Jones, J.P., Knight, T., and Pullin, A.S. (2010). The evidence base for community forest management as a mechanism for supplying global environmental benefits and improving local welfare. Scientific and Technical Advisory Panel (STAP) of the Global Environment Facility (GEF). Centre for Evidence-Based Conservation, SENRGY, Bangor University.

Boyd, J. and Banzhaf, S. (2007). What are ecosystem services? The need for standardized environmental accounting units. *Ecological Economics* 63 (2007): 616 – 626

Bradburd, D.A. (1992). Territoriality and Iranian pastoralists: looking out from Kerman. In Casimir, M.J. and Rao, A. (eds), *Mobility and Territoriality: Social and Spatial Boundaries among Foragers, Fishers, Pastoralists, and Peripatetics*. New York: Berg, pp. 309–327.

Breman, H. (1992). Desertification control, the West African case: prevention is better than cure. *Biotropica* 24(2b): 328–334.

Brouwer, J. (2009). The seasonal role of isolated wetlands in the Sahel: key resources for people and biodiversity, under pressure from global change. Paper presented at 'Seasonality Revisited', an International Conference organised by the Future Agricultures consortium at the Institute of Development Studies, Brighton, UK, 8–10 July, 2009. http://event.future-agricultures.org/index.php?option=com_docman&task=cat_view&gid=17&dir=DESC&order=name&Itemid=44&limit=5&limitstart=35.

Brouwer, J. (2010). Climate change in dryland and wetland ecosystems in the Sahel Region. In Andrade Pérez, A., Herrera Fernandez, B. and Cazzolla Gatti, R. (eds), *Building Resilience to Climate Change: Ecosystem-based Adaptation and Lessons from the Field*. Gland, Switzerland: IUCN, pp. 32–45. http://www.iucn.org/knowledge/publications_doc/publications/?6297/Building-resilience-to-climate-change--ecosystem-based-adaptation-and-lessons-from-the-field

Brouwer, J. and Mullié, W.C (1994a). Potentialités pour l'agriculture, l'élevage, la pêche, la collecte des produits naturels et la chasse dans les zones humides du Niger. In Kristensen, P. (ed.), Atelier sur les zones humides du Niger. Proceedings of a workshop, 2–5 November (1994), La Tapoa/Parc du W, Niger, IUCN-Niger, Niamey, Niger, pp. 27–51.

Brouwer, J. and Mullié, W.C. (1994b). The importance of small wetlands in the central Sahel. *IUCN Wetlands Programme Newsletter*, 9: 12–13.

Brouwer, J. and Mullié, W.C. (2001). A method for making whole country waterbird population estimates, applied to annual waterbird census data from Niger. *Ostrich*, Supplement No. 15: 73–82.

Brouwer, J. and Ouattara, M. (1995). Interactions between wetlands and surrounding drylands in the Sahel: a key to sustainable use. Paper presented at the meeting of IUCN's SAWEG (Sahelian Wetlands Expert Group), Dakar, Senegal, 21–24 May (1995).

Brouwer, J., Codjo, S.F., and Mullié, W.C. (2001). Niger. In Fishpool, L.C.D. and Evans M.E. (eds), *Important Bird Areas of Africa and Associated Islands: Priority Sites for Conservation*, BirdLife International Conservation Series no. 10. Newbury, UK: Cambridge and Pisces, pp. 661–672.

Browning, D.M. and Archer, S.R. (2011). Protection from livestock fails to deter shrub proliferation in a desert landscape with a history of heavy grazing. *Ecological Applications* 21: 1629–1642.

Bruce, J., Wendland, K. and Naughton-Treves, L. (2010). Whom to pay? Key concepts and terms regarding tenure and property rights in payment-based forest ecosystem conservation. Land Tenure Center Policy Brief 15. http://www.nelson.wisc.edu/ltc/.

Burrows, W.H., Carter, J.O., Scanlan, J.C., and Anderson, E.R. (1990). Management of savannas for livestock production in north-east Australia: contrasts across the treegrass continuum. *Journal of Biogeography* 17: 503–512.

Byers, B.A., Cunliffe, R.N., and Hudak, A.T. (2001).Linking the conservation of culture and nature: a case study of sacred forests in Zimbabwe. *Human Ecology* 29: 187–218.

Byrne, J. and Glover, L. (2002). A common future or towards a future commons: globalization and sustainable development since UNCED. *International Review for Environmental Strategies* 3(1): 5–25.

California Department of Fish and Wildlife. (2013). DFG lands viewer. http://www.dfg.ca.gov/lands/viewer/index.html (accessed 13 February 2013).

California State Lands Commission. (2013). Mission statement. http://ceres.ca.gov/wetlands/agencies/slc.html (accessed 13 February 2013).

California State Parks. (2013). About us. http://www.parks.ca.gov/?page_id=91 (accessed 13 February 2013).

Cammeraat, L.H. and Imeson, A.C. (1999). The evolution and significance of soil-vegetation patterns following land abandonment and fire in Spain. *Catena* 37: 107–127.

Campbell, B. and Shackleton, S. (2001).The organizational structures for community-based natural resources management in Southern Africa. *African Studies Quarterly* 5(3): 87–112.

Carl Bro International. (1982). An evaluation of livestock management and production in Botswana with special reference to communal areas, vols 1–111. Evaluation Unit, Ministry of Agriculture and the Commission of the European Communities European Development Fund.

Carmona, C.P., Azcárate, F.M., Oteros-Rozas, E., González, J.A., and Peco, B. (2013). Assessing the effects of seasonal grazing on holm oak regeneration: implications for the conservation of Mediterranean dehesas. *Biological Conservation* 159: 240–247.

Casas, R. (2013). Actas de la 1ª Reunión técnica sobre la trashumancia y sus problemas. León. 2013, unpublished.

Casas Nogales, R. and Manzano Baena, P. (2011). Hagamos bien las cuentas. Eficiencia y servicios de la trashumancia en la Cañada Real Conquense. In Consejería de Agricultura y Desarrollo Rural, II Congreso Nacional de Vías Pecuarias, Cáceres, pp. 302–315.

Cassinello, J. (2012) El paisaje en mosaico del Mediterráneo y su supervivencia: de la ganadería extensiva al papel desempeñado por las especies exóticas. *LYCHNOS. Cuadernos de la Fundación General CSIC* 9.

Catley, A., Lind, J., and Scoones, I. (2013). Development at the margins: pastoralism in the Horn of Africa. In Catley, A., Lind, J., and Scoones, I. (eds), *Pastoralism and Development: Dynamic Change at the Margins*. London: Routledge and Earthscan, pp. 1–26.

CDF-FRAP. (California Department of Forestry and Fire Protection, Forest and Range Assessment Program) (2003). *Changing California: Forest and Range 2003 Assessment*. Sacramento, CA: State of California Resources Agency.

CDF-FRAP. (California Department of Forestry and Fire Protection, Forest and Range Assessment Program) (2010). *California's Forests and Rangelands: 2010 Assessment*. Sacramento, CA: State of California Resources Agency.

Central Intelligence Agency (CIA) (2009). The world factbook: Botswana. https://www.cia.gov/library/publications/the-world-factbook/geos/bc.html.

Centre for Applied Research (CAR) (2006). Environmental assessment of Botswana's livestock sector. Centre for Applied Research report. Ministry of Finance and Development Planning, Gaborone.

Centre On Housing Rights and Evictions (COHRE) (2004). *Bringing Equality Home: Promoting and Protecting the Inheritance Rights of Women*. Geneva: COHRE.

Cerdá, A. (2003). Tierras marginales, abandono del campo y erosión. *Mètode: Revista de Difusió de la Investigació de la Universitat de Valencia* 1: 176–179.

Chanda, R., Totolo, O., Moleele, N., Setshogo, M., and Mosweu, S. (2003). Prospects for subsistence livelihood and environmental sustainability along the Kalahari transect: the case of Matsheng in Botswana's Kalahari rangelands. *Journal of Arid Environments* 54: 425–445.

Ciria, J. (2008). El futuro de la ganadería en Castilla y León. In Gómez, L. (ed.) *El futuro de la agricultura en Castilla y León*, Valladolid: ITACYL, pp. 91–101.

Claude, J., Grouzis, M., and Milleville, P. (1991). *Un espace sahélien: la mare d'Oursi, Burkina Faso*. Paris: éditions ORSTOM.

Clover, J. and Eriksen, S. (2009). The effects of land tenure on sustainability: human security and environmental change in southern African savannas. *Environmental Science and Policy* 12: 53–70.

Collinson, S. (2009). The political economy of migration processes: an agenda for migration research and analysis. International Migration Institute, University of Oxford.

Cooper, A., Shine, T., Mccanna, T., and Tidane, D.A. (2006). An ecological basis for sustainable land use of Eastern Mauritanian wetlands. *Journal of Arid Environments* 67: 116–141.

Corbelle, E. and Crecente, R. (2008). El abandono de tierras: concepto teórico y consecuencias. *Revista Galega de Economía* 17(2): 47–62.

Cormier-Salem, M.C., Juhe-Beaula-Ton, D., Boutrais, J., and Rousel, B. (eds) (2002). *Patrimonialiser la nature tropicale. Dynamiques locales, enjeux internationaux.* Paris: IRD Éditions.

Corrigan, S. and Granziera, A. (2010). *A Handbook for the Indigenous and Community Conserved Areas Registry.* Cambridge: UNEP-WCMC.

CDR (Council for Development and Reconstruction) (2004). National physical master plan for the Lebanese territories. Beirut, Lebanon.

Crane, T.A. (2010). Of models and meanings: cultural resilience in social–ecological systems. *Ecology and Society* 15(4): article 19. http://www.ecologyandsociety.org/vol15/iss4/art19/.

Cushman, S.A. (2006). Effects of habitat loss and fragmentation on amphibians: a review and prospectus. *Biological Conservation* 128: 231–240. doi: 10.1126/science.162.3859.1243.

Dafinger, A. and Pelican, M. (2006). Sharing or dividing the land? Land rights and herder-farmer relations in Burkina Faso and Northwest Cameroon. *Canadian Journal of African Studies* 40: 127–151.

Dahir n° 1-83-226 du 9 Moharrem 1405. (5 octobre 1984) Portant promulgationde la loi no. 24-83 fixant le statut général des coopératives et les missionsde l'Office du développement de la cooperation. http://adala.justice.gov.ma/production/html/Fr/68867.htm.

Darkoh, M. (2000). Desertification in Botswana. RALA Report No. 200 [online]. Available at: http://www.rala.is/rade/ralareport/darkoh.pdf

Davies, J. Boravast rangelands observations. International Union for Conservation of Nature (IUCN), unpublished.

Davies, J. and Roba, G. (2010) Pastoralism: shift in policy making. *Farming Matters.* March 2010. http://www.agriculturesnetwork.org/magazines/global/going-for-more-animals/pastoralism-shifts-in-policy-making/at_download/article_pdf.

Davies, J., Poulsen, L., Schulte-Herbrüggen, B., Mackinnon, K., Crawhall, N., Henwood, W.D., Dudley, N., Smith, J., and Gudka, M. (2012). *Conserving Dryland Biodiversity.* Nairobi: IUCN/UNEP-WCMC/UNCCD.

Davis, L. (1995). Opening political space in Cameroon: the ambiguous response of the Mbororo. *Review of African Political Economy* 22: 213–228.

Davis, S.D., Heywood, V.H., and Hamilton, A.C. (eds) (1994). *Centres of Plant Diversity: A Guide and Strategy for their Conservation; Vol. 1: Europe, Africa, South West Asia and the Middle East.* Cambridge: IUCN Publications Unit.

De Beaufort, F. and Czajkowski, A.-M. (1986). Zones humides d'Afrique septentrionale, Centrale et Occidentale. II Inventaire préliminaire et méthodologie. *Inventaires de Faune et de Flore,* Fascicule 35. Conseil International de la Chasse et de la Conservation du Gibier, Sécretariat de la Faune et de la Flore, Muséum National d'Histoire Naturel, Paris.

De Buys, W. (1985). *Enchantment and Exploitation: The Life and Hard Times of a New Mexico Mountain Range.* Albuquerque, NM: University of New Mexico Press.

Demay, S. (2004). Diagnostic agraire dans le Haut Atlas marocain, Territoire des Ait Ikiss. Master's dissertation, INA Paris-Grignon, France.

Dennis, P., Young, M.R., Howard, C.L., and Gordon, I.J. (1997). The response of epigeal beetles (*Col. carabidae, staphylinidae*) to varied grazing regimes on upland *Nardus stricta* grasslands. *Journal of Applied Ecology* 34: 433–443.

DFID (2006). *Eliminating World Poverty: Making Governance Work for the Poor.* London: DFID.

Domínguez, P. (2005). Ocupación del espacio y usos de los recursos naturales en el Alto Atlas marroquí: el caso de los agro-pastores bereberes Ait Ikis y el agdal del Yagour. *Perifèria* 2 (25). http://antropologia.uab.es/Periferia/catala/numero2/N2PD.pdf.

Domínguez, P. (2010). Approche multidisciplinaire d'un système traditionnel de gestion des ressources naturelles communautaires: l'agdal pastoral du Yagour (Haut Atlas marocain). PhD dissertation, École des Hautes Études en Sciences Sociales, Paris, France / Universitat Autònoma de Barcelona, Barcelona, Spain.

Domínguez, P. and Hammi, S. (2010). L'agdal du Yagour, écologieetpastoralisme. In Fernández, K. (ed.), *Proceedings of the Conference Ecología y Pastoralismo*. San Sebastián/ Donostia: KoldoMichelena, pp. 40–65.

Domínguez, P., Zorondo-Rodríguez, F., and Reyes-García, V. (2010). Relationships between saints' beliefs and mountain pasture uses: A case study in the High Atlas Mountains of Marrakech, Morocco. *Human Ecology* 38(3): 351–362.

Domínguez, P., Bourbouze, A., Demay, S., Genin, D., and Kosoy, N. (2012). Culturally mediated provision of ecosystem services: the Agdal of Yagour. *Environmental Values* 21: 277–296.

Domínguez, R. (2001). La ganadería española: del franquismo a la CEE: balance de un sector olvidado. *Historia agraria: revista de agricultura e historia rural* 23: 39–53.

Dong, S., Wen, L., Liu, S., Zhang, X., Lassoie, J.P., Yi, S., Li, X., Li, J., and Li, Y. (2011). Vulnerability of worldwide pastoralism to global changes and interdisciplinary strategies for sustainable pastoralism. *Ecology and Society* 16(2): article 10. http://www.ecologyandsociety.org/vol16/iss2/art10/

Doran, M.H., Low, A.R.C., and Kemp, R.L. (1979). Cattle as a store of wealth in Swaziland.Implications for livestock development and overgrazing in Eastern and Southern Africa. *American Journal of Agricultural Economics* 61(1): 41–447.

DOS. (2011). Jordanian Department of Statistics.

DOS. (2012). Jordanian Department of Statistics.

Dougill, A.J., Thomas, D.S.G., and Heathwaite, A.L. (1999). Environmental change in the Kalahari: integrated land degradation studies for nonequilibrium dryland environments. *Annals of the Association of American Geographers* 89: 420–442.

Dougill, A.J., Fraser, E.D.G., and Reed, M.S. (2010). Anticipating vulnerability to climate change in dryland pastoral systems: using dynamic systems models for the Kalahari. *Ecology and Society* 15(2): article 17. http://www.ecologyandsociety.org/vol15/iss2/art17/

Drent, A.K. (forthcoming). Competing practices in conflict? How nomadic Fulbe (b)order their world. Dissertation, Max Planck Institute for Social Anthropology in Halle/Saale.

Dugan, P.J. (ed.) 1990. *Conservation de zones humides*. Gland, Switzerland: IUCB.

Elard (Earth Link and Advanced Resources Development). (2010).*Climate Risks, Vulnerability and Adaptation Assessment*. Final Report. Lebanon: UNDP/MOE.

Elcome, D. and Baines, J. (1999). Steps to success: working with residents and neighbours to develop and implement plans for protected Areas. IUCN, Commission on Education and Communication. http://data.iucn.org/dbtw-wpd/edocs/1999-008.pdf.

Eldridge, D.J., Bowker, M.A., Maestre, F.F., Roger, E., Reynolds, J.F., and Whitford, W.G. (2011). Impacts of shrub encroachment on ecosystem structure and functioning: towards a global synthesis. *Ecology Letters* 14: 709–722.

Ellis, J.E. and Swift, D.M. (1988). Stability of African pastoral ecosystems: alternative paradigms and implications for development. *Journal of Range Management* 41: 450–459.

Fahrig, L. (2003). Effects of habitat fragmentation on biodiversity. *Annual Review of Ecology, Evolution, and Systematics*, 34: 487–515.

Fairfax, S.K., Gwin, L., King, M.K., Raymond, L., and Watt, L.A. (2005). *Buying Nature: The Limits of Land Acquisition as a Conservation Strategy, 1780–2004*. Cambridge, MA: MIT Press.

FAO. (2001). *Agro-ecological Distributions for Africa, Asia and North and Central America.* Consultants' Report. Rome: FAO.

FAO. (2002a). Gender and access to land. *FAO Land Tenure Studies* 4. Rome: FAO.

FAO. (2002b). Land tenure and rural development. *FAO Land Tenure Studies* 3. Rome: FAO.

FAO. (2005a). Forest Resource Assessment: Country Report Lebanon. Global Forest Resource Assessment. Forest Department, Food and Agriculture Organization, Rome.

FAO. (2005b). Irrigation in Africa in figures, Aquastat Survey 2005. http://www.fao.org/nr/water/aquastat/countries/botswana/botswana_cp.pdf (accessed March 2009).

FAO. (2006a). *Informe pecuario 2006.* Roma: Organización de las Naciones Unidas para la Agricultura y la Alimentación.

FAO. (2006b). *The State of Food Insecurity in the World.* Rome: FAO.

FAO. (2008). Monitoring the voluntary guidelines on the responsible governance of tenure of land fisheries and forests: a civil society perspective. *Land Tenure Working Paper* 22. Rome: FAO. http://www.fao.org/docrep/016/ap098e/ap098e00.pdf

FAO. (2010). Forest Resource Assessment: Country Report Lebanon. Global Forest Resource Assessment. Forest Department, Food and Agriculture Organization, Rome.

FAO. (2012). 'Invisible Guardians – Women manage livestock diversity'. FAO Animal Production and Health Paper No. 174. Rome, Italy. http://www.fao.org/docrep/016/i3018e/i3018e00.pdf

FAOSTAT. (2013). FAO Statistics Division. http://faostat.fao.org/site/573/default.aspx#ancor (accessed 20 June, 2013).

Farquhar, F.P. (ed). (1930). *Up and Down California in 1860–1864: The Journal of William H. Brewer.* New Haven, CN: Yale University Press.

Fernández-Giménez, M.E. (2002). Spatial and social boundaries and the paradox of pastoral land tenure: a case study from postsocialist Mongolia. *Human Ecology* 30: 49–79.

Fernández-Giménez, M.E. (2006). Land use and land tenure in Mongolia: a brief history and current issues. USDA Forest Service Proceedings RMRS-P-39.

Fernández-Giménez, M.E. and Le Febre, S. (2006). Mobility in pastoral systems: dynamic flux or downward trend? *International Journal of Sustainable Development and World Ecology* 13(5): 341–362.

Ferrer, C. and Broca, A. (1999). El binomio agricultura-ganadería en los ecosistemas mediterráneos. Pastoreo frente a 'desierto verde'. Actas de la XXXIX Reunión de la S.E.E.P., Almería, pp. 309–334.

Ferrer, C., San Miguel, A., and Olea, L. (2001). Nomenclátor básico de pastos en España. *Pastos* 31: 7–44.

Ferrer, C., Barrantes, O., and Broca, A. (2011). La noción de biodiversidad en los ecosistemas pascícolas españoles. *Pastos* 31: 129–184.

Fish, W.B. (1944). The Lebanon. *Geographical Review* 34(2): 235–258.

Fishpool, L.C.D. and Evans, M.E. (eds) (2001). *Important Bird Areas of Africa and Associated Islands: Priority Sites for Conservation,* BirdLife International Conservation Series no. 10, BirdLife International, Cambridge and Newbury: Pisces.

Fityani, R. and Laban, P. (2010). 'Rewarding ecosystems, rewarding people' in dryland watershed ecosystems of the West Asia and Mediterranean regions. Regional Water Resources and Dryland (REWARD) Programme, IUCN Regional Office for West Asia, Amman, Jordan.

Flintan, F. (2012). *Protecting Livestock Mobility Routes: Lessons Learned.* Rome: International Land Coalition.

Foley, J.A., Defries, R., Asner, G.P., Barford, C., Bonan, G., Carpenter, S.R., and Snyder, P.K. (2005). Global consequences of land use. *Science* 309(5734): 570–574.

Folke, C., Berkes, F., and Colding, J. (1998). Ecological practices and social mechanisms for building resilience and sustainability. In Berkes, F. and Folke, C. (eds), *Linking Social and Ecological Systems: Management Practices and Social Mechanisms for Building Resilience.* Cambridge: Cambridge University Press, pp. 414–436.

Folke, C., Pritchard, L., Berkes, F., Colding, J., and Svedin, U. (2007). The problem of fit between ecosystems and institutions: ten years later. *Ecology and Society* 12(1): article 30. http://www.ecologyandsociety.org/vol12/iss1/art30/.

Follett, R.F. (2001). Organic carbon pools in grazing land soils. In Follett, R.F., Kimble, J.M., Lal, R. (eds), *The Potential of US Grazing Lands to Sequester Carbon and Mitigate the Greenhouse Effect.* Boca Raton, FL: Lewis Publishers, pp. 65–86.

Fortmann, L. and Roe, E. (1986). Common property management of water in Botswana. Document No. 05781/10021. London: Overseas Development Institute.

Framine, N. (1994). Pisciculture des zones humides: compatabilité, exploitation et conservation. In Kristensen, P. (ed.), Atelier sur les zones humides du Niger. Proceedings of a workshop, 2–5 November (1994), La Tapoa/Parc du W, Niger, IUCN-Niger, Niamey, Niger, pp. 17–26.

Frantz, C. (1986). Fulani continuity and change under five flags. In Adamu, M. and Kirk-Green, A.H.M. (eds), *Pastoralists of the West African Savanna.* Manchester: Manchester University Press, pp. 16–39.

Frechou, H. (1966). *L'elevage et le commerce du betail dans le nord du Cameroun.* Paris: ORSTROM.

Frimpong, K. (1995). A review of the tribal grazing land policy in Botswana. *Journal of African Studies* 9: 1–16.

Frutos Mejías, L.M. and Ruiz Budría, E. (eds) (2006). Estrategias territoriales de desarrollo rural. Institución Fernando el Católico.

Funtowicz, S. and Ravetz, J.R. (1991). A new scientific methodology for global environmental issues. In Costanza, R. (ed.) *Ecological Economics: The Science and Management of Sustainability.* New York: Columbia University Press, pp. 137–152.

Galaty, J.G., Fratkin, E., Galvin, K.A., and Roth, E.A. (1994). Rangeland tenure and pastoralism in Africa. In Fratkin, E., Galvin, K.A. and Roth, E.A. (eds) *African Pastoralist Systems: an Integrated Approach.* Boulder, CO: Rienner Publishers, pp. 185–204.

Galvin, K.A. (2009). Transitions: pastoralists living with change. *Annual Review of Anthropology* 38: 185–198.

Galvin, K.A., Reid, R.S., Behnke, R.H., and Hobbs, N.T. (eds) (2008). *Fragmentation in Semi-arid and Arid Landscapes Consequences for Human and Natural Landscapes.* Dordrecht: Springer.

García, J. and Entretantos Foundation. (2011). Diagnosis for a LIFE social intervention program against Wildfire, unpublished.

García, J. and Entretantos Foundation. (2012). La ganadería extensiva y trashumante, clave en la conservación de sistemas de alto valor natural. *Cuadernos Entretantos* 1.

García De Celis, A.J. (2011). Los paisajes ganaderos 'mediterráneos' de Castilla y León: pastizales y matorrales. *Polígonos. Revista de Geografía* 21: 205–221.

García-Dory, M.A.Y. and Martínez, S. (1988): *La ganadería española ¿desarrollo integrado o dependencia?* Madrid: Alianza Editorial.

García Sanz, A. (1978). La agonía de la Mesta y el hundimiento de las exportaciones laneras: un capítulo de la crisis económica del antiguo régimen en España. *Agricultura y sociedad* 6: 283–356.

García Sanz, A. (1994). La ganadería española entre 1750 y 1865. Los efectos de la reforma agraria liberal. *Agricultura y sociedad* 72: 81–120.

García Trujillo, R. (2004). Bases ecológicas de la ganadería extensiva en España. *Sistemas de Producción Agropecuaria* 143.

Garzón, J. (1992). La trashumancia como reliquia del paleolítico. Actas Symposio. Trashumancia y cultura pastoril en Extremadura.

GEA. (2005) 'Análisis de la representación social del fuego y el desarrollo rural en los municipios incluidos en el Plan 42'. Junta de Castilla y León y Universidad de Valladolid, inédito.

GEF, Haut-Commissariat aux Eaux et Forêts et à la Lutte Contre la Désertification, IFAD, ONUDI. (2007a). Projet de lutte participative contre la désertification et de réduction de la pauvreté dans les écosystèmes arides et semi-arides des hauts plateaux du Maroc oriental – Document de Travail 1: Evaluation et valorisation des techniques et des savoir-faire locaux pour le contrôle de la dégradation des sols et de la desertification, November 2007.

GEF, Haut-Commissariat aux eaux et forêts et à la lutte contre la désertification, IFAD, ONUDI. (2007b).Projet de lutte participative contre la désertification et de réduction de la pauvreté dans les écosystèmes arides et semi-arides des hauts plateaux du Maroc oriental – Document de Travail 2: Les ressources humaines et leur impact sur la dégradation des ressources naturelles dans les hauts plateaux de l'oriental, November 2007.

GEF, Haut-Commissariat aux eaux et forêts et à la lutte contre la désertification, IFAD, ONUDI. (2007c). Projet de lutte participative contre la désertification et de réduction de la pauvreté dans les écosystèmes arides et semi-arides des hauts plateaux du Maroc oriental – Document de Travail 4: Fréquence et impact des phénomènes de sécheresse, des averses torrentielles et de l'invasion acridienne, November 2007.

Geist, H.J. and Lambin, E.F. (2004). Dynamic causal patterns of desertification. *Bioscience* 54: 817–829.

Gellner, E. (1969). *Saints of the Atlas*. London: Weidenfield and Nicholson.

Genin, D., Fouilleron, B., and Kerautret, L. (2012). Un tempo bien tempéré. Place et rôle des agdals dans les systèmes d'élevage des Ayt Bouguemmez. In Auclair L. and Alifriqui M. (eds), *Les Agdals du haut Atlas marocain: savoirs locaux, droits d'accès et gestion de la biodiversité*. Rabat: IRCAM/IRD, pp. 411–434.

Germano, D.J., Rathbun, G.B., and Saslaw, L.R. (2012). Effects of grazing and invasive grasses on desert vertebrates in California.*Journal of Wildlife Management* 76(4): 670–682.

Giraudoux, P., Degauquier, R., Jones, P.J., Weigel, J., and Isenmann, P. (1988). Avifaune du Niger: état des connaissances en 1986. *Malimbus*, 10: 1–140.

Gorte, R.W., Vincent, C.H., Hanson, L.A., and Rosenblum, M.R. (2012). Federal land ownership: overview and data. Congressional Research Service Report R42346. http://www.fas.org/sgp/crs/misc/R42346.pdf (accessed 13 February 2012).

Gómez, L. (2008). El futuro de la agricultura en Castilla y León. *ITACYL*, 91–101.

Gómez Sal, A. and Rodríguez Pascual, M. (1992). *Cuadernos de la Trashumancia 3, Montaña de León*. Madrid: ICONA.

Government of Botswana (GoB). (1975). National policy on tribal grazing land. Paper 2 of 1975, Gaborone: Government of Botswana.

Government of Botswana (GoB). (1991). National policy on agricultural development, Gaborone: Ministry of Agriculture, Government of Botswana.

Government of Botswana (GoB). (1999). Community-based natural resource management practitioner's guide, Gaborone: Department of Wildlife and National Parks, Government of Botswana.

Government of Botswana (GoB). (2002). Botswana national land policy: issues report. Ministry of Lands, Housing and Environment, Department of Lands. Gaborone: Natural Resource Services.

Government of Botswana (GoB). (2013). Annual agricultural surveys preliminary results for 2011. Gaborone: Government of Botswana. http://www. cso.gov.bw (accessed 7 June 2013.

Greenhow, T. (1978). The tribal grazing land policy and integrated land-use planning: a district view. *Botswana Notes and Records* 10: 159–168.

Gripne, S.L. (2005). Grassbanks: bartering for conservation. *Rangelands* 27: 24–28.

Gruber, J.S. (2010). Key principles of community-based natural resource management: a synthesis and interpretation of identified effective approaches for nanaging the commons. *Environmental Management* 45(1): 52–66.

Hadadin, N. and Tarawneh, Z. (2007).Environmental issues in Jordan, solutions and fecommendations. *American Journal of Environmental Sciences* 3(1): 30–36.

Haddad, F., Mizyed, B., and Laban, P. (2009).Enhancing rights and local level accountability in water management in the Middle East. In Campese, J., Sunderland, T., Greiber, T. and Oviedo, G. *Rights-based Approaches - Exploring issues and Opportunities for conservation.* Bogor Barat: CIFOR.

Haddon, I.G. (2005).The Sub-Kalahari geology and tectonic evolution of the Kalahari Basin, Southern Africa. University of Witwatersrand, Johannesburg, PhD Thesis. http://wiredspace.wits.ac.za/bitstream/handle/10539/193/Haddonthesistext.pdf.

Hammi, S., Al Ifriqui, M., Simonneaux, V., and Auclair, L. (2007). Évolution des recouvrements forestiers et de l'occupation des sols entre 1964 et 2002 dans la haute vallée des Ait Bouguemez (Haut Atlas Central, Maroc). *Sécheresse* 18(4): 271–277.

Hannam, I.D. (2007). Report to United Nations Development Program Mongolia on Review of Draft Pastureland Law of Mongolia, United Nations Development Program Sustainable Grassland Management Project, Ulaanbaatar.

Hannam, I.D. (2009). Compilation Report, Environmental Law and Institutional Framework Mongolia, UNDP Project Strengthening Environmental Governance in Mongolia.

Hannam, I.D. (2012). Working Paper 2, Legal and Policy Framework to Support Livestock/ Grassland NAMA, Mongolia, ADB R-CDTA 7534 Strengthening Carbon Financing for Regional Grassland Management In Northeast Asia.

Hannam, I.D., and Borjigdkhan, A.T.S. (2009). Feasibility study on pasture use fee and its reinvestment into local land improvement activities for ensuring sustainability of pastoral resources in Mongolia, UNDP Project, Sustainable Land Management for Combating Desertification in Mongolia.

Hardin, G. (1968). The tragedy of the commons. *Science* 162: 1243–1248.

Heras, F. (2003). *Entre tantos: guía práctica para dinamizar procesos participativos sobre problemas ambientales y sostenibilidad.* Valladolid: GEA.

Hernández, F.I. (1996). Organización de la trashumancia. *MG Mundo ganadero* 83: 68–69.

Hesse, C. (2000). Gestion des parcours: qui en est responsable et qui y a droit? In Tielkes, E., Schlecht, E., and Hiernaux, P. (eds), *Elevage et gestion de parcours au Sahel, implications pour le développement.* Stuttgart: Grauer Verlag, pp. 139–153.

Hesse, C. and Cotula, L. (2006). Climate change and pastoralists: investing in people to respond to adversity. International Institute for Environment and Development (IIED).

Hesse, C. and Macgregor, J. (2006). Pastoralism: drylands' invisible asset? Drylands Programme, International Institute for Environment and Development. http://pubs. iied.org/pubs/pdfs/12534IIED.pdf.

Hesse, C. and Pattison, J. (2013) Ensuring devolution supports adaptation and climate resilient growth in Kenya, IIED policy brief. http://pubs.iied.org/17161IIED.html.

Heywood, V.H. (1998).The Mediterranean region – a major centre of plant diversity. In:Heywood, V.H. and Skoula, M. (eds), Wild food and non-food plants: information networking. Proceedings of the second Medusa regional workshop on 'Wild food and non-food plants: information networking', 1–3 May 1997 at Port el Kantaoui, Tunisia. *Cahiers Options Méditerranéennes* 38: 5–15.

Heywood, V.H. (2000). Challenges of in situ conservation of crop wild relatives. *Turkish Journal of Botany* 32: 421–432.

Hitchcock, R.K. (1978). Kalahari cattle posts: a regional study of hunter-gatherers, pastoralists and agriculturalists in the western sandveld region, Central District, Botswana, Government Printer, Gaborone.

Hitchcock, R.K. (1980). Tradition, social justice and land reform in central Botswana. *Journal of African Law* 24(1): 1–34.

Hitchcock, R.K. (2002). Coping with uncertainty: adaptive responses to drought and livestock disease in the northern Kalahari. In Sporton, D. and Thomas,D.S.G. (eds), *Sustainable livelihoods in Kalahari Environments: Contributions to Global Debates*. Oxford; Oxford University Press, pp. 221–236.

Hollis, G.E., Adams, W.M., and Aminu-Kano, M. (eds) (1993). *The Hadejia-Nguru Wetlands. Environment, Economy and Sustainable Development of a Sahelian Floodplain Wetland*. Gland, Switzerland and Cambridge: IUCN.

Horowitz, M.M. (1986). Ideology, policy, and praxis in pastoral livestock development. In Horowitz, M.M. and Painter, T.M. (eds), *Anthropology and Rural Development in West Africa*. Boulder, CO: Westview Press, pp. 251–272.

Huntsinger, L., Forero, L.C., and Sulak, A. (2010). Transhumance and pastoralist resilience in the western United States.*Pastoralism: Research, Policy, and Practice* 1: 1–15.

Huntsinger, L., Sayre, N.F., and Wulfhorst, J.D. (2012). Birds, beasts and bovines: three cases of pastoralism and wildlife in the USA. *Pastoralism: Research, Policy and Practice* 2(12). doi:10.1186/2041-7136-2-12.

Ibarrola, P. (2008). Reflexiones sobre el pastoralismo ibérico a lo largo de la historia. *Foresta* 5: 38–39.

IFAD. (2000). Sustainable Livelihoods in the Drylands. A discussion paper for the eighth session of the Commission on Sustainable Development, United Nations.

IFAD. (2006). *Community-based Natural Resource Management*. Rome: IFAD.

IFAD (2009). *Enabling Poor Rural People to Overcome Poverty*. Rome: IFAD. http://www.ifad. org/pub/basic/finance/eng.pdf.

IGOE, J. (2004). *Conservation and Globalization: A study of National Parks and Indigenous Communities from East Africa to South Dakota*. Belmont, CA: Wadsworth/Thompson Learning.

ILRI. (1995). Livestock policy analysis. ILRI Training Manual 2, International Livestock Research Institute, Nairobi, Kenya.

Independent News. (2009). Livermore, CA. http://www.zoominfo.com/#!search/profile/ person?personId=53527832&targetid=profile.

Irvin, R.A. and Stansbury, J. (2004). Citizen participation in decision making: is it worth the effort? *Public Administration Review* 64(1): 55–65.

Institut national de la recherche agronomique, Haut-Commissariat aux eaux et forêts et à la lutte contre la désertification, ONUDI. (2011). Projet de lutte participative contre la désertification et de réduction de la pauvreté dans les écosystèmes arides et semi-arides des hauts plateaux du Maroc oriental. Etude sur la situation de références au niveau des hauts plateaux du Maroc Oriental – Rapport Final (Centre Régional de La Recherche Agronomique d'Oujda).

IUCN. (2000). Policy on social equity in conservation and sustainable use of natural resources. Adopted by IUCN Council Meeting, February 2000.

IUCN. (2009). Rewarding ecosystems, rewarding people. REWARD Strategic Workshop, Sharm Al Shaikh, May 2009. http://cmsdata.iucn.org/downloads/rewarding_ecosystems_rewarding_people__reward_sharm_al_shaikh_report__final.pdf.

IUCN. (2011a). Supporting sustainable pastoral livelihoods: a global perspective on minimum standards and good practices. Published for review and consultation through global learning fora. Nairobi: IUCN ESARO.

IUCN. (2011b). *The Land We Graze: A Synthesis of Case Studies about How Pastoralists' Organizations Defend their Land Rights*. Nairobi: IUCN ESARO office.

IUCN. (2011c). An assessment of natural resource governance in Garba Tula, Northern Kenya Project baseline report.

IUCN. (2011d). Securing rights and restoring range lands for improved livelihoods in the dadia of the Zarqa River Basin, Jordan. Base line study. Amman, November 2011.

IUCN. (2012a). Reviving Hima Case study.

IUCN. (2012b). Biocultural diversity conserved by indigenous peoples and local communities' examples and analysis, IUCN.

IUCN, UNDP-GEF and FAO. (2007) Worldwide Initiative for Sustainable Pastoralism. http://www.iucn.org/wisp/

Ives, A.R. and Carpenter, S.R. (2007). Stability and diversity of ecosystems. *Science* 317(5834): 58–62. doi:10.1126/science.1133258.

Izquierdo, J. (2005). Desarrollo rural en zonas de montaña: la propuesta del programa Pastores XXI. Gobierno del Principado de Asturias. In Frutos Mejías, L.M. and Ruiz Budría, E. (eds), Estrategias territoriales de desarrollo rural. Institución Fernando el Católico, pp. 165–176

Jackson, R.B., Banner, J.L., Jobbagy, E.G., Pockman, W.T., and Wall, D.H. (2002). Ecosystem carbon loss with woody plant invasion of grasslands. *Nature* 418: 623–626.

Jain, S.P. and Polman, W. (2007). A handbook for trainers on participatory local development: the Panchayati Raj model in India. FAO Regional Office for Asia and the Pacific, Bangkok, Thailand, August 2003.

Jodha, N.S. (1985). Market forces and erosion of common property resources. In Agricultural markets in the semi arid tropics. Proceedings of the international workshops held at ICRISAT Center, India, 24–28 October 1983, pp. 263–277.

Joubert, D.F., Rothauge, A., and Smit, G.N. (2008). A conceptual model of vegetation dynamics in the semiarid Highland savanna of Namibia, with particular reference to bush thickening by *Acacia mellifera*. *Journal of Arid Environments* 72: 2201–2210.

Joyce, H. (2007). *Women Pastoralists: Preserving Traditional Knowledge, Facing Modern Challenges*. Bonn: Secretariat of the UNCCD / IFAD.

Juneidi, J.M. and Abu-Zanat, M. (1993). Jordan agricultural sector review: low rainfall zone, Agricultural Policy Analysis Project, Phase II (APAP II), USAID, Amman, Jordan.

Junta de Castilla y León. (2000). *Directrices de ordenación del territorio de Castilla y León*. Valladolid: Junta de Castilla y León.

Junta de Castilla y León. (2006). PLAN 42. Un programa integral para la prevención de incendios forestales. Valladolid: Junta de Castilla y León.

Kari, S. and Scholte, P. (2001). La réhabilitation pastorale de la plaine d'inondation waza-logone (Cameroun): comment consolider sa réussite écologique? In Tielkes, E., Schlecht, E., and Hiernaux, P. (eds), *Atelier regional: les approches de la gestion des pâturages et les projets de développement: quelles perspectives?* Niamey (Niger): Verlag Ulrich E. Grauer, pp. 315–316.

Katjiua, M. and Ward, D. (2007). Pastoralists' perception and realities of vegetation change and browse consumption in the northern Kalahari, Namibia. *Journal of Arid Environments* 69: 716–730.

Kaufmann, D., Kraay, A., and Zoido-Lobaton, P. (1999). *Governance Matters*. Policy Research Working Paper. Washington, DC: World Bank.

Kelt, D.A., Konno, E.S., and Wilson, J.A. (2005). Habitat management for the endangered Stephens' kangaroo rat: the effect of mowing and grazing. *Journal of Wildlife Management* 69: 424–429.

Kerautret, L. (2005). Entre Agdal et Moucharika. Master's dissertation, Université de Provence, Laboratoire Population-Environnement-Développement, Marseille.

Kerven, C. (1992). Customary commerce: a historical reassessment of pastoral livestock marketing in Africa. Vol. 15. ODI Agricultural Occasional paper. London: Overseas Development Institute.

Kerven, C. and Behnke, R. (2011). Policies and practices of pastoralism in Europe. *Pastoralism: Research, Policy and Practice* 1(28). http://www.pastoralismjournal.com/content/1/1/28

Klein, J. (1979). *La Mesta: estudio de la historia económica española*: 1273– 1836. Madrid: Alianza Editorial.

Kleinbooi, K. (2013). Reshaping women's land rights on communal rangeland. *African Journal of Range and Forage Science* 30(1and2): 17–21.

Klintenberg, P., Seely, M.K., and Christiansson, C. (2007). Local and national perceptions of environmental change in central northern Namibia: do they correspond? *Journal of Arid Environments* 69: 506–525.

Köhler-Rollefson, I. (2012). Invisible Guardians – Women manage livestock diversity. FAO Animal Production and Health Paper No. 174. Rome: FAO.

Kothari, A., Corrigan, C., Jonas, H., Neumann, A., and Shrumm, H. (eds), (2012). Recognising and supporting territories and areas conserved by indigenous peoples and local communities: global overview and national case studies. Secretariat of the Convention on Biological Diversity, ICCA Consortium, Kalpavriksh, and Natural Justice, Montreal, Canada. Technical Series no. 64: 160 pp. www.iccaconsortium.org.

Kouokam, R. (1994). Application de la méthode accélérée de recherche participative 'MARP' dans la zone pilote du Projet Waza-Logone (Province de l'Extrême-Nord du Cameroun). Paper prepared for the IUCN Workshop on the Initiative on Sahelian Floodplains, Tapoa, Niger, 31 October–2 November 1994.

KPMG. (2011). Financing low carbon Investment in developing countries: public-private partnership for implementing nationally appropriate mitigation actions.

Krätli, S., Huelsebusch, C., Brooks, S., and Kaufmann, B. (2013) Pastoralism: a critical asset for food security under global climate change. *Animal Frontiers* 3: 42–50. doi: 10.2527/af.2013-0007.

Kreuter, U.P., Woodard, J.B., Taylor, C.A., and Teague, W.R. (2008). Perceptions of Texas landowners regarding fire and its use. *Rangeland Ecology and Management* 61: 456–464.

Kristjanson, P., Waters-Bayer, A., Johnson N., Tipilda A., Baltenweck, I., Grace, D., and Macmillan, S. (2010). Livestock and women's livelihoods: a review of the recent evidence. ILRI (International Livestock Research Institute also known as ILCA and ILRAD). Discussion Paper No. 20.

Kroeger, T., Casey, F., Alvarez, P., Cheatum, M., and Tavassoli, L. (2010). An economic analysis of the benefits of habitat conservation on California rangelands. Conservation Economics White Paper. Defenders of Wildlife. Washington, DC.

Laban, P. (2008). Rewarding ecosystems rewarding people in dryland watershed ecosystems of the West Asia and Mediterranean regions. IUCN Regional Office for West Asisa, Amman, Jordan.

Laiolo, P., Dondero, F., Ciliento, E., and Rolando, A. (2004). Consequences of pastoral abandonment for the structure and diversity of the alpine avifauna. *Journal of Applied Ecology* 41: 294–304.

Lambin, E.F. and Meyfroidt, P. (2011). Global land use change, economic globalization, and the looming land scarcity. *Proceedings of the National Academy of Sciences* 108: 3465–3472.

Lambin, E.F., Turner, B.L., Geist, H.J., Agbola, S.B., Angelsen, A., Bruce, J.W., and Xu, J. (2001). The causes of land-use and land-cover change: moving beyond the myths. *Global Environmental Change* 11: 261–269.

Lasanta, T. (2010). Pastoreo en áreas de montaña: estrategias e impactos en el territorio. *Estudios Geográficos* LXXI(268): 203–233.

Lasanta, T., Vicente-Serrano, S.Y., and Cuadrat, J.M. (2005). Mountain Mediterranean landscape evolution caused by the abandonment of traditional primary activities: a study of the Spanish Central Pyrenees. *Applied Geography* 25: 47–65.

Levasseur, M., Richard, L., Gauvin, L., and Raymond, E. (2010). Inventory and analysis of definitions of social participation found in the aging literature: proposed taxonomy of social activities. *Social Science and Medicine* 71: 2141–2149. doi:10.1016/j.socscimed.2010.09.041.

Li, W. and Huntsinger, l. (2011). China's grassland contract policy and its impacts on herder ability to benefit in Inner Mongolia: tragic feedbacks. *Ecology and Society* 16(2): article 1. http://www.ecologyandsociety.org/vol16/iss2/art1/.

Liffmann, R.H., Huntsinger, L., and Forero, L.C. (2000). To ranch or not to ranch: Home on the urban range? *Journal of Range Management* 53(4): 362–370.

Little, P.D., Mahmoud, H., and Coppock, D.L. (2001). When deserts flood: risk management and climatic processes among East African pastoralists. *Climate Research* 19(2): 149–159.

LUCOP. (2007). Suite de l'état des lieux des mares dans la zone pastorale. Rapport de mission pour le Projet Lutte contre la Pauvreté (LUCOP) Tillabéri et Tahoua Nord de la Coopération Nigéro-Allemande, Programme Régional Tahoua Nord, Bureau Régional à Agadez.

Lussigi, W.J. (2008). Policy failures in Afrian rangeland Development. In Rockwood, L., Stewart, R. and Dietz, T. (eds), *Foundations of Environmental Sustainability: The Coevolution of Science and Policy*. Oxford: Oxford University Press, pp. 148–156.

Lyons, R.K. and Wright, B.D. (2003).Using livestock to manage wildlife habitat. Texas Cooperative Extension System, Texas A&M University System. Publication B-6136.

Maczko, K. and Hidinger, L. (eds) (2008). Sustainable rangelands ecosystem goods and services. SRR Monograph No. 3. Sustainable Rangelands Roundtable.

Mahadi, Y., Roba, G., and Gibbons, S. (2013). *Participatory Rangelands Planning: A Practitioner's Guide*. Nairobi: IUCN-ESARO.

Mahatan, C. (1994). Etude de la filière des cultures de contre-saison, zone du PMI. SNV-Netherlands Organisation for Development Aid, Projet Mares Illela, Niamey, Niger.

Makepe, P.M. (2006). The evolution of institutions and rules governing communal grazing lands in Botswana. *Eastern Africa Social Science Research Review* 22(1): 39–61.

Mallen, I., Dominguez, P., Clavet, L., Orta, M. and Reyes-García, V. (2012). Applied research on ethno-ecology: field experiences. *Revista de Antropología Iberoamericana* 7(1): 9–32.

Mamdani, M. (1996). *Citizen and Subject: Contemporary Africa and the Legacy of Late Colonialism.* Princeton, NJ: Princeton University Press.

Mantecón, A.R., Lavín, P., and Frutos, P. (1994). Sistemas extensivos de ganado ovino. Curso de: pastos, forrajes y ganadería extensiva. Junta de Castilla y León, noviembre 1994.

Manzano, P. (2006). Trashumancia y vías pecuarias. *Ecologista* 48: 38–39.

Manzano, P., Ng'eny, N., and Davies, J. (2011a). La iniciativa mundial por un pastoralismo sostenible (IMPS) y la importancia económica, social y ambiental de los pastores a nivel global. In Consejería de Agricultura y Desarrollo Rural (ed.), II Congreso Nacional de Vías Pecuarias, Cáccres, pp. 336–343.

Manzano, P., Ng'eny, N., and Davies, J. (2011b). Changing mentalities towards pastoralism across scales: the World Initiative for Sustainable Pastoralism and other related initiatives. IX International Rangeland Congress, Rosario (Argentina), pp. 760–765.

Manzano Baena, P. (2012). Shaping policies. Science-policy interface in natural resources management. In Davies, J. (ed.), *Conservation and Sustainable Development. Linking Practice and Policy in Eastern Africa.* New York and London: Taylor & Francis and Ottawa: IDRC, pp. 107–126.

Manzano Baena, P. and Casas, R. (2010). Past, present and future of Trashumancia in Spain: nomadism in a developed country. *Pastoralism: Research, Policy and Practice (Practical Action)* 1: 72–90.

Manzungu, E., Mpho, T.J., and Mpale-Mudanga, A. (2009). Continuing discontinuities: local and state perspectives on cattle production and water management in Botswana. *Water Alternatives* 2(2): 205–224.

Markakis, J. (2004). *Pastoralism on the Margin.* London: Minority Rights Group International.

MARM. (2011). Efectos de la Reforma PAC 2003 sobre la ganadería. Análisis y prospectiva. *Serie Agrinfo* 19: 1–8.

Martín Bellido, M., Escribano Sánchez, M., Mesías Díaz, F.J., Rodríguez De Ledesma, A., Pulido, F. (2001). Sistemas extensivos de producción animal. *Arch. Zootec* 50: 465–489. 2001.

Marty, J.T. (2005).Effects of cattle grazing on diversity in ephemeral wetlands. *Conservation Biology* 19: 1626–1632.

MAE-NIGER. (1993). Annuaire des statistiques de l'agriculture et de l'élevage (1991). Ministère de l'Agriculture et de l'Elevage, Directions des Etudes et de la Programmation, Service d'Analyse des Politiques et de la Coordination des Statistiques, Niamey, Niger.

Mathuba, B.M. (2003). Botswana land policy. International Workshop on Land Policies in Southern Africa Berlin, Germany, Ministry of Lands and Housing, Botswana.

Mazvimavi, D. and Motsholapheko, M.R. (2008). Water resource use and challenges for river basin management along the ephemeral Boteti River, Botswana. In Manzungu, E. (ed.), *Towards a New Water Creed: Water Management, Governance and Livelihood in Southern Africa.* Rackwitz, Inwent and Harare, Zimbabwe: Weaver Press, pp. 65–74.

McCabe, J.T. (1990). Turkana pastoralism: A case against the tragedy of the commons. *Human Ecology* 18(1): 81–103.

McCabe, J.T. (2004). *Cattle Bring Us to Our Enemies: Turkana Ecology, Politics, and Raiding in a Disequilibrium System.* Ann Arbor, MI: Michigan University Press.

McCosker, M. (1998). *Heritage Merino.* West End: Owen Edwards Publications.

McGahey, D.J. (2011). Livestock mobility and animal health policy in southern Africa: the impact of veterinary cordon fences on pastoralists. *Pastoralism: Research, Policy and Practice* 1(14). doi:10.1186/2041-7136-1-14.

McGarigal, K. and Cushman, S.A. (2002). Comparative evaluation of experimental approaches to the study of habitat fragmentation effects. *Ecological Applications* 12(2): 335–345.

Meiggs, R. (1998). *Trees and Timber in the Ancient Mediterranean World.* Oxford: Oxford University Press.

Meine, C.D. and Archibald, G.W. (eds) (1996). *The Cranes – Status Survey and Conservation Action Plan.* Gland, Switzerland: IUCN.

Meinzen-Dick, R., Pradhan, R., Di Gregorio, M. (2005). Understanding property rights. In Mwangi, E. (ed.), *Collective Action and Property Rights for Sustainable Rangeland Management.* CAPRI Research Brief. Washington, DC: Consultative Group on International Agriculture.

Merafe, Y. (1992). Achievements, constraints and problems of livestock development and management in communal areas: the Botswana case. In Cousins, B (ed.), Institutional dynamics in communal grazing regimes. Proceedings of a workshop held in Harare, Zimbabwe.

Meyers, W.S. (1994). Australian irrigation: balancing rights and responsibilities, production and conservation. *Soils News (Newsletter of the Australian Society of Soil Science)*, 99: 1–4.

MHE-DFPP. (1991). Organisation de la production et de la commercialisation du poisson dans le Département de Tahoua. Ministère de l'Hydraulique et de l'Environnement, Direction de la Faune, de la Pêche et de la Pisciculture. Rapport de Projet.

MHE-DRE-NIGER. (1993). Liste des mares et leur régime. Ministère de l'Hydraulique et de l'Environment, Direction des Ressources en Eau, Niamey, Niger.

MHE-NIGER. (1990a–c). Synthèse des ressources en eau du Département de Tillabéri./ Zinder/Tahoua Ministère de l'Hydraulique et de l'Environnment, Direction Départementale de l'Hydraulique de Tillabéri. Projet PNUD/DCTD NER/86/001.

MHE-NIGER. (1990d–e). Les nappes aquifères à l'Ouest de l'Aïr – synthèse hydrogéologique. Première partie: les nappes paléozoiques. Deuxième partie: les nappes des grés d'Agadez. Ministère de l'Hydraulique et de l'Environnement, Direction des Ressources en Eau. Projet PNUD/DCTD NER/86/001. Niamey, Niger.

MHE-NIGER. (1991a–d). Les ressources en eau du Département de Diffa/Maradi/ Dosso/ Nord-Est Nigérien. Ministère de l'Hydraulique et de l'Environnment. Direction Départementale de l'Hydraulique de Diffa. Projet PNUD/DCTD NER/86/001. Niamey, Niger.

MHE-NIGER. (1992). Séminaire National sur l'Etat de Connaissance de Ressources en Eau du Niger. Contribution des Directions Départementales de l'Hydraulique et du Genie Rural de Maradi. Maradi, du 21 au 25 avril (1992). Ministére de l'Hydraulique et de l'Environnement, Direction Départementale de l'Hydraulique de Maradi. Maradi, Niger.

Michon, G., Nasi, R., and Balent, G. (2012). Public policies and management of rural forests: lasting alliance or fool's dialogue? *Ecology and Society* 18(1): article 30. http://www.ecologyandsociety.org/vol18/iss1/art30/

Mikesell, M.W. (1969). The deforestation of Mount Lebanon. *Geographical Review* 19: 1–28.

Millington, J.D.A. (2007). Modelling land-use/cover change and wildfire regimes in a Mediterranean landscape. Doctoral thesis, King's College London.

Ministry of Agriculture (MoA). (2003). National Action Plan to Combat Desertification. Beirut: UNCCD/UNDP/GTZ/MOA.

Ministry of Agriculture (MoA). (2001). National rangeland strategy for Jordan. Amman, Jordan: Range Department of the Ministry of Agriculture.

Ministry of Agriculture (MoA). (2013, pending public release). Revised National Rangeland Strategy. The Hashemite Kingdom of Jordan. Amman, Jordan: The Ministry of Agriculture.

Ministry of Environment, Jordan (MoE). (2006). National Action Plan and Strategy to Combat Desertification. Amman, Jordan: Ministry of Environment.

Ministry of Environment, Jordan (MoE). (2007). National Capacity Self Assessment for Global Environmental Management–MoEnv Jordan 2007. Amman, Jordan: Ministry of Environment.

Ministry of Planning (2009). Integrated Financing Strategy for Combating Desertification in Jordan. Amman, Jordan: Ministry of Planning.

Mitchell, J.E. (ed.) (2010). *Criteria and Indicators of Sustainable Rangeland Management*. Laramie, WY: University of Wyoming. Extension Publication No.SM-56.227.

Mittermeier, R.A., Robles-Gil, P., Hoffmann, M., Pilgrim, J.D., Brooks, T.B., Mittermeier, C.G., Lamoreux, J.L., and Fonseca, G.A.B. (2004). *Hotspots Revisited: Earth's Biologically Richest and Most Endangered Ecoregions*. Mexico City: CEMEX.

Mkutu, K. (2001). Pastoralism and conflict in the Horn of Africa. Africa Peace Forum/Saferworld/University of Bradford.

Moench, M., Caspari, E., and Dixit, A. (eds). (1999). *Rethinking the Mosaic: Investigations into Local Water Management*. Kathmandu: Nepal Water Conservation Foundation and Boulder, CO: Institute for Social and Environmental Transition.

Moleele, N.M., Ringrose, S., Matheson, W., and Vanderpost, C. (2002). More woody plants? The status of bush encroachment in Botswana's grazing areas. *Journal of Environmental Management* 64: 3–11.

Molina, I. (2012). *Evolución y principios para una política de ordenación territorial en las áreas rurales de Castilla y León*. Valladolid: Fundación Perspectivas de Castilla y León.

Molinero, F. (2008). La percepción social de los incendios forestales y su motivación en Castilla y León. *Ería* 76: 213–229.

Molinero, F., Cascos, C., García De Celis, A., and Baraja, E. (2008). *Dinámica de los incendios forestales en Castilla y León. Boletín de la A.G.E.* 48.

Molnar, A., France, M., Lopaka, P., and Karver, J. (2011). Community-based forest management: the extent and potential scope of community and smallholder forest management and enterprises. Rights and Resources Initiative. Washington DC.

Mongolian Centre for Policy Research. (2010). The livestock sector needs drastic policy reform. *Zuunii Medee* 17: 22 January 2010.

Mongolian Government. (2007). Draft pastureland law 20 July 2007 and brief introduction to the draft law on pastureland.

Mongolian Government. (2008). Terminal report, sustainable grassland management project, Ulaanbaatar.

Mongolian Government. (2009). Government policy towards herders, 4 June 2009, Resolution 39, Ulaanbaatar.

Mongolian Government. (2010). Mongolian second national communication under the nited Nations Framework Convention on Climate Change, Ministry of Nature, Environment and Tourism.

Montes, N., Ballini, C., Deschamps-Cottin, M., Hammi, S., and Bertaudirere-Montes, V. (2005). Conséquences écologiques de la gestion coutumière des espaces forestiers dans le Haut Atlas marocain. Le cas de la vallée des Ayt Bouguemmez. In Auclair L. and Alifriqui M. (eds), *Les Agdals du haut Atlas marocain: savoirs locaux, droits d'accès et gestion de la biodiversité*. Rabat: IRCAM/IRD, pp. 151–163.

Montserrat, P. (2004). Importancia gestora y social del pastoralismo. *Archivos de Zootecnia* 50 (192): 499.

Montserrat, P. (2007). Ganadería extensiva y ecológica. *Fertilidad de la Tierra* 30: 10–14.

Montserrat, P. and Fillat, F. (1990).The systems of grasslands management in Spain. In Breymeyer, A. (ed.), *Managed Grasslands* 17. Amsterdam: Elsevier Science, pp. 37–70.

Montserrat, P. and Villar, L. (1999). Consecuencias ecológicas del abandono de tierras y de la despoblación rural. *Investigación agraria. Sistemas y recursos forestales*. Fuera de Serie 1: 135–141.

Montserrat, P. and Fillat, F. (2004). Pastos y ganadería extensiva. Evolución reciente de la ganadería extensiva española y perspectivas. XLIV Reunión de la S.E.E.P 9–17, Salamanca.

Moreira, F., Rego, F.C., and Ferreira, P.G. (2001). Temporal (1958–1995) pattern of change in a cultural landscape of Northwestern Portugal: implications for reoccurrence. *Landscape Ecology*, 16: 557–567.

Morel, G.J. (1971). Report on the controversy between agriculture and waterfowl conservation in West Africa. Report to the Seventh Annual Executive Board Meeting of the International Wildfowl Research Bureau, Slimbridge, UK, 9–10 December 1971.

Moreno, G. and Pulido, F.J. (2009).The functioning, management and persistence of dehesas. *Agroforestry in Europe: Current Status and Future Prospects* 6: 127.

Moriarty, P., Batchelor, C.H., Abd-Alhadi, F., Laban, P., and Fahmy, H. (2007). The EMPOWERS approach to water governance: guidelines, methods and tools. INWRDAM, Jordan.

Moritz, M. (2003). Commoditization and the pursuit of piety: the transformation of an African pastoral system. Dissertation, University of California at Los Angeles.

Moritz, M. (2006a). Changing contexts and dynamics of farmer-herder conflicts across West Africa. *Canadian Journal of African Studies* 40: 1–40.

Moritz, M. (2006b). The politics of permanent conflict: farmer-herder conflicts in Northern Cameroon. *Canadian Journal of African Studies* 40: 101–126.

Moritz, M. (2008). Competing paradigms in pastoral development? A perspective from the Far North of Cameroon. *World Development* 36: 2243–2254.

Moritz, M. (2010). Crop-livestock interactions in agricultural and pastoral systems in West Africa. *Agriculture and Human Values* 27: 119–128.

Moritz, M. (2012). Pastoral intensification in West Africa: implications for sustainability. *Journal of the Royal Anthropological Institute* 18: 418–438.

Moritz, M., Scholte, P., Hamilton, I.M., and Kari, S. (2013). Open access, open systems: pastoral management of common-pool resources in the Chad Basin. *Human Ecology* 41(3): 351–365.

Moritz, M., Hamilton, I.M., Chen, Y.-J., and Scholte, P. (2014). Do mobile pastoralists distribute themselves in an ideal free distribution? *Current Anthropology* 55(1): 105–114..

Moritz, M., Soma, E., Scholte, P., Juran, T., Taylor, L., Kari, S., and Xiao, N. (2010). An integrated approach to modeling grazing pressure in pastoral systems: the case of the Logone Floodplain (Cameroon). *Human Ecology* 38: 775–789.

Morton, J.F. (2007). The impact of climate change on smallholder and subsistence agriculture. *Proceedings of the National Academy of Sciences* 104: 19680–19685.

Mosalagae, D. and Mogotsi, K. (2013). Caught in a sandstorm: an assessment of pressures on communal pastoral livelihoods in the Kalahari Desert of Botswana *Pastoralism. Research, Policy and Practice* 3(18). http://www.pastoralismjournal.com/content/3/1/18.

Mouchet, J. (1960). Enquête entomologique dans le Logone et Chari (13–25 mai 1960). I: Le Foyer de glossines du Logone et Chari. II: L'Anophélisme et les possibilités de lutte antipaludique. III: La Transhumance des 'Foulbé' dans les 'yaéré'. IRCAM.

Mpho, T.J. (2005). An analysis of the challenges facing collective management of small dams in the southwestern communal areas of the Limpopo river basin, Botswana. MSc thesis, Harare, University of Zimbabwe.

MSRM (Mongolian Society for Rangeland Management). (2012). Green gold pasture ecosystem management project annual report 1 January to 31 December, 2011.

Mullié, W.C. (1994). Capture and trade of the Red-billed quelea in the Lake Chad Basin: sustainable use of a biological resource. DFPV, Niamey, Niger (in French).

Mullié, W.C. and Brouwer, J. (1994). L'importance des zones humides au Niger pour les oiseaux d'eau afrotropicals et paléarctiques. In Kristensen, P. (ed.), Atelier sur les zones humides du Niger. Proceedings of a workshop, 2–5 November (1994), La Tapoa/Parc du W, Niger, IUCN-Niger, Niamey, Nige, pp. 57–74.

Mullié, W.C., Brouwer, J., and Scholte, P. (1996). Numbers, distribution and habitat of wintering White Storks in the east-central Sahel in relation to rainfall, food and anthropogenic influences. In Biber, O., Enggist, P., Marti, C., and Salathé, T. (eds), Proceedings of the International Symposium on the White Stork (Western Population), Basel, Switzerland, 7–10 April (1994), pp. 219–240.

Mullié, W.C., Brouwer, J., Codjo, S.F., and Decae, R. (1999). Small isolated wetlands in the Sahel: a resource shared between people and birds. In Beintema, A. and van Vessem, J. (eds), *Strategies for conserving migratory waterbirds* – Proceedings of Workshop 2 of the Second International Conference on Wetlands and Development held in Dakar, Senegal, 8–14 November (1998), Wetlands International Publication 55: 30–38.

Mullié, W.C, Brouwer, J., With Dupont, P., Codjo, F., Kounou, A. and Souvairan, P. (1994).Waterbirds and wetlands in the Sahel: a threatened resource. Results of three years' monitoring (1992–1994) in the Republic of Niger. Report submitted to IUCN-Niger.

Muzila, M., Sethogo, M., Moseki, B., and Morapedi, R. (2011).An assessment of Prosopis, L., in Bokspits Area, South-Western Botswana, based on morphology. *The African Journal of Plant Science and Biotechnology*, 5 (1), 75–80.

Myers, N., Mittermeier, A.R., Mittermeier, C.G., Da Fonseca, G.A.B., and Kent, J. (2000). Biodiversity hotspots for conservation priorities. *Nature* 403: 853–858.

National Agricultural Statistics Service. (2007). Arizona. Statistics by State Bulletin 5. http://www.nass.usda.gov/Statistics_by_State/Arizona/Publications/Bulletin/07bul/pdf/pg52.pdf

Naughton, L. and Day, C. (2012) Lessons about land tenure, forest governance and REDD+. Case Studies from Africa, Asia and Latin America. Madison, WI: UW-Madison Land Tenure Center,USAID. www.rmportal.net/landtenureforestsworkshop. The Land Tenure Center: http://nelson.wisc.edu/ltc/publications.php.

Naveh, Z.Y. and Kutiel, P. (1990). Changes in the Mediterranean vegetation of Israel in response to human habitation and land use. In Woodwell, G.M. (ed.), *The Earth in Transition: Pattern and Processes of Biotic Impoverishment*. Cambridge: Cambridge University Press, pp. 259–299.

Neely, C., Bunning, S., and Wilkes, A. (eds). (2009). Review of evidence on drylands pastoral systems and climate change. Land and Water Discussion Paper, 8. Rome: FAO.   http://www.fao.org/fileadmin/user_upload/rome2007/docs/Drylands_pastoral_systems_and_climate%20change.pdf

Nelson, F. and Agrawal, A. (2008). Patronage or participation? Community-based natural resource management reform in Sub-Saharan Africa. *Development and Change* 39: 557–585.

Nelson, R.H. (1995). *Public Lands and Private Rights*. Lanham, MD: Rowman and Littlefield.

Neves-García, K. (2004). Revisiting the tragedy of the commons: ecological dilemmas of whale watching in the Azores. *Human Organization* 63: 289–300.

Niamir-Fuller, M. (1998). The resilience of pastoral herding in Sahelian Africa. In Berkes, F., Folke, C. and Colding, J. (eds), *Linking Social and Ecological Systems: Management*

Practices and Social Mechanisms for Building Resilience. Cambridge: Cambridge University Press, pp. 250–284.

Niamir-Fuller, M. (ed.) (1999) *Managing Mobility in African Rangelands: The Legitimization of Transhumance*. Exeter: IT Publications.

Niger Bird Database (2013). NigerBirdDataBase. www.nibdab.org (accessed 2 September 2013).

Nori, M., Switzer, J., and Crawford, A. (2005). Herding on the brink: towards a global survey of pastoral communities and conflict. International Institute for Sustainable Development (IISD).

Notenbaert, A.M.O., Davies, J., De Leeuw, J., Said, M., Herrero, M., Manzano, P., Waithaka, M., Aboud, A. and Omondi, S. (2012). Policies in support of pastoralism and biodiversity in the heterogeneous drylands of East Africa. *Pastoralism* 2(14). http://www.pastoralismjournal.com/content/2/1/14

Nuzum, R.C. (2005). Report: using livestock grazing as a resource management tool in California. Contra Costa Water District report, Concord, California, USA. www.ccwater.com/files/LivestockGrazingFinal72005.pdf.

Nyong, A., Adesina, F., and Elasha, O. (2006). The value of indigenous knowledge in climate change: mitigation and adaptation strategies in the African Sahel. *Mitigating Adaptation Strategies to Global Change* 12: 787–797

Oba, G., Sjaastad, E., and Roba, H.G. (2008). Framework for participatory assessments and implementation of global environmental conventions at the community level. *Land Degradation and Development* 19: 65–76.

Ochieng, O.M. (2012) 'The unrelenting persistence of certain narratives: an analysis of changing policy narratives about the ASALs in Kenya', IIED/Ford Foundation.

Olaotswe, K.E. (2006). Effects of climate change variability on livestock population dynamics and community drought management in Kgalagadi, Botswana. Norwegian University of Life Sciences, Department of International Environment and Development Studies (NORAGRIC), Master Thesis.

Ollagnon, H. (2000). La gestion en patrimoine commun de la qualité de l'eau dans un basin. In Falque, M. and Massenet, M. (eds), *Les ressources en eau. Droits de propriété, économie et environnement*. Paris: Dalloz, pp. 325–345.

Omosa, E. (2005). The impact of water conflicts on pastoral livelihoods: the case of Wajir District in Kenya. International Institute for Sustainable Development (IISD). Winnipeg, Manitoba, Canada. http://www.iisd.org/publications/impact-water-conflicts-pastoral-livelihoods-case-wajir-district-kenya

Oppermann R., Beaufoy, G., and Jones, G. (eds) (2012). *High Nature Value Farming in Europe*. Ubstadt-Weiher, Germany: Verlag Regionalkultur.

OPTIMA (Optimisation for Sustainable Water Resources Management Project) (2006). Presentation of Jordan Case Study Zarqa River Basin to the Third Management Board Meeting May 18–19, 2006 Gumpoldskirchen, Austria.

Ostrom, E. (1990). *Governing the Commons: The Evolution of Institutions for Collective Action*. Cambridge: Cambridge University Press.

Ostrom, E. (1999). *Crafting the Institutions for Self-governing Irrigation Systems*. San Francisco: Institute for Contemporary Studies.

Ostrom, E., Gardner, R., and Walker, J. (1994). *Rules, Games and Common-pool Resources*. Ann Arbor, MI: University of Michigan Press.

Parés, M. and March, H. (2013). Guide to evaluating participatory processes. Short Guides for Citizen Participation, 3. Department of Governance and Institutional

Relations. Innovation and Democratic Quality Programme. Government of Catalonia. Barcelona, June 2013.

Parr, C.L., Lehmann, C.E.R., Bond, W.J., Hoffmann, W.A., and Andersen, A.A. (2014). Tropical grassy biomes: misunderstood, neglected, and under threat. *Trends in Ecology and Evolution* 29: 205–213.

Pastor, J., Dewey, B., Moen, R., Mladenoff, D.J., White, M., and Cohen, Y. (1998). Spatial patterns in the moose-forest soil ecosystem on Isle Royale, Michigan, USA. *Ecological Applications* 8: 411–424.

Pavanello, S. (2009). Pastoralists' vulnerability in the horn of Africa. HPG Literature review. HPG. London, April 2009.

Pavanello, S. (2010). Working across borders. HPG Policy Brief 41. HPG-EU, July 2010.

Pelican, M. (2008). Mbororo claims to regional citizenship and minority status in North-West Cameroon, Africa. *The Journal of the International African Institute* 78: 540–560.

Perkins, J.S. (1996). Botswana: fencing out the equity issue. Cattle posts and ranching in the Kalahari Desert. *Journal of Arid Environments*, 33: 503–517.

Piaton, H. and Puech, C. (1992). Apport de la télédétection pour l'évaluation des ressources en eau d'irrigation pour la mise en valeur des plans d'eau à caractère permanent ou sémi-permanent au Niger. Rapport de synthèse. Avec J.Carette, Ecole Polytechnique Fédérale de Lausanne, Suisse. Comité Interafricain d'Etudes Hydrauliques, Ouagadougou, Burkina Faso.

Picardo, A. (2011). Natural resource management and common Land: examining the Plan-42 project in Northern Spain. High nature calue grasslands: securing the ecosystem services of European farming post-2013. Plovdiv. International conference, EFNCP.

Pimber, M. and Pretty, J.N. (1995). Parks, people and professionals: putting 'participation' into protected area management, UNRISD, IIED, WWF. Discussion Paper No. 57, February 1995. UNRISD, Geneva.

Pleasants, A.B., Mccall, D.G., and Sheath, G.W. (1995). The management of pastoral grazing systems under biological and environmental variation. *Agricultural Systems* 48(2): 179–192.

Plieninger, T., Ferranto, S., Huntsinger, L., Kelly, M., and Getz, C. (2012). Appreciation, use, and management of biodiversity and ecosystem services in California's working landscapes. *Environmental Management* 50: 427–440. doi:10.1007/s00267-012-9900-z.

Porter-Bolland, L., Ellis, E.A., Guariguata, M.R., Ruiz-Mallen, I., Negrete-Yankelevich, S. and Reyes-García, V. (2012). Community managed forest and forest protected areas: an assessment of their conservation effectiveness across the tropics. *Forest Ecology and Management* 268(SI): 6–17.

Poteete, A.R. (1999). Disaggregating state and society: accounting for patterns of tenure change in Botswana 1975–1996. PhD dissertation, Duke University.

Prévosto, B., Dambrine, E., Coquillard, P. and Robert, A. (2006). Broom (*Cytisus scoparius*) colonization after grazing abandonment in the French Massif Central: impact on vegetation composition and resource availability. *Acta Oecologica* 30: 258–268.

Primack, R. (2002). *Essentials of Conservation Biology*, 3rd edn. Sunderland, MA: Sinauer Associates.

Prugh, L.R., Stoner, C.J., Epps, C.W., Bean, W.T., Ripple, W.J., Laliberte, A.S., and Brashares, J.S. (2009). The Rise of the Mesopredator. *BioScience* 59: 779–791.

Pyke, C.R. and Marty, J. (2005). Cattle grazing mediates climate change impacts on ephemeral wetlands. *Conservation Biology* 19: 1619–1625.

Ramsar Bureau. (2004). Site information sheet for Tabalak wetland. http://ramsar. wetlands.org/Database/SearchforRamsarsites/tabid/765/Default.aspx (accessed 23 August 2013).

Rao, K. and Geisler, C. (1990).The social consequences of protected areas development for resident populations. *Society and Natural Resources* 3: 19–32.

Rappoport, A. (1985). Applications of game theoretic concepts in biology. *Bulletin of Mathematical Biology* 47: 161–192.

Raverdeau, F. (1991). La contre saison au Niger. Etude des systèmes de culture dans les départements de Tillabery et Dosso. Université de Niamey, Faculté d'Agronomie. Niamey, Niger.

Ravetz, J. and Funtowicz, S. (1999). Post-normal science. An insight now maturing. *Futures* 31: 641–646.

Raynaut, C. (2001). Societies and nature in the Sahel: ecological diversity and social dynamics. *Global Environmental Change* 11: 9–18.

RBALE. (2011). Plan estratégico. Plan de acción (2011–2013). Reserva de la Biosfera de los Ancares Leoneses.

RCC. (2006). Dispositif agroenvironnemental appliqué à la prévention des incendies de forêt en région méditerranéenne. RCC N° 11: 2006.

Reason, P. and Bradbury, H. (2008).*The SAGE Handbook on Action Research. Participative Inquiry and Practice*. London: Sage.

Reed, M.S. (2008). Stakeholder participation for environmental management: a literature review. *Biological Conservation* 141(10): 2417–31. doi:10.1016/j.biocon.2008.07.014.

Reed, M.S. and Dougill, A.J. (2008). Participatory land degradation assessment. In Lee, C. and Schaaf, T. (eds),*The Future of Drylands*. Paris and Berlin: UNESCO and Springer, pp. 719–729.

Reed, M.S., Dougill, A.J., and Taylor, M.J. (2007). Integrating local and scientific knowledge for adaptation to land degradation: Kalahari rangeland management options. *Land Degradation and Development* 17: 1–19.

Reed, M.S., Dougill, A.J., and Baker, T.R. (2008). Participatory indicator development: what can ecologists and local communities learn from each other? *Ecological Applications* 18: 1253–1269.

Reid, R.S., Galvin, K.A., and Kruska, R.S. (2008). Global significance of extensive grazing lands and pastoral societies: an introduction. In *Fragmentation in Semi-arid and Arid Landscapes*. New York: Springer, pp. 1–24. http://link.springer.com/chapter/10.1007/978-1-4020-4906-4_1.

Reinhardt, E.D., Keane, R.E., Calkin, D.E., and Cohen, J.D. (2008). Objectives and considerations for wildland fuel treatment in forested ecosystems of the interior western United States. *Forest Ecology and Management* 256: 1997–2006.

Rey Benayas, J.M., Martins, A., Nicolau, J.M., and Schulz, J.J. (2007). Abandonment of agricultural land: an overview of drivers and consequences. *CAB Reviews: Perspectives in Agriculture, Veterinary Science, Nutrition and Natural Resources* 2: 1–14.

Reynolds, J.F. and Stafford Smith, M. (2002). Global desertification: do humans create deserts? In Stafford-Smith, M. and Reynolds, J.F. (eds), *Do Humans Create Deserts?* Berlin: Dahlem University Press, pp. 1–22.

Ribot, J. (2004). Waiting for Democracy: the Politics of Choice in Natural Resource Decentralisation, World Resources Institute Report, Washington DC. http://pdf.wri.org/wait_for_democracy.pdf

Ribot, J.C. and Peluso, N.L. (2003). A theory of access. *Rural Sociology* 68: 153–181.

Ringrose, S. (1996). The use of integrated remotely sensed and GIS data to determine causes of vegetation cover change in southern Botswana. *Applied Geography* 16: 225–242.

Ringrose, S., Chanda, R., Nkambwe, M., and Sefe, F. (1996). Environmental change in the mid-Boteti area of north-central Botswana: biophysical processes and human perceptions. *Environmental Management* 20: 397–410.

Ríos Osario, L.A., Lobato, M.O., and Del Castillo, X.A. (2005). Debates on sustainable development: towards a holistic view of reality. *Environment, Development and Sustainability* 7: 501–518.

Rissman, A. and Sayre, N.F. (2012). Conservation outcomes and social relations: a comparative study of private ranchland conservation easements. *Society and Natural Resources* 25: 523–538.

Robinson, J. (2008). Being undisciplined: transgressions and intersections in academia and beyond, *Futures* 40: 70–86.

Robinson, L.W. and Berkes, F. (2011). Multi-level participation for building adaptive capacity: formal agency-community interactions in Northern Kenya. *Global Environmental Change* 21: 1185–1194. doi:10.1016/j.gloenvcha.2011.07.012.

Robinson, J. (2008). Being undisciplined: transgressions and intersections in academia and beyond. *Futures* 40: 70–86.

Robinson, R.A., Learmonth, J.A., Hutson, A.M., Macleod, C.D., Sparks, T.H., Leech, D.I., Pierce, G.J., Rehfisch, M.M. and Crick, H.Q.P. (2005). *Climate Change and Migratory Species*. Thetford: British Trust for Ornithology.

Rodríguez Pascual, M. (2011). Trashumancia, cañadas y merinas: una visión histórica. Simposium Hispano Luso sobre razas autóctonas en peligro de extinción. San Vitero (León).

Rodríguez Ruiz, L.A. (2013). Análisis de la rentabilidad en las explotaciones de ovino de leche en Castilla y León. PhD thesis, Facultad de Veterinaria, Departamento de Producción Animal, Universidad de León.

Roe, E., Huntsinger, L., and Labnow, K. (1998). High reliability pastoralism. *Journal of Arid Environments* 39: 39–55.

Roe, D., Nelson, F., and Sandbrook, C. (eds). (2009). Community management of natural resources in Africa: impacts, experiences and future directions. *Natural Resource Issues* No. 18, International Institute for Environment and Development, London.

Rohde, R.F., Moleele, N.M., Mphale, M., Allsopp, N., Chanda, R., Hoffmann, M.T., Magole, L., and Young, E. (2006). Dynamics of grazing policy and practice: environmental and social impacts in three communal areas of southern Africa. *Environmental Science and Policy* 9: 302–316.

Röling, N.G. and Engel, P.G.H. (1991). Information Technology from a Knowledge System Perspective: concepts and issues. In Kuiper, D. and Röling, N.G (eds.) *Proceedings of the European Seminar on Knowledge Management and Information Technology*. Wageningen Agricultural University, Dept. Extension Science, Wageningen, The Netherlands.

Romero Calcerrada, R. and Perry, G.L. (2004). The role of land abandonment in landscape dynamics in the SPA encinares del río Alberche y Cofio, Central Spain, 1984–1999. *Landscape and Urban Planning* 66: 217–232.

Rook, A.J., Dumont, B., Isselstein, J., Osoro, K., Wallisdevries, M.F., Parente, G., and Mills, G. (2004). Matching type of livestock to desired biodiversity outcomes in pastures – a review. *Biological Conservation* 119: 137–150.

Rota, A. (2010). Women and Pastoralism. IFAD Livestock thematic papers. www.ifad.org/lrkm/index.htm.

Rota, A. and Sperandini, S. (2009). Livestock and Pastoralism. IFAD Livestock thematic papers. www.ifad.org/lrkm/index.htm.

Ruiz-Mallen, I. and Corbera, E. (eds). (2013). Community-based conservation and traditional ecological knowledge: implications for social-ecological resilience. *Ecology & Society* 18(4):12.

Ruiz-Mallen, I., Dominguez, P., Clavet, L., Orta, M. and Reyes-García, V. (2012). Applied research on ethno-ecology: field experiences. *Revista de Antropología Iberoamericana* 7(1): 9–32.

Ruiz-Mirazo, J. (2011). Las áreas pasto-cortafuegos: un sistema silvopastoral para la prevención de incendios forestales. PhD thesis, Universidad de Granada, abril 2011.

Ruiz-Mirazo, J., Robles, A.B., and González-Rebollar, J.L. (2009). Pastoralism in Natural Parks of Andalusia (Spain): a tool for fire prevention and the naturalization of ecosystems. *Options Méditerranéennes* A, 91: 2009 – Changes in sheep and goat farming systems at the beginning of the 21st century.

Ruiz-Mirazo, J., Martínez-Fernández, J., and Vega-García, C. (2012). Pastoral wildfires in the Mediterranean: Understanding their linkages to land cover patterns in managed landscapes. *Journal of Environmental Management* 98: 43–50.

Runge, C.F. (1981). Common property externalities: isolation, assurance and natural resource depletion in a traditional grazing context. *American Journal of Agricultural Economics* 63: 595–606.

Runge, C. F. (1984). Institutions and the free rider: the assurance problem in collective action. *Journal of Politics* 46: 154–181.

Runge, C.F. (1986). Common property and collective action in economic development. National Research Council, Proceedings of the Conference on Common Property Resource Management. National Academy Press, Washington, DC.

Saandar, D. and Gunin, D.D. (1993). Ecological mapping and evaluation of Mongolian nature based on remote sensing data, Geoscience and Remote Sensing Symposium, IGARSS '93, Better Understanding of Earth Environment.

Sallu, S.M., Twyman, C., and Thomas, D.S.G. (2009). The multidimensional nature of biodiversity and social dynamics and implications for contemporary rural livelihoods in remote Kalahari settlements, Botswana. *African Journal of Ecology* 47: 110–118.

Sally, L., Kouda, M., and Beaumond, N. (eds). (1994). *Zones humides du Burkina Faso. Compte rendu d'un séminaire sur les zones humides du Burkina Faso*. Gland, Switzerland: IUCN Wetlands Programme.

Samarakoon, J. with Maeve Nightingale, M., Hermes, R., Joseph, B.L. and Salagrama, V. (2011). *Review of Community-based Integrated Coastal Management: Best Practices and Lessons Learned in the Bay of Bengal, South Asia*. Colombo: Ecosystems and Livelihoods Group, Asia, IUCN.

Sankari, M. (1993). Maintenance and development of the rangeland in Arabic countries. In Radwan, M.S. (ed.) *Workshop on Maintenance and Development of the Rangeland, Its Role in Combating Desertification of the Arab World*. Amman, Jordan, FAO, pp. 180–297.

Santos, L. (Ed.), Herrera, P., De Las Rivas, J.L., and Vázquez, G. (2011) *Plan de adecuación y usos de la Sierra de Atapuerca*. Valladolid: Junta de Castilla y León, Consejería de Cultura y Turismo. Dirección General de Patrimonio Cultural.

Saraza Ortiz, R., Sotillo, J.L., Serrano, V., Tejón, D., Pérez, T., and Cuellar, Y.L. (1975). *Ganadería española*. Madrid: Editorial Nacional.

Sattout, E. (forthcoming). *Valuation of Lebanese Forest Ecosystems Services and Goods: Guiding Best Conservation Policies and Management Practices*. GIZ Regional Project Silva Mediterranea-CPMF. Lebanon: Ministry of Agriculture/GIZ.

Sattout, E.J. and Abboud, M. (2007). *National Self Capacity Assessment for Global Management. Thematic Biodiversity Profile*. Lebanon: GEF/UNDP/MOE.

Sattout, E.J., Talhouk, S., and Kabbani, N. (2005). Lebanon. In Maurizio, M. and Croitoru, L. (eds), *Valuing Mediterranean Forests: Towards a Total Economic Value.* Wallingford: CABI Publishing, pp. 161–176.

Savory, A. (1999). *Holistic Management: A New Framework for Decision Making*, 2nd edn. Washington, DC: Island Press.

Sayre, N.F. (2002). *Ranching, Endangered Species, and Urbanization in the Southwest: Species of Capital.* Tucson, AZ: University of Arizona Press.

Sayre, N.F. (2005). *Working Wilderness: The Malpai Borderlands Group and the Future of the Western Range.* Tucson, AZ: Rio Nuevo Publishers.

SCET-SCOM. (2008). Actualisation de la situation de référence, Projet De Développement Des Parcours Et De L'élevage Dans L'oriental (PDPEO) – Phase II, Assistance Technique et Conseil pour la Mise a Niveau d'un Système de Suivi-Evaluation et L'actualisation d'une Situation de Référence, 2008.

Scherr, S.J. (2000). A downward spiral? Research evidence on the relationship between poverty and natural resource degradation. *Food Policy* 25: 479–498.

Schilling, J., Opiyo, F., Wasonga, O., and Mureithi, S. (2012) Resource-based conflicts in drought-prone Northwestern Kenya: The drivers and mitigation mechanisms. *Wudpecker Journal of Agricultural Research* 1(11): 442–453.

Schlager, E. and Ostrom, E. (1992). Property-rights regimes and natural resources: a conceptual analysis. *Land Economics* 68: 249–262.

Scholte, P. and Brouwer, J. (2008). The relevance of key resource areas for large-scale movements of livestock: developing the KRA-concept based on examples from Sahelian floodplains. In Prins, H.H.T. and van Langevelde, F. (eds), *Resource Ecology: Spatial and Temporal Aspects of Foraging.* Wageningen: Springer, pp. 211–232.

Scholte, P., Kari, S., Moritz, M., and Prins, H. (2006). Pastoralist responses to floodplain rehabilitation in Northern Cameroon. *Human Ecology* 34: 27–51.

Schuster, B. and Steenkamp, C. (2007). *Creating Synergies Between CBNRM and UNCCD. Lessons Learnt from a Regional CBNRM Assessment in Southern Africa.* Washington,DC and Pretoria: IRG and IUCN.

Scoones, I. (ed.). (1991). *Wetlands in Drylands: The Agroecology of Savanna Systems in Africa. Part 1: Overview – Ecological, Economic and Social Issues.* London: International Institute for Environment and Development.

Scoones, I. (1995).Exploiting heterogeneity: habitat use by cattle in dryland Zimbabwe. *Journal of Arid Environments* 29: 221–237.

Scott, J.C. (1998). *Seeing like a State: How Certain Schemes to Improve the Human Condition have Failed.* Yale Agrarian Studies. New Haven, CT: Yale University Press.

Segosebe, E.M. (1997). Pastoral management in Botswana: a comparative study of private and communal grazing management in the Kweneng and Southern district. PhD dissertation. Clark University.

Seignobos, C. and Iyébi-Mandjek, O. (eds). (2000). *Atlas de la Province Extrême-Nord Cameroun.* Paris: IRD & MINREST.

SELDAS. (2004). *Strengthening the Environmental Legislation, Development, and Application System in Lebanon.* Beirut: MOE/UOB/ELARD/LIFE.

Serrano, E. and Mantecón, A.R. (2003) Bases para un desarrollo ganadero sostenible: la consideración de la producción animal desde una perspectiva sistémica y el estudio de la diversidad de las explotaciones. *Estudios Agrosociales y Pesqueros* 199: 159–191.

SGAA. (2011). *La trashumancia en España.* Libro Blanco. DGDRPF. Madrid: Ministerio de Agricultura, Alimentación y Medio Ambiente.

Shahrani, M.N. (2002). *The Kirghiz and the Wakhi of Afghanistan: Adaptation to Closed Frontiers and War*, 2nd edn. Seattle, WA: University of Washington Press.

Shanahan, M. (2012). Why following the herd can be good for Kenyan media. IIED Blog. http://www.iied.org/why-following-herd-can-be-good-for-kenyan-media

Sheppard, E., Porter, P.W., Faust, D.R., and Nagar, R. (2009). *A World of Difference: Encountering and Contesting Development*, 2nd edn. New York: Guilford Press.

Sidahamed *et al.* (2011). MOA report compiled for IFAD Evaluation Mission April 201!.

Sierra, I. (1996). Los sistemas extensivos, las razas autóctonas y el medio natural. XXXVI Reunión de la S.E.E.P., Logroño, pp. 17–31.

Silberbauer, G.B. (2013). Kalahari – Encyclopaedia Britannica. http://global.britannica.com/EBchecked/topic/309972/Kalahari (accessed 25 September 2013.

Sing, K. (n.d.) *Introduction of Religion and Conservation*. World Wide Fund for Nature, India.

Sluiter, R. (2005). Mediterranean land cover change. Modelling and monitoring natural vegetation using GIS and remote sensing. Doctoral thesis, University of Utrecht.

Society for Range Management. (2003). Rangelands and global change. http://www.rangelands.org/pdf/Global_Issue_Paper.pdf.

Sommerhalter, T. (2008). Multi-stakeholder forums for co-management of pastoralism in Niger. *Nomadic Peoples* 12: 165–177.

Sporton, D. and Thomas, D.S.G. (2002). *Sustainable Livelihoods in Kalahari Environments: Contributions to Global Debates*. Oxford: Oxford University Press.

Starrs, P.F. (1998). *Let the Cowboy Ride: Cattle Ranching in the American West*. Baltimore, MD: Johns Hopkins University Press.

Steinfeld, H. (2006). *Livestock's Long Shadow: Environmental Issues and Options*. Rome: Food and Agriculture Organization of the United Nations.

Stenning, D.J. (1957). Transhumance, migratory drift, migration; patterns of pastoral Fulani nomadism. *The Journal of the Royal Anthropological Institute of Great Britain and Ireland* 87: 57–73.

Sulak, A. and Huntsinger, L. (2002a). Sierra Nevada grazing in transition: the role of Forest Service grazing in the foothill ranches of California. A report to the Sierra Nevada Alliance, the California Cattlemen's Association, and the California Rangeland Trust. University of California, Berkeley: Sierra Nevada Alliance, California. http://www.sierranevadaalliance.org/publications/Sierra%20Nevada%20Grazing.pdf.

Sulak, A. and Huntsinger, L. (2002b). The importance of federal grazing allotments to central Sierran oak woodland permittees: a first approximation. General Technical Report – Pacific Southwest Research Station, USDA Forest Service PSW-GTR-184:43–51.

Sulak, A. and Huntsinger, L. (2007). Public lands grazing in California: untapped conservation potential for private lands? *Rangelands* 23(3): 9–13.

Swallow, B.M. (1990). Strategies and tenure in African livestock development. LTC paper #140. Madison, WI: Land Tenure Center, University of Wisconsin.

Swatuk, L.A. (2008). Paradigms in conflict: water resources management in Botswana. In Manzungu, E. (ed.), *Towards a New Water Creed: Water Management, Governance and Livelihood in Southern Africa*. Rackwitz: Inwent and Harare, Zimbabwe: Weaver Press, pp. 1–10.

Swift, J. (1991). Local customary institutions as the basis for natural resource management among Boran pastoralists in Northern Kenya. *IDS Bulletin* 22(4): 34–37.

Swift, J.J. (2007). Case study: institutionalizing pastoral risk Management in Mongolia: lessons learned. Prepared under the overall guidance from the Rural Institutions and Participation Service, FAO Project Pastoral Risk Management Strategy, TCP/MON/0066.

Swyngedouw, E. (2010). Apocalypse forever? Post-political populism and the spectre of climate change, *Theory, Culture & Society* 27: 213–232.

Tasser, E., Ruffini, F.V. and Tappeiner, U. (2009). An integrative approach for analysing landscape dynamics in diverse cultivated and natural mountain areas. *Landscape Ecology* 24: 611–628.

Taylor, C. (2005). Prescribed burning cooperatives: empowering and equipping ranchers to manage rangelands. *Rangelands* 27(1): 18–23.

Taylor, M. (2007). Rangeland tenure and pastoral development in Botswana: is there a future for community-based management? www.cassplaas.org.

Tennigkeit, T. and Wilkes, A. (2008). Carbon finance in rangelands: an assessment of potential in communal rangelands. IUCN, the International Union for the Conservation of Nature. https://cmsdata.iucn.org/downloads/microsoft_word___carbon_finance_english.pdf.

Texas General Land Office. (2013). The Land Office. http://www.glo.texas.gov/GLO/index.html.

Texas Parks and Wildlife. (2004). A guide for wildlife management associations and co-ops. http://www.tpwd.state.tx.us/publications/pwdpubs/media/pwd_bk_w7000_0336.pdf.

Teyssier, A., Hamadou, O., and Seignobos, C. (2003). Expériences de médiation foncière dans le Nord-Cameroun. *Land Reform*, 1: 90–115.

Thirgood, S., Mosser, A., Tham, S., Hopcraft, G., Mwangomo, E., Mlengeya, T., Kilewo, M., Fryxell, J., Sinclair, A.R.E., and Borner, M. (2004) Can parks protect migratory ungulates? The case of the Serengeti wildebeest. *Animal Conservation* 7: 113–120.

Thomas, D.S.G. (2002). Sand, grass, thorns, and . . . cattle: the modern Kalahari environment. In Sporton, D. and Thomas, D.S.G. (eds), *Sustainable Livelihoods in Kalahari Environments: Contributions to Global Debates*. Oxford: Oxford University Press, pp. 21–38.

Thomas, D.S.G. and Shaw, P.A. (1991). *The Kalahari Environment*. Cambridge: Cambridge University Press.

Thomas, D.S.G. and Twyman, C. (2004). Good or bad rangeland? Hybrid knowledge, science and local understandings of vegetation dynamics in the Kalahari. *Land Degradation and Development* 15: 215–231.

Thomas, D.S.G., Sporton, D., and Perkins, J. (2000). The environmental impact of livestock ranches in the Kalahari, Botswana: Natural resource use, ecological change and human response in a dynamic dryland system. *Land Degradation and Development* 11: 327–341.

Thomas, D.S G., Knight, M., and Wiggs, G.F.S. (2005). Remobilization of southern African desert dune systems by twenty-first century global warming. *Nature* 435: 1218–1221.

Tielkes, E., Schlecht, E., and Hiernaux, P. (eds). (2001). Elevage et gestion de parcours au Sahel: implications pour le développement. Comptes-rendus d'un atelier régional ouest-africain sur 'La gestion des pâturages et les projets de développement: quelles perspectives? qui s'est tenu du 2 au 6 octobre 2000 à Niamey, Niger. La gestion des pâturages et les projets de développement: quelles perspectives? Stuttgart: Verlag Grauer.

Tortell, P., Borjigdkhan, A.T.S. and Naidansuren, E. (2008). Institutional structures for environmental management in Mongolia. UNDP Project Strengthening Environmental Governance in Mongolia.

Traore, N. (2010). Les pasteurs face à la crise fourragère : l'impact des aménagements de bas-fonds et mare sur la survie des petitis pasteurs. Report for SNV-Niger, Netherlands Development Organisation, Niamey, Niger.

Tsimako, B. (1991). The tribal lands grazing policy ranches performance to date. Agricultural Information and Public Relations Division, Gaborone, Botswana.

Turner, B.L., Lambin, E.F., and Reenberg, A. (2007). The emergence of land change science for global environmental change and sustainability. *Proceedings of the National Academy of Sciences* 104(52): 20666–20671.

Turner, M.D. (1999). The role of social networks, indefinite boundaries and political bargaining in maintaining the ecological and economic resilience of the transhumance systems of Sudano-Sahelian West Africa. In Niamir-Fuller, M. (ed.) *Managing Mobility in African Rangelands.* London: IT Publications, pp. 97–123.

Twyman, C., Dougill, A.J., Sporton, D., and Thomas, D.S.G. (2002). Community fencing in open rangelands: a case study of community self-empowerment in Eastern Namibia. *Review of African Political Economy* 28: 9–26.

Tyler, N.J.C., Turi, J.M., Sundset, M.A., Strømbull, K., Sara, M.N., Reinert, E., and Corell, R.W. (2007). Saami reindeer pastoralism under climate change: applying a generalized framework for vulnerability studies to a sub-Arctic social-ecological system. *Global Environmental Change* 17(2): 191–206.

Tyson, P.D. (1986). *Climatic Change and Variability in Southern Africa.* Oxford University Press, Oxford

Ubels, J. and Horst, L. (eds). (1993). *Irrigation Design in Africa.Towards anInteractive Method.* Wageningen and Ede: Wageningen Agricultural University and Technical Centre for Rural and Agricultural Co-operation.

United Nations. (2012). World urbanization prospects, the 2011 revision: highlights. United Nations, Department of Economic and Social Affairs, Population Division New York..

UNCCD. (1994). United Nations Convention to Combat Desertification. Geneva, Switzerland.

UNDP. (2005). Economic and ecological vulnerabilities and human security in Mongolia. United Nations Development Program.

UNDP. (2007). *Strengthening of National Capacity and Grassroots In Situ Conservation for Sustainable Biodiversity Protection.* Lebanon: GEF/UNDP/MOE.

UN-HABITAT. (2008). Secure land rights for all. UN-HABITAT – United Nations Human Settlements Programme, Global Land Tool Network.

UN-HABITAT. (2010). Land inventory in Botswana: processes and lessons. United Nations Human Settlements Programme (UN-HABITAT), Kenya. UNON, Publishing Services Section, Nairobi, ISO 14001:(2004)-certified.

USAID. (2010). USAID country profile, property rights and resource governance, Botswana. http://usaidlandtenure.net/botswana (accessed 25 September 2013).

USDA-FWS (United States Department of the Interior Fish and Wildlife Service). (1997). Draft recovery plan for the Stephen's kangaroo rat, Region 1. United States Department of the Interior Fish and Wildlife Service, Portland, Oregon, USA. [onlinehttp://ecos.fws.gov/docs/recovery_plan/970623.pdf .

USDA-FWS (United States Department of the Interior Fish and Wildlife Service). (2010). San Joaquin kit fox (Vulpes macrotis mutica), five year review: summary and evaluation. US Fish and Wildlife Service, Sacramento, CA. http://ecos.fws.gov/docs/five_year_review/doc3222.pdf.

Valdivielso, J.L. (1996). Los pastores trashumantes en la provincia de Burgos. *Revista de Folklore* 183(16a): 89–95.

Vallentine, J.F. (2000). *Grazing Management.* Amsterdam: Elsevier.

Voisin, A. (1988). *Grass Productivity.* Washington, DC: Island Press.

Wade, R. (1987). The management of common property resources: collective action as an alternative to privatisation or state regulation. *Cambridge Journal of Economics* 11: 95–106.

Wagner, M.W., Kaiser, R.A., Kreuter, U.P., and Wilkins, R.N. (2007a). Managing the commons Texas style: Wildlife management and ground-water associations on private lands. *Journal of the American Water Resources Association* 43(3): 698–711.

Wagner, M.W., Kreuter, U.P., Kaiser, R.A., and Wilkins, R.N. (2007b). Collective action and social capital of wildlife management associations. *Journal of Wildlife Management* 71(5): 1729–1738.

Wana Forum Publication (2012). The Human Integrated Management Approach (Hima) Global Initiative: Hima's Role in Conflict Resolution & Peace-Building.

Washington, R., Downing, T.E., New, M., Ziervogel, G., Bharwani, S., and Bithell, M. (2005). Climate outlooks and agent-based simulation of adaptation in Africa. Tyndall Centre for Climate Change Research Report T2.32. University of East Anglia, Norwich.

Weber, K.T. and Horst, S. (2011). Desertification and livestock grazing: the roles of sedentarization, mobility and rest. *Pastoralism: Research, Policy and Practice* 1(19). http://www.pastoralismjournal.com/content/1/1/19

Weber, K.T. and Gokhale, B. (2011). Effect of grazing on soil-water content in semiarid rangelands of Southeast Idaho. *Journal of Arid Environments* 75: 464–470.

Weiss, S.B. (1999). Cars, cows, and checkerspot butterflies: nitrogen deposition and management of nutrient-poor grasslands for a threatened species. *Conservation Biology* 13: 1476–1486.

West, P., Igoe, J., and Brockington, D. (2006). Parks and peoples: the social impact of protected areas. *Annual Review of Anthropology* 35: 251–277.

White, C. and Conley, C. (2007). Grassbank 2.0. *Rangelands* 29: 27–30.

White, R. (1993). *Livestock Development and Pastoral Production on Communal Rangeland in Botswana*. Gaborone: The Botswana Society.

White, R., Murray, S., and Rohweder, M. (2000). *Pilot Analysis of Global Ecosystems: Grassland Ecosystems*. Washington, DC: World Resources Institute.

Wilcox, D. (1994). The guide to effective participation. Joseph Roundtree Partnership. http://www.partnerships.org.uk/guide/index.htm.

Wilkins, R.N., Snelgrove, A.G., Fitzsimons, B.C., Stevener, B.M., Skow, K.L., Anderson, R.E., and Dube, A.M. (2009). Texas Land Trends. Texas A&M Institute of Renewable Natural Resources, College Station, TX. http://www.txlandtrends.org (accessed November 2012).

World Bank. (1995). Rangeland development in arid and semi-arid areas: strategies and policies, Middle East and North Africa (MENA) Region, November 1995. Washington, DC.

World Bank. (2009). World Development Indicators. Washington DC: The World Bank. http://ddp-ext.worldbank.org/ext/DDPQQ/member.do?method=getMembers&userid=1&queryId=137 (Accessed 18 May 2010).

Ziébé, R., Thys, E., and De Deken, R. (2005). Analyse de systèmes de production animale à l'échelle d'un canton: cas de Boboyo dans l'Extrême-Nord Cameroun. *Revue d'élevage et de medecine veterinaire des pays tropicaux* 58: 159–165.

Electronic resources

FIDA. Graines d'innovation: gestion communautaire des parcours. http://www.ifad.org/operations/projects/regions/pn/infosheet/IS2_Morocco_f.pdf

FIDA. Agriculture paysanne durable: innovations et meilleures pratiques aux fins de transposition et de reproduction à plus grande échelle. http://www.ifad.org/climate/resources/gef_brochure.pdf

Index